War Isn't the Only Hell

War Isn't the Only Hell

A New Reading of World War I American Literature

KEITH GANDAL

Johns Hopkins University Press
Baltimore

Printed in the United States of America on acid-free paper
9 8 7 6 5 4 3 2 1

Johns Hopkins University Press
2715 North Charles Street
Baltimore, Maryland 21218-4363
www.press.jhu.edu

Library of Congress Cataloging-in-Publication Data

Names: Gandal, Keith, author.
Title: War isn't the only hell : a new reading of World War I American literature / Keith Gandal.
Description: Baltimore : Johns Hopkins University Press, 2018. | Includes bibliographical references and index.
Identifiers: LCCN 2017034504 | ISBN 9781421425108 (hardcover : alk. paper) | ISBN 9781421425115 (electronic) | ISBN 1421425106 (hardcover : alk. paper) | ISBN 1421425114 (electronic)
Subjects: LCSH: American prose literature—20th century—History and criticism. | World War, 1914–1918—United States—Literature and the war. | War and society—United States—History—20th century.
Classification: LCC PS374.W65 G38 2017 | DDC 810.9/358403—dc23
LC record available at https://lccn.loc.gov/2017034504

A catalog record for this book is available from the British Library.

Special discounts are available for bulk purchases of this book. For more information, please contact Special Sales at 410-516-6936 or specialsales@press.jhu.edu.

Johns Hopkins University Press uses environmentally friendly book materials, including recycled text paper that is composed of at least 30 percent post-consumer waste, whenever possible.

For J.L.V.

War isn’t the only hell.

—VICTOR DALY, *Not Only War: A Story of Two Great Conflicts* (1932)

CONTENTS

Acknowledgments xi

Introduction: The Shock of War and Meritocracy 1

PART ONE: WAR LITERATURE BY NONCOMBATANT MALES 33

1 Noncombatant Mobilization Wounds: The Postwar Masterpieces of Hemingway, Fitzgerald, and Faulkner 35

2 The Horrors of War Mobilization: The Early Works of Hemingway, Fitzgerald, Faulkner, and Dos Passos 46

3 Saved by French Arrest and Imprisonment: E. E. Cummings's *The Enormous Room* 69

4 Hemingway's Thrice-Told Tale: *A Farewell to Arms* and Noncombatant Fantasy 78

PART TWO: WAR LITERATURE BY FEMALE PARTICIPANTS AND NONPARTICIPANTS 101

5 The Mobilization of Young Women: Soldiers, Noncombatants, and Women from a Female Perspective in Porter's "Pale Horse, Pale Rider" 103

6 "A Miracle So Wide": Ellen La Motte, Willa Cather, and the War's Opportunity 114

PART THREE: COMBATANT WAR LITERATURE 133

7 A War Hero in an Antiwar Tale? Thomas Boyd's *Through the Wheat* 135

8 The Intimate Seductions of Meritocracy: Laurence Stallings's *Plumes* 154

9 Not Only What You Would Expect: The Inside Story in Victor Daly's *Not Only War* 172

10 Too Glorifying to Tell: The Unspeakable in William March's *Company K* and Hervey Allen's *Toward the Flame* 200

Conclusion: War *and* Meritocracy Literature 223

Notes 229
Index 263

ACKNOWLEDGMENTS

Several scholars have contributed to this book. Ichiro Takayoshi helped get me focused on the project by inviting me to contribute to an anthology, and he also read and responded to a chapter of this manuscript. Pearl James gave me excellent editorial suggestions on a couple of chapters, and her enthusiasm for the project was a great encouragement. My friend Max played the role of a sounding board as I developed some of the chapters. Brian Bruce, David Davis, and Chad L. Williams spoke with me about their work, and Nancy Gentile Ford and Jennifer Keene generously gave their time, shared their knowledge, and expressed interest in the project. Steven Trout did the same and also provided unswerving support. Eric Sundquist, who has played a central role in all of my scholarship, was again a wonder of assistance from the very beginning and all the way through, reading and commenting on the entire manuscript. Once more I want to thank my editor at Johns Hopkins University Press, Elizabeth Sherburn Demers, for her advocacy of my work. I would also like to acknowledge the superb work of the production team at and affiliated with Johns Hopkins University Press. And most of all, I want to thank my wife, Jen, who was endlessly patient and supportive as I wrote it.

Financial support was generously provided by a sabbatical fellowship leave from the City College of New York, CUNY, without which this book simply could not have been written. Institutional support was provided by Tulane University, which granted me library privileges as a visiting scholar, and for this I would like to thank in particular the chair of the Tulane English Department, Michael Kuczynski. A version of chapter one (along with a limited number of short passages from other chapters) was previously published as "The Great War" in *American Literature in Transition, 1920–1930*, ed. Ichiro Takayoshi (New York: Cambridge UP, 2017).

War Isn't the Only Hell

Introduction

The Shock of War and Meritocracy

IT IS A WELL-KNOWN FACT that Ernest Hemingway and William Faulkner each lied about his service in World War I. After the war, they both tampered with their uniforms and attempted to "pass" as military veterans. Faulkner told people his plane had been shot down in France and affected a limp.[1] Hemingway made up a heroic story about his wounding: in this fantasy, he miraculously carried a man to safety after being hit by shrapnel.[2] He also told people he had been in the Italian infantry, a fabrication that even ended up on the book jackets of *The Sun Also Rises* (1926) and *A Farewell to Arms* (1929).[3]

The truth was that each had wanted but could not get a commission in the US Army air corps because of physical disqualifications: Hemingway had a bad eye and thus did not even try.[4] Although Faulkner did try—he gained weight and even attempted to stretch himself—he was too short and light.[5] Though too young to be drafted during the first draft call in 1917 (when the initial requirement was 21 years of age), they were both old enough in the summer of that year to have enlisted as privates in the army, but apparently neither attempted to do so—probably out of caution about ending up in trench or infantry warfare.[6] The author of *Through the Wheat* (1923), Thomas Boyd, who was born the year after Faulkner, did enlist as an 18-year-old and saw as much frontline action as just about any American soldier in World War I.

Hemingway joined a Red Cross ambulance unit, and Faulkner joined the Canadian Royal Air Force. Faulkner never made it to Europe during the war. Hemingway did serve as an ambulance driver on the Italian front and was injured there, but, when he was hit by a trench-mortar shell while delivering "cigarettes, chocolate, and postcards" to Italian soldiers, he was the one who had to be carried to safety by stretcher bearers.[7] He never served in the Italian army.

These facts about Hemingway and Faulkner have long been familiar, but we have fundamentally failed to comprehend why these famous authors lied about their war records. Yes, we understand that they made up stories to make themselves look better. But that understanding is only the tip of the iceberg. We have concentrated on the individual authors, but we have tended not to compare their similar experiences, and, most significantly, we have paid little attention to the historical moment. These writers' embellished war records tell us little about them—precisely because it was extremely common for men to lie about their World War I service. So why did they, along with so many others, find themselves having been in wartime positions that they felt the need to embellish? Why was there social pressure to fabricate their records?

The answer to these questions lies in the little-known, and recently recovered, history of the US mobilization for World War I, a chapter of American history that eventually changed this country forever. The mobilization was for various reasons unprecedented. To begin with, it relied on conscription to a degree that no other American army had, and the government produced a state-of-the-art propaganda campaign to promote the draft that tied masculinity to military service, and to combat service in particular. But most important, and most shocking, the army conducted, in its selection and utilization of recruits and its assembly of an officer corps, America's first, large-scale national experiment with meritocracy. Though the army was notoriously discriminatory against African Americans, it nonetheless made a groundbreaking attempt to extend egalitarian treatment to other ethnic groups, as well as to the poor and working class. Understanding this historical moment helps clarify not only Hemingway's and Faulkner's motivations for lying but also the major American prose literature of World War I. This literature includes famous works from the 1920s by the principal male Lost Generation authors, all noncombatant participants from privileged backgrounds—Hemingway, Faulkner, F. Scott Fitzgerald, John Dos Passos, and E. E. Cummings. It also includes several of the lasting works by combat-soldier writers, those of Thomas Boyd, Laurence Stallings, Hervey Allen, William March, and Victor Daly, some of whom had poor or troubled upbringings and one of whom was African American. And finally, it includes a few of the well-known texts of women writers, two of whom, Katherine Anne Porter and Willa Cather, experienced the home front and one of whom, Ellen La Motte, was a frontline nurse. We have long misunderstood American World War I literature due to a limited knowledge of the historical context and a basic failure to distinguish between the very different wartime experiences of male combatants and noncombatants.

Recovering this historical moment and reconsidering these writers' lives and their works in that context allows us to come to a different understanding of the American encounter with World War I, and especially the experience of male participants. These male noncombatant, male combatant, and participant and nonparticipant female writers all had remarkable, intense, disturbing, confusing, and representative wartime experiences, which were in fundamental ways unprecedented and which these authors were left to work out on their own, which they attempted to do through their writing. This powerful writing speaks to us today in part because of the sometimes excruciating, sometimes exciting intensity of that attempt to come to terms with modern warfare, modern social organization or control in the forms of massive propaganda and especially meritocracy, and the beginning of the breakdown of white, Anglo, male supremacy. By an examination of this writing, the authors' lives, and the times, we can rediscover a fascinating and formative chapter in American history that has long been forgotten—overshadowed by a bigger, more recent world war but also fundamentally unknown because of a buried military-historical record and a literature that, for various reasons, is cryptic or was tailored mostly for insider audiences.

The American army in the First World War was unlike any previous US military force, and its revolutionary nature begins with the unprecedented Selective Service Act of 1917. When President Woodrow Wilson signed the act into law on May 18 of that year, in preparation for America's entrance into World War I, he stated: "This is not the time for any action not calculated to contribute to the immediate success of the war. The business now in hand is undramatic, practical, and of scientific definiteness and precision."[8]

Wilson's seemingly modest and unmemorable statement, in conjunction with the Selective Service Act itself, might be classed with the Declaration of Independence and the Gettysburg Address as one of the great pronouncements of our national heritage and the working out of our national destiny. Though Wilson's words hardly strike one as impressive or inspiring—and much the same might be said of the language of the Selective Service Act—his call for practicality along with "scientific definiteness and precision" in the prosecution of the Great War draft, along with the regulations of the act, effected a sea change in the mobilization of the army, a suddenly massive national institution with unmatched prestige and reach. Wilson's words and the act also signaled the beginning of America's national embrace of meritocracy, a conception of status and a practice of governance that had roots in the founding principle of human equality and that would move the country toward an understanding of equality not simply as equality of political rights but also as equality of socioeconomic rights, or equality of opportunity for advancement.

The scope of the draft itself was unique in American history for a couple of reasons. First, never before had an American army been raised largely through conscription. Second, Wilson's draft was, in contrast to that of the Civil War, somewhat egalitarian: though it allowed exemptions, it pertained to all men between the ages of 21 and 31 (in September 1918, that range would be extended to all men between 18 and 45). In the Civil War, men were allowed to pay substitutes to go in their places or simply to buy their way out of service if they could afford to (thus the wealthy were privileged with the option of exemption), and conscription provided a small minority of the troops on both sides. Only 8 percent of the Union Army was made up of drafted men; that number was somewhere between 10 and 21 percent for the Confederate force. Both sides considered draftees unpatriotic and untrustworthy in battle and turned to conscription out of desperation.

In World War I, the draft was instituted more or less at the start of American involvement in the war and eventually provided 72 percent of the men in the nation's first mass army.[9] The Selective Service Act of 1917 expressly stated: "No person liable to military service shall hereafter be permitted or allowed to furnish a substitute for such service; nor shall any substitute be received, enlisted, or enrolled in the military service of the United States; and no such person shall be permitted to escape such service or to be discharged therefrom prior to the expiration of his term of service by the payment of money or any other valuable thing whatsoever as consideration for his release from military service or liability thereto."[10] Wilson came to favor conscription because it was seen as an efficient and equitable way to raise an army.[11]

The Selective Service Act and Wilson's statement, though marking a decisive break with American military tradition, did not come out of the blue but was in keeping with the thinking of the Progressive Era, which most historians date from around 1890. In a sense, the act represented a culmination of Progressivism, given the extensive reach of the draft. Wilson's conception of the draft was informed by the Progressive Era ethos of social organization and systematization.[12]

Wilson's eventual decision to rely on a draft (despite his own initial opposition) was also a reaction to realities of the moment. In spite of his famous words about a war "to end all wars" and the need "to make the world safe for democracy," American men "did not rush to enlist. A million men were needed, but in the first six weeks after the declaration of war only 73,000 . . . volunteered."[13] Initial enlistment brought the total number of men in the army (regular army plus National Guard) to only around 360,000.[14]

The determination to use conscription also resulted from the United States sitting out the first two and a half years of the war and watching other nations make mistakes. American authorities had observed the Europeans and Canadians and recognized that "England offered an especially compelling example" of how not to mobilize for war. "The British had refused until 1916 to resort to the draft. In the first two years of the war they had seen their best-educated and most talented young men rush willy-nilly to the colors and as quickly and haphazardly die in the mud in Flanders. That non-policy wrought a terrible loss of leadership cadres that seriously crippled the British military effort."[15] It also misused or wasted men essential to certain sectors of the economy or qualified as technical experts by allowing them to end up on the front lines. Wilson and his aides wanted to do things differently. He characterized his embrace of the draft as representing not only a means to draw "men into the military service of the Government but the virtual assigning of men to the necessary labor of the country. Its central idea was to disturb the industrial and social structure of the country just as little as possible."[16]

It is no coincidence that Wilson put aside his doubts about the draft and made his remarks specifically in response to what he considered a "dramatic," "impractical," and "unscientific" proposal for a volunteer division made by his political rival Theodore Roosevelt, the old Rough Rider of the Spanish-American War. Roosevelt's idea was steeped in elitist traditions of the nation and the military: "Some staff positions [Roosevelt] intended to offer to scions of the French nobility. . . . But most of the officers—indeed most of the enlisted men—would be Ivy Leaguers. Places of special distinction were reserved for the descendants of prominent Civil War generals. There would be a German-American regiment and a black regiment (officered by whites)."[17]

And there is no question that Wilson's rather vague pronouncement accompanying the launching of the national draft was interpreted as an appeal for meritocracy by the War Department and the military. Secretary of War Newton D. Baker, for example, echoed Wilson's call for an approach with "scientific definiteness" but did so with a good deal more specificity when he remarked: "We have to have a selective process by which we will get round men for the round places, the strong men for the strong tasks, and the delicate men for the delicate tasks. . . . Some system of selection of talents which is not affected by immaterial principles or virtues . . . , something more scientific than the haphazard choice of men, something more systematic than preference or first impression, is necessary to be devised."[18]

Indeed, the US Army in World War I was different from any previous American military force—for the first time in US history, an army was to some degree mobilized and organized on the basis of "scientific" personnel methods imported from business and industry or developed by psychologists, such as interviews and qualification cards for recruits that recorded "occupational, educational and military" experience; trade tests that evaluated the occupation skills of those claiming specialized abilities; rating systems that evaluated officers or identified potential ones; and intelligence tests that identified potential officers and excluded men who were deemed "feebleminded."[19] Wilson's and Baker's approach translated into the country's first mobilization attempted in part according to "modern" personnel procedures.

Even before the US entry into the war, the National Defense Act of 1916 aimed to "professionalize" the armed forces, "root out inefficiency," and put the selection of officers on a rational, meritocratic basis that would result in a "capable" officers' corps. To this end, it included provisions that "federalized" the control of officer appointments in National Guard units; though such units had been given to the federal government in the Civil War, state governors still retained the power to appoint officers for their own reasons, which were generally political and favored the privileged. With the act of 1916, which was part of the "Preparedness Movement" in case of war, the national military took over this prerogative, and, when the country entered the war, National Guard units were for the first time entirely federalized.[20]

In the course of the US participation in the war, agencies such as the Committee on Classification of Personnel in the Army in the Adjutant General's Office and the Committee on the Psychological Examination of Recruits, as well as the Foreign-Speaking Soldier Subsection of the Military Morale Section of the Military Intelligence Branch, were developed and sometimes coordinated to help distribute recruits, including immigrants and ethnic Americans, to appropriate ranks and jobs in the military. Echoing Baker's comment, the Committee on Classification of Personnel in the US Army recognized "the necessity of utilizing to the last degree every available bit of human material," which meant for this committee evaluating, classifying, distributing, and using men on a "more careful and scientific basis" than was even the general practice in business and industry.[21]

By the war's end, the army had interviewed and created qualification cards for 3.5 million men, transferring nearly a million into technical units based on the information garnered, and it had given 1.7 million men intelligence tests and 130,000 trade tests.[22] One index of the importance to the army of "personnel" matters, or the identification of talents and abilities, is that Walter Dill Scott, a businessman involved in identifying effective salesmen before the war and who headed the Committee on Classification of Personnel, which was ultimately responsible for these managerial practices, was awarded the esteemed Distinguished Service Medal.[23]

As Raymond Dodge, an original member of Scott's team, explained, the Committee on Classification of Personnel's careful assignment and utilization of manpower played a significant role in winning the war.

> In an address at the Personnel Officers' School . . . [the] Director of Organization of the British army, spoke very frankly of the serious mistake of Great Britain in recruiting her skilled labor indiscriminately into fighting units. They made good soldiers, but the plan seriously interfered with the development of technical units and the "output of many vital things."
>
> If it had not been for the great American reservoir of skilled labor it would have probably cost the war. That the United States did not make a similar, and with the exhaustion of the reservoir, a disastrous mistake in the military distribution of our skilled labor is due primarily to the Committee on the Classification of Personnel in the Army.[24]

The fact is that the US Army quietly inaugurated a social revolution the likes of which the world had never known. The military attempted to raise and mobilize troops and an officer corps on largely meritocratic principles, blind to ethnicity and class—in the end, and against the military's initial plans for "no racial discrimination in the National Army,"[25] the experiment in meritocracy would mostly exclude African Americans. In short, World War I introduced new categories of "human resources" and conceptions of status—such as those concerned with talents or abilities and capacities—into national consciousness, profoundly shaking up traditional American hierarchies based on class, ethnicity, and gender. These changes would initially be limited essentially to the military alone but would eventually, after a similar but even larger mobilization in World War II, followed by the fully egalitarian GI Bill provision concerning education that extended to African Americans as well, come to ripple out to society as a whole. Meanwhile, other national militaries, including Germany's and Britain's, would, in World War II, follow the example of America in World War I.[26]

And despite the military's institutionalization of racism and segregation under pressure from the government, the status of African American men was also to a degree shaken up by their mobilization in the World War I army. Though the Wilson administration made military leaders adjust their initial plan of "no racial discrimination," they did not simply cave in to white southern demands. The ultimate policy adopted by the army concerning African Americans did not please black leaders, but it displeased white racist leaders as well. Some high-profile white southern civilian leaders wanted no African Americans drafted, and none wanted black commissioned officers, black troops trained in combat, or black recruits stationed in southern states. But the military, though it acquiesced in some ways—most notably in instituting segregation and assigning most black recruits to labor units—insisted on a black draft, commissioned a limited number of black officers, put some black troops into combat, and did station black recruits in southern states.[27]

Thus, at a moment when the public was staunchly xenophobic, anti-German, and suspicious of ethnic Americans and immigrants, insisting on a harsh and uncompromising attitude of complete assimilation or "100 percent Americanism," the army ended up taking a completely different and very welcoming approach to ethnic-minority populations, extending to them equal opportunity for promotion as well as respect for their cultures.[28] This was not out of a concern with social justice. Rather, its purpose was not to waste the hundred thousand non-English-speaking immigrants the government had drafted and spent the first six months of the war doing little with besides housing and feeding.

The military brass became convinced that a program of meritocracy was necessary for the successful prosecution of the war, partly because the morale of immigrants and ethnic Americans, who made up a third of the population and thus of the draft (as well as that of the poor and working class, which made up an even larger proportion) was instrumental to their willing participation in the army.[29] Half a million immigrants alone would end up serving in the army.[30] Given that reality, ethnic American discrimination was essentially seen as a peacetime luxury that the military leadership could not afford, without perhaps losing control of the army, especially on top of the government-mandated prejudice against and alienation of African Americans, who made up about 13 percent of the draft.

But the army did not generally advertise this program concerning ethnic Americans, which included selecting, training, and promoting to commissioned officer rank qualified bilingual men who could lead language- and "ethnic-specific companies" of immigrants who did not speak English, and which came to be known as the Camp Gordon Plan.[31] It is impossible to know for sure why the program was not publicized. The army then (as now) had no obligation to make itself transparent to the civilian population, but perhaps the military brass, aware that it was radically out of touch with the rest of the nation and specifically with a jingoistic public that would have raised an outcry about such an approach to immigrants, including German Americans, saw no reason to stir the pot, especially as there was already plenty of public controversy to deal with surrounding the army's limited and segregated involvement of African American troops, which nonetheless alarmed white southern officials. For decades, evidence of the army's social revolution that gave essentially equal opportunity to working-class and ethnic American men existed only in the military papers in the National Archives, in the memories of men who served, and in often oblique references in the literary works of the era.

Some of those works with oblique references are among the most well-known and painstakingly analyzed in our national literary canon, including F. Scott Fitzgerald's *The Great Gatsby* (1925) and Hemingway's *A Farewell to Arms*. Yet these allusions have been missed, not only because, again, the army history had been until recently unknown or hidden but because the authors or their narrators seem to have a curious reluctance or allergy to explaining or even naming the shockingly new army practices.[32] For example, late in *The Great Gatsby*, the narrator Nick Carraway corrects Gatsby's undoubtedly bogus account of his army promotions stateside in a tiny detail that sheds little light on the subject, declaring that Gatsby "was a captain before he went to the front" (158). Weirdly, we never learn how the man whose real name was Gatz, born poor and ethnic American, and probably from a German background, became a commissioned officer in the US Army fighting Germany.[33]

Our famous World War I literature, that of the Lost Generation, has long been interpreted as an outcry over the horrors of modern warfare and a revulsion from the patriotic propaganda about a moral crusade and great adventure that the government mobilized to promote the war and the draft. But this seems a misinterpretation that comes out of deduction based on the understanding of the European literary response to the war and also ignorance about the history of the US mobilization and the organization of its World War I army. Indeed, the term "Lost Generation" originates in an epigraph in *The Sun Also Rises*—"You are all a Lost Generation"—attributed to Gertrude Stein, who got it from her Parisian car mechanic, who had used the term to describe French, not American, veterans. Apparently, Hemingway did not take the epigraph seriously.[34] Similarly, Ezra Pound's famous postwar poem "Hugh Selwyn Mauberley" (1920), which is often cited for its classic presentation of the theme of postwar disillusionment with propaganda and with modern civilization—"disillusions as never told in the old days . . . /There died a myriad,/and of the best, among them,/For an old bitch gone in the teeth,/For a botched civilization"[35]—is about Europe and England in particular, not about the United States. Pound had been living abroad (mostly in London) for the previous twelve years.

Lost Generation fiction and memoir by men—again, all written by Anglo-Americans of privilege who ended up as noncombatants—is largely a dismayed and disillusioned response, not to the war but to the mobilization of the new American army. On the one hand, it reacts against the army's unprecedented use of meritocratic procedures for the evaluation and selection or rejection of recruits; for the assignment of tasks or the utilization of men in different enterprises, many in support not battle; and for the promotion of officers. On the other hand, it is shaped by a groundbreaking propaganda campaign linking masculinity to participation in the armed forces. American prose modernism about the war by Anglo-American women as well as men is principally about the shock of encountering not modern, technological warfare but new systems of power and publicity deployed in war's mobilization. These systems have in common the tactic of controlling men by identifying them with positions or roles, classifying men not on the traditional basis of who they are or where they come from—their families, classes, and ethnicities—but on what they do and what they are deemed able to do.

More generally, World War I American prose literature—including the famous, the less well-known, and the all-but-forgotten portions—offers us not only a view of the experience of modern combat but also that of the new army and its mobilization. What we find in these works, and perhaps nowhere else, are sustained—though also sometimes cryptic—accounts of the way men and women of different classes, ethnicities, and races experienced and felt about not only the war and the battlefield but also this sudden and limited social revolution, our nation's first widespread encounter with meritocracy. Indeed, much of this literature was meant primarily for a veteran audience, whom the authors could count on to understand their cryptic references and know the information being withheld. At the same time, the authors themselves have their own particular social or psychological reasons for not explaining certain things.

As transformative as it was, the injection of meritocracy into a body politic with little previous exposure to it is only part of the social status shake-up instigated by the American army in World War I. Wilson's mobilization program produced another culture shock on a different social front: namely, masculinity and gender roles. Because Wilson did not want a repeat of the Civil War draft riots (an event that partly accounted for his initial doubts about conscription), his government aggressively sold the war and the draft through an unprecedented propaganda campaign, identifying masculinity with army service, and specifically with service as a combat soldier, often using promises of female sexual attention to sell the draft. And despite the president's promise that the draft would be an undramatic business, the propaganda offensive was often quite dramatic.[36] "GEE!! I WISH I WERE A MAN—I'D JOIN THE NAVY—BE A MAN AND DO IT," read a typical poster about joining up, which featured a "Christy Girl" (drawn by Howard Chandler Christy) with bobbed hair wearing a navy uniform and striking a provocative pose and expression. Other sexually implicit "ads" for enlisting or complying with the draft that featured Christy Girls in "military drag" read, "IF YOU WANT TO *FIGHT!* JOIN THE *MARINES*" and the more direct "*I WANT YOU* FOR *THE NAVY*."

With World War I, "propaganda for the first time became [an] all-important and formal branch of government," as Ralph D. Casey put it.[37] Recruiting posters were considered so important that the notorious wartime federal agency known as the Committee on Public Information formed a Division of Pictorial Publicity in 1917, led by the famous American illustrator Dana Gibson, whose "Gibson Girl" was the precursor to the Christy Girl.[38] Journalist George Creel, who headed the committee, initially sold the agency to President Wilson as "a plain publicity proposition, a vast enterprise in salesmanship, the world's greatest adventure in advertising."[39] For the task of selling the war and the draft, the government contracted out to experts. On a scale never seen before, it enlisted, in an official capacity, professional advertisers with years of experience in manipulating public sentiment. Consequently, their pitch in ads papered across newspapers, cable cars, movie theaters, churches, office buildings, windows in homes, and department stores went beyond typical appeals to glory and patriotism.[40] James Montgomery Flagg, who created in 1917 probably the most famous recruitment poster in history, of "Uncle Sam" pointing to the viewer, with the caption, "I want YOU for U.S. Army," said after the war, "A number of us who were too old or too scared to fight prostituted our talents by making posters inciting a large mob of young men who had never done anything to us to hop over and get shot at. . . . [W]e sold the war to youth."[41]

The draft itself was, in one important way, class-blind: in the Civil War, rich men on both sides had had the opportunity to buy their way out of service (for $300), and most did. This practice probably had as much to do with the assertion of status as it did with cowardice. The buyout was a status acknowledgment the military was offering then. That possibility was closed down in the World War I draft, and privileged men naturally looked for new ways to assert their superiority, and they would find it either in opportunities for status within the army or in exemption from service: in the special application process for officer training school offered to college men (college was still largely a privilege of the wealthy) or in deferments based on having indispensable jobs or dependents. Poor, unskilled laborers, including blacks "historically barred from skilled trades," would tend not to qualify for exemptions on either grounds, as the modest army pay and the family allotment would actually increase the income of many lower-class families.[42]

With the second wave of the Industrial Revolution after the Civil War, older forms of masculinity, notably that of self-reliance, had become untenable for many, and there was a "crusade for masculinity" beginning in the 1890s as men searched for new avenues to prove and experience their manhood.[43] But the combination in World War I America of the masculine "call" of the battlefield, the government's hard sell of the draft, and its elimination of the option of buying out meant that army service quite suddenly and effectively became a requisite for masculinity in some social quarters—again, predominantly among younger men of draft age. Once the draft got going, and US involvement was well on, it was possible to tell instantly which men were recruits and which were not: soldiers were in uniform, and in many communities, draft-age men not in uniform (whether by choice or not) were seen as unmanly and were sometimes subject to "slacker raids," or round-ups, by self-appointed patriotic groups that the Wilson administration did little to restrain.[44]

And the recasting of the masculine experience went further still. Because of the way selective service worked, men, especially those from the middle and upper class, were put in a historically atypical position for their gender: they were in general asked to be passive and wait to be drafted. One of the results of Wilson's rebuff of Roosevelt's plan for a volunteer division, along with the president's more general commitment to an organized, systematic mobilization, was to shut down almost all forms of volunteering.[45] After the initial two months after the declaration of war, there was another short window for volunteering, between June 5, 1917, when 10 million men famously registered for the draft on a dramatic day of patriotic events throughout the country, and December 15, 1917, after which the possibility of enlistment ended for all but those with very special skills that the army needed.[46]

Of course, many men, and in fact most of the 24 million who eventually registered for the draft, were happy to take advantage of their right to ask for a deferment because of their occupations or their support of dependents.

Over 65 percent of all the men who registered received deferments (and 43 percent of these were married men who were sole providers).[47] Thus, most men could be said to have exercised agency when it came to the draft—in getting out of it. And while most of these men meanwhile attempted to publicly safeguard their appearance of patriotism and masculinity by openly registering for the draft and privately requesting a deferment, that balancing act was sometimes difficult to pull off in the context of a war hysteria that could target draft-age men not in uniform as "slackers" evading their duty.[48]

That so many men were glad to get deferments might seem to contradict the idea that there was an enthusiasm for the war. Remember, however, that the government specifically "sold the war to youth," and that older men in the draft-age range were more likely to have significant or long-term jobs, wives, and children. They were less susceptible to the propaganda because they were more mature and had lives that would be interrupted by going to war; they also had occupations and domestic responsibilities that made them feel adequately masculine without serving. And, to be sure, some of these even slightly older or more mature men who did not have family obligations before America entered the war quickly sought them out to avoid service. When the United States joined the conflict, the writer Henry Miller got a job in Washington as a clerk in the War Department in the hopes of getting a draft deferment; when he nonetheless got a letter requiring him to register, he returned home to New York and promptly married his girlfriend—he was 25 at the time.[49] As Faulkner's biographer Frederick R. Karl writes, "Even as men married, had children, and did what they could to avoid the draft," 19-year-old Faulkner put in a lot of "effort . . . to get into the war."[50] Of the ten male war-participant writers being discussed in these pages, all but one of them were between the ages of 17 and 23 when the United States joined the conflict in the spring of 1917. And Hervey Allen, who was 27, had previously served in the National Guard in the 1916 border war with Mexico.

For those who registered and were drafted, and did not qualify for a deferment—again, the overwhelming majority of those who served—the process meant being evaluated (physically and sometimes mentally as well) and then either rejected or selected and designated combatant or noncombatant. After being assigned to a particular branch of the army, one might be evaluated further before being deployed. In December 1917, the Selective Service administrator, Provost Marshal Gen. Enoch H. Crowder, "introduc[ed] a classification system, designed to sort the registrant pool . . . scientifically into five classes of varying suitability for service."[51] Men who enlisted between April and December of that year and stated a desire to be in combat could choose the branch of the army they would serve in, such as the infantry, artillery, or air corps; however, they still faced examination and possible rejection. The same was true for men who wanted to enlist in the Marines: they had to pass physical examination.

So, to look at the Lost Generation writers who had encounters with the US army but ended up as noncombatants: Faulkner tried to enlist in the air corps but was rejected because he failed to meet the height and weight specifications. Dos Passos, who was drafted and wanted to get back to the war zone where he had been volunteering with an ambulance unit, found himself, because of "restricted vision," relegated to the Services of Supply (SOS).[52] Cummings, who was drafted but desired to avoid the front line and suggested he could serve as an interpreter, given his ambulance service in France, was assigned to the infantry. He was even promoted to acting corporal on the basis of a high intelligence test score, but the war ended before he could be shipped over.[53] Fitzgerald, who enlisted with hopes of combat service, was able on the basis of his college education to take and pass a written exam for officer candidates, but his military career stalled at the rank of lieutenant because of poor officer training camp performance; moreover, because his superiors had doubts about his ability for command, he was shuttled around from one training camp to another but never shipped over to Europe.[54] Much has been made of the way World War I's unprecedented trench warfare undermined traditional battlefield opportunities for masculine assertion and bravery.[55] But the United States also saw the undermining of typically male prerogatives before men ever reached the front, or even a training camp.

Moreover, much of what men experienced in training camp (if they were selected) and even in Europe (if they got there, and more than half of the 4 million who enlisted or were drafted did not) was not the "adventure" promised on billboards or at recruiting stations but mundane activities or work under almost constant supervision and the requirement of obedience. It was another submission that did not exactly square with traditional notions of masculine agency and power among the privileged classes, especially as masculinity had been imagined in the context of previous wars and was portrayed in government advertising to promote the current war effort. Men in the American Expeditionary Forces (AEF) found themselves constantly ordered about by their superiors, and most would never have the opportunity to counter or exorcise this submission by exercising their masculine traits on the battlefield with a gun.

In previous American wars, including the Civil War, something like 90 percent of the men who joined the army saw combat because the army relied on civilian contractors to do the labor necessary to support the fighting force.[56] That was not the case in World War I. The army quickly realized that there was no French labor force left to tap (able-bodied men were in the army), and bringing over and paying American civilian workers would have been too expensive. So the army essentially decided to provide all the labor it needed from its own ranks.[57] The result was that most recruited men were channeled into support, and only about 40 percent of non-black troops (and 10 percent of black troops) were designated as combat soldiers.[58]

This momentous decision about the utilization of men had an unintended effect. To be assigned to noncombatant service was potentially emasculating, because in the public imagination, reaffirmed by government propaganda, only combat service was considered fully manly. And the military, though aware of the morale problem among the noncombatant troops, tended to reinforce this perception by giving most official rewards to fighting men.[59] Meanwhile, combat soldiers sometimes "displayed contemptuous indifference and open hostility to noncombatant soldiers, whom they viewed as purposefully evading the really arduous work of subduing the Germans."[60]

As Jennifer Keene, the preeminent social-military historian of the US experience in World War I, puts it,

> the army became the victim of its own success in fostering the notion that a courageous performance on the battlefield served as the truest test of manhood and patriotism. . . . The warrior image of soldiering fostered in wartime propaganda, the stories expected by families at home, and the physical expressions of masculinity championed in the training camps through recreational activities like boxing haunted noncombatants who became increasingly disillusioned when their military experience failed to live up to this ideal. The contradiction between their expectations and what military service actually entailed for noncombatants precipitated an unforeseen crisis for these men within the wartime army.[61]

Historian Richard S. Faulkner observes the "chasm" that opened up in World War I between the "teeth" and "tail" of the US army: "Those who served behind the lines understood that the combat soldiers thought of them as lesser beings and may have viewed themselves as SOL"—shit out of luck, a popular wartime term and one that appeared in a well-known SOS song—"for their assignments."[62] Many men were left in the slightly shameful position of trying to justify their support service by comparing the hazards they faced to those encountered by combat soldiers.[63] Others, including Hemingway and Faulkner, embellished or lied about their war roles.

Because masculinity was during the war identified with armed service, and especially with combat experience, and because men had to be selected for the army, as well as for commissioned or noncommissioned officer (NCO) status, and faced the possibility of rejection in each case, many men—mostly among the privileged—found themselves in the position of a passive object. Women (of the upper classes) had long occupied such a position when it came to their feminine status, which depended on a marriage proposal and to moral judgments of their chastity. This gender reversal mostly pertained to privileged men, who were not only used to exercising choice but expected, because of their social status, to be officers. Such men had of course long been the final arbiters of femininity in their social worlds—because, if nothing else, they exercised the prerogative of proposing marriage, as a group legitimating some women and stigmatizing others. But now such men found the tables turned. It was women who now had the power to confirm or deny a man his masculinity, to determine his quotient of manhood, simply by affirming the military's judgments about masculinity in their choices not of husbands but of sex or romance partners—as the "unusual conditions" of wartime provoked America's first sexual revolution.

The sexual outbreak, or hysteria or revolution, that accompanied World War I and all but swept aside longstanding American inhibitions against casual sex, at least temporarily, has been well documented. The wartime Commission on Training Camp Activities (CTCA) reported: "The 'lure of the uniform' is more than a phrase; it is an actuality. Girls often lose their heads in a whirl of emotion brought about by these unusual conditions."[64] Those conditions included wartime and the gathering of thousands of uniformed men in American training camps all over the country. These women and girls were sometimes referred to as "charity girls" because they were not charging soldiers for sex.[65] An internal CTCA report on the problem at Camp Dix, New Jersey, explained: "In all towns, both large and small, in the vicinity of the camp or accessible to the soldiers by jitney, trolley or train, there still is considerable volume of 'charity' intercourse. There seems to be a psychological feature to this particular evil in that young girls between the ages of 14 and 20 are inordinately susceptible to any man in uniform whether he be an officer or one of lesser rank."[66] The amplitude of the "charity girl" phenomenon was not a paranoid fantasy of a moralistic government agency; it was also observed by journalists, reform groups, academic researchers, American novelists, concerned citizens, and soldiers themselves. An article in *The Survey* magazine stated: "The social hygiene problem created by this war is not a problem of commercialized prostitution. It is a problem of the individual soldier and the individual girl—the man cut away from his ordinary amusements and social life, the girl responding to the unusual and romantic glamour of the uniform."[67] A reform organization recorded in 1917 that under the "lure of the uniform, [girls were] picking up soldiers on the street, going to shows and ice cream parlors with them, and gradually becoming demoralized." A postwar psychological study came to the surprising conclusion that World War I "wrought its greatest influence . . . in the field of sexual relationships." It created "a vast emotional tension which tends to break conventionalities and outer restraints."[68] Faulkner described this dynamic in his first novel, *Soldiers' Pay* (1926). A woman who married a soldier she knew for three days says: "You remember how it was then—everybody excited and hysterical, like a big circus. . . . [A]ll soldiers talking of dying gloriously in battle without really believing it or knowing very much about it, and how women kind of got the same idea, like the flu—that what you did to-day would not matter to-morrow, that there really wasn't a to-morrow at all."[69] As one citizen wrote in a letter to an officer in the army, not sure what to conclude, "The girls of Scranton [Pennsylvania] it seems . . . have lost all the sentiment of decency that is proper of the sexes, giving another exhibition of immorality hunting for men like a bunch of sea dogs in the season of love. Maybe they were sacrificing themselves on the altar of the fatherland, which I believe is not asking so much of the patriotism of their women. Never before [have] . . . I witnessed such a debauche."[70] At the age of 105, Lloyd Brown, at that point the last known surviving US navy veteran of World War I, still remembered, some nine decades later, why he'd snuck into the service at age 16 (the minimum age for enlistment was 18): "Most all the young people were doing it at that time. When we went into the war, why, it was quite a popular thing for young man to do. . . . Very popular among the young ladies too."[71]

Here again, the army was a victim of its own success in propagating the idea that masculinity was now equivalent to service in the armed forces and to combatant status in particular. But other "unusual conditions" played a role as well in this sexual outpouring. Thousands of young men were arriving in small cities and towns. Not only had these men been vetted in some sense by the military; they were cut loose from the normal ties and surveillance of family members and neighbors. For the first time in the lives of the local girls and women, there were lots of available young men. These men were not only strangers, but they would not be hanging around long. Not only that, these men might be going off to die. The possibilities for clandestine sex, and sex without consequences, were not only plentiful, they were highly romantic.

In most of the towns and small cities where there were army bases, nothing so exciting had ever happened. And it must have seemed that nothing so exciting might ever happen again. For many women and soldiers, it seemed a once-in-a-lifetime moment not to be missed. Fitzgerald's future wife, Zelda, an upper-class 18-year-old woman at the time, remembered that "there was scarcely a ripple in our lives. . . . Then the war came and we had the inescapable feeling that all this beauty and fun—everything—might be over in a minute. We couldn't wait, we couldn't afford to wait, for fear it would be gone forever, so we pitched in furiously, dancing every night."[72]

In any case, the army found itself with what it considered a vast health and moral problem—the hundreds of thousands of women and girls having sex with soldiers and the concomitant rise in venereal disease rates. The CTCA responded by providing recruits with alternative leisure activities and trying to educate them, but most ignored the advice.[73] The military authority, given special powers by the Justice Department due to the national emergency of war, also responded by arresting and locking up women and girls who were presumed to be attempting to pick up soldiers. The army ended up incarcerating somewhere between 15,000 and 30,000 women, only a third of whom were charged with prostitution; most were merely found to have violated a sexual code that could extend to speech, clothing, and styles of dancing.[74]

Although this first American sexual revolution has been much discussed, historians have focused on sexual liaisons between soldiers and local women and girls, identifying the "charity girl" phenomenon as involving mostly working-class females.[75] Not only did it include women of all classes, but this focus on sex leaves aside a larger phenomenon. Romantic liaisons cut across classes—involving upper-class women and working-class men—due to the meritocratic selection of combat soldiers, especially officers. This "shocking" reality was not lost on F. Scott Fitzgerald. As one of his biographers, Arthur Mizener, wrote in describing Zelda's wartime experience, "Camp Sheridan and Camp Taylor filled up with officers from all over the country and from what was for those times . . . a startling range of social classes. Overnight the social life of Montgomery [Alabama] took on an excitement, a feeling that anything was possible. . . . It only added to the excitement that you never knew whether the handsome officer who cut in at the Country Club was a streetcar conductor, like the Earl Schoen of Fitzgerald's story, 'The Last of the Belles,' or a Harvard man of distinguished Boston ancestry."[76] Or an ethnic American man from a poor farming family, like Gatsby. Literary critics have not adequately examined how girls' and women's flocking to soldiers for sex or romance, or both, across all classes, their shunning men who were not in uniform, and their showing less interest in recruits who were noncombatants and most in men of officer rank—women as a group accepting and thus effectively vetting the military's judgments and assignments of men—affected female and male experience and, at least temporarily, altered—and to a degree reversed—gender roles, especially among the privileged classes.

To understand the American experience of World War I, it is important to recognize that for men in the army a noncombatant war experience, with its potential embarrassments, was overwhelmingly the norm. Partly due to the army's providing its own support personnel and partly due to happenstance, the vast majority of recruits did not end up being combat soldiers at any point in their service, regardless of their designation: 2.1 million American soldiers were sent overseas out of the mobilized army of almost 4 million, and only 1.1 million were involved in combat.[77] The reason there were so many men who made it to training camps but not to France, including men who were designated for combat but never experienced it, was due to the happenstance that the US government had no idea when the war was going to end and was in fact surprised by the "sudden" armistice in November 1918.[78]

Of those who enlisted or were drafted and not rejected, around a quarter actually served in combat. If one includes the men turned away at draft boards among the ranks of the noncombatants, that percentage is smaller still. As for those who made the commissioned officer ranks, whether serving in Europe or stateside, that group was even more exclusive. There were only 200,000 such officers.[79] Thus, America's first large-scale experiment with meritocracy was—like our contemporary version—a highly competitive one that left most men feeling they had not made the grade. This reality has to do with the lasting relevance of Lost Generation writing: almost a hundred years later, it continues to feel surprisingly modern or contemporary in certain ways, not because it expresses "universal" truth but because it represents a social world similar to our own.

Hemingway, Fitzgerald, Faulkner, and John Dos Passos—because they ended up as noncombatants frustrated in their military ambitions—had quite common experiences of the war. It is not a stretch to say that, whether they were actually in the American army or not, they were in a real sense "typical doughboys."[80] And in their fictions, they also expressed their disillusionment with their treatment by the army or their paramilitary outfits. These male writers of the Lost Generation had a special talent to express commonplace frustrating experiences shared by millions of men—whose discussion otherwise had no other outlet in public discourse partly because criticism of the army, even after the war, could be controversial and, most of all, because the experiences were embarrassing.

This is not how these authors and their fictions have generally been seen. Their literature has long been considered as presenting an elite or intellectual antiwar response, and thus out of touch with the masses, including average American soldiers, who supposedly preferred upbeat, patriotic accounts of the war even after it was over. (And this preference may have been true among that minority of American veterans who served in combat.) But it actually makes more sense to see the Lost Generation works as reflective of and speaking to the typical, noncombatant veteran who had disappointing experiences in the army—and little other affirmation of his difficulties and grievances. The relative commercial success of Dos Passos's *Three Soldiers* (1921) and Hemingway's *The Sun Also Rises*, not to mention the phenomenal bestselling status of *A Farewell to Arms*, might have something to do with their appeal to noncombatant veterans.

In particular, the relationship between Hemingway's representation of the noncombatant experience and his incredible commercial success with *A Farewell to Arms*, the only American novel of World War I that was a runaway bestseller, is tantalizing. Hemingway kept cracking away at the same basic story—a relationship between a nurse and a wounded soldier—until he produced a book that was a hit. With "A Very Short Story" in *In Our Time* (1925), *The Sun Also Rises*, and *A Farewell to Arms*, Hemingway tells a variant of the story three times, and each one involves a distinct permutation of the wartime status of the soldier. This was a story with personal meaning for him. He himself had been wounded in the war and had a relationship with a nurse. But it also seems that he knew he had a kernel of an important tale on his hands, and he was dogged because he sensed that commercial success and real fame were just a matter of getting the details of the formula "right." In any case, when one looks at these Hemingway works from the point of a view of a noncombatant, they open up in striking ways, and longstanding mysteries about the author's narrative decisions seem to resolve themselves.

On first glance, it seems odd that the canonized male American literature of World War I should be written entirely by noncombatants, two of whom (Faulkner and Fitzgerald) never even made it to Europe. This was not the case in Britain or Europe. But when one takes into account that the noncombatant experience was by far the most common for American recruits (hardly the case in European armies), it becomes understandable. Chance alone would dictate that most of the best writers, or the most stylistically modernist ones, would thus come from the much larger noncombatant group. But perhaps representativeness played a role, too. It is debatable whether any of the combatant authors deserve to be included in the canon, but the work of Thomas Boyd and William March is at once strikingly modernist and accomplished.

Lost Generation literature is not only written by former noncombatants but predominantly about the noncombatant experience. Thus, one might reasonably assume, it was appealing at the time to noncombatant veteran readers—especially because these men found that the discomfort of their wartime status did not disappear when the war was over. The commander of the Services of Supply attempted to reassure his troops that their work in support was valuable, that they "did more for their country by living for it than they could possibly have done by dying for it," but he himself admitted that noncombatants were "doomed to spend the rest of their lives explaining why they served in the Services of Supply."[81]

One SOS doughboy anticipated his coming sense of alienation in a song he sent to Stars and Stripes in April 1918:

> When this cruel war is over, and the boys go marching home,
> I'm afraid I'll be an outcast, and forever have to roam;
> When wound chevrons they exhibit, and their service stripes of gold,
> And they tell admiring lassies, of their doughty deeds and bold,
> I'll be missing from the circle, and nobody there will hear,
> How I—I was but hero, in the SERVICES OF THE REAR.
>
> *Chorus*:
>
> For I'm a S.O.R. boy—also an S.O.L.
> I never pulled a trigger, or sent a Boche to hell;
> I never saw a dugout, in fact was never near—For I performed my duty in the SERVICES OF THE REAR.[82]

Indeed, one of the surviving noncombatant veterans of World War I interviewed by Richard Rubin for his book *Last of the Doughboys* (2013) still felt, more than eighty-five years later, that in being assigned to an AEF forestry unit, instead of a combat division, he had failed to measure up.[83]

The fiction of the era may offer us the best window on what noncombatant men truly underwent and felt because the reality of experiencing military rejection or even assignment to noncombatant positions was for many so uncomfortable that it was often not spoken of, or it was lied about. This seeming paradox—that fiction is a particularly important resource here in terms of finding or putting together the full truth, because fiction always involves the comfort of plausible deniability by an author who can of course claim that his main character or narrator is not him—is neatly suggested by *A Farewell to Arms*. The biographical note about the author tells the lie that Hemingway was in the Italian infantry (this lie would continue to appear in this book and *The Sun Also Rises* through the 1970s). Meanwhile, the fictional tale presents a narrator-protagonist whose position as an ambulance driver and experience of getting wounded in an unheroic way is close to the truth of Hemingway's.

The full noncombatant story was not told in any other public forum—not in newspapers or magazines, not even in the *American Legion Magazine*, which featured articles praising the work of noncombatants but did not explore their marginalization or alienation.[84] According to historian Jennifer Keene, "the unspoken story of World War I, and indeed all modern American wars, is the noncombatant experience."[85] Again, given World War I propaganda as well as previous US wars, the American public associated military service with fighting, and support activity was not recognized by the average citizen as legitimate military service. Meanwhile, the American Legion veterans organization, in which a former head of the Services of Supply was active,[86] wanted to obscure this distinction between combat soldiers and support servicemen, in the interest of promoting solidarity among veterans—specifically, to keep noncombatants from feeling alienated. For example, when the subject of whether adjusted compensation after the war should apply only to combat soldiers or to everyone in uniform, the Legion decided that it should be universal, extended even to men whose service was entirely in training camps. As Keene concludes, "in official public forums, the distinction between combatant and noncombatant in World War I was ignored or obscured," but, when it was acknowledged privately or casually, "the noncombatant experience was belittled."[87]

What this means about Lost Generation literature is that, first of all, it is significant—in a way that has not been recognized—for revealing an otherwise missing chapter of American history, namely as telling a version of the noncombatant story in World War I (or any modern American war) that has hardly been told anywhere else. Second, it suggests that Lost Generation literature was probably intensely meaningful for members of the large population of American men who served as noncombatants—and who had no other public forum which specifically recognized their difficult experience and alienated point of view.

The Lost Generation male authors' fictional representations of men's wartime experiences allowed them to examine feelings that were shameful, even to transform them, through the alchemy of storytelling, into something more psychologically acceptable. Dos Passos's *Three Soldiers*, Fitzgerald's

The Beautiful and Damned (1922), Hemingway's "A Very Short Story," and Faulkner's *Soldiers' Pay* explored and aired shameful feelings fairly straightforwardly, without significant transposition of the authors' own positions in the military. These authors' subsequent works *1919* (1932), *The Great Gatsby*, *The Sun Also Rises* and *A Farewell to Arms*, and *The Sound and the Fury* (1929) all involved fundamental transmutations of the authors' military circumstances and an alteration in tone, from the early works' bitterness to tragedy—ingenious and symbolic fictionalizations that arguably gave birth to these writers' distinctive prose modernisms. By triangulating these authors' fictions, their own experiences, and the historical record of the US army and the mobilization, we can make sense of these works and also get insight into what noncombatants actually underwent and felt—about themselves, the army, and young women. Regarding the noncombatant take on young women, most of these authors create uncaring or even man-eating females—Luz in "A Very Short Story," Brett in *The Sun Also Rises*, Daisy in *The Great Gatsby*, Margaret Powers in *Soldiers' Pay*, Genevieve Rod in *Three Soldiers*. These characters seem to follow from the authors' "mobilization wounds" to their masculinity. In other words, the female characters involve traceable projections by the authors.

Another distinct angle of approach to the noncombatant experience in general, and to noncombatants' projections onto women in particular, is provided by Katherine Anne Porter's autobiographical novella "Pale Horse, Pale Rider" (1939), which gives us a view of such men from a female protagonist and female author. Written by a mature woman who experienced the war at home and featuring a sensitive female main character, the story is revealing not only about a young woman's experience of World War I but about the defensiveness, resentment, and aggression that noncombatant men manifested in their interactions with young women.

In short, we have long thought about American World War I literature in the wrong way. Much Lost Generation literature is a specific kind of writing—hardly comparable to novels written principally for a general audience and read chiefly for entertainment, edification, or a good story. Many of the 1920s works of the Lost Generation might be thought of as a therapeutic literature for both the noncombatant writer and noncombatant readers who share a specific traumatizing experience that is historically new and thus recognized and addressed nowhere else.

Something similar might be said of some of the American war literature of World War I written by combat veterans. The combat experience was also traumatizing, in ways that we are generally more familiar with—but here also the new meritocracy played a role we have largely missed. While magazine stories, books, plays, and movies validated the combat soldier's experience, many of them were unrealistically idealistic. These depictions, though flattering, would only have a limited psychological utility for the combat veteran who was shell-shocked or suffering from other traumas of war.

Literal shell shock of the sort suffered in World War I was a new experience—because shelling had never before been so continuous and profound. It was noticed during the war that several hours of shelling could actually put men to sleep.[88] Much the same might be said about the machine-gun warfare, which was also unprecedented. The carnage veterans underwent, precipitated, and witnessed in this first mechanized war was mind-boggling. Writing was sometimes the only therapy. William March's biographer maintains, "There is no doubt that for March the gradual composition of *Company K* [finally published in 1933] was in some part an exercise in self-therapy."[89]

As combat veteran Hervey Allen recuperated for more than a month in the hospital from injuries sustained in battle, "he was," his biographer wrote, "tortured by night with the hallucination that people were whispering about him. Truthfully, having seen so many die, he was, for a time, ashamed to have survived at all." He even "contemplated suicide."[90] His psychological troubles continued after the war. "After returning home in 1919," Allen wrote in a preface to a 1934 edition of his memoir, *Toward the Flame* (1926), "I found myself much troubled at night by memories of the war and often unable to sleep. It occurred to me then that I might rid myself of my subjective war by trying to make it objective in writing." Putting together "notes jotted in rough diary" and his letters home, "I whipped the whole into shape without any thought at the time of publishing it. The medicine worked."[91] As his biographer summarizes, "what finally jogged him out of shellshock was externalizing it in prose and poetry."[92]

Our critical apprehension of the combatant literature of World War I has also tended not to see this literature for what it is. We have tended to want to identify it ideologically or intellectually, as, for example, protesting modern war; criticizing the army for its institutional injustice, inhumanity, and ineptitude; or making a case for full African American equality. But all of the combat literature being considered is shaped by intense, sometimes overwhelming emotional responses to the almost unimaginable combination of the traumas and stresses involved not only in violent combat, unceasing discipline, and sometimes also racial prejudice as well, but also to those involved in the guilt of receiving promotions and commendations while fellow soldiers are dying or being maimed.

All of the soldier-writers being considered here were not merely selected to be combatants, which was unusual enough in itself among recruits in the World War I American army (and it was even more unusual, as discussed, for black recruits, of which Daly was one). They were all distinctive, special, or affirmed in other ways by the American or French militaries or both. Stallings, Allen, and Daly were commissioned officers (Boyd and March were promoted to noncommissioned officer rank during or after the war). Stallings was made a captain after the armistice, and Daly was one of the extraordinarily elite 639 African American men who were chosen for and graduated from the single, segregated black officers training class at Fort Des Moines, Iowa. Stallings, Boyd, and March were in the Marines, a select fighting force that made up just over 1 percent of all American troops. Boyd experienced more combat than the overwhelming majority of American soldiers who fought in France during the war.[93] All five men were awarded major decorations: they all received the Croix de Guerre from France,[94] and Stallings, Boyd, and March were also decorated by the American army. Daly arguably deserved such a distinction as well but, being black, was denied it.[95] March received a combination of medals from the American army "that to anyone with a knowledge of the military services, is literally mind-defying."[96]

While we are more familiar with combat as opposed to noncombat trauma, there were some forms of trauma for American World War I combat troops that were not only new but different from those of European soldiers—who were not experiencing a military engaged in an unprecedented meritocratic experiment as well as a vicious discrimination against African Americans.

Probably all five of these combat writers experienced post-traumatic stress (of various kinds). Allen, March, and Boyd had documented mental, emotional, or nervous problems; Stallings was crippled for life; about Daly, we simply lack the information. The books they produced are shaped or twisted by their ongoing, postwar emotional struggles. What writers of autobiographically based accounts experience and what they are able and prepared to say about it are always, of course, two different things, but when it comes to the experience of combat and the army, the difference, due to trauma, is exaggerated and often quite dramatic. And it requires special treatment, a treatment these American World War I combatant texts have rarely if ever received. Contemporary feminist criticism of women war writers is more attuned to psychological realities here: for example, in appraising World War I memoirs about nursing by Mary Borden and Ellen

La Motte, critics Sandra Gilbert, Dorothy Goldman, and Jane Marcus demonstrate that these nurses' literary approaches are shaped by a need for "dissociating . . . from the unbearable reality," the result being narratives characterized by "numbness," "neurasthenia," or an "anaesthetic esthetic."[97] Perhaps when it comes to assessing the works of men who never achieved the status of great writers, there is a lingering cultural and gender bias about American male soldiers that leads to their emotional vulnerability being ignored or underestimated. (Artistic stature seems to matter here, as Hemingway, for example, who was wounded as a noncombatant, is sometimes extended this understanding and special treatment.)[98] It is hard, otherwise, to comprehend the almost complete absence of such considerations when it comes to apprehending the aesthetics of these narratives by male combatants, four of whom were definitely wounded, one maimed (again, Daly we do not know about, though he probably was not wounded, at least not seriously[99]), and all of whom participated in killing or wounding men on the other side, as well as witnessed the deaths and drastic injury of their comrades—while they also all received major decorations. Meanwhile, it seems absolutely impossible to come to grips with most if not all of the combatant writers here—Stallings, Allen, Daly, and March, to be sure—without considering the impact of psychological trauma in the shaping of their aesthetics.

Some American war literature written by combat veterans was meant to be therapeutic for the writer, but it could function that way for the combat-veteran reader as well. Robert Graves, a British World War I veteran and author of the bestselling war memoir *Good-bye to All of That* (1929), who suffered from shell shock, or "neurasthenia," after the war, came to "regard . . . poetry as, first, a personal cathartic for the poet suffering from some inner conflict, and then as a cathartic for readers in a similar conflict." (Graves went so far as to conclude that "writing poetry of 'universal appeal' " was in fact an "impossibility.")[100] Combat veterans desired and needed such war writing often because they were suffering from troubles that no one but other World War I veterans knew anything about. Perhaps they had an even greater need to come to terms with their harrowing experiences once the US Congress refused to ratify the fraught Versailles peace treaty, and it became unclear what all the bloodshed and their suffering had been for.

It is a strange truism first asserted a few years after the war by publishers and repeated by literary critics today about the early 1920s that there was not a big enough market to justify publishing war novels or that "the public was surfeited with war."[101] World War I tales, in the form of books, Broadway plays, and movies, broke records throughout the 1920s and into the 1930s.[102] Dos Passos's *Three Soldiers* made a huge splash in 1921, though it was predicted that being a war book, it would not sell.[103] Though the publisher of Willa Cather's *One of Ours* (1922) could not sell the serial rights to any major magazine in large part because "the war aspects discouraged interest," the book turned out to be a bestseller and won the Pulitzer Prize in 1923.[104] Thomas Boyd's *Through the Wheat* sold 5,000 copies in the first two and a half months of 1923, reaching the *Chicago Tribune*'s bestseller list a month later.[105] Laurence Stallings's *Plumes* (1924) ran through eight printings in its first six months.[106] Hemingway's *The Sun Also Rises* (1926) was another bestseller, with 8,000 copies purchased in less than two months, 3,000 more copies the next month, and a total of 20,000 within nine months.[107] Hervey Allen's memoir *Toward the Flame* did well when it came out in 1926 and by 1933, when the publisher felt a new edition with a new forward was called for, the book had sold over 30,000 copies.[108] At the end of the 1920s, Hemingway's *A Farewell to Arms* was a phenomenal bestseller, moving 100,000 copies in a year. March's *Company K* (1933), which came out during the Depression, though it had trouble finding a publisher and one critic "weary" of war stories had "gone so far as to pronounce that it would be preferable to fight another war than to have to read another war book," sold 3,000 copies in the first month and a half, much better than the publisher had hoped for "in these tough days."[109] As Thomas Boyd flatly put it to editor Max Perkins, when his novel was initially rejected by Scribner's because war books supposedly lacked a market (Fitzgerald later prevailed upon the publishing house to take it), "I think that the belief that people are sick of war books is false."[110] Obviously, today's critics are mistaking public, political, editorial, and critical discourse for the private tastes of the reading public.[111]

Though most readers soon enough had had their fill of a war that became unpopular in America soon after it ended, veterans—combatants and noncombatants alike—continued to crave works that could help them deal with psychological traumas for which, especially as most Americans wanted to forget the darker side of the war, if not the war entirely, there was little other help—or medicine. If "America" had had enough of the war, many veterans were not quite done with it. As late as 1932, the Bonus March attracted 17,000 veterans and their families to Washington to agitate for back pay promised by the government. More than 4 million American veterans survived the war, which alone—not considering their family members and friends—was a considerable percentage of the population of the entire country (around 100 million).

This book presents the varied responses to World War I and the new American army, but it does not attempt to be comprehensive in its coverage of American writing of the war; to begin with, it is limited to thirteen authors who wrote and published book-length prose works.[112] A comprehensive project devoted to writers who produced prose concerning World War I, one that employs both close readings of the literature and detailed discussions of the author's experiences—which are, along with the detailed reconstruction of the historical context, essential to this project—would be beyond the scope of a single volume. There are several reasons why such a study as this one has not previously existed. First and foremost is the fact that the history of the American army in World War I has only recently been recovered. But another important reason is that the books of the combatant authors discussed here have rarely if ever been given the close, sustained attention they require and deserve. Finally, the task of assessing only the 1920s masterpieces of Hemingway, Fitzgerald, and Faulkner (namely *The Great Gatsby*, *The Sun Also Rises*, and *The Sound and the Fury*) in what amounts to an essentially new historical context required an entire book on its own, which had to be done before this project could be undertaken. Chapter one here is thus, for the most part, a summary of that book, my previous monograph, *The Gun and the Pen: Hemingway, Fitzgerald, Faulkner and the Fiction of Mobilization* (2008). As an encapsulation, it compresses arguments and includes less detail than the other chapters here. (I should add that Faulkner and Fitzgerald get relatively brief treatment in this volume because I have said at length what I have to say about their most renowned 1920s works in that monograph.)

The selection of the thirteen authors, beyond the inclusion of the five most famous Lost Generation authors who produced books on World War I—a group including Dos Passos and Cummings, who would naturally appear in any serious revision of World War I American literature—requires a bit of explanation. The five combatant male authors considered here are only a portion of the group of American soldier-writers who produced postwar books of prose. I have chosen these combat-veteran writers because expert commentators consider them important. Military historians consider the works of Boyd, March, and Allen to be the most significant.[113] Daly's novel is uniquely important by virtue of the fact that it is the only book of the war published by an African American combat veteran. In addition, all of these authors' books under consideration here, including Stallings's, have been recently reissued—essentially the results of decisions by literary critics and university press publishers—which puts them in a special category.[114] Meanwhile, the female authors included have been chosen because they all experienced or witnessed the war as well as confronted in their writing, in one way or another, issues of meritocracy in the wartime context.[115] (This criterion applies to the male writers considered here as well, but the men naturally meet it because all of them had wanted to serve, and thus all of them encountered the reality of a meritocratic US Army. Since American women writers were not subject to the draft and could not enlist in the army, they did not necessarily encounter the American military or write about meritocracy.) Here it is perhaps less obvious whom to include or exclude, but my contention is that Porter, Cather, and La Motte produced the richest and thus most revealing books by American women writers of World War I when it comes to those issues. And as with the combatants' texts, the women writers' books have also been recently reissued—again indicating their reputation among critics and publishers. (The fact that all of the volumes being discussed here are easily available is also something I consider desirable, as interested readers of my book can consult the original texts.)

This book is divided into three parts: (1) noncombatant, participant male writers, (2) participant and nonparticipant women writers, and (3) combatant male writers. The categories are based on my contention that these groups had fundamentally different wartime experiences that derived from differing social pressures and judgments. But this organization also reflects to a significant degree—and not entirely accidentally—differences in social privilege predicated on family, gender, race, and class. Most obviously, the women writers of this era faced discrimination in the workplace based on gender, regardless of their class. But whereas the Lost Generation, noncombatant male writers of part I all came from privileged families, three of the authors in part II had disadvantaged backgrounds, because of family situation, race, or class. Of course, the relative lack of accident in this large overlap between social background and wartime role is not because meritocracy in military selection and rejection simply inverted traditional hierarchies, making it more likely that privileged men would not qualify as soldiers while disadvantaged men would. Instead, privileged and educated men who found themselves excluded from favored positions in the military underwent a greater trauma—and were thus more likely to write about it—than working-class noncombatant men who did not experience the same sense of demotion and also lacked the educational training or familial financial support to be writers. Conversely, men who had disadvantaged backgrounds (and somehow still managed to get decent educations) but found themselves receiving extraordinary recognition in wartime were perhaps more motivated to write about their experiences than privileged men who enjoyed elite ranks in the army.

Part I on noncombatant male writers opens with chapter one, in which I present the argument that the 1920s masterpieces of Ernest Hemingway, F. Scott Fitzgerald, and William Faulkner were motivated not by their experiences of the horrors of war but instead by their failure to have had those experiences; this chapter examines three of the most familiar postwar American novels—*The Great Gatsby*, *The Sun Also Rises*, and *The Sound and the Fury*—in the unfamiliar context of the World War I mobilization and explains why all of these authors transmuted their own wartime experiences into tragic stories involving similar love triangles comprising a desirable Anglo female, an Anglo male, and an outsider (in two cases an ethnic American) male. Chapter two looks at earlier works of these three writers as well as John Dos Passos's *Three Soldiers*, which likewise tell similar tales—in this case of recruits who suffer in love and war. Here the stories are closely based on the authors' own experiences and do not involve fundamental transmutations. Chapter three addresses E. E. Cummings's *The Enormous Room* (1922), which alone among these Lost Generation male texts is a "happy" one, and the happiness—surprisingly—stems from the narrator's being removed from his American ambulance unit and imprisoned by the French government on suspicion of sympathizing with the enemy. Why this should be the occasion for a happy noncombatant experience turns out to have everything to do with the difference between newfangled American military systems of organization and traditional French types. Chapter four considers how Dos Passos transmuted his miserable wartime experience in *1919* and examines what Hemingway was up to in telling three different versions of the story of a wounded soldier and a nurse in "A Very Short Story," *The Sun Also Rises*, and *A Farewell to Arms*.

Part II takes up women writers. Chapter five discusses Katherine Anne Porter's suffocating vision, in "Pale Horse, Pale Rider," of total or home-front mobilization and the seeming inescapability of falling prey to the hysteria about masculinity involved in the mobilization and propaganda. Chapter six examines Willa Cather's *One of Ours* (1922) and Ellen La Motte's *The Backwash of War* (1916), two books that could not be more different in their attitudes to war and yet profoundly coincide when it comes to issues of opportunity central to women.

Part III turns to combatant writers. Chapter seven evaluates Thomas Boyd's apparently paradoxical *Through the Wheat*, which seems to present a wartime meritocratic success story, or the tale of a modern combat hero, within an antiwar narrative. Chapter eight takes up Laurence Stallings's *Plumes* and the book's discomfort with the new realities of meritocratic promotion and recognition when it comes to a soldier who experiences these boons but is then maimed in combat. Chapter nine reveals the traumatic and taboo inside stories in Victor Daly's *Not Only War*, about serving in a schizophrenically racist and meritocratic military and about sexually crossing the color line in France. Lastly, chapter ten examines the highly unusual narrative aesthetics of Hervey Allen's *Toward the Flame*, which ends abruptly in the middle of a dramatic battle scene, and William March's *Company K*, which has 113 narrators. Motivated by post-traumatic stress, both of these authors find extreme literary devices that allow them to write about the war but at the same time to omit central experiences of their own that are too troubling to touch upon.

PART ONE

War Literature by Noncombatant Males

The officers and men who wore the shoulder insignia of the SOS [Services of Supply] . . . may not have been within range of the enemy guns but did more for their country by living for it than they could possibly have done by dying for it. . . . [However, they are nonetheless] doomed to spend the rest of their lives explaining why they served in the Services of Supply.

—MAJ. GEN. JAMES G. HARBORD,
US Commander of the Services of Supply

CHAPTER ONE

Noncombatant Mobilization Wounds

The Postwar Masterpieces of Hemingway, Fitzgerald, and Faulkner

We know there is a huge disjunction between Victorian morality and faith in progress, on the one hand, and the bloodbath and savagery of World War I, on the other. But there are other, literary, disjunctions in the famous 1920s works of Ernest Hemingway, F. Scott Fitzgerald, and William Faulkner. These novels present mysteries: the reader is often left baffled by strange holes in the stories, marooned in an alien social world that is never explained and which even the writers do not seem to understand. It is as if these writers had been struck by dissociative episodes in the midst of writing. More likely, the dissociation is intentional and functions like a euphemism; there is a polite suppression of uncomfortable details that they know a special segment of their audience, namely noncombatant veterans, does not need to be told because it is all too familiar to them. Critics tend to ignore or explain away these flaws or oddities—after all, these are the great writers.

For example, the whole story of *The Great Gatsby* hinges on the fact that Jay Gatsby, from a poor, German American background, becomes a commissioned officer in a US Army fighting Germany. It is only in this capacity that he is able to meet wealthy Anglo Daisy Faye on an equal footing and get involved with her romantically. But while Fitzgerald is otherwise exhaustive in presenting Gatsby's backstory, we are never told how he obtains that commission. Given his class and ethnic background, Gatsby's becoming an officer seems extremely unlikely. Daisy's rich husband, Tom Buchanan, will be "damned" if he sees how Gatsby—this "Nobody from Nowhere"—"got within a mile of [Daisy] unless [he] brought groceries to the back door."[1]

To take another example, why does Cadet Lowe, the main character of the first chapter of Faulkner's first novel *Soldiers' Pay*, continually subject himself to being judged by a woman who is a perfect stranger, even though she is incredibly patronizing and her judgment is extremely humiliating? (It cannot be that he has been emasculated by the experience of modern industrial warfare—a common critical interpretation of modernist male characters who are veterans of World War I—since the war ended before he finished training, and he never made it over to Europe.)

Or why, in Hemingway's *The Sun Also Rises*, is Jewish Robert Cohn even temporarily included in the other characters' exclusive social circle, since all the other men are Anglos who dislike and stereotype Jews and they are also all veterans of the war while Cohn is not? They eventually exclude him because he behaves badly in a way that they consider characteristically Jewish. So why was he there in the first place? Critics have dealt with Cohn's anomalous presence by ignoring his centrality to the story, and, though Cohn is undoubtedly one of the main characters—he is the first character described in the novel—the book is still generally seen as a portrait of the Lost Generation of men and women whose lives were disrupted by World War I. Yet such an interpretation does not accommodate Cohn.

These mysteries only resolve themselves when we understand the unprecedented way in which President Woodrow Wilson's American army mobilized for the war—and how radical and thus shocking its approach was at the time. Something similar might be said about the racist and anti-Semitic material that marks the postwar works of Hemingway, Fitzgerald, and Faulkner: critics have long noticed this material, but they have tended to excuse or dismiss it (as prejudice typical of the era) or to misinterpret it.[2]

Faulkner, Hemingway, and Fitzgerald were motivated not by their experiences of the horrors of war but instead by their failure to have had those experiences. A sense of diminishment and loss pervades these novels, a feeling of mourning for fallen worlds—symbolized by Jay Gatsby's "pre-war" romantic dream that cannot be retrieved in *The Great Gatsby* (1925), Jake Barnes's impotence received in combat in *The Sun Also Rises* (1926), Benjy's idiocy and Caddy's loss of innocence in *The Sound and the Fury* (1929). These stem not from disillusionment brought on by the catastrophe of the Great War and the concomitant alienation from the traditional values of a failed civilization but instead from personal frustration with the US Army. Fitzgerald, Hemingway, and Faulkner each desired to be part of the military's elite in what some American wartime posters referred to as the "Big Game," the "Big Show," what Fitzgerald called "the big time."[3] But they were all deemed unsuitable as candidates for the air corps or command in the field, and the ultimate consequence was that they felt themselves "emasculated." They were also disappointed that they had missed out on or been excluded from what Stephen Crane had called the "mysterious fraternities born out of smoke and danger of death."[4] In short, they were alienated, not because of their experiences of trench warfare in a modern, mass army or their awareness of mechanized mass slaughter but because they either got nowhere near the war zone or because they got there in "minor," noncombat roles on marginal fronts.

Furthermore, the disappointment of their military ambitions happened in the context of the US Army's unprecedented, if partial, experiment with meritocracy, its adoption of methods of evaluating men for positions that were indifferent to class and ethnic difference—though not racial, or black-white, difference. For decades, the common wisdom about the war years has been that they were *thoroughly* repressive toward not only African Americans but also ethnic Americans, in an era when Anglo nativists considered immigrants from southern and eastern Europe, including Jewish Americans, to be racially different.[5] There is no doubt that the army segregated black soldiers and assigned most of them to labor detail, and that the number of black men allowed to become commissioned officers was purposefully kept very small. It is also undeniable that, in the civilian social world, immigrants and second-generation Americans were subjected to obligatory assimilation. But, again, we today know that this ugly record of racism and nativism is only *part* of the wartime story.[6]

Given the military's extension of equal treatment to working-class and ethnic Americans, the demeaning failure to get into the air corps or to be promoted in the army was for Hemingway, Fitzgerald, and Faulkner also a defeat by people they considered their social inferiors. Thus we find in their famous novels a deep resentment—not of modern war and an archaic military that did not prepare them for a protracted, mechanized conflict of attrition—but of a modern military that rejected them with meritocratic personnel methods, and especially of the ethnic Americans the military welcomed. These writers—all expecting their social privilege to be operative in the military—experienced a culture shock and a status crash.

In Fitzgerald's *The Beautiful and Damned* (1922), the Anglo protagonist's privileged friends feel "strangely exalted and reproachless" when they apply for officers' training camps: "they chattered to each other, like college boys, of war's being the one excuse for, and justification of, the aristocrat, and conjured up an impossible caste of officers, to be composed, it appeared, chiefly of the more attractive alumni of three or four Eastern colleges."[7] But for Anthony Patch, the protagonist, who is rejected from officer training on the basis of a medical exam, these expectations are dashed, and, in the army, he must appeal to a "short swarthy Italian" for a place to sit on the train, and his "tent-mates" include a "a big, scared Pole, and [a] disdainful Celt" (261). "For the first time in his life he was in constant personal contact with the waiters to whom he had given tips, the chauffeurs who had touched their hats to him, the carpenters, plumbers, barbers and farmers who had previously been remarkable only in the subservience of their professional genuflections" (268–69). Wrenching experiences of failing to measure up in the new army meritocracy—shared by Hemingway, Fitzgerald, and Faulkner—explain the racist and anti-Semitic material in certain of their 1920s books. Feelings of social demotion and dislocation also explain the disjunctions in their books.

With perhaps less obvious resentment, these novels also depicted women as promiscuous, and socially or ethnically indiscriminate in their choice of men. During the war the authors had watched women flock around training camps in such numbers that the army deemed it a national problem of hygiene and morality and ended up locking up tens of thousands of women (see introduction).[8] The jailed women were not only prostitutes but what were called at the time "charity girls."[9] The military had during World War I essentially the power to confer or deny masculinity—and they conferred it, along with desirability, on many ethnic and lower-class Americans. Thus, at the heart of these authors' most famous postwar novels are "love triangles" involving Anglo male characters outdone in love and war and thus downgraded in their masculinity; attractive and sexually active Anglo females whom the Anglo males cannot possess; and ethnic or outsider upstarts affirmed in some way by the military, who are rivals of the Anglo men and (at least temporarily) get the Anglo girls.

All three authors imagined being aviators, the stars of the war, but none of them were.[10] Hemingway and Faulkner could not get commissions in the air corps because of physical disqualifications. Again, Hemingway ended up in a Red Cross ambulance unit and Faulkner in the Canadian Royal Air Force. Fitzgerald, who was old enough to be drafted in the fall of 1917, actually made officer in the US Army—he passed a written entrance exam open to college students that made him a candidate, and he successfully earned his infantry commission—but once in camp he hit roadblocks to promotions and combat service. At Camp Leavenworth, his fellows remembered him as "the world's worst second lieutenant."[11] And he was not given the platoon he was supposed to receive at Camp Zachary Taylor because "his superior officers felt he couldn't be entrusted with a command." At Camp Sheridan, where he finally got his only promotion, from second to first lieutenant, his fellow officers mocked him and pulled pranks on him. He remained in training camps for the duration of the war.[12]

Only Hemingway made it to the war zone, and he was famously wounded, but as an ambulance driver who was delivering cigarettes and chocolate to the troops on a minor front. After the war, he and Faulkner, as we have seen, lied about their war records. Fitzgerald, in his essay "The Crack-Up" (1936), named "not getting overseas during the war" as one of the "juvenile regrets" that bothered him in the 1920s. In a 1920 short story he wrote of a man who never gets to the front: "It was not so bad—except that when the infantry came limping back from the trenches he wanted to be one of them. The sweat and mud they wore seemed only one of those ineffable symbols of aristocracy that were forever eluding him."[13]

Jake Barnes's phallic war wound in *The Sun Also Rises*, usually seen to symbolize emasculation in the face of the horrors of modern war, is, from its introduction, tied to status issues: "Well, it was a rotten way to be wounded and flying on a joke front like the Italian."[14] In fact, Barnes and Hemingway both experience demotion in masculine status over the course of the war: Barnes begins as a pilot, a star of the military, while Hemingway got notoriety as the first American wounded on the Italian front while serving as a Red Cross ambulance driver.[15] By the end of the war, Barnes has because of his injury been diminished as a man; likewise, Hemingway was to find that his status had plummeted, as ambulance driving came to be seen as women's or boy's work.[16]

Jake Barnes finds himself in a rivalry with Jewish Robert Cohn for the affections of desirable Lady Brett Ashley. And the point of Hemingway making Robert Cohn a character who is physically manly (a boxer) and inwardly emasculated (nervous, emotional, and controlled by women) is to have a precise foil to Jake, who is, both outwardly and inwardly, the opposite. One of the reasons the gang of characters in *The Sun Also Rises* goes to the bullfights is to assert that Cohn is comparable to a castrated bull, while Jake, though literally missing part of his genitals, is not. (Hemingway asserted, in an interview with George Plimpton of the *Paris Review* years after the novel came out, that Jake was not castrated like a steer. Meanwhile, in a letter to Fitzgerald, he called the book "THE SUN ALSO RISES [LIKE YOUR COCK IF YOU HAVE ONE]."[17])

Jake, then, does not lack testicles, and thus, in the familiar metaphor, guts: he has an inner manliness that serves him in war and makes him generally "hard-boiled." It is quite evident from the novel that Jake is not suffering from shell shock. (Hemingway makes this absolutely clear by describing such a character, Brett's previous husband, Lord Ashley, who sleeps every night on the floor holding a loaded revolver.) When it comes to his narrator, Hemingway is not interested in symbolizing, by Jake's physical wound, the inner loss of masculinity brought about by World War I's mechanized warfare. What Hemingway is trying to represent is something quite different, what might be termed a social emasculation.

Jake has his "balls" but lacks the private part that matters to women, especially to his sexually hungry true love, Lady Brett. This metaphor is less familiar. Jake has suffered an exterior loss of masculinity because of the war. What Jake has been deprived of, through no fault of his own, no failure of inner strength or courage, is the phallus as masculine status, as male attractiveness, as sexual viability to the opposite sex. Something similar happened to Hemingway: because of the hysterical definitions of masculinity operating by the end of the war, which women bought into—whereby only combat soldiers qualified as men—Hemingway, though seriously injured in the line of duty, was deemed, because of his position as ambulance driver, a mere boy.[18]

There are passages in the Hemingway oeuvre that are clear-cut about issues of status in the military. In a telling scene in *A Farewell to Arms* (1929), a minor character questions the narrator's right to his medals. Frederic Henry has been decorated for being wounded while working with an ambulance service, which is to say, in circumstances resembling those in which Hemingway was famously wounded. Lieutenant Moretti, an Italian American infantry officer who on the basis of "merit of war" is about to be made captain, and thus to outrank Henry, questions Henry's decorations. Making the nature of Henry's competition with this ethnic American even more explicit, the novel goes on to establish that bilingual Moretti would outdo Henry in the US Army as well because Moretti "can command a company in Italian." Henry is left shaken by the encounter and asks his love interest, Catherine Barkley, "Wouldn't you like me to have a more exalted rank?"[19]

Henry finds himself in competition and at a loss with an ethnic American in the military, just as in *The Sun Also Rises* the narrator finds himself in competition with Robert Cohn, whose Jewishness is constantly commented on by the other characters and who attended "military school" and received egalitarian treatment there: "at the military school . . . no one ever made him feel he was a Jew, and hence any different from anybody else" (4). (Military schools were of course not officially part of the US military, but they tended then as now to reflect its current ethos.)[20] If Robert Cohn is being considered for membership in Jake's Anglo clique, despite its anti-Semitism, it is because, though the book only obliquely suggests this at the very beginning, the US military has included Jews on an equal footing—

something any reader who had been in a training camp would be familiar with. And Jake finds himself at a disadvantage in the sexual competition (over his promiscuous love interest and Anglo princess, Lady Brett Ashley), since Cohn has a good body, is a talented athlete, and is not impotent, and since Brett, to Jake's dismay, follows the lead of the American military and is ethnically nondiscriminating.

For similar reasons, the darling of the military, and of Daisy, in *The Great Gatsby* is a German American (from a poor family), whom Daisy's husband, Tom, calls "Mr. Nobody from Nowhere" and implies he does not consider white (137). Fitzgerald's Anglo-American narrator, Nick Carraway, is quite interested in how Gatsby achieves his military ranks and decorations. But while Nick eventually corrects Gatsby's romantic saga of his promotion from lieutenant to major at the front as a result of his combat performance, he does so cryptically, only adding, "He was a captain before he went to the front" (158). He never explains *how* Gatsby made captain, or even lieutenant for that matter—though once he learns that James Gatz invented a distinguished family named Gatsby, the latter's story about being offered a commission on the basis of his family falls to pieces.

Captain is precisely the rank Fitzgerald desired and had fantasies about, but never achieved in training camp.[21] The military's own records concerning the ethnic makeup of recruits at Camp Taylor, the training camp where Fitzgerald places Gatsby, indicate that Fitzgerald likely watched German Americans make that rank of captain and pass him by. Camp Taylor had nearly 1,500 German Americans—the largest ethnic group at the camp—around the time Fitzgerald was there.[22] And, despite the fact that the United States was fighting Germany, German Americans were well represented in the army's officer ranks. This reality surprised French soldiers at the time. As one described US troops in France in 1917, "You could not imagine a more extraordinary gathering than this american [*sic*] army, there is a bit of everything, Greeks, Italians, Turks, Indians, Spanish, also a sizable number of boches [Germans]. Truthfully, almost half of the officers have German origins."[23]

Likewise, in *The Sound and the Fury* (which never so much as mentions World War I and seems to have nothing to do with it), effeminate Quentin has incestuous fantasies about his sister Caddy and, trying to play the protective brother, faces off with her lover, an outsider named Dalton Ames, whose status as a war veteran with combat experience most critics ignore; he so intimidates Quentin that he faints in Ames's presence. Meanwhile, Quentin's brother Jason jokes about their "idiot" brother Benjy, whom he has castrated: "you can send Ben to the Navy I says or to the cavalry anyway, they use geldings in the cavalry."[24] It is significant that Jason imagines *this* particular absurdity of Benjy going into the military when Benjy is unqualified to do so many things.

US Army papers documenting its mostly forgotten personnel practices record that, first, the military's intelligence testing program was originally instituted to eliminate the "feebleminded," men such as Benjy.[25] Second, in order to make use of non-English speaking troops, specific programs were developed to identify qualified bilingual immigrants and ethnic Americans to lead them—just as Moretti suggests in *A Farewell to Arms*.[26] Third, the army also developed and used meritocratic classification methods for identifying potential officers, and in particular captains, including intelligence test scores. This explains how a man of Gatsby's ethnic and lower-class background could become an officer and a captain in the training camps, information that any man who had been in a training camp would know. It turns out that Camp Taylor, one of the many camps where Fitzgerald ended up spending time—not the one where he met Zelda (that was Camp Sheridan in Alabama) but the one where he decided to put Gatsby—was one of four training camps where the military first experimented with intelligence tests.[27] A real recruit with fictional Gatsby's timeline, who shipped out in the winter of 1917–1918, would have been given such a test at Camp Taylor, and a man with Gatsby's background would have been poised to excel on these tests because, in an era when the average non-black recruit born in the United States had 6.9 years of schooling, Gatsby had finished high school, and success on the test correlated strongly with level of education.[28]

In short, military records reveal that the mobilization extended equal opportunities to ethnic Americans, which meant that, on meritocratic grounds, ethnic Americans such as Moretti or Gatsby might indeed be promoted while Anglo-Americans such as Benjy might be rejected. Though the public was largely xenophobic, the military leadership, as we have seen—dedicated to winning the war and already bowing to civilian pressure to exclude black men from combat and segregate them—was not.[29] Despite the traditional critical take, the "past" that Gatsby desperately wants to "repeat" with Daisy is not actually prewar but wartime. For Gatsby, the ideal moment was that of the national emergency when he suddenly could, as never before, gain entrance to Daisy's mansion thanks to his status as an army officer.

The World War I intelligence tests have a thoroughly bad name—as blunt instruments of prejudice in the name of science—but this is due to a misunderstanding and, again, a failure to consult the military records. The tests were indeed culturally biased against immigrants, and there is no doubt that invidious and racist publications about the intelligence test results after the war famously helped achieve the passage of the Immigration Restriction Acts of 1921 and 1924, which all but shut off immigration from eastern and southern Europe. Stephen J. Gould, in *The Mismeasure of Man* (1981), among others, has drawn attention to the way the psychological testing program results were compiled after the war and dubiously analyzed to "prove" that immigrants from eastern and southern Europe (as well as African Americans) were mentally inferior to Nordics. Gould demonstrated that the army tests did not really measure intelligence but rather correlated with education and years of American residence.[30] But the immediate postwar interpretation of the tests—the psychologists' false claims to have measured individual intelligence and to have discovered proof of Nordic mental superiority—did not mean that in practice during the war the tests selected only for Anglo men and were not in part meritocratic. Precisely because they correlated most closely with education and American residency, in practice they selected for ethnic Americans such as Gatsby, who was American born and raised, had much more than the average amount of schooling, and received that education in the North where schools were better.[31]

Records show that in the case, for example, of Jewish Americans—who did badly on the tests overall (presumably because in the army there were many more immigrant Jews than Jews born in America) and against whom there was by all accounts a robust Anglo prejudice during the era—the army was even-handed regarding officer commissions, except perhaps at the very highest ranks. There were perhaps as "many as 200,000 . . . American Jews in service during the war," and the "army, Navy and Marine Corps altogether had nearly 10,000 Jews as commissioned officers," including "more than a hundred colonels and lieutenant colonels" (as well as "a really tremendous number of non-commissioned officers").[32] That proportion of all Jewish commissioned officers to all Jewish soldiers—namely one to twenty—is similar to, and if anything slightly greater than, the proportion of all American officers to all American soldiers (around 200,000 to around 4.4 million).

The inclusion of ethnic Americans and immigrants in the military and the officers' corps explains why all of these famous Anglo novels express anti-Semitism and anti-ethnic feeling, and why Hemingway and Fitzgerald's novels make sure their "upstart" ethnic Americans with military connections who sleep with Anglo princesses have a comeuppance. It is because Gatsby, Moretti, and Cohn succeed on the military's terms—Gatsby and Moretti are obviously war heroes, but military-school graduate Cohn excels in the sports institutionalized by the military in the camp athletic programs, such as football and boxing—that these novels disqualify ethnic

Americans on other grounds. So *The Sound and the Fury* attacks Wall Street "eastern jews" as swindlers; Gatsby's Jewish associate Meyer Wolfshiem is a criminal mastermind who fixed the 1919 World Series; Gatsby himself is a bootlegger who, from time to time, wears the expression of a murderer; Cohn is a neurotic boor; and Moretti is similarly an unmannered bore and a bully. And Cohn gets ostracized from the group, and Gatsby gets killed. Not simply expressing a general xenophobia of the period, these novels enact a backlash against the military's sudden extension of equal opportunity to ethnic Americans and immigrants.

In their early works of fiction (on which, see chapter two), these modernist writers indulged in self-pity and sometimes directed bitterness toward the military for their rejections and frustrated ambitions. In their "mature," stylistically sophisticated, and most famous fictions, Hemingway, Fitzgerald, and Faulkner learned to disguise their wounds of rejection and transfigure them as irony, tragedy, and symbolism.

Cadet Lowe of *Soldiers' Pay* (1926), who like Faulkner got flight training but never saw action, whines to the desirable war widow Powers that he, too, would have been wounded, like the dying Mahon, if only he'd been given the chance. But despite his "slobbering and moaning," she treats him like a child.[33] When next we hear of "slobbering and moaning" from Faulkner, it will be in regard to the idiot Benjy, and the pathetic rejection of Lowe by Powers will transform into the impossible and thus tragic love of siblings Quentin and Caddy. Meanwhile, the military frustration and rejection will have been transfigured and all but hidden: Faulkner's rejection on physical grounds will metamorphose into Benjy's highly symbolic mental disability, and Quentin's antagonist and "rival," Dalton Ames, will be a veteran of an unnamed war (as World War I is still in the future when Caddy is involved with Ames).[34]

The protagonist Anthony of Fitzgerald's *The Beautiful and Damned*, who like Fitzgerald goes to training camp but never to war, is court-martialed for his camp slip-ups and expresses his hatred for the army. After the war he calls a Jewish sexual rival (who, like Gatsby, Anglicizes his name) a "God-damn Jew" (357) and gets punched out for it. Meanwhile, Fitzgerald's narrator Nick Carraway will see service in the war and will not be a rival of Gatsby's; he will be an ironically detached observer of the Tom-Gatsby competition as Daisy's cousin, and his fussing over the details of Gatsby's military career will be in the interest of dispassionate truth telling.

Hemingway's protagonist of "A Very Short Story," compensating sexually when thrown over by his love interest for a senior officer, picks up a girl in Chicago and gets venereal disease, a phallic wounding as a result of degraded love, not yet a phallic wounding that will be transfigured, in *The Sun Also Rises*, into the tragic predicament of a love that due to a war wound can never be consummated. Thus, out of a compulsion to both explore and hide their "mobilization wounds," which were at once unavoidable and humiliating, these American writers devised their famous modernist prose, with its mythic symbolism.

CHAPTER TWO

The Horrors of War Mobilization

The Early Works of Hemingway, Fitzgerald, Faulkner, and Dos Passos

JOHN DOS PASSOS'S NOVEL *Three Soldiers* (1921) begins with an epigraph from Stendhal, in French: "Les contemporains qui souffrent de certaines choses ne peuvent s'en souvenir qu'avec une horreur qui paralyse tout autre plaisir, meme celui de lire un conte."[1] Dos Passos was not the only modernist writer to have an untranslated bit of foreign language in his work. Such a device is considered a mark of "high" modernism. T. S. Eliot is famous for having done so. His untranslated epigraphs for *The Waste Land* (1922) and "The Love Song of J. Alfred Prufrock" (1915), in Greek and medieval Italian respectively, essentially serve as signposts indicating the relevant poems are meant for an elite literary audience. Was Dos Passos's epigraph meant to function in the same way? It is hard to believe that was the case. Dos Passos is seen as writing for a broader audience, and though controversial, as the first "World War I novel of protest," the book, as noted in the introduction, was a popular success.[2] Did Dos Passos use an untranslated epigraph for another reason?

Perhaps the average American was no more familiar with French than with Greek, but is it possible that Dos Passos was reaching out to a particular US population that had some French, namely the more than 2 million veterans who had recently served in France? After all, many veterans, because they were encouraged to by the military, or for their own reasons, spoke what they called "A.E.F. French."[3] And if a particular veteran reader had not learned enough of the language to puzzle out the epigraph, which is not especially difficult French, he probably knew a comrade who had. Learning some French was in no way limited to intellectually minded soldiers, as knowing a bit of the language was a real help in picking up French women, which was a common pastime among American troops despite its being against the rules set by the US military authority. An experienced soldier advises the protagonist in Willa Cather's *One of Ours*, "Are you quick with your French? . . . You'd better brush up on it if you want to do anything with French girls."[4]

But even if Dos Passos was addressing veterans here by communicating in the language of the country where most men in the American Expeditionary Force (AEF) served, why not translate it as well? E. E. Cummings strategically uses "the privacy" of French—and rather simple French in fact—at points in *The Enormous Room*: some extended racy comments made by a French speaker, which might worry an American publisher concerned with censorship, are left untranslated. But censorship is not Dos Passos's concern here; the quote from Stendhal translates as: "Contemporaries who suffer certain things can only be reminded of them with a horror that paralyzes every other pleasure, even that of reading a story."[5] Is Dos Passos telling his insider readers that he is going to remind them in this book of certain things that will make them relive a horror? Is this a way of immediately connecting with his fellow veterans? Even if this is the case, it does not explain why the author wants to communicate privately with his target audience.

Why the coded message? Why the privacy or secrecy? Dos Passos's book exposes "bitterness against army life" with its brutal and punitive discipline—as Stanley Cooperman puts it in his landmark study. But as Cooperman also points out, a lot of World War I American literature does so, including Thomas Boyd's *Through the Wheat* and William March's *Company K*.[6] These authors did not see the need to communicate with veterans at the start of their books in untranslated French or in some other coded way. Victor Daly has a forbidding prologue in his *Not Only War* that likewise precedes the story proper, but it is in English.

It seems this mystery can only be solved, and Dos Passos's book can only be fully comprehended, when we consider the possibility that he was writing for a more particular, but still huge, audience—not all veterans, but the majority of that group, who were designated as noncombatants—and realize that he was describing not only the horror of discipline but another horror as well, one that applied only to noncombatants, a suffering absolutely central to *Three Soldiers*. Dos Passos was himself a noncombatant: he served as an ambulance driver and, later in the war, just after the armistice, returned to France as a member of the Services of Supply in the Army Medical Corps. In that latter service, he would feel slighted and abused by the US military in more than one way.

Dos Passos's untranslated French appears to be motivated by the same sort of trauma and embarrassment—or, to put it another way, a similar sensitivity to this specific readership's feelings—as Fitzgerald's purposeful withholding of the explanation of how a man with Gatsby's background became a captain: information about the processes of army selection and promotion that noncombatants were all too familiar with—because these processes did not favor them and in many cases demeaned them. *Three Soldiers*—just like the World War I texts of Hemingway, Fitzgerald, and Faulkner—has been misunderstood by being interpreted alongside combatant works in a generalized category of literature by veterans or male war participants. But, as I suggested in the introduction, the experiences of male noncombatants and combatants were significantly different, even for those noncombatants who saw combat or the human devastation that resulted from it. Combatants were validated by the army and the larger society while noncombatants were not.

Early in their careers, Hemingway, Fitzgerald, Faulkner, and Dos Passos all produced tales or episodes about recruits who suffer in both love and war, or, more accurately, in both love and the army. Not surprisingly perhaps, given the social stigma and potential emasculation attached to noncombatant status, the stories all involve the same two related elements: these characters experience, in one way or another, the lowliness of their military rank or position—in three of four cases, they are clearly noncombatants—and matters are made worse by their getting involved with women who cause them further problems. Women pop up as antagonists, or as "trouble," for these characters because noncombatants saw women as contributing to their emasculation by affirming the military's judgments of masculinity.

In the stories by Fitzgerald and Dos Passos, those problems concern falling afoul of army regulations. The two of these four writers who served in the US Army, they explore in some detail their protagonists' intense mental suffering as a result of encounters with meritocratic procedures of evaluation, which do not favor them, and military discipline, which becomes punitive and even brutal when they break the rules. In *Three Soldiers* and the wartime portion of *The Beautiful and Damned*, the genre of the tale seems to veer at points into psychological horror. The depiction in *Three Soldiers* is especially harrowing. Arguably, *Three Soldiers* is the "truest" fictional account of the noncombatant experience.[7] Like these early texts by the other Lost Generation authors, it is raw and little transformed from actual experience; in distinction to those texts, it is sustained and detailed. The extent of the trauma suffered by Dos Passos's protagonist in particular gives readers a sense of the profundity and suddenness of the social dislocation and demotion that men from privileged backgrounds could find themselves confronting. In this way, it may shed light on the baffling gaps or cryptically discretionary omissions one sometimes encounters in other Lost Generation novels.

In Faulkner's sometimes awkward first novel, *Soldiers' Pay*, the opening chapter focuses on the immediate postwar experience of a character named Cadet Lowe, who does not feature in the rest of the novel. Lowe is introduced as being distraught because "they had stopped the war on him" before he got into combat.[8] At the armistice, he had yet to finish flight training, so he never got his "wings" (pilot's insignia on his uniform) or a chance to prove himself in battle. Faulkner had the same basic experience: he was training in Canada with the Canadian Royal Air Force when the war ended.[9] From the first lines of the novel, 19-year-old Lowe is already suffering over his insufficient status on the train home from army camp. Gilligan, a 32-year-old private who saw action, rubs it in by calling him "General" and "Lootenant" (3). Lowe encounters the slightly older Margaret Powers, a "charity girl" turned officer's wife turned war widow (when the man she married after a few days of acquaintance is killed), who is now caring for a gravely wounded British pilot named Mahon. The attentions she extends to Mahon exacerbates Lowe's sense of inadequacy and intensifies his envy of the man's "wings" as well as his wound. "To have been him! he moaned. Just to be him. Let him take this body of mine! To have got wings on my breast, to have wings; and to have got his scar, too, I would take death tomorrow" (41). Lowe carries on about "wings" and a "scar" three more times, the last time out loud to Margaret: "you don't like him better than me because he has wings and a scar, do you?" (48). His "passionate disappointment" gets so bad that he starts "[s]lobbering and moaning" (42).[10]

Though it redoubles his humiliation, he cannot help vocalizing his envy as well as trying to justify himself to her, protesting that he never had the opportunity to prove his skills or his bravery. He claims that he would have been an ace, a talented flyer, and was quite ready to have been wounded or worse. "I would have been killed . . . if I could, or wounded like him, don't you know it? . . . I would have been, if I'd had the chance" (48). Though he thereby wants to impress Powers with his masculine credentials, his immaturity and whininess about having missed his chance only confirms his status as a child. Powers "treats me as a child," he tells himself twice (46); later, she calls him "sweet child" (49) and "dear boy" and allows him only to kiss her on the cheek and embrace her legs (as he hugs the seated Powers while on his knees). Meanwhile, she kisses him "as his mother" does (50) and makes him promise to return straight home to her. In short, his lack of military rank and experience, and the emasculation it implies, is only made worse by his unconfident and embarrassing approach to Powers—in begging for a validation he knows he will not get. "He knew he was acting the child she supposed him to be, but he couldn't help it" (48).

The characters' names in this first section of the novel are transparently symbolic. There is the lowly Lowe—whom Faulkner almost always refers to as "Cadet Lowe"; singularly among the characters, his "rank" or position is repeated over and over to emphasize the mere trainee status that haunts him (the same is not true of Private Gilligan). Mahon is the model "man," and Mrs. Powers has the power to judge manliness and to treat men according to their rank, position, war experience, and battle scars.[11]

Hemingway's "A Very Short Story," which appears in the collection *In Our Time* (1925),[12] is, like *Soldiers' Pay*, closely based on the author's own experience. And it is another tale of a main male character finding himself bested in love by a higher ranked and more accomplished foreign officer, and treated like a boy by the woman he desires. A wounded American, presumably a soldier (the only information specified about his position is that he is serving at "the front" [65], and he is evidently Nick Adams, who figures in a number of stories in *In Our Time*, but his name does not appear in this story), has a love affair with his nurse named Luz, and they talk of getting married. But after the war, she wants him to get a job back in the States before she joins him, and in the meantime she meets an older, and much more highly ranked Italian (a major) who is also a member of the elite storm troops called the *arditi* (66). She gets engaged to the Italian major and writes Nick a "Dear John letter."[13] In it, she adds insult to injury by gratuitously belittling their relationship, telling him that their love was "only a boy and girl affair" (66). Her name, too, has significance. Luz means "light" in Spanish, and it is in the light of this woman's attention and judgment that the masculinity of each man is revealed. Luz seems also to be a pun on "loose": no doubt the rejected American soldier comes to see her as a "loose" woman.

Hemingway's experience is in many details identical. He got involved with a nurse, an American woman eight years older named Agnes von Kurowsky, who, uneasy about their age difference, called him "Kid."[14] Hemingway told her he wanted to marry her. When he was back in the United States and she was still in Italy, she hinted in a letter that she might marry him in a year or so, a hint he took as a "solemn pact."[15] She eventually wrote him that she had fallen in love with a titled Italian lieutenant, Duca Domenico Caracciolo.

> Now, after a couple of months away from you, I know that I am still very fond of you, but, it is more as a mother than as a sweetheart.
>
> So, Kid (still Kid to me, & always will be) can you forgive me some day for unwittingly deceiving you? . . . But, I am now & always will be too old, & that's the truth, & I can't get away from the fact that you're just a boy—a kid. . . .
>
> I tried hard to make you understand a bit of what I was thinking on that trip from Padua to Milan, but, you acted like a spoiled child, & I couldn't keep on hurting you.[16]

As one of Hemingway's biographers concludes, "Ernest had lost his nurse to a more experienced rival."[17]

Though the differences between the fiction and reality are slight, they are worth noting. In the story, Luz is not established as being older, so her condescending to the soldier is more presumptuous and gratuitous. In a similar vein, Luz's betrayal is more intense, since she, unlike Agnes, is not hesitant to commit to her young American but seemingly just as invested as he is in their prospective marriage. Finally, the titled Italian lieutenant becomes in fiction an Italian major with the *arditi*: just as age difference is removed as an issue, social class is also downplayed, while military rank, prowess, and experience are emphasized. Luz's new lover bests the narrator to a degree on the basis of his being Italian: "she had never known Italians before" (66). (Perhaps Hemingway is toying with the stereotype of Italian male sexual charm.) More importantly, however, is his rank. Major is quite a jump from lieutenant, and the *arditi* implies exalted military status. In the world of the story, the woman chooses a man—or a man's appeal as a mate is determined—almost entirely on the basis of his position in the military.[18]

In Hemingway's story the American recruit's experience of his relatively lowly status and his emasculation is effected by the woman; in Faulkner's novel it is merely confirmed by her, and it is Lowe's misguided but apparently irresistible approach to her that makes matters worse. Nick seems to have no problem with his status or masculinity before Luz's condescending rejection. After all, he sees action and is wounded.

But true to the form of this particular story that all of these Lost Generation authors share, Nick's subsequent involvement with a second woman gives him a further problem, which echoes that first injury. Presumably smarting from Luz's rejection and looking to compensate for the wound it has caused to his sense of masculinity, Nick has sex in a taxicab with "a sales girl from a loop department store" and "contract[s] gonorrhea" (66) from her. A physical injury to his "manhood" is now added to the emotional one. As in Faulkner's story, the male character "doubles down" after an initial bruise to his status and masculinity by approaching a woman who might alleviate his pain, but the result is further degradation.

Dos Passos and Fitzgerald take a different tack. Instead of a recruit facing condescension or rejection from a woman, the noncombatant protagonist, who is already feeling the lowliness and ignominy of his position, pursues an involvement with a woman as an escape from or antidote to the suffering inflicted by his wartime experience. But that involvement, while initially providing relief, eventually gets him in trouble with the army authorities for breaking rules. And he thereby finds himself experiencing the penal end of the military system—and further humiliation. Again, the main characters' experiences resemble those of the writers, but in both cases the characters achieve less success and undergo more punishment in the army than their authors.

In a sustained and discrete wartime section of *The Beautiful and Damned*, the Anglo main character, Anthony Patch, like Fitzgerald, does not make it to Europe. But unlike Fitzgerald, who stalled at the rank of first lieutenant, Patch never gets a commission at all, despite his expectations as a result of his high social standing and college education. He is peremptorily excluded from "officers' training camp" because of "low blood pressure," which nonetheless does not prevent him from being drafted.[19] His lowly status as a regular recruit is so painful for him that "he hate[s] . . . every officer," and frequently his "eyes . . . turned precipitously inward upon the indignity of his position. . . . [L]ife was unendurable" (262).

His involvement with a lower-middle-class girl nicknamed Dot, who has already had an affair with a "naval officer" and two local men in a period of eight months, is for him about a "rest" from and "alleviat[ion]" of "the morbid . . . poundings of his imagination" (265). Because of Anthony's social superiority—and despite his lack of a commission—she looks up to him and gives him "worship[ful] . . . glances" (271) that at least momentarily reduce the sting of the status crash the army has meant for him.

Though Anthony does get promoted to corporal—"He was to be one of the quarter million selected for that consummate trust," quips the narrator with bitter irony (273)—and then sergeant, and is in fact on the verge of making it to officers' training camp after all, his status "comeback" is short-circuited when Dot essentially tricks him into being out of camp after curfew. Desperate to see him, she phones him late one evening and pretends she is breaking up with him. Now desperate himself—since she seems to be the only thing standing between him and "a hundred disordered and prowling thoughts" (265)—he rushes out to dissuade her. Immediately upon reaching her he realizes she only "shouted 'wolf'" in order to have some time with him, but it is too late for him to get back to camp in time, and he "collapse[s] . . . sobbing beside her" (283–84).

Convinced that he has to sneak back into camp because if he is caught coming in late "again his name would probably be stricken from the list of officer candidates" (284), he lies about his identity to the officer of the guard. A couple of days later, he is apprehended by the military police. Now he faces a punishment much more severe: he is "reduced to ranks without trial, and confined for a month to the limits of the company street." And things soon get even more drastic: "With this blow a spell of utter depression overtook him," and, when he is "caught down-town . . . in a drunken daze," he is sentenced to the "guard-house" for three weeks (285). Anthony's experience and punishment are similar to Fitzgerald's, but worse. Fitzgerald was once confined to camp for getting into trouble with a girl.[20] But he was not court-martialed, nor was he imprisoned.

Like Fitzgerald, Dos Passos came from a wealthy and privileged background (despite being an illegitimate child).[21] He attended an Ivy League college (Harvard). And like Hemingway, he served as a volunteer ambulance driver. He was also, later in the war, still eager to participate at the front.[22] But the army assigned him to the Services of Supply, and, because of his experience in that capacity, his postwar works were motivated by a sense of having been misused by the military. Also like Hemingway, he had "restricted vision," which was why the army classified him for "special service" when he managed to convince the draft board medical examiner to pass him on his eye exam, despite his not being able even to "read the *E* on the top line" on the chart.[23] He ended up in the Army Medical Corps, a unit, as he portrayed it, to which "characters whom other outfits found indigestible tended to sift down. . . . All were misfits and oddballs of various kinds." At training camp, "the sergeants found us too awkward to drill so they set us to washing windows" and other menial tasks.[24] Things did not get better for him in Europe. Since his unit was in transit in the Atlantic Ocean on the day of the armistice, there was little call for ambulance work, and he experienced mostly drilling. Though he was promoted to quartermaster sergeant because he could type, Dos Passos was unceremoniously stripped of his rank when he ordered the men he was drilling, in front of a colonel, to march into a stone wall. After that he remained a private, never even making private first class (unlike almost all the men he had gone to France with).[25]

Three Soldiers, based on his experience in the army, has been interpreted as staunchly antiwar, though in fact it depicts little of the violence of the battlefield. Though only novella length, Dos Passos's earlier work, *One*

Man's Initiation: 1917 (1920), which came out of his volunteer service in the Norton-Harjes Ambulance Corps, shows a good deal more of the destruction of modern combat.

The US military is the real enemy in *Three Soldiers*, just as the allied Italian military is the real enemy in Hemingway's *A Farewell to Arms* (see chapter four). Dos Passos does not scapegoat ethnic Americans in his novel. Rather, his poor and ethnic American soldiers (Chrisfield and Fuselli) and his privileged soldier (Andrews) all get along, and they all suffer at the hands of the rule-obsessed military. One goes AWOL, another serves time in a punitive labor battalion, and the third does both.

Fitzgerald's Anthony realizes in the army, though he had never thought of it "once in his lifetime" before, that "he had been a civilian . . . , white, free, and well" (274). John Andrews in *Three Soldiers* is, immediately after his mobilization, "appalled by the loss" of his "liberty" and "utterly in the void"; he, too, recognizes that he has departed "the glittering other world" of the wealthy and descended into "the lower half of the pyramid" (17). Though he had enlisted in the army to "humble himself" (13), "forget himself," and escape his "bored[om] with himself," "he had not foreseen" the extent of the "slavery" (17) that was the common lot in the military. Andrews finds himself constantly taking orders and doing menial work, such as "washing windows" (239). In his lowly position, he experiences both "terror" and "degradation." Though he early on tells himself "he must not let himself sink too deeply into the helpless mentality of the soldier" and "he must keep his will power" (17), he soon enough almost entirely fails to do so.

Like Anthony, Andrews seems for a short while to be bouncing back. He begins to recover some well-being and reconnect to his previous upper-class life, when he gets assigned to a postwar "School Detachment" in which he can continue musical studies at the Sorbonne. It is in Paris that he meets a couple of women, and in particular an educated, upper-class woman named Genevieve Rod, with whom he can talk about his experience of "slave psychology" (241) and feel recognized as a musician. He begins to be able to experience relief from his almost constant feelings of "helpless despair" and "slavery" (241), to "forg[e]t everything in the great wave of music" (246).

But his involvement with Rod soon lands him in much worse trouble, and more profound servitude. He decides, like Anthony, to break the rules to spend time with his female interest. He goes outside Paris without a pass and is apprehended by the military police. Andrews's punishment is worse than anything Anthony has to endure, however: he finds himself a "prisoner"

(255) in a labor battalion after being punched in the face for failing to salute a superior officer.

Andrews escapes the labor battalion by leaping in the water one day when the prisoners are on a boat, and he then decides to shed his army uniform—essentially to desert—an offense that can lead to life imprisonment. He refuses the aid of friends in the military but instead follows Genevieve out to the countryside, where the military police eventually pick him up again. The book ends with this second arrest.

While Dos Passos himself experienced army discipline and menial tasks (in particular window washing), and even grueling work in a labor battalion, and though he did at one point go AWOL as well, Andrews's arrests and incarceration are worse than anything his creator underwent. Dos Passos found himself in a labor battalion in a discharge camp as he waited to be demobilized, not because he broke the rules pursuing a woman, and he actually went AWOL for a day to help expedite his official demobilization, which had hit a bureaucratic snag.[26]

Lost Generation war literature by men might be better labeled noncombatant literature—and its authors might more accurately be thought of as men who, like most American recruits in World War I, "lost out" in the competition for wartime status. The characters in these stories may well have "lost" moral direction, but not at all, or not principally (this depends on their particular experiences), as a result of the horrors of the battlefield. Rather, they have been "losers" in the suddenly meritocratic competition for military rank and position, on the one hand, and women, on the other. The failure in the first regard generates failure in the second. (In these stories, either can lead to a loss of direction.)

Though their failure in the competition for women is not as obvious as with Faulkner's Lowe and Hemingway's Nick, both Anthony and Andrews have new vulnerabilities in this arena, determined by their relatively lowly military status. After we follow his miserable camp experience, we learn that Anthony's status failure in the military has created distance—indeed, a kind of social distance—between himself and his upper-class wife, Gloria. While Anthony struggles in camp, at home he is being humiliated in absentia by various pilots—commissioned officers and the cream of the military—who flirt with his wife. Though Gloria initially takes new pride in Anthony when he is drafted and is later annoyed that her friends are "unimpressed" with his making corporal (303), she ends up spending time with "an ancient flame, a young man whom at one time she had fully intended to marry" who is now in "the Aviation Corps" (301).

The married couple's estrangement, it becomes clear, is not only a function of Anthony's being away but also his social demotion. The distance between them is exacerbated when Anthony lets his wife know that he does not want her to visit him at camp, presumably because of his lowly rank, as well as his having turned to Dot who, though she is his social inferior, is now better suited to him. In Gloria's presence he would inevitably be embarrassed by his failure to obtain a military position commensurate with his civilian social standing. Meanwhile, Gloria, sensing Anthony's having pulled away, meets and occupies herself with "several [more] aviators" (301–2).

A similar dynamic undermines Andrew's relationship to Genevieve Rod and leads to the listlessness that allows him to be arrested for desertion. Though they are both from the upper classes (of their respective nations), Andrews, due to his status demotion and humiliation in the army, begins to imagine that she treats him with little respect; he cannot help but feel beneath her socially. "His first thought was how long he had to wait that day to see Genevieve. . . . Was it worth while going to see her at all, he asked himself. And very gradually he felt cold despair taking hold of him." He suddenly thinks back to Jeanne, the working-class woman he was previously seeing, with her "grimy, overworked fingers," and wonders how she would have treated him. He concludes in his mind that "those who road in the great car"—that is, Genevieve Rod—"could never feel as the others felt"—including himself now that he is no longer protected by his upper-class civilian status—"the toads hopping across the road" (303).

What is ultimately most striking about Fitzgerald's and Dos Passos's portraits of military life is that each of their main characters experiences extreme mental distress. Both approach mental breakdowns as a result of their army humiliations.

In lock-up,

> the conviction took root in [Anthony] that he was going mad. It was as though there were a quantity of dark yet vivid personalities in his mind, some of them familiar, some of them strange and terrible, held in check by a little monitor, who sat aloft somewhere and looked on. The thing that worried him was that the monitor was sick, and holding out with difficulty. Should he give up, should he falter for a moment, out would rush these intolerable things—only Anthony could know what a state of blackness there would be if the worst of him could roam his consciousness unchecked. (285)

Such a "state of blackness" comes over him when Dot visits during work detail during the second week of his term in the brig. Anthony experiences "a sort of terror" and then blacks out ("the earth tipped back and forth to a babel of shouting and confusion" and "when next he became conscious he was back in the guard-house"). He only realizes days later that she was there, but he is able to do so because, as his sentence winds down, "the cloud that oppressed him had lifted." He is left in "a deep, dispirited lethargy," but "the conscious mediator, the monitor who kept that fearsome menage of horror, grew stronger." Dot does send a letter that threatens to unnerve him again, but he gets sick with influenza, and "the sickness" turns out to be "providential," saving him from "a hysterical relapse" (286–87).

As psychologically damaged as Anthony gets, his trauma is over when the war ends and he leaves the army, and his mental state is restored to the point that he can "rejoice . . . to see general and field-officers riding desolately about the barren camp deprived of their commands. He rejoiced to hear the men in his company laugh scornfully at the inducements tendered them to remain in the army" (305). Dos Passos's protagonist Andrews, by contrast, experiences a trauma he seemingly cannot shake off and does not recover from.

Andrews's passivity and even fatalism seem at first hard to understand. He turns down offers of help from fellow soldiers who are confident that, through connections they have, his AWOL stint can be "fix(ed) . . . up on the records" and thus he can return to the army without further punishment. He also declines to join or copy an army friend who is leaving the country. As one of his soldier pals says to him, "for God's sake don't ruin your whole life on account of stubbornness, and some damn fool anarchistic ideas" (279). Other characters in the book are unable to comprehend him and get exasperated with him for his refusal to help himself. "All right; do what you goddamn please; I'm through with you," another of his soldier friends snaps (280).

Andrews explains that the army is "not the sort of thing a man can make good in" (290), but the book does not finally bear out that conclusion. Though it is affirmed by the ultimate trajectories of the title characters, it is also undercut in the text. While the army is experienced as an unmitigated demotion by wealthy, college-educated, and Anglo Andrews, it seems at first to offer opportunities of advancement to Italian American Fuselli, who is promoted to private first class, and the poor farm kid Chrisfield, who makes corporal. Even upper-class Andrews enjoys an army benefit when he takes advantage of the opportunity to attend the Sorbonne.

While the army might be in many ways strict and unyielding, there are plenty of loopholes to exploit. Dos Passos introduces us at different points to men who enjoy the war for just this reason, such as Dan Cohen, who spends the war pursuing outrageous hijinks, including going on joyrides in army vehicles. Though he faces court-martial several times, he always manages, because he has connections, to come out all right. The three soldiers of the title, and some others who find themselves in trouble, have themselves partly to blame because they have experienced failures of patience, cleverness, nerve, or will. Fuselli is tripped up not by having repeated sexual contact against regulations but by contracting venereal disease, and Chrisfield goes AWOL seemingly out of sheer paranoia, after literally getting away with murder: he frags a sergeant he believes has been "pickin' on" him (14). Likewise, Andrews carelessly flouts the terms of his plum position in the School Detachment by venturing outside of Paris without a pass and, after managing a death-defying escape from the labor battalion, refuses to help himself further and eventually waits around to be nabbed by the military police again.

The book further suggests, despite Andrews's experience of the army as relentless humiliation, that military discipline might not seem nearly as bad for someone coming from an unprivileged background. Though Andrews maintains that the hard treatment doled out by the army makes the educated and uneducated suffer just the same, a soldier also serving in the labor battalion disagrees, commenting, "a feller who's led a rough life can put up with an awful lot" (261). Readers and critics have tended to take Andrews's critique of the military as Dos Passos's, and no doubt this is basically correct. Andrews shares the author's first name (John) and resembles him in his background, education, artistic interest, and army assignments (such as being in the medical corps and doing menial labor). In addition, Dos Passos complained bitterly about the army in his letters, in terms similar to Andrews's.[27] But the book also maintains some ironic distance on Andrews's "sensitive" (301) and upper-class conclusions, sometimes entertaining a more balanced, broader, "trans-class" view of the army and the military experience. Dos Passos seems to be aware that "a working class background . . . might have given men a better chance at surviving [and] thriving in the rough masculine culture and world of arbitrary authority within the wartime army."[28]

Andrews's analysis of army organization may not apply to all men, but it applies to many. Andrews is not an everyman, but he speaks to a traumatic experience that many noncombatants and some rank-and-file combat soldiers had, and presumably some of Dos Passos's readers shared. *Three Soldiers* received many outraged and hostile reviews that considered his book slander on the American army and soldier, including two that appeared in the *New York Times Book Review* from reviewers who had served in the Canadian and American militaries. But some reviews praised the book's honesty. H. L. Mencken wrote: "At one blast it disposed of oceans of romance and blather. It changed the whole tone of American opinion about the war; it even changed the recollections of actual veterans of the war. They saw, no doubt, substantially what Dos Passos saw, but it took his bold realism to disentangle their recollections from the prevailing buncombe and sentimentality."[29]

Dos Passos does not represent the average American combatant. As the reviewer of a typically upbeat soldier memoir wrote in 1921: "the 'doughboy' . . . was . . . not the morbid, introspective neurotic and constitutional rebel against his officers and the government, such as Dos Passos portrays in *Three Soldiers*, but a light-hearted fun-maker. Even when the work he was called upon to do was disagreeably hard and in the tensest moments he joked and played. For every book like that of Dos Passos hundreds of these will be written, for every man like the characters in his book, thousands of fun-loving soldiers will refute his imputations."[30] But even if this reviewer is right and that, out of every hundred combat soldiers, only one would share Dos Passos's attitude, it is still true that for every thousand "fun-loving" combatants, there were some 3,000 noncombatants who missed out entirely on those "tensest moments" and thus the chance to be playful in the face of danger. As literary historian Steven Trout has discovered, giving support to Mencken's claim, "*Three Soldiers* inspired testimonials—one actually signed by 'three soldiers'—in numerous magazines and newspapers. Many veterans wrote that Dos Passos's sour recollections of life in the AEF, albeit camouflaged as fiction, were consistent with their own."[31] One young war veteran sent his copy of the novel to a friend in New Orleans, having written in the flyleaf, "This is the truest damn book ever written."[32]

In addition to embodying a common experience, Andrews is in one obvious way an impressive and even a brave figure. Though Andrews may be "morbid, introspective" and "neurotic," he is not a coward, as one of the *New York Times* reviews asserts.[33] He puts his money where his mouth is and does what many recruits who were disillusioned and disgusted with the army, including Dos Passos himself, fantasized about but were terrified to do.[34] In his ultimate and shocking refusal to submit to the army, and, instead, not only to go AWOL but to throw off his uniform, he becomes a specific sort of noncombatant hero: a principled deserter.

As Dos Passos realizes, army discipline and humiliation is more effective on some men than on others. To work effectively, men have to accept its authority—at least for a while. Andrews acknowledges that "he had . . . given himself up, that he had . . . let the grinding discipline have its way with him." And he attempts to resolve to "give up this cowardly cringing before external things. He would be recklessly himself" (136). He meets soldiers "no war could down," such as Dan Cohen and the 17-year-old "Kid" with whom he escapes the labor battalion. While in the army, Kid had stolen a Ford and sold it "for five hundred francs, and gone on a party with a man who'd stolen an ammunition train, and he wanted to write for Italian movies" (270).

But it is not easy for Andrews any longer to "be recklessly himself." In this one year in the army, he feels, "all the other years of his life had been blotted out" (136). Once this disciplinary and degrading power gets a foothold, it is hard to disengage from, even after the "boredom and abasement were over." On his way to his School Detachment in Paris after the war ends, Andrews tries to envision "the vivid life he was going to live. . . . He was free to work [on his art] and hear music and make friends." But he realizes that "he might go far away out of sound of the tramp of marching, away from the smell of overcrowded barracks where men slept in rows like cattle, but he would still be one of them. He would not see an officer pass him without an unconscious movement of servility, he would not hear a bugle without feeling sick with hatred" (187). Other soldiers are also aware of this syndrome, which is created by being "ordered around all day long" (270) for months on end: as one of them puts it, "The fellers in that camp was so damned skewed they jumped if you snapped yer fingers at 'em. It's the discipline . . . , it gets a feller in the end" (258). As Chrisfield concludes to Andrews—surprisingly, given that he has been capable of murdering an officer he did not like—"Fellers like us ain't got it in 'em to buck the system" (284). Andrews is what we would call post-traumatic, not suffering from shell shock but rather what might be termed "order shock."

In explaining why he will not return to the army after he deserts, Andrews says, "I'm not being heroic. . . . It's a purely personal matter. I've got to a point where I don't give a damn what happens to me. I don't care if I'm shot, or if I live to be eighty. . . . [suspension points in original] One more order shouted at my head is not worth living to be eighty . . . to me [suspension points in original]. That's all. . . . I've got to be free now. I don't care at what cost. Being free's the only thing that matters" (279). He ends the discussion with his friend by stubbornly declaring that he "shall never put a uniform on again" (280).

Much like a shell-shocked man who refuses to return to the front lines because he cannot abide the gunfire and bombing anymore, Andrews will not return to the army because he cannot any longer endure "order[s] shouted at my head." Of course, the difference is that a shell-shock victim is escaping a return to ungovernable terror while Andrews is avoiding a return to uncontrollable feelings of humiliation.[35] As he tells Genevieve, "A man told me at the labor battalion . . . that they'd tortured a friend of his by making him swallow lighted cigarettes; well, every order shouted at me, every new humiliation before the authorities, was as great an agony to me" (301). Andrews's "order shock" is so severe that he does not need to "see an officer" or "hear a bugle" to suffer what we would call today post-traumatic stress. Out in the countryside with Genevieve, he cannot "get it out of my mind . . . those tramping feet, those voices shouting orders" (293, suspension points in original).

And though Andrews sounds fatalistic in these passages, he has in mind a loose plan of survival and recuperation. "It's not in one day that you can unbend a slave's back," he says to Genevieve. But he figures that if he stays with her in the countryside, "after a while the rhythm of legs all being made the same length on drill fields, the hopeless caged dullness will be buried deep in me by gorgeousness of this world of yours." In addition, he imagines that his pursuit of music will help him: "If I could manage to express all that misery in music, I could shove it far down into my memory" (292). As for survival: "If I can pull through six months, I'm safe. The army will have gone. I don't believe they extradite deserters" (305).

But another form of "shock"—this one fairly specific to noncombatants—stands in the way of John Andrews's recovery. There is, in addition to discipline, another facet to his subjection by the army—and a different psychological suffering accompanying it—that is crippling him, namely his being measured and his information being kept on file. Fitzgerald touches briefly on the subject as well in *The Beautiful and Damned* but does not develop it at all. Anthony is given a medical examination and found to have a blood pressure abnormality that initially disqualifies him from officer training, yet not from service as a private; however, neither the thought of having "faulty blood-pressure" nor this "preposterous incongruity" (261) recurs later, once he is in camp. Andrews, too, is measured, and presumably he is found to be somewhat undersized. Yet he cannot get the "scene of measurement" out of his head and has absolutely haunting visions of both his "skinniness" and his personnel file.

Andrews and Anthony both undergo a practice of power distinct from the subordinating discipline that leaves Andrews traumatized. What Dos Passos sees in the new, meritocratic army procedures for evaluating men—and therefore what Andrews experiences—is a sort of power that is demeaning by different means. Unlike continual orders, which work by repeated shocks to the system, this power ties one's identity to an army measure or classification. It is a single branding, objectification, or stigmatization of one's person that is recorded and maintained. For Dos Passos, the power involved in these new techniques, the power to evaluate and create a file on a man, can give him a new and unshakable identity from that moment of measurement on. A couple of times in the text, Andrews flashes back on "the day he stood naked in the middle of a base room while the recruiting sergeant prodded him and measured him" (136). The phrase "while the recruiting sergeant prodded him and measured him" is later repeated word for word (296), and we have been witness to the original scene as well: "John Andrews stood naked in the center of a large bare room. . . . [H]e stood tamely being prodded and measured, feeling like a prize horse at a fair" (8). As psychologically debilitating as the long-term effects of military discipline can be, "order shock" is only part of Andrews's ongoing psychological problem.

While meritocracy attempts to be selective on the basis of talent and ability rather than class-standing or character, it inevitably has its own arbitrariness that can have little to do with merit or capacity. Anthony in Fitzgerald's novel refers to a "preposterous incongruity" in the system: why should his blood pressure condition disqualify him from being a commissioned officer but not from serving as a private or a noncommissioned officer? Perhaps there is a logic here. Perhaps commissioned officers have that much more responsibility than privates or even noncoms, so the health risk presented by Anthony's blood pressure problem is acceptable if he has only a lesser position. But there were plenty of "incongruities" in the system, to use Fitzgerald's word. American army standards or qualifications were not fixed but rather fluctuated in the course of the war. The personnel "system" was in many ways a work in progress during the nineteen months of US involvement, and a recruit was more likely to face (or enjoy) rejection on physical grounds earlier on; as the conflict continued and the army became more desperate for bodies, the military lowered the bar for acceptance.[36]

To take an example of obvious arbitrariness in the system, why should Faulkner's height and weight matter to his being a pilot? After all, he is physically able and big enough to operate a plane; maybe he would even be gifted at doing so—and so the Canadian Royal Air Force does accept him. Faulkner presumably would not have been disqualified from the American cavalry in previous wars, on the grounds of his size, before technological advancements allowed the cavalry to take to the air; no doubt a horse could have been found to accommodate his build; he could have brought such a horse to war with him. His disqualification from the American air corps comes from a certain arbitrariness based on the nature, and cost, of the complex, mass-produced machinery that an airplane is: the cockpit size will be standard, as will the pilot's seat, and so on. Someone of Faulkner's size may have a bit of trouble seeing over the dashboard and operating the controls—without a booster seat and maybe other appendages that add unnecessary parts and risks to the operation. And it is cost-ineffective to make custom-made planes to also accommodate smaller men who are talented at aviation; there's no dearth of taller men who qualify, so why would the army bother? The point is that meritocracy, even when functioning without corruption, does not always select on the basis of merit or talent.[37] Yet because it is a system designed to be egalitarian, rather than exclusionary or aristocratic, and because it has aspirations to being scientific and fair, its judgments are hard to dismiss or reject as arbitrary or prejudicial (as opposed to, say, race, gender, or class discrimination). This may explain why Andrews's physical evaluation cuts so deeply and is impossible for him to shake.

In one of the most provocative passages of *Three Soldiers*, Dos Passos makes an observation about identity in the new regime of the army that seems more postmodernist or poststructuralist than modernist—something one might expect to find in a Thomas Pynchon novel or an essay by Michel Foucault:

> Then [Andrews] thought of the Major's office that morning, and of his own skinny figure in the mirrors, repeated endlessly, standing helpless and humble before the shining mahogany desk. Even out here in these fields where the wet earth seemed to heave with the sprouting of new growth, he was not free. In those office buildings, with white marble halls full of the clank of officers' heels, in index cards and piles of typewritten papers, his real self which they had the power to kill if they wanted to, was in his name and number, on lists with millions of other names and other numbers. This sentient body of his, full of possibilities and hopes and desires, was only a pale ghost that depended on the other self, that suffered for it and cringed for it. He could not drive out of his head the picture of himself, skinny in an ill-fitting uniform . . . (246)

One might expect Dos Passos to call Andrews's "sentient body, full of possibilities and hopes and desires," his real self and the self created by index cards, typewritten records, names, and numbers to be labeled artificial. But Dos Passos pointedly refers to Andrews's officially constructed identity as "his real self," to which his body and his feelings are subordinated. Moreover, his body and feelings are "depend[ent] on the other self": they suffer and cringe for it.

Though jarring on first read, this passage (which begins and ends with Andrews's image of himself as "skinny" but seems to take up a separate issue of personnel files in the middle) is not, actually, incoherent: he sees himself in the last line as "skinny" in relation to the uniform the army has clothed him in, which comes in "standard" sizes, or, more broadly, "skinny" in terms of the army's classification of him. In other words, this self-image, which he "could not drive out of his head," is an effect of the "real self" that has been constructed in his written file, where his physical measurements are included and he is, presumably, "skinny" according to the size and weight standards that the army has established.

Dos Passos intriguingly suggests—like a poststructuralist critic—that meritocracy works by giving its subjects new identities based on measurements in the context of standards or norms, of which physical evaluations are just one part. When Andrews's body is being "prodded and measured" and his heart tested, he hears a clerk at a typewriter recording the mental evaluations of another recruit (or several), based on the notorious intelligence tests: "imbecility," "mental deficiency," "scores ten years . . . in test B," "m-e-n-t-a-l-i-t-y that of a child of eight." There is also a psychological evaluation being typed out: "No . . . record of sexual dep . . . . ravity or alcoholism," "immature," "responds to no form of per . . . suasion" (suspension points in original). The recruit (or one of the recruits) at issue receives a "recommendation for discharge" (8).

Andrews's being measured is another instance of humiliation. But Dos Passos does not make clear how the subjection to measurement affects Andrews beyond his being haunted as a result of his treatment like an object or an animal and his experiencing a new and alien sense of himself as "skinny." Perhaps his "skinniness" makes him feel weak and less able to combat the other humiliation of continually being ordered about, but this connection is never explicitly made. It does not seem to threaten his masculine confidence or affect his sense of self in relation to women: he has no trouble beginning relationships with two women, and his eventual sense of not being Genevieve's equal seems to come out of his low rank and constant subordination to superiors, not this newly branded "real self" or its residence on paper or index cards. Even less clear is what Andrews or Dos Passos means by the claim that "they had the power to kill [his army-constructed 'real self'] if they wanted to." How would that killing be effected or realized? What would that mean for that "real self" to be killed?

Three Soldiers is fairly exhaustive and markedly repetitive about the experience of army discipline and subordination, and its overarching metaphors about the resulting standardization and mechanization, as well as breakdown of human beings, are thoroughly explained (the section titles of the novel include "Making the Mould," "The Metal Cools," "Machines," and "Rust"). Against this thorough and indeed repetitive rhetorical technique, Dos Passos's suggestive but enigmatic assertion about the army's creation and potential destruction of a "real self"—a claim that is not repeated, referred to again, or explained—stands out as anomalous. It almost seems as if the author has something in mind that he will not share with the reader.

To understand this cryptic passage, one apparently needs to move beyond the domain of the novel, and the obvious place to go is Dos Passos's own experience in the army since he draws so heavily from that experience. Indeed, an event in his service seems to have been the inspiration for this meditation. When Dos Passos went AWOL, he did so not to rebel but to expedite the army's bureaucratic process of letting him go. At the discharge camp awaiting demobilization, Dos Passos's "discharge had been inexplicably held up," as his biographer puts it. It was then, assigned in the meantime to a labor battalion, in which he was daily ordered to move the same piles of scrap iron pointlessly back and forth across the depot, that he considered going AWOL out of what he called "stupid despair." He wrote in a letter, "It really needs constant restraint to keep from fleeing pell mell across the fields and hedges, away from all this hideousness." Earlier on, in an army office in Paris, he had seen his application for discharge stamped with approval, but the paper had not been processed by the local discharge office. Awaiting the bureaucratic resolution, he became certain that he was going to die of hard labor in what he called his current situation of "non-being."[38]

It is easy to imagine how Dos Passos got from his actual predicament and the words he used about himself to the language of the passage in *Three Soldiers*. The army's hold on his constructed "real self" meant that his lost papers—his "non-being" in the system of records—had occasioned his limbo in the discharge camp: with the disappearance of key papers in his personnel file, no action would be taken on his case, and being thus stuck might literally translate to his death through hard labor.

Grasping his situation—which resembled a tale of his contemporary Kafka—Dos Passos went AWOL for 22 hours, making his way to the army headquarters in Tours in order to locate his discharge papers, which had gone missing, and thus to make possible his release by the military. Afterward, he did precisely what Andrews refuses to do to avoid punishment: he slipped back into the army without anyone in charge at his camp knowing that he had broken the rules.[39] Dos Passos ended up freed and Andrews incarcerated.

Not only does Dos Passos's biography cast light on a fairly cryptic portion of his novel. It also reveals his artistic mode or strategy, essentially his decision to make Andrews's story a modernist romance of hopeless rebellion in the name of freedom "from the system"—as opposed to his own story of postmodern irony, in which freedom can only come from submission to a system that ordains one's identity. Despite its momentary poststructuralist insight that meritocratic power gives individuals new identities and controls them in part through their identification with standardized measurements, and that, in this new meritocratic system, one's personnel file, managed by bureaucracies, becomes the ultimate arbiter of one's place in the world, the book does not maintain this outlook.

Andrews may fail in his rebellion against the system; he may fail to have "lived up to the name of John Brown" with whom he identifies during his latter AWOL stint. But he nonetheless is "revolting hopelessly" against "organizations growing and stifling individuals" (300) in the name of individual freedom. As he says to Genevieve Rod, "I, by pure accident, have made a gesture, feeble as it is, towards human freedom" (301). So when it comes to his being a "deserter," he is not "ashamed" but "rather proud of this" (305). Andrews muses that most men would be "battered into servility. . . . And those that were not sheep? They were deserters; every rifle muzzle held death for them; they would not live long. And yet other nightmares had been thrown off men. Every man who stood up courageously to die loosened the grip of the nightmare" (297). Andrews may be captured again at the end by the military police, but the important thing for him is that he has not willingly submitted. Though he claims earlier on that he is not being heroic, he comes to think of himself in precisely these terms. He is a martyr.

His cause is the freedom of the authentic, nonstandardized self: of the "inquisitive . . . mind" (297) and the "sentient body . . . , full of possibilities and hopes and desires," that in most of the book represents the "real self," despite that one anomalous and unsynthesized passage. John Andrews clearly has an authentic self that the army has not succeeded in subordinating, has not managed to turn into a "pale ghost that depended on" the identity constructed by the military bureaucracy (246). It is manifested not only in his stubborn desire to revolt but in his talent as a musician, an identity that the army has not given him and an ability it has not measured. It is significant that during his desertion Genevieve recognizes Andrews as an "artist" (301) and that he is working on his music. The last image in the book is of papers left behind when Andrews is arrested and not, significantly, the "typewritten papers" of personnel files in "office buildings"

(246). These abandoned papers "litter[ing]" the floor may be a desolate image, but the papers are "broad sheets" recording original music, and they represent that unique self the army cannot kill or imprison.

Both Dos Passos and Fitzgerald give searing portraits of the psychological trauma of sudden subordination for a man used to social superiority. And they both decided to do so by imagining characters who had worse experiences in the US Army than they themselves had. Perhaps their intention was to conjure up humiliations and punishments worse than the ones they underwent because they had an awareness that the feelings they experienced might be perceived by readers as "unwarranted" by their actual circumstances. Or perhaps they described men worse off than themselves because that was satisfying, a way of alleviating their own humiliation by imagining those whose plights were more drastic. In any case, these portraits of subordination and the concomitant psychological trauma no doubt allowed other former noncombatants, especially those from privileged backgrounds—some of their readers—to feel validation and also some relief in seeing their suffering, or likewise suffering worse than their own, conjured up in print.

But Dos Passos seems to anticipate in his epigraph that such readers might also re-experience their own pain, or be vulnerable to post-traumatic sensations, in reading such realistic—such straight, naked, and untransformed—accounts. Maybe that is why the veteran who gave the book to a friend in New Orleans called it not simply the "truest book" but the "truest *damn* book."

It is almost as if Dos Passos has included the untranslated epigraph as a warning to insiders, that is obviously "coded" in a foreign language they have special knowledge of. Likely both an invitation and a heads-up, Dos Passos's epigraph is privately letting noncombatant veteran readers know that he is one of them, that they may well find their real experiences represented in this book, and that reading this story will thus likely be intense and difficult. And he is doing so secretly because these real experiences were embarrassing and traumatizing—and he probably wants to give his target reader the opportunity to consume this book in a private fashion, without his friends or loved ones also knowing that this book depicts the actual "certain things" he suffered and can still suffer from being reminded of.

No doubt this book was also meaningful for combatants who felt abused by the army as well. But given the centrality of the repeated scene of meritocratic evaluation, in which Andrews does not measure up, there is no question that this book speaks in particular to veterans who did not make the combat grade.

Dos Passos's epigraph suggests why the latter World War I–related works of Hemingway, Fitzgerald, and Faulkner all involved significant transpositions of their own noncombatant experiences. It may also help explain why and how Hemingway—who is known for his exceptional ability to reflect his times and, by implication, his readers' desires or needs—kept working and re-imagining his basic love story about a wounded soldier and his nurse.

CHAPTER THREE

Saved by French Arrest and Imprisonment

E. E. Cummings's *The Enormous Room*

HOW IS IT THAT E. E. CUMMINGS, apparently alone among the Lost Generation male writers, escaped feelings of emasculation and insufficiency—though he, too, was a noncombatant? It is true that Cummings was "enough of a pacifist" that he had no desire to bear arms, so he did not consider ambulance work as a second best to some form of combat service. Rather, for him, ambulance service meant he could get a deferment from the draft and the undesirable possibility of infantry assignment. But he most likely could have secured, alternatively, conscientious objector status "due to his father's influence," only he did not "relish the idea of alternative service that would probably have kept him stateside."[1] Like the other Lost Generation authors, he preferred a more dramatic, exciting, or glamorous wartime role at the front. And like them, he found his noncombatant experience humiliating, as is abundantly clear in *The Enormous Room*, his "documentary account," or memoir, of the war.[2]

How did Cummings avoid feelings of oppression and despair when he, like Anthony in F. Scott Fitzgerald's *The Beautiful and Damned* and Andrews in *Three Soldiers*, by John Dos Passos, was imprisoned for falling afoul of the military authorities? Unlike those characters, that incarceration experience is precisely what makes his "real" story about his wartime "travels" a tale of "happiness."[3] To make the question more specific, why is it that Cummings's imprisonment allows him to produce an autobiographical story about a noncombatant in wartime that is a happy one?

Cummings shared a similar wartime role with Dos Passos, Fitzgerald, William Faulkner, and Ernest Hemingway—and similar feelings about that role. Nevertheless, he did not produce the storyline that was common to these other four authors: featuring a recruit-protagonist who experiences the lowliness of his position and then makes matters worse by getting involved with a woman. Cummings served in the same ambulance outfit as Dos Passos, the Norton-Harjes Ambulance Corps. Moreover, *The Enormous Room* starts out much the same as Dos Passos's and Fitzgerald's tales: Cummings's main character and narrator (who shares his name) feels put down and mistreated in his mundane routine and undistinguished position. He chafes under the discipline of the leaders of his unit, Mr. A. and Mr. P., who emulate American army order, efficiency, and cleanliness. He does not like being crowded together with a bunch of other men. He disrespects his superiors, questions their right to order him around, and flouts the rules of his outfit—the result being that one day he is arrested by military authorities.

Here the similarities with *Three Soldiers* and *The Beautiful and Damned* end. Cummings does not experience his arrest and imprisonment as an intensification of the discipline he chafed under or as a further humiliation. Instead he sees it as a salvation, "a *deus ex machina*." His arrest yanks him "from the putrescent banalities" of his service role and throws him "into a high . . . adventure" (7). In fact, when a prison door closes on him for the first time, with a "hideous crash" reminiscent of an "earthquake," he feels "[a]n uncontrollable joy," proclaiming, "I was myself and my own master" (22).

Is he delirious, the reader wonders. Has he lost his mind and become insensitive to what is really happening to him? Or is he being completely ironic? Neither is the case: he is both coherent and essentially sincere about his repossession of himself. But then how can he feel joy and confidence upon being locked up in a dirty and dismal cell?

Maybe he is gratified by taking an "antiwar" stand. When he is arrested by French authorities, he experiences a "new dignity" in front of one of his unnamed American comrades who asks if he did "something to get pinched"; he is "proud" of being identified as a wrongdoer or "criminal" (9). It seems possible at this moment that he, like John Andrews in *Three Soldiers*, is bent on individual rebellion, and that only the identity of a war resister will satisfy him after his "miserable" experience of being "bossed and herded" (4, 23). But, on further consideration, that reading does not hold up.

It simply is not the case that he is determined to rebel and establish himself as an antiwar resister. The reader has already learned that before being arrested, Cummings and his ambulance corps companion B. were trying to enlist in the "l'Esquadrille Lafayette," the French Aviation service (17). Yes, he is "excited and proud" (9) to be a criminal, but he would likewise be happy and proud to be a pilot. (This reality even seems to throw into question Cummings's supposed "anti-war" and "pacifist" sentiments.)[4] Perhaps Cummings is simply interested in a more exalted war role. Criminal and pilot perhaps have this in common: in either capacity, he would be distinguished from the herd of ambulance drivers. But that interpretation does not square with the facts either. He has stated that he would also be satisfied to stay in his ambulance unit, if he was merely treated better and entitled to the same privileges as everyone else. He would be mollified if a "Monsieur Norton, the supreme head of the Norton-Harjes fraternity, who had known my father in other days," would send an "emissary" to their boss to "demand an explanation" for his and B.'s poor treatment, and also to "secure our long-delayed *permission*" for leave (5–6). In fact, this is what he initially thinks, with satisfaction, is happening when the French authorities show up.

So what has happened that makes Cummings's happy feelings explicable? When the prison door shuts on him, he says, "An uncontrollable joy gutted me after three months of humiliation," generating a "delirium of relief" (22–23). We understand that he is glad to be out of his ambulance unit, but how does he know that his term of "humiliation," of "being bossed and herded and bullied and insulted," has come to end? How does he know that his incarceration will not continue this experience, or even intensify it? The answer is that Cummings realizes he has passed from American to French control, and—on the basis of the interrogation he has already undergone with the French police, along with his sustained experience of the French support crew attached to the ambulance unit—he knows that this makes a world of difference.

This answer sheds light on the American army's techniques of control, from which Andrews suffers so intensely: the grueling discipline and also the individualizing "branding" involved in meritocratic assessment, classification, and assignment. It perhaps also makes clearer why Andrews ends up choosing doomed tactics of resistance. Briefly put, Cummings's narrator's arrest by French authorities is a deus ex machina that lifts him out of his difficult, but short, American experience and relocates him in a "traditional" French police and prison system that, in its non-disciplinary and non-individuating procedures, is a world away from the US Army—and highly preferable to Cummings. For him, the stark, and humane, differences between "how they do things" (3) in France and in the American army exhibits the US military's unprecedented, modern techniques of control.

In the first chapter of *The Enormous Room*, the narrator describes his transition from *American* paramilitary control to *French* government incarceration. The first operation—his ambulance unit—is arranged along disciplinary lines, and he and his friend B., due to their failures in "personal appearance" and their insistence on "fraternization" with the French, are deprived the "privilege" of driving in an ambulance together (4) and receive a "daily lecture" on cleaning up their "dirty . . . habits" and "*keep[ing] away from them dirty Frenchmen*" (65). The narrator and B. have taken to boarding with the French support crew (attached to the ambulance unit) that their superior has told them not to associate with. When the narrator is arrested, he passes officially into French hands, and though he is a prisoner, he feels more comfortable because the French police and the French prison system clearly share with the French army and support crew an undisciplined, disorganized nature—at least by the standards of his ambulance corps boss, who would like to "show those [French] bastards how they do things in America" (3).

The narrator knows too that he will not be remaining alone in that jail cell, and he is soon transferred to an "internment center" at La Ferte Mace (iii).[5] The authorities there do not, however, attempt to separate the narrator and his friend B. but rather allow them to bunk right next to each other. This is surprising given that the French police have arrested them both for treachery and consider B. to be a corrupting influence on the narrator. But the "makeshift internment center," or "Camp du Triage" (324), they are assigned to was "strictly speaking . . . not a prison."[6] It does not have cells but rather one "enormous room" in which the prisoners themselves decide where they will sleep: the undifferentiated space of the "enormous room" is the antithesis of the "panoptic" disciplinary machine described by Foucault in *Discipline and Punish*. Inmates are allowed to wear their own clothes and keep their belongings (the narrator has a sturdy fur coat). They also have their own money, which allows the narrator and B. to buy things most others cannot afford.

The narrator's arrest is obviously essential to his recovery of himself. Importantly, he has not been arrested for any traitorous act of his own. He is being held because he is friendly with B., whom the French accuse of sympathizing with the Germans. The police interrogators do give the narrator the opportunity to clear himself in the course of questioning him—"To walk out of the room a free man I had merely to say yes" to the question, do you hate the Germans or "*boches*" (19). However, he refuses to make a statement that will ensure that "my friend and myself" should have "different fates" (20). But the crucial point is that the French army authority that calls for the narrator's arrest does not "individualize" men; it does not assess each of them separately or distinguish between them on the basis of individual attributes and behaviors. It may be arbitrary; it may be unfair; it may arrest a man simply because his friend is under suspicion—but that very arbitrariness and unfairness embody its non-individualizing approach.

The French military authority gives the narrator the opportunity to choose solidarity with his friend—and in this way to assert a corporate identity antithetical to the sort of individual identity that the American army is assigning to men. Moreover, the French police approach is consonant with the French military authority; they, too, recognize and express interest in the narrator's social connections and his identity outside of his wartime position.

But first it is important to underline that the narrator has *not* been in the US Army and has not experienced either the punitive, relentless discipline or the traumatic branding that Dos Passos and his fictional Andrews do. As much as the volunteer ambulance corps leaders—Mr. A. and, before him, Mr. P.—seem to emulate the US military in their attempt to encourage neatness, order, and discipline, they also appear to have little power to enforce these "ideals" (4). Though the narrator and B. openly disregard Mr. A.'s instructions, they are not punished, beyond being routinely lectured and denied "the privilege of acting as *conductors*" or drivers (4) as well as the "*permission de sept jours*," a leave of seven days (5). And so they are able to continue their disobedience—their slovenliness and fraternization with the French. Moreover, the narrator has not been subjected to the physical and mental measurement practiced by the army. There is no army file on him that identifies him as physically subpar or a "misfit."[7] In short, he has not been stigmatized with the sort of army-constructed "self" that Andrews is haunted by—and is perhaps trying to erase in his particular brand of rebellion.

The narrator speaks of his "official non-existence" in the ambulance corps. He sleeps with "forty huddling Americans" (4), or, rather, he stops doing so and tries in this way, and in fraternizing with the French in general, to remove himself as much as possible from the undifferentiated herd of men in his outfit. He and B., faced with the expectation of conforming to the "American" norms of group behavior, try as a pair to distinguish themselves. While he may feel insulted and unrecognized, and forced to undergo the daily round of "putrescent banalities" that make him feel "non-existent" in the ambulance corps, he is not forced to change his habits, nor is he subjected to a battery of individual examinations and saddled with a demeaning, army-generated "official" identity. His problem is not that he has been tied to an individual identity he finds alien but that he is associated with a group he cannot identify with and subordinated to leaders who subject him to "sundry insults and indignities" (5).

So what to make of the "new dignity" the narrator experiences when French authorities arrest him in front of one of his fellow American ambulance drivers? Crucial to his being "excited and proud" (9) is his liberation from the American group. He seeks this liberation by several means. Again, he and B. have already attempted to enlist in the "l'Esquadrille Lafayette," the French Aviation service (17). He would likewise be satisfied if the head of the entire ambulance operation, whom his father knows, would take his side in his differences with the unit leader. The narrator is looking for respect as well as deliverance from harassment by his ambulance-corps leader. He will take it as a prisoner of the French authorities, as a French pilot, or even as a member of a "reformed" American ambulance corps, entitled to customary leave (and he has no problem with falling back on his elite family connections to get him that respect and that right).

In an introduction added to *The Enormous Room* a dozen years after its initial publication, Cummings asserted that the book is about "[t]he individual," and that "[t]hanks to . . . my art I am able to become myself" (viii, ix). No doubt his art was to a degree a comfort during his service and internment, but the 1922 text suggests a different reason why he was "able to become myself" once he was arrested and removed from American control. Cummings's statement that the book is about "[t]he individual" is likewise unconvincing.

Such a claim may describe Dos Passos's story about Andrews, who seems determined, as one critic has put it, "to create his own vision of existence independently of friends, foes, family, society, and tradition."[8] Conceivably, Andrews goes down that path because the army has so effectually isolated or individualized him by his subjection to its measurement and assessment. In other words, if Andrews asserts his individuality to his own peril—and eventual self-destruction—it may be because the army has, shockingly, assigned him an identity that he must escape from in order to recover any chance of happiness. But, again, the narrator of *The Enormous Room* does not undergo this army branding. Nor does he find salvation in an asocial individuality or artist's identity.

Instead, he discovers dignity and identity in his associations. Not only do the French authorities acknowledge his friendship to B., they also express interest in the narrator's ethnic background and family, thus recognizing another of his corporate identities and allowing him to proudly assert his exalted family history. "'You are Irish by family?' . . . 'Your name it is Irish?'" he is asked in the interrogation. "'Cummings is a very old Scotch name . . . ,'" replies the narrator; "'it used to be Comyn. A Scotchman named The Red Comyn was killed by Robert Bruce in a church. He was my ancestor and a very well-known man.'—'But your second name [Estlin], where have you got that?'—'From an Englishman, a friend of my father.' This statement seemed to produce a very favourable impression" on one of the interrogators, "who murmured 'Un ami de son père, un anglais, bon!' [a friend of his father's, an Englishman, good!]" (14).

It may seem a contradiction that while the narrator is happy to be arrested and imprisoned by the French government, the foreword to the book includes outraged letters by Cummings's father, one to President Woodrow Wilson (no less), concerning what, in his view, is his son's "prolonged injustice at the hands of France" (xiii). Sensing this contradiction, the narrator, somewhat defensively, insists that "I do . . . very strenuously object to the assumption" that this story has a "Happy Ending" that comes with his release from captivity: "I have proved to my own satisfaction (if not anyone else's) that I was happier in La Ferte Mace . . . than the very keenest words can pretend to express" (313).

But this contradiction is more apparent than real. For one thing, it probably turned out to be fortuitous that Cummings was rescued before being transferred to an actual penitentiary, Precigne, whose environment would hardly have been so comfortable and lax as that of La Ferte. Also, the foreword establishes Cummings's elite family identity, which has "powerful and willing friends on both sides of the Atlantic"—powerful enough to secure his release (xi). That is, deeper than the contradiction is the continuity: at the beginning of the story, the narrator expects his family to intervene in his difficulties, and they eventually do. (Cummings was in touch with his family "regularly" by mail during his internment, so he was aware of his father's ongoing efforts to free him, though he did not include this detail in the narrative.[9] No doubt this knowledge made Cummings's actual experience in La Ferte much more tolerable than it otherwise would have been.) He is sprung from La Ferte when one day an official letter arrives directing that "Edward E. Cummings . . . should report immediately to the American Embassy, Paris" (324).

It is not the case that Cummings's art restores him to himself. What allows him to "become myself" again after his alienating experience with the ambulance corps is instead his associations with and connections to not only his colorful fellow inmates at La Ferte, whom the majority of the book is focused on, but most of all his American friend B. and his family. In fact, and despite the continued presence, support, and concern of fellow inmates, the narrator loses himself again when B. is transferred to Precigne prison: he is "knock[ed] for a loop" and experiences "depression" and "nearly" a "mental catastrophe" (314). Here enters, briefly, the despair that Dos Passos's Andrews and Fitzgerald's Anthony fall prey to in lockup. Only the timely intervention by his family saves him from a complete mental collapse.

Among all the male writers of the Lost Generation, Cummings came from the most "powerful" family, and the tale he tells in *The Enormous Room* is shaped by the same "economic forces" that he blithely scoffs at in the 1932 introduction to the reissued text (even though he is aware that his denial of socioeconomic factors makes him sound "childish," deluded, ignorant, and absurdly "Highbrow" [x]). If his narrator's wartime story goes from bad to better, unlike those tales of the other Lost Generation male writers, it is because of his particularly elite social identity, combined with his distinctly non-American experience of the war. He is spared the subjection of the US Army.[10] His three-month stint with the American ambulance corps is relatively brief. And he has the good fortune of being arrested and incarcerated with a close friend in a haphazard, undisciplined, and non-individualizing "French" camp.

Some five months after the 23-year-old Cummings was freed from French prison and returned to America (on January 1, 1918), he got his draft notice. Two months after that he was inducted into the US Army after all. However, this experience is not represented in *The Enormous Room*, which ends with his ship reaching American soil: what he calls the "land of the flea, home of the dag—dago of course" (331).[11] (For all his acceptance and embrace of racial, ethnic, and national otherness in the book—one of his most beloved fellow prisoners is a black man he calls "Jean Le Negre"—Cummings indulges in some typical ethnic slurs of his era; he also refers to a couple of the Jewish inmates as "Sheeneys." And in a letter to his mother about his first few days in the army, he refers to the "Yid" who wrote down his personal data.[12])

According to his biographer, Cummings did not enjoy his service at Camp Devens in Massachusetts. He was assigned to the infantry; he offered that he could serve as an interpreter, but this suggestion was ignored. To make matters more difficult, he did not "find a soulmate, like Brown" (or B., as he is referred to in *The Enormous Room*).[13] Instead, "out of the 250 more or less male bipeds with whom I cohabited night and day," he found only "a pair of human beings."[14] Though he certainly had to endure being herded and disciplined, his subjection to army measurement and classification was not stigmatizing, even if it had inconvenient results, given his service preferences.

Unlike Dos Passos, whose military evaluation and assignment made him feel a "misfit" and an "oddball," Cummings was found physically fit for combat duty. Not only that, because he performed so well on the mental examination, he was selected to "'go to school' for non-commissioned officers," as he wrote home. This, too, was inconvenient for Cummings—he told his "captain about my temperament, my occupation, my equivocal behavior under fire, etc.," claiming he was not suited to be an infantry officer. Yet his words made "no impression whatever, as expected." He wrote to his mother that he had been made acting "corporal on basis of 'very high psychological examination,' " or the IQ test.[15] The fact was, the army's meritocratic standards selected for Cummings, both physically and mentally, and one has the feeling that in these letters to his family, his complaints also contain elements of pride.

Maybe the army's validation of his personal traits and abilities helped him endure his military service. "Despite his gripes," as his biographer puts it, "Cummings endured his training without landing himself in the stockade. He was by no means a model soldier; he simply figured out how much in step he had to be."[16] Cummings clearly understood that American army incarceration would have been nothing like his French experience. He wrote to his father what he had been told by his lieutenant: "You men ought to take a look at what they do to a man at the military prisons, Jay, New York; Leavenworth, Kansas; Fort Angel (?) California. . . . When a man comes to Fort Jay, the first thing they do is give him a g.d. fine beating. They black his eyes for him. They do that on principle down there."[17] (This is more or less the treatment Andrews gets from the military police in France in *Three Soldiers*—not on principle but because he fails to salute an officer.)

Cummings's most famous wartime poem is about a blond-haired, pacifist recruit he met who ended up in trouble with the authorities on the basis of his "refusal to pick up a gun."[18] In these lines Cummings expresses no illusions about US army prisons. Because "Olaf glad and big," is "a conscientious object-or," he suffers physical abuse at the hands of military officers, including "knocking on the head." Despite the torture, the attempt to instill "allegiance per blunt instruments," Olaf proclaims, "I will not kiss your fucking flag." The poem concludes,

> unless statistics lie he was
> more brave than me:more blond than you.[19]

The poem gives no illusions about the limits of its author's own bravery when it comes to bucking US authorities in wartime. Though he shares Olaf's rebellious attitude and admires his resistance, Cummings—whom other reliable "statistics" have deemed physically fit and mentally exceptional—is careful not to end up, like him, in the disciplinary and individualizing *American* military penal system.

CHAPTER FOUR

Hemingway's Thrice-Told Tale

A Farewell to Arms and Noncombatant Fantasy

THE END OF ERNEST HEMINGWAY'S *A Farewell to Arms*, in which the protagonist-narrator's love interest, the nurse Catherine Barkley, dies in childbirth, in a Swiss hospital outside the war zone, has been much discussed.[1] What has been discussed less—and what is quite curious—is the narrator's extended thought when he learns that the baby is stillborn and concludes, "Now Catherine would die."[2] Though often quoted, this passage is under-analyzed. Frederic Henry, reasonably angry at the human condition and the seemingly arbitrary injustice of a young, healthy person unexpectedly dying, thinks to himself: "That was what you did. You died. You did not know what it was about. You never had time to learn" (232). Then, Henry's train of thought seems to leave his dying girlfriend behind and instead reverts to the war he and Catherine had managed to escape. This movement of mind makes sense, as war is the great generator of the death of young people in Henry's experience. However, in contemplating the ways that "you died" in war, he does not name the most obvious sort of death in war, namely being killed by enemy forces. "They threw you in and told you the rules and the first time they caught you off base they killed you. Or they killed you gratuitously like Aymo [who dies by friendly fire]. Or gave you the syphilis like Rinaldi. But they killed you in the end. You could count on that. Stay around and they would kill you" (232). The "they" here, though not identified, is clearly one's own military in the first two examples, and not so obviously in the third as well since collecting thousands of men in camps and war zones spreads venereal disease. In short, all of his examples of the ways "you died" are deaths caused by one's own army.

In order to come to grips with the end of *A Farewell to Arms*, and with the novel generally, this mental rant has to be confronted—especially as it is hardly the only cryptic or seemingly unexplained passage in the book. *A Farewell to Arms* is dotted with such enigmatic passages. Moreover, this is also not the only scene in which Henry starts thinking in the second person. At an earlier climactic moment, when Henry has escaped being executed by his own army and so decides he is through with the war, there is an entire paragraph narrated in the second person, which concludes: "You were out of it [the war] now. You had no more obligation" (167).

The simplest, most straightforward, and most convincing way to make sense of Henry's oddly narrow contemplation of the ways one died, along with Hemingway's use of the second person at this other key moment as well, is that he is not referencing the thoughts of a universal "one" but rather a particular "you"—a particular sort of reader who would follow Henry's seemingly idiosyncratic train of thought immediately.

What sort of reader would that be? Let us look more closely at the scene of Henry's escape from execution—the final war action in the novel. There is a conundrum connected to this part of the book as well: Why did Hemingway choose for the climactic military action of his novel the retreat from Caporetto—an event that predated his posting to Italy—when he had his own experience to reference? He had seen action as a noncombatant and had enough to draw on from his own service.

No doubt the story of the retreat from Caporetto allowed Hemingway to give Henry a good reason for leaving the war and famously declaring a "separate peace" (173). In the chaos of what some elements in his Italian army consider a shameful retreat, his own battle police have tried to kill him, and he has managed, with some resourcefulness, to free himself. But if Hemingway wanted Henry to have a justifiable way out of a brutal and senseless war, why have his own army try to kill him and thus give him a good reason to desert? Why not, for example, make him a principled dissenter prepared to protest a war that had gotten out of hand—say, as British soldier-writer Siegfried Sassoon was in reality and his alter-ego George Sherston is in *Memoirs of an Infantry Officer* (1930)?

Could Hemingway, in this scene and others, have been trying to appeal specifically to combat veterans? This seems doubtful. A decade after a war that had come to seem fairly pointless to Americans, perhaps something along the lines of Sassoon's story might have had a limited appeal to combat veterans. But it is hard to imagine Frederic Henry's story having much appeal at all, as combat veterans tend not to like deserters. Likewise, to return to Henry's meditation in the hospital, a combat veteran would connect death, and certainly death in war, first and foremost with the enemy, not his own army. Why does Hemingway's novel insist that the real enemy is one's own military? Americans in general did not see things that way, and combat veterans did not either.

But there is one specific sort of reader to whom such an insistence makes immediate sense: a noncombatant veteran, who has a lingering resentment against his own army for its underestimation and poor treatment of him. And once one starts thinking about Hemingway as writing with a noncombatant readership in mind, longstanding conundrums about *A Farewell to Arms*, and *The Sun Also Rises* as well, begin to resolve themselves.

The idea that Hemingway, F. Scott Fitzgerald, and William Faulkner were, in words of the preeminent social-military historian of World War I, Jennifer Keene, "spokesm[e]n for the average doughboy" is an unfamiliar notion. The standard take on the relationship between Lost Generation literature and the average American soldier has, of course, been quite different. As Keene summarizes it, "David Kennedy, in *Over Here: The First World War and American Society*, the oft-cited standard-bearer for understanding the war and the home front, asserts that the postwar novels of protest, including Hemingway's, exposed a brutal, alienating war that differed dramatically from the romantic and upbeat assessment of the war's purpose and fighting that average doughboys often saw in their own memoirs and veterans' magazines. Kennedy asserts that the wide divide between intellectuals like Hemingway and the masses made this elite-produced postwar literature unrepresentative of the average soldiers' experience." Keene suggests, by contrast, a way "to reconnect the Lost Generation writers to their fellow veterans."[3]

> These writers articulated the sense of disillusionment and disappointment that many soldiers shared, not about the experience of combat or fighting but about their failure to serve along the frontlines. Men commonly lamented their noncombatant role, as Everett Taylor did, with the assertion that "it was not my fault I was behind the line." Having experienced firsthand the frustration of spending the war among the noncombatant ranks, Hemingway, F. Scott Fitzgerald, and William Faulkner were perfectly positioned to speak for a majority of the wartime generation and their anger at the powers that be that relegated them to the rear.[4]

Something similar might be said of John Dos Passos as well.

There is an obvious similarity between Taylor's comment, "it was not my fault I was behind the line," and Cadet Lowe's assertion in Faulkner's *Soldiers' Pay*: "I would have been killed . . . if I could, or wounded . . . , don't you know it? . . . I would have been, if I'd had the chance."[5] Noncombatant Paul Maxwell wrote a memoir called "Diary of a Dud."[6] Were the works written in the first person, the phrase would be an apt title for Cadet Lowe's chapter, the section in Fitzgerald's *The Beautiful and Damned* that sees his protagonist humiliated in a training camp, or much of Dos Passos's *Three Soldiers*. It is impossible to know, but one can imagine that a noncombatant with Everett Taylor's or Paul Maxwell's feelings would find it privately validating to come across the noncombatant degradation of Cadet Lowe, Anthony Patch of *The Beautiful and the Damned*, or Andrews and Fuselli of *Three Soldiers* in a *published* work. Meanwhile, one can further imagine that it might have been something more than validating, something recuperative, to come across Hemingway's Frederic Henry or Richard Savage in Dos Passos's *1919* (1932): characters that have dramatically transcended the humiliation of the noncombatant experience and come out as winners.

Many wartime and postwar books and magazine articles glorified the war and the combat soldier's experience, and this media onslaught would be all the more reason why publications like those by Faulkner, Fitzgerald, Dos Passos, and Hemingway would be meaningful to noncombatants who discovered that the embarrassment of their wartime status did not end when the war did. Both Hemingway and Dos Passos continued to write about noncombatant characters a decade after the war's end, turning from thinly veiled depictions of their own embarrassing experiences to fully fictionalized tales of empowered and powerful noncombatants.

The seemingly insignificant chitchat involved in the first exchange between Frederic Henry and Catherine Barkley at the start of *A Farewell to Arms*, about Henry's position in the Italian army, might likewise be quite meaningful for noncombatants. Though ostensibly about why Henry, an American, ends up in the Italian army, the conversation captures the uncomfortable moment of explanation or self-justification that noncombatants often found themselves in. It seems hardly a coincidence that Hemingway leads up to this passage with a series of fairly repetitive observations by Henry about the insignificance and fraudulence of his wartime role: "It evidently made no difference whether I was there to look after things or not. . . . Evidently it did not matter whether I was there or not. . . . The whole thing seemed to run better while I was away. . . . It was one of those things that gave you a false feeling of soldiering" (16–17).

Immediately after they meet, Catherine Barkley comments on Henry's situation, and Henry is not only put on the defensive but must admit that he has a noncombatant position:

> "What an odd thing—to be in the Italian army."
>
> "It's not really the army. It's only the ambulance."

"It's very odd though. Why did you do it?"

"I don't know," I said. "There isn't always an explanation for everything." (17)

Once one understands that most Americans who served ended up as noncombatants, that this group of men was quite large, numbering about 3 million, and that this service turned out for many to involve a humiliation that outlasted the war, the Lost Generation postwar literature takes on a new appearance. Maybe one of the reasons that Fitzgerald does not account for ethnic American Gatsby's stateside promotions in the army or Hemingway does not explain Jewish American Robert Cohn's presence in *The Sun Also Rises* is that they do not feel they need to. Perhaps they were assuming a readership partly made up of veterans, especially of noncombatant veterans. As with Dos Passos's untranslated epigraph in *Three Soldiers*, there would have been a private communication going on with such readers in the know, who would surely have appreciated a book with certain passages that implied a special solidarity with them—and at the same time was discreet about a reality that had caused them suffering. Nick's seemingly elliptical comment that Gatsby "was a captain before he went to the front" was probably such a passage.[7] Whereas the general reader would not know exactly what to make of this limited information, men who had been in an American training camp would immediately understand exactly how a German American man from a poor background could make captain before shipping out. Similarly, in *The Sun Also Rises*, as the characters begin to realize their dislike for Cohn, the narrator's friend Bill asks him, "How did you ever happen to know this fellow anyway?"[8]—and it is a question that is never answered. The point is that Anglo-American veterans would not need an answer because they would have understood, in general, how the military, indifferent to the civilian social hierarchy, suddenly and unexpectedly brought Jews into "personal contact" with them (to borrow Fitzgerald's phrase from *The Beautiful and Damned*)—and this had been a particularly uncomfortable experience for those noncombatant veterans who felt passed over for Jewish, German, or other ethnic Americans, or found themselves commanded by such men. The resentment, and the racial slurs, this phenomenon provoked among Anglo-American recruits is something that Dos Passos represents in *Three Soldiers*—directly and without discretion. "Ah didn't get in this here army to be ordered around by a goddamn wop," mutters Chrisfield, about "the corporal, a bandy-legged Italian."[9]

Similar passages in *A Farewell to Arms* that strike a contemporary reader as gratuitous and cryptic would have been immediately comprehensible to veterans, especially resonating with noncombatants. For example, at one point, Henry is commenting on American newspapers and specifically the baseball news, in the middle of which he throws in a quick, enigmatic digression: "The American news was all training camps. I was glad I wasn't in a training camp" (100). This subject never recurs, and his reason for being glad is never explained. Yet a readership with a particular World War I experience would not require an explanation. Conceivably they could understand this comment about the training camps as an assurance that the author is communicating privately with them.

Reading Hemingway's 1920s novels with a knowledge of the noncombatant veteran's plight suggests the extent of these secret communications. The noncombatant experience is going to be conjured up, but obliquely, at a certain remove, and with some transposition that allows the reader—and writer—a comfortable distance from what was painful and humiliating. To accomplish this, to address this special audience with its particular vulnerabilities and needs, Dos Passos and Hemingway create fictional protagonists whose positions in the army involve significant transpositions from their own experience—transpositions not found in their earlier, more autobiographical, war stories. Hemingway was unquestionably up to something quite purposeful and determined: he took up the same love-story kernel, about a wounded soldier and his nurse, three times, experimenting with different permutations.

Because the noncombatant experience was embarrassing, noncombatants tended either to avoid discussing their wartime role or to embellish it. So it is reasonable to imagine that when noncombatants found books that addressed their predicament, their consumption of these books was intensely private. If that was in fact the case, for noncombatant readers a particularly accommodating feature of Hemingway's 1920s novels and Dos Passos's *1919* was that the authors' transpositions made the reading experience that much more removed from public scrutiny. While outsider readers of *Three Soldiers* could hardly miss the miserable rendition of the noncombatant experience and would conclude that a noncombatant reader who loved the book shared Andrews's discontent with the army, outsider readers of, say, *A Farewell to Arms* are not likely to notice its noncombatant theme but are rather going to perceive a straightforward war and love story, and will assume that all appreciative readers are moved by these aspects.

Despite some of the claims of publishers at the time, repeated by critics to this day, war books, plays, and films sold well throughout the 1920s into the 1930s, and a number were huge hits (see introduction). Perhaps this persistence from a public that more or less quietly continued to consume war stories is explained by the presence of a significant but predominately "silent" group of war veterans in the public—the silent portion being the more than three-quarters of veterans that were noncombatants—for whom the war was still a live issue.

If noncombatant veterans continued to write about the army and the war throughout the 1920s, it was partly because they were still occupied with that experience.[10] And conceivably an emotional reaction that was true for noncombatant veterans who were writers was also true for noncombatant veterans who were not. The success of these books, especially of Hemingway's, plausibly has something to do with their appealing to millions of noncombatant veterans. And in his bestselling *A Farewell to Arms*, Hemingway offers a story that could appeal on different frequencies to two very different groups of readers: a romance for women and a fantasy for noncombatants.

In Richard Ellsworth Savage, one of the protagonists of *1919*, the second volume of the *U.S.A.* trilogy, John Dos Passos creates a noncombatant character who is not a victim but rather a "player." The early portions of Savage's story are largely Dos Passos's own: Savage goes to Harvard, then joins the American Norton-Harjes ambulance unit and gets into some trouble with the Red Cross authorities by writing antiwar letters. Then he returns to the war for a second leg with the Services of Supply (SOS). At that point, however, his story starts to deviate dramatically from his creator's. Instead of a lowly, humiliated private who is traumatized by being measured and evaluated, primarily used for menial tasks, and constantly ordered about, Dick Savage effortlessly finds himself a cushy position as an SOS "bigwig."[11]

He makes lieutenant and then captain, partly on the basis of personal attributes that his superiors value and partly on the basis of his exalted military-family past: his commanding officers "got so they couldn't do without Dick who knew how to order a meal comme il faut, and the proper vintages of wine and could parleyvoo with the French girls and make up limericks and was the grandson of the late General Ellsworth" (657–58). Dos Passos nods to the fact that the "guys at the front" say denigrating things "about the S.O.S.," but that does not bother Dick too much because "somebody's got to handle the supplies and the ordnance. . . . And the mademosels and the vin blanc" (658). Dos Passos's humiliation of being designated unfit for combat is transformed here into a smart-alecky irony about magically finding oneself in the plumb position of a clever operator safe behind the lines: as Dick's combat-soldier brother, whom Dick has the power to get a commission, remarks, "Well, of all the goddam lousy grafts . . .

I don't know whether to be proud of the little kid brother or to sock him in the eye" (658).

In order to effect this transposition, Dos Passos could be said to turn the clock back on US military history, as the army Dick is succeeding in seems to be largely a nepotistic one, in which powerfully connected relatives fix things up for him: "It must have been Mother's doing. . . . Honestly, I forgot that granpa was a general" (658).[12] It is no accident that this noncombatant fantasy—in which the aristocratic protagonist never experiences the shocking equality of the US army—brings with it, in striking in contrast to the democratic and socially conscious attitude of *Three Soldiers*, an elitist, racist, and anti-ethnic tone (for example, the terms "wop" [524, 672] and "nigger" [658] are casually tossed out).

In short, the novel adopts the attitude that noncombatant operatives (who enjoy safety and fringe benefits), and not combat soldiers, are the real winners in the American Expeditionary Force, essentially reversing not only public perception but Dos Passos's wartime and immediate postwar feelings. This cynical attitude, which contemporary readers might associate with the Vietnam era, no doubt existed during World War I, but it was uncommon on elite college campuses and much more likely to be found among older draft-age men, perhaps especially men who had previous experiences of class or social oppression. *Three Soldiers* could be said to figure a couple such characters—the Kid and Dan Cohen—who "consume" the war as opportunists out for a good time. But they have minor roles in the story. Dick, a major character in *1919*, also resembles Dan Cohen—and not Andrews—in his attitude toward women. While Andrews gets serious about the aristocratic Genevieve Rod, Dick seduces a proper "Texas girl," does not get too emotionally involved (it is she who asks him to "Say you love me" [675]), and is relieved to get away from her.

Dos Passos's final stratagem in his fantastical idealization of the noncombatant experience is to find a way to put Dick at the heart of the action, a tricky feat given that the Services of Supply operates, by definition, in a backup role and usually away from the front lines. The device is to make Dick a player not in the war but in the peace—in a clever twist, Dos Passos has him become an international dispatch courier during the peace negotiations, attending "various official functions" and getting "near enough the President's party" (676) to hear Woodrow Wilson himself discuss matters with foreign emissaries. Though Dick remains cynical about this role and is dubious about the prospects for true peace, it is crucial to Dos Passos's project here that his noncombatant character rubs elbows with important men. *A*

Farewell to Arms, which preceded *1919*, is likewise committed to imagining a way to take the noncombatant out of his support capacity and to put him into a role that is front and center.

Starting with the publication of *The Sun Also Rises* in 1926, the publisher included a biographical note that identified Hemingway as having "served as an ambulance driver and infantry man with the Italian army."[13] (Hemingway maintained a couple of lies about his service: He embellished the story of his actual wounding to make himself appear heroic rather than the victim of an "accident."[14] That he had been in the Italian army was a complete invention that he started to tell in his hometown of Oak Park, Illinois, in 1919, when he claimed that "after a tour of duty with the American Volunteer Ambulance Service he had joined the 69th Infantry, Brigata Ancona as a first lieutenant and had fought in three major battles: along the lower Piave, on Monte Grappa and at Vittorio Veneto." He continued to relay this lie in Chicago and Paris in the early 1920s.[15]) Hemingway's own fabrications about his infantry service had made it onto his novels' dust jackets.

The success of Hemingway's falsehoods of course played a role in his becoming a masculine icon. But what has not been considered is the effect that this lie would have had on noncombatant readers. Hemingway was identified on the book jacket as both a noncombatant and a combatant. Thus, his *A Farewell to Arms* would have been perceived as a novel extraordinary, if not unique, by virtue of the fact that a combatant (who also knew the noncombatant experience) had decided to write an entire novel about a noncombatant—and in particular a noncombatant who is admirably brave and tough, is loved by a beautiful British woman, and rises to the occasion when things get thorny. A central aspect of the humiliation of the noncombatant experience was that combat soldiers looked down on them. That a combat soldier had decided to write a novel about a noncombatant would have been in itself validating for noncombatants; that this noncombatant is a heroic figure would have been intensely vindicating for them. *A Farewell to Arms* would have been a noncombatant's dream novel, and its appeal to noncombatant readers was in part an ironic consequence of Hemingway's own quite common noncombatant coping mechanism (of lying about the terms of one's service).

Critics have long been aware that Hemingway wrote three versions of the love story of a wounded soldier and his nurse: in "A Very Short Story," *The Sun Also Rises*, and *A Farewell to Arms*. Critics have also long understood that this story was based on Hemingway's own experience with his nurse, Agnes Von Kurowsky. But what has not been explored is how the various versions of this story would have appealed in different ways to noncombatants. No doubt Hemingway had a tremendous personal investment in that story. No doubt, too, the versions of the story changed as he developed as a person and as an artist. But that personal stake and development does not mean that he was not aware that he had a tale with potentially mass popular appeal. So he took three shots at it until he had not only produced a critically acclaimed novel that established him as a major writer (namely *The Sun Also Rises*) but finally had a tremendous bestseller on his hands with *A Farewell to Arms*.

Hemingway's intuitive artistic savvy has been much commented on by literary critics. Edmund Wilson called him the "moral barometer" of his time.[16] Critics have paid much more attention to that "barometric" ability than to the time he registered, a historical context we are finally in a position, thanks to the work of social military historians, to place against his artistic works.

"A Very Short Story" differs in one significant way from similar tales of a recruit who suffers in both love and in war, as a result of his relatively lowly position in the army. In Hemingway's story, the woman who demeans the recruit experiences a pointed comeuppance, and the humiliated soldier is to a degree vindicated. Luz, who dismissed her relationship with the protagonist as "a boy and girl love," gets dumped by the high-ranking and militarily-experienced Italian officer she expected to marry. This comeuppance is not an invention of Hemingway's—his love interest, Agnes, had the same experience.[17] But including it in the story gives Hemingway's version a distinct conclusion and thus an ultimate trajectory that the other stories lack.

In *The Beautiful and Damned*, Anthony Patch gets a "tear-swollen" letter from his training-camp girlfriend, Dot, that he does not answer. But Anthony lets "it slip from his inert hand and drowsed back into a nebulous hinterland of his own" (287). At the point that he gets the letter, he is, like her, broken, and his actions are hardly conscious: their tale ends in a separately experienced but similarly crippling despair. Meanwhile, Hemingway's story finishes on an angry, bitter, and actively vengeful note. His character not only leaves Luz's letter unanswered but goes out and has casual, retaliatory sex in a taxicab—he has the satisfaction not only of seeing the woman who demeaned him brought down but of rejecting her in turn. So in Hemingway's first version of the soldier-nurse love story there is already an element of satisfaction for a reader who shares the experience of status humiliation in the army.

When Hemingway has a second go at the story, in *The Sun Also Rises*, he makes some major transpositions. This time the wounded American is

Jake Barnes, a pilot who has been literally emasculated while fighting on a "joke front" (31). Pilots were the stars of the war. Not only were men in the air corps officers, but their dog-fight exploits made them heroic and romantic figures (almost uniquely so in a war where the infantry mostly fought cowering in the trenches). Hemingway has his narrator of *A Farewell to Arms* express a competitive dislike for "aviators." Wearing civilian clothes because he has had to flee a vigilante military police force that has set itself up and targeted high-ranking officers and suspected spies after the retreat from Caporetto, Henry encounters "some aviators" in a train "compartment who did not think much of me. They avoided looking at me and were very scornful of a civilian my age. I did not feel insulted. In the old days I would have insulted them and picked a fight" (173). These "old days" of Henry's, when he could be made to feel insulted, are not otherwise referred to in the novel. But the point is that Hemingway could count on noncombatants sharing this resentment of aviators.[18]

So why write a novel about a pilot who is not only brought down a notch by his posting to a minor front but literally emasculated by an injury he gets there? It is impossible to know whether Hemingway worked things out consciously or instinctively, but consider the satisfaction involved for a noncombatant writer or reader. What could be more pleasurable for a lowly noncombatant than to see a star warrior of the army thus roundly humiliated—turned, quite literally, into a male "dud"?

At the end of the portion of *The Beautiful and Damned* that chronicles Anthony's wartime humiliation, there is a section called "Discomfiture of the Generals," in which, after the armistice but before he is discharged, Anthony "rejoiced to see general and field-officers riding desolately about the barren camp deprived of their commands" (305). Fitzgerald gives noncombatant Anthony and the noncombatant reader this little moment of vindication after pages and pages of noncombatant humiliation. Hemingway's approach in *The Sun Also Rises* would have been not only more satisfying but more comfortable for the noncombatant reader: Watch the humbling of one of the army's elite (rather than of a noncombatant whose position in the army resembles his). Call up the feeling of emasculation he experienced but distance it by giving it to a pilot the reader would naturally resent. Thus, Hemingway treats the painful subject of the noncombatant's humiliation and emasculation in an enjoyable way.

This is an ingenious stratagem. Perhaps Hemingway had gotten the idea from *The Great Gatsby*, in which Fitzgerald had arguably done something similar. Hemingway read *Gatsby* "just a few months before" beginning *The Sun Also Rises*.[19] According to Hemingway biographer Michael Reynolds,

"Fitzgerald's *Gatsby* had been there when Hemingway most needed a rough model for *Sun*," and he was "consciously competing with Fitzgerald" in its writing.[20] In *Gatsby*, Fitzgerald had created as his title character a man with a poor, ethnic American background who does phenomenally well in the American army—a natural target of resentment for a noncombatant, especially an Anglo-American noncombatant brought up to believe in his ethnic superiority. Such a reader might experience some satisfaction at seeing Gatsby outed as a criminal, ultimately rejected by the Anglo princess Daisy, and then destroyed.

But this stratagem of bringing down a character who is one of the army's chosen elite presents novelistic difficulties when that character is the protagonist, as is the case with both Gatsby and Jake Barnes. A reader must get close to and sympathize with the protagonist for a story to hold his or her interest over the length of a novel. And how does a reader both sympathize with Gatsby and wish for his comeuppance, or get close to Jake and continue to take pleasure in his emasculation? Critics have noted that the reader never gets too close to Gatsby, and many consider this a major failing of the book. (One critic has even argued that Nick Carraway is the protagonist since the reader watches him go through a transformation at the end, but, given Nick's quite minor role in the story, this claim demonstrates just how problematic it is for this reader to consider the title character of Fitzgerald's *The Great Gatsby* the protagonist.)[21] If the book was created by a noncombatant writer who had a noncombatant readership at least partly in mind, then Fitzgerald's "failure" here is no failing at all but a result of the book's unusual *need* to keep a particular readership distanced from the main character.

Hemingway eventually lets the reader get close to Jake and creates sympathy for him. But this results in a different problem by complicating things emotionally for a noncombatant reader who initially enjoys Jake's emasculation. Could such a reader transition from taking pleasure in Jake's humiliation to rooting for Jake? Could the book even be meant to work that way?

Jake's having been a pilot is referred to only once, and rather early on in the novel, when the reader does not know Jake very well. We learn no details about his combat experience beyond the simple fact that he was "wounded . . . flying on a joke front . . . the Italian." It is directly after we are informed of Jake's genital wound that his mental suffering over it is revealed, especially in regard to his relationship with Brett, and "then all of sudden," in the privacy of his room, he "started to cry" (31). It is plausible that a noncombatant reader could find satisfaction in Jake's tears and humiliation—he has not been a very sympathetic character up to this point.

Jake's opening narration does not cast him in a likable light. The first sentence introduces the reader to Robert Cohn, and specifically his collegiate middleweight boxing title, which Jake immediately belittles in the second sentence. After a full paragraph detailing Cohn's boxing experience at Princeton, Jake then tells us that he doubted that Cohn had ever "been middleweight boxing champion" there (a title he is "not . . . very much impressed by" anyway) and leaks some additional animus, wondering if Cohn had rid himself of his Jewish nose and gotten an "improved," flattened one because, instead, "perhaps a horse had stepped on his face, or that maybe his mother had been frightened or seen something, or he had, maybe, bumped into something as a young child." The entertainment of all these possibilities comes off as catty, especially once Jake admits that he later learned that his "suspicion" was completely unfounded and that Cohn was actually telling the truth about his boxing title (1–2). When the chapter concludes with Jake commenting of Cohn, "I rather liked him" (7), we also have the sense that Jake is not very self-aware. In short, in the first several pages, Jake is presented as ungenerous, resentful, petty, and a bit ridiculous.

After the sequence in Jake's room that reveals the nature of his wound, he never ruminates again on the subject, and he does not cry again either. (The reader of course will not forget about his wound because it is instrumental to his relationship to Brett and to his role in the love polygon that includes Robert Cohn; Brett's fiancé, Mike; and the bullfighter, Romero.) Additionally, Jake's having been one of the army's select never comes up again, though his having been in the war is referred to a few more times. (By contrast, Gatsby's exceptional wartime status—his army ranks and promotions, battlefield heroics, and decorations—gets a lot more play in Fitzgerald's novel and recurs at various points well into the book.) Hemingway's reader is not, like Fitzgerald's, reminded of the protagonist's once-exalted military status, and thus Jake's emasculation becomes effectively separated from his elite military past.

When male crying recurs in the novel, it comes from Cohn—and it is not in private. As the novel goes on, Cohn takes over the role of the obnoxious, ridiculous, and humiliated character, which was Jake's at the start. Cohn's sleeping with Brett is the first occasion for some ugliness on his part; he cannot help letting everyone know and acting "superior" about it (95, 96). Then Cohn decides to "hang . . . about" and "follow Brett around" (141). He stares at her even after she has been joined by her fiancé, something that is uncomfortable for both Brett and Mike. Cohn's lack of "manners" (142) eventually leads to Mike's verbally attacking him at the bullfights and Mike's accusation that he resembles a "steer," a castrated bull (141). Cohn's humiliation over Brett reaches a climax when he bursts into Romero's hotel room and punches out the bullfighter. This is the juncture at which he cries over Brett, but his humiliation is worse than Jake's was because he breaks down quite publicly.

As Cohn becomes more irritating and demeaned, Jake becomes progressively more sympathetic, even self-possessed. His new likability inheres partly in the fact that he becomes self-aware, especially as relates to his bad behavior toward Cohn. When Cohn starts projecting "an air of superior knowledge" in regard to Brett, Jake is "irritated" (95) and angry. He then begins to "enjoy . . . Cohn's nervousness," but now Jake's pettiness is mitigated by his consciousness of it. "It was lousy to enjoy it," he comments, "but I felt lousy" (98).

Jake never turns into a saint, but he does become honest with himself and the reader about some of his ugly feelings. Earlier in the book, Jake is "angry" at the group of homosexuals who accompany Brett when she first appears and wants to "swing on one" (20). He likewise feels hostility, expressed through racist imagery and language, including the word "nigger," toward a black drummer in a nightclub who waves at Brett (62). In neither case does he acknowledge that he is jealous of Brett's attention. But as Cohn becomes obnoxious about his having slept with Brett, Jake admits this reason for hating him, even though his first instinct is to pretend—reminiscent of the Jake who opens the book—that he does not know why. This admission represents a transitional moment for Jake, and it makes for an odd series of sentences, in which he contradicts himself: "Why I felt the impulse to devil him I do not know. Of course I do know. I was blind, unforgivingly jealous of what had happened to him" (99).

Two emasculated characters follow Brett around; one demonstrates a growing self-consciousness, the other's behavior devolves. Hemingway's stratagem with Jake and Cohn here is fairly involved. But, in one sense, what he seems to have done is effectively split Fitzgerald's Gatsby in two. Jake, like Gatsby, was once one of the army's elite; Cohn resembles Gatsby in other obvious ways: they are both moneyed ethnic American outsiders trying to mix with Anglos; they both mistakenly idealize high-class, desirable Anglo females with whom they have sexual relationships; in addition, both have egalitarian experiences connected with the military (Gatsby in the army and Cohn in military school).

Gatsby himself represents an amalgam of two figures in *The Beautiful and Damned*, rivals of Anthony for the affections of his wife, Gloria. These two figures align quite directly with Jake and Cohn, a pilot and a Jewish man: there are the aviators who flirt with Gloria while Anthony is in camp, and there is a rich, Jewish film producer named Joseph Black, born Bloeckman (like Gatsby, he Anglicizes his name), who punches out an Anglo rival. Black levels Anthony; Cohn decks both Jake and Mike after hammering Romero. So Hemingway arguably has broken Gatsby back down into the component parts Fitzgerald originally invented. Or perhaps Hemingway was also getting ideas from Fitzgerald's earlier novel.

Hemingway is certainly counting on Cohn to become an object of the reader's disdain, along with most of the characters', but his demise might in particular be satisfying for an Anglo-American noncombatant veteran who not only shares in the common nativist anti-Semitism of the era but has a special dislike, as Hemingway arguably does, for ethnic Americans in the military.[22] Cohn might be especially irritating for a noncombatant veteran. Not only did he enjoy the army's egalitarian ethos at military school, where "no one had made him race-conscious. No one had ever made him feel he was a Jew, and hence any different from anybody else" (4). He did so without ever "having to pay for it" by enduring the drudgery and humiliation of being in the army. We also learn in the first few pages that Cohn has been married and "had three children" (4), from which we can surmise that Cohn was one of the many men who used the fact of his marriage or children to get a deferment.[23] Men who escaped service in this way were objects of resentment for veterans bitter about the terms of their own service, and the implications of Cohn's situation would not have escaped veteran readers.

In short, in *The Sun Also Rises*, Hemingway offers up to a noncombatant reader the pleasure of watching the humiliation and emasculation of two characters, both of whose roles in the war that reader might naturally resent. Hemingway's approach in the novel is a departure from that of *Three Soldiers*, *The Beautiful and Damned*, *Soldiers' Pay*, and "A Very Short Story"—all of which directly showed noncombatants or soldiers of lesser rank suffering embarrassments and indignities. For noncombatant readers, it might have been therapeutic to see their unsung and inglorious experience being taken seriously in these earlier stories. Such readers could also take comfort in that fact that the authors seemed to share their lingering mental duress. But reading these tales might also have been painful, in that it likely involved revisiting their own humiliations, perhaps reopening their mobilization wounds.

In *The Sun Also Rises*, Hemingway is copying Fitzgerald's cunning tactic in *The Great Gatsby*—clever because it would have spared the noncombatant reader a renewal of the trauma—of representing the humiliation and disgrace of characters whom a noncombatant would have resented on the basis of their war service. Hemingway may have tried in *The Sun Also Rises* to solve a problem in *Gatsby* by finding a way for the noncombatant reader to get close to a protagonist who was a member of the army's elite. *The Sun Also Rises* allows such a reader to initially enjoy that protagonist's suffering yet later to sympathize with him when another character the reader also resents takes over the role of the character whose humiliation will be pleasurable.

But Hemingway was not yet done with his story of a doomed love between a wounded soldier and his nurse. *A Farewell to Arms* took an entirely new approach to the problem of how to treat the issue of the noncombatant—and presumably how to most effectively appeal to a noncombatant reader. The dust jacket copy on *The Sun Also Rises* that identified Hemingway as a member of the Italian infantry may have "embarrassed" him, as his biographer Reynolds claimed.[24] Nevertheless, he never took any action to remove it, and it remained on the jacket for more than fifty years—indeed, for a couple of decades after his death. But this mischaracterization of his wartime service provided him with an opportunity he did not have as long as he was identified as a "mere" ambulance driver, a noncombatant. Since he was now writing as a former combatant, he for the first time had the status and authority to validate noncombatants as potential heroes. It is not simply the case that it took Hemingway three attempts and a decade of writing to come up with the tack he takes in *A Farewell to Arms*. A noncombatant writing about a noncombatant protagonist who proves himself in the heat of battle would have been easily derided as a fantasy imagined by a man who had never fired a gun or took death-defying action.

As we have seen, noncombatant memoirists and fictional noncombatant characters alike defended themselves by pointing out, as Everett Taylor did, that "it wasn't my fault I was behind the line" or claiming, as Faulkner's Cadet Lowe does, that had he been given "a chance," he would have been just as ready to be wounded or die as any frontline soldier. Lowe also claims that he would have been just as effective: "I am as good a flyer as any ever was at the front—flying or any other way" (47). Chester C. Nash Jr., an army hospital cook, wrote in his diary: "I would prefer to get into a man's unit, get out of this baby affair. Then I might be a real man." Nash was one of the many noncombatants who put in multiple requests for transfer to combatant units.[25] Validating as it might have been for actual noncombatants to hear fictional noncombatant characters echoing their complaints and self-justifications, it would have been much more satisfying to observe a noncombatant character being brave and effective when taken out of the "baby affair" and put to the test.

And that is precisely what Hemingway offers up in *A Farewell to Arms*. Reynolds seems to miss crucial aspects of both the novel and the times when he claims of *A Farewell to Arms*, "by 1928, when America was no longer interested in war-heroes and trench adventures, Hemingway modified his experience to fit what the age demanded."[26] The main character, Henry, though officially an ambulance driver with only a "false feeling of soldiering," has in the course of the novel the very chance that noncombatants longingly talked about and some attempted to attain: to undergo perilous frontline adventures and prove himself heroic.

Hemingway develops Henry's noncombatant discomfort and sense of fraudulence quite fully, even repetitively, in the first several chapters of the book. Henry feels "embarrassment" when he has to salute (21). The paraphernalia of war makes him feel awkward because he is in no real danger: he feels he is playing at war and is almost surprised to find that the equipment is not fake as well. "We were supposed to wear steel helmets . . . but they were uncomfortable and too bloody theatrical in a town where the civilian inhabitants had not been evacuated. I wore one when we went up to the posts, and carried an English gas mask." It is "a real mask" (25). His gun gives him a similar sense of "shame" and "ridiculousness," and he feels the need to justify his wearing it. "Also we were required to wear an automatic pistol; even doctors and sanitary officers. . . . You were liable to arrest if you did not have one worn in plain sight." He also mocks himself for initially being excited about having one.

> Rinaldi [an experienced noncombatant] carried a holster stuffed with toilet paper. I wore a real one and felt like a gunman until I practiced firing it. It was an Astra 7.65 caliber with a short barrel and it jumped so sharply when you let it off that there was no question of hitting anything. I practiced with it . . . trying to master the jerk of the ridiculous short barrel until I could hit within a yard of where I aimed at twenty paces and then the ridiculousness of carrying a pistol at all came over me and I soon forgot it and carried it flopping against the small of my back with no feeling at all except a vague sort of shame when I met English-speaking people. (25)

This thorough conjuring up of the noncombatant's sense of uselessness and humiliation is typical of Lost Generation writing, but in this novel, it is all a setup for the complete transformation—to real danger, real bravery in the face of grave injury, real shooting, and real daring in the face of almost certain death—that is to come.

Fairly early on, Henry is wounded. Though the damage to his leg is serious and he handles it stoically and even heroically, at times more concerned with others' wounds than his own, he insists on treating it as a noncombatant injury. But now this insistence on his noncombatant status functions in a new way, as impressive modesty. At the hospital, when his friend Rinaldi tells him, "You will be decorated," he responds, "What for?"

> "Because you are gravely wounded. . . . Did you do any heroic act?"
>
> "No," I said. "I was blown up while we were eating cheese."
>
> "Be serious. You must have done something heroic either before or after . . ."
>
> "I did not."
>
> "Didn't you carry anybody on your back? Gordini says you carried several people on your back but the medical major at the first post declares it impossible."
>
> "I didn't carry anybody. I couldn't move." (50)

By this point, Henry's transition from untried noncombatant to cool-headed and understated hero is already well under way, for he did behave as heroically as a man so badly injured he is unable to move could. Right after he realizes his "knee wasn't there" and "was very afraid" and prays to "God . . . to get me out of here," he thinks, "however, that there had been three others." And when he is finally picked up off the ground by stretcher bearers, the first thing he says is, "There are three others" (45). In the dressing station, he selflessly tells a British ambulance driver, "I'd rather wait. . . . There are much worse wounded than me. I'm all right," to which the Englishman responds, "Come, come. . . . Don't be a bloody hero" (47).

Recent critics have observed that the scene in the hospital with Rinaldi ironically sets straight, under cover of fiction, Hemingway's lie about having carried people to safety after being hit by shrapnel. But at the time, and for many decades after, people would have interpreted it as a striking act of modesty by a writer who was supposed to have been heroic in precisely the way Henry insists he was not. More to the point, this sequence allows Hemingway to create for his unlikely hero a noncombatant's special brand of humility: the familiar pathetic lament, "given the chance I would have been wounded" or "given the chance I would have been just as heroic" becomes the impressive understatement, "oh, no, I wasn't heroic; I was merely seriously wounded while doing my unimportant job."

Also validating for a noncombatant reader would be the fact that Henry—like Hemingway—*is* decorated for being injured while doing his noncombat job. Most medals went to combat soldiers. (Perhaps at this point, ten years after the fact, Hemingway realized that his getting a medal as an ambulance driver was a personal experience with meaning to the average noncombatant, who was not recognized in this way. Therefore, he gives his own validation directly, and unchanged, to Henry.)

Indeed, a noncombatant reader will hardly be surprised—in fact, one imagines he will be expecting—that a combat soldier will at some point in the narrative materialize to challenge or mock the ambulance driver's decoration. Making this confrontation particularly charged for a noncombatant American veteran, the combat soldier who plays this antagonistic role is an Italian American officer (in the Italian army).

Ettore Moretti, "a wop from Frisco" (88), as someone calls him, has been wounded three times and is about to be promoted to captain, and thus to outrank Henry, on the basis of "merit of war" (91). Moretti taunts Henry by asserting that he himself had to "work for [the] decorations" (89) Henry got simply by being hit by shrapnel. Moretti makes it clear that he is also one-upping Henry by making captain in just two years, while Henry, who is not being promoted, has been in service three years. But the noncombatant reader will be pleased that Henry comes off the winner in this sequence. Crucially, it is Catherine who says about Moretti, "We have heroes too . . . But, usually, darling, they're much quieter." She tells Henry that Moretti is "the type of boy I don't care for" though "you can picture him at the front and you know he's useful"; that "he's a dreadful, dreadful boy really." She finally reassures Henry that she "wouldn't like [him] to have some more exalted rank" (91–92). Catherine here essentially breaks ranks with the military's ranking of men, asserting an alternative scale of masculinity, in which other values enter in, and in which Moretti comes out, importantly, as a "boy"—the term is repeated for emphasis. This exchange reverses the way things play out in the parallel scene in "A Very Short Story" where Luz, following the military's valuations, prefers the man with higher rank and more intense combat experience and deems Nick a boy. Catherine's words would be music to a noncombatant's ears.

Starting with the scene of his injury, Henry changes from an insecure and vaguely ashamed noncombatant to a "real man" (as Chester Nash, the hospital cook who tried to have himself transferred to a combat unit, might have put it). First, he bravely goes through surgery without "say[ing] anything silly," even under the anesthetic (80). Later, as he and his ambulance men get caught up in the war, he is no longer "embarrassed" by his position but rather—like a seasoned soldier who has been inundated with battlefield mutilation and death—by the "abstract words" that governments used to justify the slaughter, such as "sacred, glorious, and sacrifice" (133). During the chaotic retreat from Caporetto, he takes on the authority that his rank of lieutenant (previously all but honorary) demands as he tries to shepherd his scared crew members to safety while German bombers fly overhead, and he wisely keeps off the main roads to avoid being hit. One of their cars gets stuck in a muddy side road, and he orders a couple of sergeants traveling with him to help him dig out. When they refuse and walk off, he orders them to "halt." They refuse to acknowledge his authority and keep going, and, as they start to move off "faster," he simply takes out his gun and starts firing. They run, and he "drop[s] one" (146–47). Though he has presumably shot a man merely for disobeying his orders, Henry—who initially felt ridiculous even carrying a gun—appears utterly unfazed, even after one of his men, Private Bonello, happily finishes the man off and takes pleasure in killing a superior. This killing of a superior, one imagines, provides a satisfying moment for a noncombatant reader who felt bossed around and abused. (The scene is reminiscent of the sequence in *Three Soldiers* in which Chrisfield murders a sergeant who he feels has picked on him, but Hemingway's fictional setup makes the murder more justified, as Bonello has a legitimate, impersonal reason for an execution, even if it gives him personal satisfaction.) Henry evinces no emotional reaction either at the moment or later: he seems somehow to have already become, by the occasion of his first act of violence, a hardened killer.[27]

The climax of the war-story portion of *A Farewell to Arms* seems tailor-made for a noncombatant reader. In this sequence, Henry is apprehended by the self-appointed "battle police," a group of "officers and carabiniere" who are summarily executing officers that have deserted or lost the soldiers in their charge or men that they accuse of being "German agitators in Italian uniform" (160, 162). And so begins a scene that must have been intensely cathartic for the noncombatant with a chip on his shoulder—as Hemingway himself arguably still was a decade after the fact.[28]

Henry has just proved himself a fearless and clever officer in the face of real danger, but the men in charge of the army fail to recognize him for what he is. Hemingway has cleverly found a way in the situation of the retreat from Caporetto to reprise at the climactic moment the disrespect and mistreatment of the noncombatant, even after this noncombatant has shown what he is capable of on the front lines. "Don't you know you can't touch an officer?" Henry says, now simply asserting the status he was previously embarrassed by, to the men who seize him (160). (Henry's reaction to being grabbed by the "battle police" would in itself be a nice little pleasure for a noncombatant reader: military policemen were intensely disliked, and it is no coincidence that they also play the role of antagonist for Fitzgerald's Anthony and Dos Passos's Andrews. Here Henry gets in a couple of choice shots when he is grabbed, punching one "carabiniere" in the face, drawing blood, and kneeing another in the groin.)

Henry gets to pass judgment on the stupidity of his "illegitimate" superiors as he waits in line to be executed. "I was obviously a German in Italian uniform. I saw how their minds worked; if they had minds and if they worked" (162). Again, this situation would resonate with a noncombatant reader and have special meaning for him. Henry is facing the stupidity and cruelty of decision-making men who have appointed themselves the leaders of an army, and they fail to identify him for what the reader knows he truly is: a loyal, brave, and effective soldier and officer.

The highlight of this sequence for the noncombatant reader is not Henry's daring getaway from the murderous clutches of his own army, exciting though this is—like Dos Passos's Andrews, he escapes into a river: he runs for it and, again like Andrews, swims away under fire as he contends with "very cold" water (162). Rather, it comes when Henry—turning the tables on the army, for himself and for the noncombatant reader—gets to reject the army that rejected him. First he "cut[s] the cloth stars [indicating his officer rank] off my sleeves" (164), literally to avoid recapture and not as a "point of honor" (167) but, symbolically, very much as a point of honor, in a gesture of rejecting the army's system of ranking men. Then he gets to righteously turn his back on the whole affair, an act he invites the reader to participate in by writing at points in the second person: "You were out of it now. . . . [I]t was not my show anymore" (167).

Henry has gone through a cleansing that the noncombatant reader can potentially share in. "Anger was washed away in the river along with any obligation. . . . I was not against them. I was through." As well as cleansing or baptism, Hemingway presents also the metaphor of death and rebirth. "Piani would tell them they had shot me. . . . They might call me drowned. I wondered what they would hear in the states. Dead from wounds and other causes" (167).

Perhaps no book could fully relieve the noncombatant of his shame and anger. But in this climactic section of the novel, the narrator also seems to be describing a way to proceed, in lines that would be suggestive for noncombatant and combatant readers alike: "Doctors did things to you and then it was not your body anymore. The head was mine, and the inside of the belly. It was very hungry in there. . . . The head was mine, but not to use, not to think with; only to remember and not too much remember" (166).

This returns us to the book's ultimate climax, Catherine Barkley dying in childbirth in a Swiss hospital. Though the scene is set far beyond the war zone and focused on the relationship between Henry and his one-time nurse, the predicament of the noncombatant is conjured up one final time, in his contemplation of the ways that "you died"—always at the hands of one's own military. Perhaps Henry blames Catherine's death on the Italian military as well. Their fleeing his own army has put stress on Catherine in obvious ways, including physically (she did some of the rowing as they crossed a lake on their way to Switzerland [196]). Or perhaps Henry is what we could call today "post-traumatic" due to all the horrors he has faced.

In any case, despite the way many readers have taken it, this morbid meditation is not simply a soldier's brand of pessimism. No, what the reader gets five pages before the end of this story of love and war is, strikingly, a noncombatant's lament because the bogeymen—the unnamed "they"—are precisely one's own armed forces. Though it has a universal feel, this summarizing passage speaks especially to a very specific experience, and spoke at one time to a very particular audience. And though it may seem not to fit the occasion of a lover's death in childbirth, it is fitting for a book dedicated to validating and redeeming the noncombatant.

Hemingway's ingenuity here is to link the highly emotional death of a lover and a potential child to the losses and missed opportunities the noncombatant underwent. It may be that Hemingway was only thinking of his own loss of his love with Agnes Von Kurowsky, transmuted from the bitter comedy registered in "A Very Short Story" into a sentimental tragedy in his final World War I book. But nonetheless, this ending would have been cathartic for a noncombatant reader as well. This conclusion licenses nothing less than mourning—and allows tears—over a suffering that had no public ritual or recognition, and was given no treatment by the Veterans Bureau.

Leslie Marmon Silko's *Ceremony* (1977) describes the ritual, invented by an unorthodox medicine man, that a Native American veteran of World War II enacts to heal not only his "battle fatigue" but the social demotion or "demobilization wounds" experienced when, after the war, returning "Indian" soldiers took off the American military uniforms that had momentarily granted them a significant measure of equality and social acceptance, and they were returned to discrimination. Hemingway's novel might be said to present a *virtual* ceremony for noncombatants who were still suffering after World War I from their "mobilization wounds."

PART TWO

War Literature by Female Participants and Nonparticipants

We women of America tell you that America is not a democracy. Twenty million women are denied the right to vote.

—ALICE PAUL, *suffragist*

CHAPTER FIVE

The Mobilization of Young Women

Soldiers, Noncombatants, and Women from a Female Perspective in Porter's "Pale Horse, Pale Rider"

KATHERINE ANNE PORTER'S LONG SHORT story set during World War I on the home front, "Pale Horse, Pale Rider" (1939), provides a more balanced view of the wartime changes in gender roles and in relations between young women, combatants, and noncombatants than the male writers of the Lost Generation offered.[1] Porter's story is, like theirs, based to some degree on her own experience. Porter became very ill during the 1918 influenza epidemic that swept the country; she may also, during the war, have fallen in love with "a boy, an army lieutenant" who died of the flu that almost killed her as well.[2] But she wrote the story twenty years later, from the point of view of a mature adult in her late forties who had plenty of distance on that World War I experience.

"Pale Horse, Pale Rider" seems to be a straightforward indictment of the almost terroristic wartime patriotic hysteria, especially as it affects women. The main character, Miranda, is met with male hostility from almost every direction; sometimes she is openly bullied and menaced.

Her first encounter with this malice occurs when two men selling Liberty Bonds lay siege to her at the newspaper office where she works—aggressively sitting on her desk—in an attempt to extort an exorbitant sum of money from her in support of the war effort. When she balks, understandably given that a bond would cost her nearly three weeks' salary, they threaten her. "[Y]ou can lose a lot if you don't," one says, acting like a "little thug."[3] She wonders if she could lose her job—or worse. "She would have to raise that fifty dollars somehow, she supposed, or who knows what can happen? She was hardened to stories of personal disaster, of outrageous accusations and extraordinarily bitter penalties that had grown monstrously out of incidents very little more important than her failure—her refusal—to buy a Bond" (153).

Later, when she visits the wounded, because it is one of the expectations put on her as a young woman, she is met there with the icy, "hostile" stare of a young, injured veteran who clearly resents her presence and the feeble attempt she is supposed to make to cheer him up with flowers and "sweets and cigarettes" (152). She would like to avoid performing this uncomfortable and seemingly futile service in the future, but she fears being branded insufficiently patriotic and becoming a pariah. She would at least like to share her feelings with "another girl" at the hospital, who says, "I don't like this, do you?" But they are both too "cautious" (153) and afraid to talk further. She would in fact like to speak out against a war she sees as destroying the lives of young men and making some older men rich—"Suppose I were not a coward, but said what I really thought? Suppose I said to hell with this filthy war?" (147)—but she is absolutely terrified, given the prevailing jingoistic attitude, to voice the slightest criticism.

In addition, her male colleague at work, Chuck, a man rejected by the army because of a bad lung, looks at her with a defensive and "sidelong" glance that accuses her of her being a "bloodthirsty female" (171) because women presumably look on him, or any man in civilian garb, as a slacker and a coward. Moreover, he may perhaps resent her presence in the workplace because he would like her job as a theater critic.

At the theater, between acts, she must sit quietly and listen to a pro-war speech given by yet another self-important Liberty Bond salesman. He repeats the usual propagandistic phrases: "the WAR to end WAR, war for Democracy for humanity, a safe world forever and ever." All she can do is grit her teeth and think to herself, "Coal, oil, iron, gold, international finance, why don't you tell us about them, you little liar?" (175).[4] Another time, a theater performer she has "panned" in a review confronts her in the street because he sees her as threatening his reputation and livelihood. "If you was a man, I'd knock your block off," he tells her (168, 169).

To make matters worse, the wartime frenzy is driving her boyfriend, Adam, who is in the army waiting to be shipped out, to almost certain death, given his expected duties as a "Second Lieutenant in an Engineers Corps" (156). The two of them try to be brave and "laugh" about the fact that supposedly "the average life expectation of a sapping party . . . after it hits the job" at the front is "nine minutes," but "tears" come to her eyes because his apparently probable death is no joke. "She liked him, she liked him, and there was more than this but it was no good even imagining, because he was not for her or any woman, being beyond experience already, committed without any knowledge or act of his own to death" (161–62). She tries to tell herself, later, as they dance, to accept things as they are: "The music was gay; and life is completely crazy anyway, so what does it matter? This is what we have, Adam and I, this is all we're going to get." But she is hurting body and soul. "She wanted to say, 'Adam, come out of your dream and listen to me. I have pains in my chest and my head and my heart and they're real. I am in pain all over, and you are in such danger as I can't bear to think about, and why can we not save each other?' " (178). However, she knows that part of the wartime hysteria that has them trapped is the ideology that has tied masculinity to armed service. He has already told her, "If I didn't go . . . , I couldn't look myself in the face" (177).

After the confrontation with the angry actor, given the terror she is living with and the almost unremitting aggression and animosity visited on her by men of just about every stripe, she momentarily loses the will to go on and breaks down. This encounter is tangential to her main worries, and certainly not central to her suffering, but seems rather to push her over the edge. She says at this point, "I'd like to sit down here on this curb . . . and die. . . . I wish I could lose my memory and forget my own name" (169). Her soon getting sick with the flu is also no surprise given the emotional stress she is under. When she recovers, against the odds, she is hardly happy and has to pretend "how gay and what a pleasant surprise it was to find herself alive" (205). When she learns that Adam has "died of influenza"—presumably he contracted the disease while caring for her—she feels, since she "came back for" him, "deceived" and even more depressed. She is so traumatized that his "ghost" was "at once . . . there beside her . . . more alive than she was" (208).

But Miranda is not merely a victim of prevailing wartime attitudes that she herself abhors and resists sharing. Her participation in the war effort goes beyond her professional obligations as a journalist to "write pieces advising other young women to knit and roll bandages and do without sugar and help win the war" (157). Yes, she wishes she could somehow stop the process that has Adam "infinitely buttoned, strapped, harnessed into a uniform as tough and unyielding as a strait jacket" (155). She wants to ask Adam, "why can we not save each other?" But the story also makes clear that the main reason that *they* cannot save each other is that each is busy dooming the other.

For one thing, Miranda finds this same "strait jacket" of a uniform sexy: "She told him how *squish* he was looking in his new soldier suit" (155, emphasis added). Postwar readers familiar with the slang of the time can get Porter's pun that his "squish" uniform is "squishing" the life out of him. But

Miranda is oblivious. She also does not see that her falling in love with a soldier she has only known for ten days (157)—despite the fact that she finds him alien and "monstrous" (156) in certain respects—contributes to the vicious cycle that makes it impossible for him to refuse to go to war. "If I didn't go, I couldn't look myself in the face," he says, because if he had not been in uniform, had not been going, she (and other women) would not have looked at his face either.

After listening to the Liberty Bond man at the theater, Miranda openly admits she hates "these potbellied baldheads, too fat, too old, too cowardly, to go to war themselves" (176). In her view, these men are consigning Adam to go instead. Perhaps one reason that Porter includes two separate encounters with Liberty Bond men, one early in the story and one fairly late, is to point out that their aggression toward Miranda in her office is not only self-important posturing but resentment based on the way young women look at them with disgust. Their pugnacious manner—seemingly gratuitous the first time around—appears now to come out of a need to compensate for the loss of masculinity they have suffered by being disqualified from service and thus deprived of female attention.

Adam, who has a typical combat soldier's attitude to noncombatants though he himself has seen no combat yet, condescends to them, too. In reference to the "Liberty Bond salesman" (174) that Miranda disparages, Adam says, "Now what could the poor sap do if they did take him? It's not his fault . . . , he can't do anything but talk. What *could* you expect of him?" Porter is obviously interested in representing the wartime social dynamic that has put men and women of different ages and capabilities into their particular roles and that leads them to behave according to type—despite what they may think of the war and the ugly nationalism. Adam shares Miranda's antiwar outlook, and specifically her skepticism about the propaganda. But just as she does not see the way in which her immediate attraction to a soldier supports the war effort, he is caught up in the "pride" that comes from his being a soldier and officer. Adam's "contempt for that unlucky being [the Liberty Bond salesman] breathed out of his very pores as he strolled, straight and relaxed in his strength" (176).

If the reader at this point thinks back to Miranda's encounter with the "young fellow" in the cantonment hospital, his "unfriendly bitter eye" (152) for her will also make more sense. Maybe, like a lot of young men, this recruit got into the war in part because he knew that young women were attracted to soldiers and because army propaganda found ways to use the promise of female sexual attention to sell the draft. Now wounded, this soldier is getting a kind of female attention he did not bargain for—sisterly tenderness and pity—and he may just resent the women who no longer look at him as a sexual being, and for whom he has become, if not exactly another sort of reject, then a different kind of desexualized man.

Adam and Miranda—the officer in training camp about to ship out and his girl—reflexively make noncombatants the butt of their jokes, as do Miranda and her female colleague, Towney, and Porter's book provides more evidence for the social-military historians' accounts of the way noncombatants were routinely put on the defensive. Talking with her workmates about the rumor that the flu epidemic of 1918 was spread by "germs" being "sprayed over the city" of Boston by a German ship, creating "a strange, thick, greasy-looking cloud," Miranda jokes, "It was a noncombatant saw that cloud" (163). And when she asks Adam who determined the life expectancy of a sapping party, he snaps back, "A noncombatant . . . , a fellow with rickets" (161).

In Miranda's colleague and supposed friend Chuck, we get a sense of the experience of a man who has in fact been rejected by the army on physical grounds (not because of rickets but rather a bad lung). His resulting masculine self-doubt and reflexive defensiveness with women is similar to that of William Faulkner's Cadet Lowe from *Soldiers' Pay*. Chuck "fretted a good deal about missing the show" (165), and he is regularly on the defensive around Miranda and Towney, who needles him about his noncombatant status. Much like Cadet Lowe, he talks tough about soldiers on the battlefield, seemingly out of a need to compensate for his failure to be inducted into the army. "'You can talk,' said Towney, with a slantwise glance at him. 'What's the idea?' Chuck asked, flushing and hunching his shoulders. 'You know I've got this lung . . .'" (166)

In a further effort to compensate, Chuck dresses in a way that he hopes makes him appear butch. He wears "peasoup tweed plus fours and . . . hobnailed tan boots which he hoped would help disguise the fact that he had a bad lung and didn't care for sports" (167). Chuck also steps in aggressively to protect Miranda when she is verbally assaulted by the "show business" fellow she has panned. "Chuck got up . . . and lounged over, taking his hands out of his pockets, and said, 'Now you've done your song and dance and you'd better get out. Get the hell out now before I throw you downstairs'" (169).

In Miranda's perception of Chuck's attitude toward women, we learn that rejected men see women as bloodthirsty.[5] "All the rejected men talked like that, thought Miranda. War was the one thing they wanted, now they couldn't have it. Maybe they had badly wanted to go, some of them. All of them had a sidelong eye for the women they talked with about it, a guarded resentment which said, 'Don't pin a white feather [representing cowardice] on me, you bloodthirsty female. I've offered my meat to the crows and they won't have it'" (170–71).

Chuck's defensiveness with Miranda is motivated not simply out of paranoia or in response to the treatment he has received from other women but also by Miranda's own attitude toward him. Miranda intuits Chuck's plight, but she does not reassure him, nor does she quite sympathize with him, apparently because she can never be sure that he had really "wanted to go." "Some of them" did, but some of them, her thought implies, are only pretending they wanted to. Miranda may be aware of the men who publicly registered for the draft but privately sought deferments.[6] It is theoretically possible that Chuck is lying about how his non-service came about; perhaps he was not rejected as a result of his induction physical but sought a deferment knowing he had a bad lung. But if Chuck is telling the truth, then he resents Miranda because he evidently feels, not exactly mistakenly, that his military rejection has rendered his manhood questionable in her eyes as well.

Male cooperation with the draft is going strong because Miranda and her female cohort are playing the role of the "bloodthirsty female" without realizing it. She is deluded about being purely opposed to the war. She may not be literally handing out white feathers to humiliate draft-age men not in uniform, as women did in England during World War I.[7] Nevertheless, she and women like her are playing a key role in the forces pushing men into service by instantly falling in love with soldiers and being suspicious of men not in uniform. Though Porter's heroine is on a conscious level completely opposed to the war, she cannot resist the social and sexual forces let loose by the war and the army's mobilization and vetting of men. While the charity girl phenomenon mainly involved working-class women and girls, others were caught up in the erotic excitement, if not participating sexually. Porter writes of society women "fresh from the country club dances, the morning bridge, the charity bazaar, the Red Cross workrooms." Miranda hears one of them saying, "Yes, and some of [the soldiers in the cantonment hospitals] are the cutest things you ever saw, I didn't know there were so many good-looking men in this country" (150). Miranda cannot help being seduced by, embracing, and thus affirming the army's valuations of masculinity—and perhaps also the power that comes to young women in their new role of judges of men. Thus she ends up contributing to the peer pressure that is driving men to enlist or comply with the draft.

But Miranda's unwitting participation in the mobilization effort does not mean she herself is not suffering from various causes. Part of Porter's "sociological" insight in this story seems her recognition that everyone on the home front is caught up in playing an almost inescapable role in the "total" mobilization for the war, determined by one's age, gender, and, in the case of draft-age men, military status. No position is free from discomfort, but each has its particular agonies.

Of course, Miranda's plight is completely different from Chuck's. Miranda's emotional breakdown, which anticipates her getting the flu, comes in her professional capacity as theater critic for a newspaper, when she is confronted by the dramatist whom she has apparently panned. Why does it occur at that point? Miranda is most of all tortured by the thought of losing Adam to the front and early death and secondly by what she calls at one point the "the worst of war": "the fear and suspicion and the awful expression in the eyes you meet . . . as if they had pulled down the shutters over their minds and their hearts and were peering out at you, ready to leap if you make one gesture or say one word they do not understand instantly" (176, suspension points in original). Should these not be the immediate cause of her crisis?

Miranda's occupation as a critic is relevant here. With the mobilization, women have been thrust into the role of "critic" or judge of men and manliness. It is also apropos that she is a theater critic, given that young men in general are trying to perform masculinity and dressing the part, whether in army uniform or otherwise.[8] Perhaps Miranda's momentary breakdown here comes out of a guilt that is at least partly unconscious. A sensitive and educated woman, she is tortured by this new and powerful role of masculinity "critic" that is simultaneously appealing and liberating for many women who are used to having their femininity morally judged by men. It seems both socially meaningful and symbolic that Miranda not only works in a journalistic profession once reserved for men but specifically as a critic and that it is in that new and unfamiliar role that her despair is triggered.

Miranda's getting sick with the flu, though terrifying from the start, provides the opportunity for Adam to "come out of [his] dream" (178). Miranda has been looking for a way to shake Adam out of his "pure" unquestioning acquiescence—his acceptance, without "resentment or revolt" (177), of the role of "sacrificial lamb," of the heroic, patriotic soldier who will die on the battlefield—and her illness does just that. Miranda's disease saves Adam from the general hysteria that has him under its spell, much as the flu "saved Anthony from a hysterical relapse" in *The Beautiful and Damned*.[9] Adam now allows his role to shift: rather than being a soldier "on leave because his outfit expected to be sent over shortly"—visiting "camp for a lot of inoculations" (180) or making out his "will" (156) or dancing with his "girl"—he is functioning in the capacity of nurse: "look[ing] after her" and bringing her medicine (184). And though this task also involves a braving of death he is seemingly committed to—"'You're running a risk,' she told him. . . . 'Never mind,' said Adam" (184)—it does not involve the kind of bravery that is, at this wartime moment, socially recognized for men.

Miranda and Adam react to the awareness that she, too, might die. They sing an "old spiritual" together and joke that they might "get up an act" (189). He allows himself to join her in playfully imagining, too, that they "Go in Hut Service . . . [to] entertain the poor defenseless heroes Over There," as she puts it. "We'll play banjos," he says (190). In other words, he allows himself to imagine being a noncombatant amusing the troops. Hut Service refers to the YMCA activities and concessions in France for soldiers, and "Y-men" were looked down on and often resented by soldiers. In the era's hierarchy of manliness, they were even lower than military noncombatants; moreover, soldiers often perceived them to be irritatingly moralistic as well as profiteering (they charged for items the soldiers sometimes felt should be cheaper or free).[10] Given Miranda's desire to awaken Adam out of his "dream" of being a sacrificial war hero, it makes sense that she jokes in this particular fashion, but his response is a far cry from the seriousness with which he has so far treated his intention to "go over" as a soldier.

There may be a deeper irony both to Miranda's trying to bring Adam out of his sacrificial dream and to his subsequent imagination of Hut Service. His "dream" of intense danger and almost certain death may be mostly that, a dream. As a member of "an Engineers Corps" (156), he would technically be a noncombatant soldier, and, even if his particular corps is attached to a combat unit (every combat division contained an engineer regiment), the fact was that most engineers, as Steven Trout explains, "did not face 'certain death'":

> Far from it. Thus, in a manner consistent with other noncombatants, Adam is almost certainly exaggerating the potential hazards of his overseas service—service that would likely have been spent far from the front line. Even in combat divisions . . . , casualties among engineers were, with some notable exceptions, infrequent. And I find this business about the brief lifespan of engineers assigned to dig a sap (a shallow trench extending into no-man's land) highly dubious. Prior to their involvement in the major battles of the summer and fall of 1918, AEF combat divisions were placed in relatively peaceful trench sectors, where little dangerous sap-digging would have been done (by engineers or anyone else).[11]

There is no question that to some in the army—combat soldiers for certain—the Engineers Corps would be viewed as support troops who had safe and easy assignments. But as Richard S. Faulkner points out,

> It is interesting to note that the "rear" of an army is always relative to the beholder. . . . Even when it came to noncombatant soldiers, there was a pecking order that separated them from those supposedly enjoying the greater comforts of the rear. Thus the doughboys working in the regimental and division supply, ammunition, and sanitary trains, whose duties often exposed them to shellfire and the hardships of the front, looked down on those slightly further to the rear in the depots of the Advance Section of the SOS. Of course, the troops in the Advance Section of the SOS resented the easy life of those timid souls working in the SOS Intermediate and Base Sections, while the personnel in those sections looked askance at the troops still in the United States.[12]

Adam's exaggerations of his role and the danger he will face form part of a wartime masculine persona that he cannot (and most noncombatant soldiers could not) resist adopting—and that Miranda, as a young woman, though a journalist and a nonbeliever in the war cause, cannot help finding convincing. The irony of this late sequence in the story is that Miranda is trying to coax Adam out of a commitment to self-sacrifice that is largely a fantasy and a pose.

Miranda and Adam alight on the spiritual they sing after considering a number of consoling "prayers" they might recite. He mentions the "Lord's prayer"; she references "Hail Mary," but that is "Catholic" and he is "Presbyterian." He does not seem to know "Bless the bed I lie upon," and "Now I lay me down to sleep" "doesn't sound right, somehow" to him, though it is eerily appropriate. (Miranda is afraid if she falls asleep she may never wake up, and he recites, "If I should die before I awake, I pray the Lord my soul to take.") Miranda suggests "a prayer beginning O Apollo," but he does not want to hear it and thinks she is joking. The "old spiritual" they settle on begins, "Pale Horse, Pale Rider, done taken my lover away." Adam "heard Negroes in Texas sing it," and Miranda "heard them sing it in a cotton field" (189). This spiritual comprehends their relationship as well as Miranda's possible death.

But the song also suggests a further departure from the points of reference that have circumscribed the couple's existence in this wartime moment. Christian prayers and themes are often deployed in the official patriotism and propaganda. The choice of an African American spiritual, however, indicates an arrival at an artifact and a sensibility that belongs not to the powerful but to the downtrodden, not to the ruling classes but to the lowest American caste—in fact, the only group that has been excluded from the equal opportunity that the army extended to every other minority group as part of its meritocratic experiment. Because of the racial discrimination the government imposed on the military, black men were segregated, and a disproportionate number of them ended up as noncombatants. And so again here we have the breaking down of boundaries that the wartime moment has established or confirmed: between black people and white people, between noncombatant and combat soldier.

If Adam had lived, it is hard to know if Miranda's brush with death and his momentary transformation might have translated into a changed attitude about the inevitability of playing his assigned role, of going off to war to die—or, perhaps, of pretending that that is his fate. But a final irony of the story is that Adam gets influenza and dies before seeing combat. This was a common death for American soldiers: as John Dos Passos's biographer puts it, "half as many soldiers died in army camps" as a result of the influenza epidemic "during the fall and winter of 1918–1919 as those mortally wounded in combat during the entire war." Observing the influenza cases at his training camp, Dos Passos thought there was something humiliating about a recruit dying before getting to the war zone, and he was not alone.[13] In a war in which "Better dead than diseased" was a message of the military propaganda concerned with preventing VD, "there would be," as social historian of venereal disease Allan Brandt has observed, "moral and immoral injuries, moral and immoral deaths."[14] Likewise, with an army ethos and a public atmosphere in which the distinction between those who fought and those who worked in support was given so much importance, there was also a hierarchy of deaths. Adam, after having escaped in life the shame of "not going," and being seen as a "rejected man" or a noncombatant, and probably having played up the danger his role would entail, dies, in the eyes of the public he was trying to impress or appease, a noncombatant death.

The irony goes further. Adam evidently contracts the flu from Miranda, while caring for her. As we have seen, the army was deeply concerned about men being infected by women—albeit with venereal disease, not flu—and consequently demonized women and imprisoned tens of thousands of them during the war. Thus, Miranda's feelings of guilt, previously an unspecific anxiety about a new power to judge men, and Adam's sacrificial dream involving his own death, both put briefly aside during her illness and before he gets sick, come back in nightmare fashion by the end of the story. Things turn out even worse than what he portrayed as inevitable: rather than managing to save him from a battlefield death that was in reality by no means certain, she has played a role in hastening his demise; he dies all right, but, because he dies in an army "camp hospital" (206) stateside, his sacrifice does not receive the honor or recognition he was anticipating or conjuring up.

Porter reportedly felt the same anxiety and guilt over a recruit she met during the war. She came down with influenza in 1918, and a soldier in a local training camp, Alexander, who shared Adam's last name, took care of her while she was sick.[15] Porter at one point communicated that she felt responsible for Alexander's death, as he was—like Adam, a "monster" of fitness who "never had a pain in his life" (156)—according to her, a large, healthy, outdoorsy kind of man, who except for her might not otherwise have come into contact with the disease.[16]

The closeness and nature of Porter's relationship with Alexander Barclay is impossible to know, partly because Porter gave different accounts of it over time, but her biographer Joan Givner thinks Porter invented most of it. In particular, Givner doubts that they were in a chaste love relationship as Porter fairly consistently claimed: "Porter was not a shy young girl [like Miranda] but a twenty-eight-year-old divorcee for whom unconsummated love affairs were unlikely."[17]

Whatever Porter's relationship was with the actual "army lieutenant," she idealized it and fantasized about it for her entire life. Thirty years after she wrote the short story, and fifty years after her own experience it was based on, Porter told the *Baltimore Sun* in an interview: "He died. And no one seems to think that was important, and it was one of the most important and terrible things that ever happened to me."[18]

CHAPTER SIX

"A Miracle So Wide"

Ellen La Motte, Willa Cather, and the War's Opportunity

ANYONE WHO IS FAMILIAR WITH Willa Cather's most famous novel, *My Antonia* (1918), will find her World War I novel *One of Ours* (1922) surprising, if not shocking. These two books are so different that one may even wonder if they were written by the same person. In *My Antonia*, a largely realistic novel, the most impressive major characters—Antonia, Lena, and Tiny—are women; they are physically strong as well as sensual, and two of them become successful entrepreneurs and do not marry. The main male character is passive and marries a rich woman who can advance his career with a corporation—namely a railroad—that is supposedly modernizing the world for the betterment of people but actually wiping out the rural West. And though that character, Jim Burden, is also the narrator, one feels that Cather chose a man to narrate partly as a tactic to legitimate the gender reversals of the book and an alternative perception of women that might at the time have been dismissed as female fantasy.

In contrast, *One of Ours* is almost absurdly romantic and traditional. The hero, Claude Wheeler, is a sensitive and chivalrous soldier who dies a glorious battlefield death in a war that is totally valorized and associated with generosity. His wife, Enid, is depicted as cold, prudish, and obsessive. She, too, is independent, but her independence is portrayed as part of her coldness and remoteness. Her one passion, the cause of Prohibition, to which she almost entirely devotes herself and for which she neglects her personal connections, including her marriage, seems extreme and compulsive. It issues out of her "dislike . . . [for] ardour of any kind."[1] Her father's liberal-minded disapproval of her sister Carrie's missionary work in China seems also to apply to her temperance lecturing, especially as she decides to join her sister in the Far East when Carrie becomes ill (rather than help her father to convince her to come home). The father tells Claude, "I don't believe in one people trying to force their ways or their religion on another" (98). In short, in this novel, the man is the idealized and idealistic character who sacrifices himself for a worthy cause while his wife and her sister are the ones devoted to reforming the world, supposedly for the better, but in reality out of "meanness" (205).

When *One of Ours* came out, it received mixed responses. The public loved it: the book was a bestseller, and Cather for the first time enjoyed financial success; it went on to win the Pulitzer Prize. At the same time, it was sharply criticized publicly and privately. Hemingway notoriously attacked it. He wrote, "Nobody had any damn business to write about [the war] . . . that didn't at least know about it from hearsay. Literature has too strong an effect on people's minds. Like this American Willa Cather, who wrote a book about war where all the last part of it was taken from the action of the 'Birth of a Nation' and ex-servicemen wrote to her from all over America to tell how much they liked it."[2]

Some reviewers were equally dismissive. Edmund Wilson thought it was a complete failure. Sidney Howard wrote in the *Bookman*, "She did not know the war for the big bow-wow stuff it is. She should stick to her farms." Heywood Broun of the *New York World* snarled: "The hero loses his life and finds his soul. We happen to believe that there is such a thing as setting too high a price upon souls and war is too high a price."[3] Perhaps the most stinging rebuke Cather received came, before the book was even completed, from her good friend Elsie Sergeant, who served as a war correspondent for the *New Republic* and was seriously injured by an unexploded shell while touring a battlefield.[4] Sergeant actually anticipated the response of some of these critical reviewers, according to one of Cather's biographers: "When Elsie Sergeant came home, hobbling on crutches, Willa besieged her to talk about the war. Elsie, however, did not entirely sympathize with Willa's curiosity. She could not escape the feeling that the war, which had injured her so cruelly, was only a story to Willa. It seemed to her that Willa showed a lack of sensitivity to the true cost of those four years."[5]

Was Cather simply pandering to the conventional sensibilities of a mainstream, patriotic audience in order to have a commercially successful novel? That turns out not to have been the case. In fact, Cather's emotional investment in the book was so intense, and her identification with the hero Claude was so profound, that she "allowed unfavorable reviews to upset" her to a greater extent than ever before.[6] So, one wonders, did something happen to Cather to change her dramatically during the few-year span between the writing of *My Antonia* and that of *One of Ours*? Or are the obvious and seemingly important differences between the novels somehow trumped by other, less blatant but more profound, values that they share?

Ellen La Motte's career during the Great War presents a puzzle. A highly trained and successful professional nurse with experience in hospital administration, she went over to France in 1914 looking to lend her expertise to helping the wounded. Her shockingly frank documentary, *The Backwash of War: The Human Wreckage of the Battlefield as Witnessed by an American Hospital Nurse* (1916), is as antiwar and as serious as any book of its time. Its frank depiction of the "human wreckage" of the conflict got it banned in England, France, and, when America entered the war, the United States.[7] Moreover, in the book she criticized dilettantes, male and female, who were participating in hospital work partly for an adventure, experience, or a good story, a criticism she leveled at the female director of her hospital, Mary Borden.[8]

La Motte left Borden's surgical field hospital in 1916, just after the book came out. Was she in part a thrill-seeker herself, simply ready for a new and different adventure? Upon leaving the hospital she did not seek another nursing post, but left the European war zone entirely, and immediately went off to China to investigate another international crisis, the opium trade. Gertrude Stein portrayed La Motte as a bit of an adventure- or story-seeker, and maybe even aware of it. Stein recounted how La Motte first worked at the American Ambulance, a hospital in Paris, but left there because—though "gun shy," as Gertrude Stein put it in *The Autobiography of Alice B. Toklas* (1933), with some ironic repetition and detail that seem to belittle or question La Motte's motives—she "wanted to nurse near the front"; "she did want to nurse near the front"; and she "did for a few months nurse at the front."[9] As Margaret Higgonet posits, in commenting about a journal article La Motte wrote about the Paris hospital, she "concedes her potential complicity, as a writer herself, with the story-seeking socialites." Higgonet writes that part of her problem with the American hospital in Paris was that it "was equipped with an ironically wasteful surplus that made her restless to move to a hospital closer to the battlefields."[10] The implication is that she wanted a more difficult, more adventuresome situation.

Stein seems to be making a similar point in writing that La Motte did nurse at the front "for a few months," exaggerating the brevity of her front-line service. Actually, La Motte served as a nurse at the front not for a few months but for more than a year, from the summer of 1915 to the fall of 1916.[11] Though it is possible that Stein simply got her facts wrong, it is unlikely, since she knew both La Motte and Mary Borden, who also appears in *The Autobiography of Alice B. Toklas*. Moreover, Stein had communication with La Motte after the war as well.

Stein makes other comments implying that La Motte's activities were trivial, perhaps even in bad taste, presenting her as just the sort of story-seeking dilettante she criticizes: "Ellen La Motte collected a set of souvenirs of the war for her cousin Dupont de Nemours. The stories of how she got them were diverting. Everybody brought you souvenirs in those days, steel arrows that pierced horses' heads, pieces of shell, ink-wells made out of pieces of shell, helmets, some one even offered us a piece of a Zeppelin or an aeroplane, I forget which, but we declined."[12] Significantly, Stein does not mention La Motte's hard-hitting and government-censored book. As Higgonet comments, "The sketches in *The Backwash of War* are not, in any case, diverting souvenirs. Unlike many wartime medical reminiscences that collect sentimentalized portraits of wounded soldiers, these pages were not token bits abstracted for propagandistic or nostalgic purposes."[13]

La Motte's criticism of adventure- or experience-seekers recurred in her writing. It came into the first journalistic piece she wrote about the war from Paris in 1915, "An American Nurse in Paris," in which she refers to "young society girls gathering experiences which will tell well in next year's ball-rooms" and those who are "animated . . . by nothing more lofty than a craving for new sensations."[14] The theme continues in *The Backwash of War*. One of its episodes, a story titled "A Surgical Triumph," concerns a Parisian hairdresser's horribly maimed son. La Motte comments that, as for the hair salon trade during the war, there were "a good many American heads to be washed, from time to time—rather foolhardy, adventurous heads, curious, sensation hunting heads, who had remained in Paris to see the war, or as much of it as they could, in order to enrich their own personal experience."[15] Her criticism of heiress Borden, founder and *directrice* of the hospital, is particularly pointed. In a story called "A Belgian Civilian," Borden summons and then lectures a Belgian mother with several children at home to care for and a business to help run that she ought to see and then stay the night in the hospital with her wounded and dying child. La Motte slyly observes, "The *Directrice* . . . seemed to feel that a mother's place was with her child, if that child was dying. The *Directrice* had three children of her own whom she had left in England over a year ago, when she came out to Flanders for the life and adventures of the front. But she would have returned to England immediately, without an instant's hesitation, had she received word that one of those children was dying" (24–25). She says plainly that Borden is after "adventures," a term elsewhere in the book associated with "sensation hunting" and foolhardiness.

Given La Motte's airing this theme of adventure seeking a few times, in no uncertain terms, then, if she was herself animated even in part by similar motives, her hypocrisy is fairly profound. Was La Motte a hypocrite? It is impossible to know what motivated La Motte at every moment, but that is not finally the issue here. The issue is really a matter of usefulness or purpose. The reason La Motte can accuse Borden of adventure seeking is that the latter's presence in the hospital she funds has no real purpose connected to medical care. Borden is not a trained nurse; the nursing skills she has learned are rudimentary.[16] What Borden contributes to the hospital, in terms of true usefulness, is her money; she need not be present to make that contribution. Borden's presence is, if anything, a potential distraction: it distracts at times from the real work of the clinic. In a story called "A Citation," La Motte describes a patient whose life is pointlessly prolonged and knows "that it would be better for him to die." She writes, "There was some sense in saving other people's lives, but there was no sense in saving his. But the surgeon, who was working for a reputation, worked hand in hand with the *Directrice* who wanted her hospital to make a reputation for saving the lives of the *grands blesses* [seriously wounded]."[17] Conversely, La Motte sees an indisputable medical purpose to her own presence at Borden's Hôpital Chirurgical Mobile No. 1 because she "was probably one of the most highly trained nurses of her generation."[18]

However, there are other actions of La Motte's to address. More specifically, what were La Motte's motives first for leaving the American Hospital (to go to Borden's surgical unit near the front) and later for abandoning the task of nursing in the middle of the war and heading instead off to the Far East? What of Stein's insinuations about her war-souvenir hunting? Was she adventure seeking in these instances, or did these moves and activities stem from other motives?

La Motte and Cather would have hated each other's books. La Motte would have seen *One of Ours* as dangerously romanticizing a horrific war. Meanwhile, *The Backwash of War* told a truth that spoiled Cather's idealism about the conflict. But I want to suggest that Cather was not pandering with her novel, and La Motte was not hypocritical. Both of these mature women (born in the same year, 1873) were true to what mattered to them most; moreover, their highest values coincided. In short, both were profoundly committed to meritocracy, so much so that it blinded them to other matters.

Whether Cather could credibly write about World War I combat is up for debate.[19] She underestimates or ignores wartime physical and mental suffering. Nevertheless, she was knowledgeable about the meritocratic opportunities for geographic and social mobility that World War I provided women and average non-black men—because this phenomenon, and its effect in particular on young American males, could be observed and learned about on the home front as well as the battlefront. And it was arguably the major factor in her enthusiasm for the war. In *One of Ours* she calls it a social "miracle" (140).

The model for Claude Wheeler, the protagonist of *One of Ours*, was Cather's cousin G. P. Cather, who died in the spring of 1918 leading his men into battle. Willa happened to be staying on G. P.'s father's farm when war broke out. She knew him rather well, had taken care of him sometimes when he was little (he was ten years younger than she) and "felt a kinship with him" because, as Cather biographer Phyllis C. Robinson indicates, he, too, felt the need for "escape" from the confining social and economic world of his early-twentieth-century hometown. But he could not embrace "her way of escape" through writing. "He couldn't escape the misery of himself except in action, yet it seemed that whatever he did turned ridiculous"—until he found his opportunity in the war.[20]

Cather's own meritocratic opportunity had come in the competitive field of journalism. She earned her big break in her career as a writer when her prodigious work for the *Nebraska State Journal* and another Lincoln paper—during her last two semesters at university, she had nearly one hundred pieces in the *Journal*—came to the attention of a publisher of a new woman's magazine, the *Home Monthly* in Pittsburgh. He hired her as editor, and she left her home state of Nebraska, never to live there again.[21]

Indeed, *One of Ours* is essentially a paean to the momentous opportunity for mobility and meritocratic status opened up by US entry into the war. World War I, for Cather's male characters, though obviously fatal for many, is nothing less than an escape from and cure for the "death in life!" that is existence "at home," working on the farm or in a factory. "What's left of men if you take all the fire out of them?" asks a pilot Claude meets. The answer is nothing but being "afraid of everything" (138). "You don't want to be back on the farm," a military doctor observes of Claude. And he is not alone; "most of [the recruits], like Claude Wheeler, felt a sense of relief at being rid of all they had ever been before and facing something absolutely new. Said [one soldier] . . . , 'Whoever likes it can run for a train every morning, and grind his days out in the Westinghouse works; but not for me anymore!' " (139). The war was "a miracle so wide in its amplitude that . . . the Wheelers and the roughnecks and the low-brows were caught up in it. Yes, it was the rough-necks' own miracle . . . ; it was their golden chance" (140).

Part of that chance is, for the first time, to "be somebody" (118). Like G. P. Cather, Claude is a misfit or a nobody before the war; he has never before been recognized as being particularly talented at anything, even in his own family. But the army clearly sees something in him and makes him a lieutenant. One evening away from the front in France, he listens to a fellow officer who has been trained on the violin, and he reflects about his own lack of training before the war came along: "If he had been taught to do anything at all, he would not be sitting here tonight a wooden thing amongst living people. He felt that a man might have been made of him, but nobody had taken the trouble to do it; tongue-tied, foot-tied, hand-tied" (187). Of course, Cather's point is that the army offered men like Claude a chance precisely because it *had* taken this trouble.

Cather recognizes what the war can mean for unprivileged men who have been grinding it out on the farm or in the factory, and her imagination of their point of view may well be made possible by her own second-class social status, as a woman, who could see what the war was likewise offering women. The same evening of Claude's reflection on his lack of training before the war, he hears about the opportunities that French women have gained because of it: they are working in hospitals and for the Red Cross; they are meeting and marrying exotic men from overseas; they are performing acts of heroism. For these women, to "have one's faculties, was to be in the war" (186)—because the war offered them an unprecedented chance to use their faculties. In another part of the book, we hear about a female *German* pilot shot down by an American aviator. The aviator respects her so much that he is willing to risk his life to take to the German side of the line a letter she "dictated . . . to her people" while dying (129). For Cather, social advancement for qualified women here trumps the war cause of defeating Germany.

It is the war's—or the US army's—extension of opportunity to the working class and to women that links *One of Ours* to *My Antonia*. In the earlier and more famous novel of the prairie, Cather valorizes the similar opportunity for advancement that the unsettled West provided to pioneers. In *My Antonia*, the main female characters are all immigrants whose families struggle financially when they are young and who, in their youth in America, work the land alongside their male relatives. Though female, they, too, are "low-brows" or even "rough-necks," seen as unfeminine or inappropriately masculine by many of the Anglo-Americans who live in the nearby town. But their rough, outdoor, pioneer upbringing makes them strong and self-confident and translates in adulthood into the ability to defy traditional American social expectations for women and to lead successful lives on their own terms. As if to drive the point home that the West at the end of the nineteenth century offered opportunities specifically to "low-brows" and "rough-necks," Antonia's father, who experienced a highbrow, cultured existence back in Europe simply cannot cope with the challenges and deprivations of prairie life and kills himself. It might even be argued that, for Cather, World War I provides the first widespread democratizing opportunity the nation has known since the closing of the frontier and essentially the elimination of pioneer life that *My Antonia* also anticipates, as the characters age and the railroad brings prosperity but also the hegemony of town life with its more confining social strictures. In that sense, *One of Ours* is perfectly consistent with *My Antonia*, as Cather chronicles the American history of social opportunity at different points in her lifetime.

La Motte belongs to one of the groups of women engaged "in the war" that Cather specifically cites (though La Motte was American and not French). More to the point, La Motte's decisions about where to serve during the war embrace, and in fact insist on, meritocratic organization. It is her commitment to meritocracy that ties her to Cather.

La Motte had no involvement with the unique American military mobilization, either on the home front or in Europe. All of the experiences that were the basis for *The Backwash of War* predated US involvement in the war, as did her writing and publishing it. After America entered the war, the government censored the book.[22] As La Motte put it in an introduction to a slightly expanded 1934 edition, her book was "suppressed in the summer of 1918," being "considered damaging to the morale. In the flood of war propaganda pouring over the country, these dozen short sketches were considered undesirable." La Motte asked her publishers why her sketches were censored. "They are true," she protested. "That is exactly the trouble," was the reply.[23] A reviewer of the 1934 edition agreed that her work had been censored because of its honesty: "It is easy to see why these stories by an American nurse were suppressed during the war. They describe far too truthfully for the interests of war propagandists the human wreckage that was carried off the battlefield into the squalor of a French field hospital."[24]

Despite La Motte's lack of any personal encounter with the American army's mobilization, her work is relevant to the US experience of war *and* meritocracy. It is relevant because La Motte, who had collegiate training as well as significant and even remarkable experience practicing nursing in the states—a field that had been professionalizing rapidly in the United States since the late nineteenth century[25]—wanted to put her professional expertise to use in the war effort and purposefully sought out a hospital whose personnel organization or management was based on meritocratic principles.

Her wartime trajectory is just the inverse of E. E. Cummings's, who, disgruntled with the American-army-inspired organization of his ambulance unit was relieved to find himself thrown into a traditional French prison system. La Motte began her wartime nursing at a hospital that was not organized on professional or meritocratic grounds and, dissatisfied with this lax arrangement, went looking for one that was.

In "An American Nurse in Paris," La Motte admits having trouble with the American Ambulance hospital for its wastefulness (as Higgonet asserts), as well as (as Stein implies) the fact that "the hardships of war are psychologically and practically as far removed from it as if they did not exist." But her critique only begins here, and the article comes to focus on the problem of the personnel "system," which not only comprehends that some volunteers are there merely "for new sensations" but also that "any man or woman who expresses a wish to care for the wounded is at once taken on in some capacity or other, regardless of the need for their services or their fitness or ability to perform the work." The result is that "[t]his system floods the institution with a mass of unskilled labor, some of which is useful, much superfluous, and some a positive menace to the patients themselves. For the auxiliaries are seldom long content with the humble tasks they are capable of performing, such as emptying vessels, cleaning dressing basins, dusting bedside tables, running errands, and the like. Most of them aspire to such work as doing surgical dressing. But since the technical work is beyond them, the result is an idle person with no occupation."[26]

La Motte's critique of the haphazard personnel system at the American Ambulance is absolutely in keeping with the thinking that led to a US Army organized at least in part on a meritocratic basis (see introduction). She cites specific examples of useless "auxiliaries": "One auxiliary settled her problem very satisfactorily. . . . She sat peacefully in the ward writing endless letters most of the day! When the doctor came to do dressings, however, she became alert . . . At the end of three weeks this little lady had acquired enough experience, plus pull, to be sent to the front. For the French standard of nursing is low." La Motte goes on to tell a story of a "rather beautiful young woman, blessed with all the attributes of charm and sunshine," who would have innocently and accidentally killed a "desperately injured man" had La Motte "not by chance appeared upon the scene." This woman, who "was in temporary charge of the ward," decided to move the wounded soldier so she could make his bed—though "his life depended upon his being kept absolutely motionless."[27]

La Motte next presents a conversation she has with the doctor in charge of the "English ambulance." He tells her that at the American hospital,

"Your nursing standards are very low. Your patients are not properly cared for." The American institution may have "ninety-five graduate nurses"—as La Motte, mock-innocently "protests" to the English doctor—but, as he explains, "their work is hindered at every step. Your whole nursing standard is dragged down to the level of the inefficient, who are given duties and responsibilities they are totally unfitted for. . . . No war hospital can be run on a basis of efficiency or economy if a large or any portion of the nursing care is entrusted to incapable hands."[28]

La Motte ends the article by recounting a somewhat comic run-in she has with a wealthy male orderly who simply refuses to help with tasks he finds unpleasant. La Motte asks for his help "irrigating" the wound of an injured soldier. "'I'd do anything I could for the dear fellow,' he began, 'but I really can't do that, it's too disagreeable.' 'But the man's an ill man,' I exclaimed, 'and it takes two people to do this dressing—I certainly shouldn't ask you if I could manage it alone.' 'It's very disagreeable,' he returned. 'I really must refuse.' Later on, when the dressing was safely over, he returned to the ward, and going up to the patient in question, presented him with a photograph of a beautiful old Norman chateau, remarking, '*This* is where your orderly lives!'"[29] It is probably no accident that La Motte ends her critique on this absurd exchange with a volunteer who is not only rich but male. As critic Hazel Hutchison writes about La Motte's stint at the American Hospital, "Its patrician atmosphere offended both her nonconforming views about the position and potential of women in society, after her long years of medical training and experience."[30]

It is hard to see La Motte as seeking adventure in China. After leaving the European war zone, she spent the next two years "writing and campaigning against the exploitation of colonised people, and most particularly the opium trade"—a campaign she carried on for a decade, mostly after returning to Europe.[31] According to various sources, she was tireless in this pursuit. "The cause became all consuming for La Motte during the 1920s. She was always [as she herself put it] 'in a great rush—opium all the time.'"[32] Her work earned her significant awards from both the Chinese Nationalist Government and the Japanese Red Cross.[33] It also provides another link between her values and Cather's. Both were critical of Westerners who "under the banner of civilization and Christianity, were taking advantage of the natives and victimizing them," as Keiko Sugiyama wrote of La Motte.[34] The words echo those of Claude's father-in-law in *One of Ours* criticizing his daughter's missionary work in China.

And what of La Motte's decision to leave the war zone and nursing the wounded, in the midst of the war? Perhaps after her book came out, revealing her criticisms of Borden, she was no longer welcome at the rich American's surgical unit, but why did she not seek out another frontline hospital? Given that *The Backwash of War* was also unmistakably critical of French military ideology and that the French government had banned it, she might have had trouble finding a position at any hospital in France. In a story called "Pour la Patrie" (For the Country), La Motte ironically mocks the "exchange" in which a dying man's life is paid for by a medal and a pension, delivered by a general who "might have put a little more feeling into" the "brief little" decoration "ceremony . . . not made it quite so perfunctory. Yet he's done this so many, many times before. It's all right, he does it differently when there are people about, but this time there was no one present—just the doctor, the dying man, and me" (51).

A sketch added at the end of the book for the 1934 edition is revealing here. The story "Esmerelda," as Higgonet describes it, "depicts a little goat who knocks down a French general inspecting the hospital with the *Directrice*, and who must therefore be disposed of."[35] The female goat, whose name like La Motte's begins with an *E*, is simply trying to get past the two of them—"the Directrice, in her immaculate starched skirts, and . . . the General commanding all that region"—blocking its usual "passage, her joyous, springing passage along the *trottoir* [pavement]." The goat is the narrator's "beloved . . . little pet," and it is the narrator, "acting upon orders," who must get rid of the animal.[36] (The narrator gives the goat to the Belgian women working in the laundry, who, much to her dismay, end up making a meal of Esmerelda.) Higgonet concludes: "This scapegoat may symbolize La Motte's own departure from the hospital following her portrayal of Borden and her attack upon militarized ideology in *The Backwash of War*."[37] It might also have symbolized La Motte's persona-non-grata status with the French military authority generally. In any case, there was a personal factor in La Motte's departure as well. Emily Chadbourne, La Motte's partner—with whom she would spend the rest of her life—wanted to get out of the war zone and head to the Far East. "For nearly a year, this had been Emily's plan to escape war," art historian Robert S. Nelson writes.[38]

And what about Stein's observation that La Motte hunted up souvenirs of war for her cousin Du Pont de Nemours—implying that her relationship to the war was partly touristic or sensational? Here, too, it helps to know the context. Alfred I. Du Pont de Nemours was the person who made it possible for La Motte to offer her nursing expertise to the war effort, and thanks to him, as Nelson writes, "she was able to give up her nursing job [in Baltimore] and transform herself into a writer."[39] Whether Du Pont asked La Motte for souvenirs or La Motte simply collected some knowing he would be pleased, she obviously did so for him, not herself, presumably out of gratitude.[40]

Given that the evidence about La Motte suggests an uncompromisingly serious writer, a highly qualified health practitioner, and a person profoundly dedicated to the causes she undertook and wrote about, one wonders what motivated Stein to portray her as she did. Did La Motte for some reason get under Stein's skin? Stein's investment in La Motte was fairly significant, as the *Autobiography* indicates: "Ellen La Motte turned up, she was very heroic but gun shy." (This epithet—"very heroic but gun shy"—seems another snipe at her.) "She wanted to go to Servia and Emily Chadbourne wanted to go with her but they did not go. Gertrude Stein wrote a little novelette about this event."[41] That Stein should have devoted a novelette to this event, or, more properly, "non-event," with La Motte as "the undecided protagonist,"[42] indicates quite an interest in La Motte. Most critics take it for granted that, if the La Motte–Stein connection is meaningful, it is because Stein's writing might have had a stylistic influence on La Motte's, which arguably has certain modernist qualities. But perhaps their crossing paths made more of an impact on Stein than on La Motte.

It is not hard to imagine that La Motte made Stein feel uncomfortable once one learns that La Motte knew Stein from her Johns Hopkins days—when Stein flunked out of medical school and La Motte was about to graduate from the Johns Hopkins Training School and "was a nurse of growing distinction in Baltimore."[43] In the *Autobiography*, Stein makes it clear that she became "bored" with her own medical studies toward the end of them; however, rather than withdraw or quit, she takes her exams and fails to pass. "You have no idea how grateful I am to you," she says in the book to the professor who fails her, after which she confesses her disinterest to him—"you don't know how little I like pathological psychology, and how all medicine bores me." She drops her plans for a medical career and moves to Paris to become a writer.[44]

Stein wants to present the incident as a fortunate failure, but other details in the *Autobiography* indicate that the episode was not so cut and dried, that Stein's pride was wounded. For example, she insists that "all the big men [at the medical school] were ready to pass her," and only this one evidently unimportant professor stood in her way.

> The big men like Halstead, Osler etcetera knowing her reputation for original scientific work made the medical examinations merely a matter of form and passed her. But there were others who were not so amiable. Gertrude Stein always laughed, and this was difficult. . . . However they did

> question her from time to time and . . . what could she do, she did not know the answers and they did not believe that she did not know them, they thought that she did not answer because she did not consider the professors worth answering. It was a difficult situation, as she said, it was impossible to apologise and explain to them that she was so bored she could not remember the things that of course the dullest medical student could not forget.

What emerges is a somewhat agonized self-portrait of a mature woman who wants the story to attest to her youthful brilliance even though she failed and of a young woman who wanted to get the degree despite the fact that she had stopped working for it. Moreover, there is some guilt attached to Stein's failure, as Stein is poised to become one of the few women doctors at the time: "Her very close friend Marion Walker pleaded with her, she said, but Gertrude Gertrude remember the cause of women." It is only years later, according to her book, that Stein tells this friend, "Not . . . that she at all minds the cause of women or any other cause but it does not happen to be her business."[45]

Enter Ellen La Motte: she not only knew Stein back then, at that inevitably uncomfortable, transitional moment when her first career plans had derailed and before she had succeeded as a writer, but, in addition to La Motte's being a highly successful medical practitioner, she is devoted to causes, including the advancement of women in the medical field.[46] And now wants to be a writer as well. Moreover, she too is homosexual and also has what will turn out to be a successful, long-term lesbian relationship. It is not hard to imagine that Stein, despite her huge success as a writer, felt competitive with La Motte—who is just about Stein's age (a year older)—and even a bit intimidated by her.

La Motte may have been, by her own admission, "gun shy." An article she wrote for the *Atlantic Monthly* mentions her decision not to accompany a fellow nurse who is looking for a relative "all the way to the entrenchments" in the "forbidden zone"—ironically, she finds herself "nonetheless exposed to more German shelling than her friend."[47] But La Motte was hardly blood shy, gore shy, mutilation shy, or death shy: she stoically confronts and treats "the backwash of war." Her title is, fittingly, a hard-hitting and grotesque metaphor rather than a euphemistic or romantic one. (Compare the title of Mary Borden's own book, published in 1929, *The Forbidden Zone*.) La Motte writes in the introduction to the 1916 edition, "It is very ugly. There are many little lives foaming up in the backwash. They are loosened by the sweeping current, and float to the surface, detached from their environment, and one glimpses them, weak, hideous, repellent" (3).

This passage is abstract and tame by comparison with what comes later in the book. The story "Alone" begins: "Rochard died to-day. He had gas gangrene. His thigh, from knee to buttock, was torn out by a piece of German shell." From there, the descriptions of his injuries become even more horrifying—sickening to read about let alone see, smell, and treat. The flesh was

> torn away . . . down to the bone, and the stench was awful. The various students came forward and timidly pressed the upper part of the thigh, the remaining part, all that remained of it, with their fingers, and little crackling noises came forth, like bubbles. Gas gangrene. Very easy to diagnose. . . .
>
> The *Medecin Chef* [Chief Doctor] took a curette, a little scoop, and scooped away the dead flesh, the dead muscles, the dead nerves, the dead blood-vessels. . . .
>
> So all night Rochard screamed in agony, and turned and twisted, first on the hip that was there, and then on the hip that was gone, and on neither side, even with many ampoules of morphia, could he find relief.

That was only one of his wounds; a second serious injury "would have been fatal" had not this first one killed him. "Rochard had a fractured skull as well. Another piece of the shell had pierced his ear, and broken into his brain and lodged there. . . . [It] had made one eye blind. There had been a haemorrhage into the eyeball which was all red and sunken, and the eyelid would not close over it, so the red eye stared into space. And the other eye drooped and drooped, and the white showed, and the eyelid drooped till nothing but the white showed, and that showed he was dying" (13–17).

Stein must have known about La Motte's unflinching toughness, but she instead chose to cite La Motte's fear of being shelled. If La Motte's nursing story has everything to do with meritocracy—and her insistence on the meritocratic system in institutions engaged in serious work—then it is altogether fitting that Gertrude Stein, who suffered a meritocratic rejection in the medical field, should play the role here of a slightly bitter commentator. It may be hard to believe that the famous writer Stein was still suffering from a "meritocracy wound" some fifteen years after leaving medical school, especially as her failure was in an area she abandoned. But consider that Hemingway was evidently still suffering ten years after the war, and a few years after his writing career had taken off, from his own "mobilization wound" (his failure in the war to have been nothing more than "a very sort of minor camp follower" as he put it later in life).[48] Meritocratic rejections or wounds are hard to shake off. They seem to be judgments on one's fitness, intelligence, or ability. Jack Kerouac, though one of the most famous writers in the world in the years before he died, was still intensely suffering from his failures decades before to make the grade in college football and to qualify as a navy pilot during World War II—he flunked a mathematics aptitude test.[49]

La Motte and Cather were both so dedicated to meritocratic opportunity that it desensitized them to other issues. La Motte could have told Cather in no uncertain terms how disturbingly and irresponsibly wishful her sentimentalization of the war was. She probably would have agreed with Hemingway that Cather, who had not seen bodies on or fresh from the battlefield, had no business writing about combat.

La Motte, meanwhile, was so dedicated to usefulness and efficiency that she was at times incapable of politic compromise and or even perhaps humaneness. Mary Borden, in a story from *The Forbidden Zone* called "Moonlight," depicts a night nurse who is presumably La Motte.[50] Under the pressure of working at the front, the nurse has allowed herself to become "a machine," a fate Borden dreads for herself and attempts to resist:

> She is no longer a woman. She is dead already, just as I am. . . . Her heart is dead. She killed it. She couldn't bear to feel it jumping in her side when Life, the sick animal, choked and rattled in her arms. Her ears are deaf; she deafened them. She could not bear to hear Life crying and mewing. She is blind so that she cannot see the torn parts of men she must handle. Blind, deaf, dead—she is strong, efficient, fit to consort with gods and demons—a machine inhabited by the ghost of a woman—soulless, past redeeming, just as I am—just as I will be.[51]

There is plenty of evidence for La Motte's inability to compromise, in addition to her treatment in print of Borden and the fundamentally professional hospital she directed. (Borden, for good reason, was awarded British medals and the Croix de Guerre; she was also "named a member of the French Legion of Honor.")[52] Before coming to France to serve as a frontline nurse, La Motte had been superintendent of the Baltimore Health Department, but, as Christine Hallett has written, her success in her field "masked a controversial" set of stances that she took and that upset her colleagues. Her departure from the United States for the war may have been partly motivated by her having alienated some of "her physician colleagues by virtually accusing them of exploiting their patients by withholding information"—and also some of her nursing colleagues by taking a hardline stance on quarantining tuberculosis patients who did not comply with preventive measures.[53] La Motte dedicated her book to "MARY BORDEN-TURNER, 'The Little Boss' TO WHOM I OWE MY EXPERIENCE IN THE ZONE OF THE ARMIES,"[54] and even in this ostensible term of endearment, "The Little Boss," one can sense La Motte's condescension to a younger woman (about fifteen years her junior) she no doubt felt lacked the credentials to be her superior in a medical institution.

But La Motte's devotion to efficiency neglected other emotional realities that fuel people's altruism and dedication. Borden would probably never have funded a hospital if she had not been able to reside there and participate in the care of patients—and in that case would never have been able to provide La Motte with the opportunity to practice her nursing skills in a well-equipped and highly functional surgical unit "in the zone of the armies." And La Motte's tunnel vision maybe did not allow her to imagine that Borden's principal personal reason for nursing in France was probably not, after all, a search for adventure. Borden sought a way out of a difficult situation of her own. In 1914, she needed to find an immediate, and socially acceptable, escape from a failing marriage to George Douglas Turner, a Scottish missionary whom she had met on a tour of the Far East. After going to France, she would never really return to that marriage or her three daughters, the oldest around five, the youngest not even a year old when she left. While at the front, she became involved with Brig. Gen. Edward Louis Spears, whom she married in 1918, after Turner, who discovered their affair, separated from her and took custody of the children. La Motte, given her own later travel, research, and campaign related to the opium trade, might have come to have sympathy with Borden's difficulty in getting along with a partner who was a Western missionary. No doubt Cather would have understood Borden's situation as well. As with her character Claude in *One of Ours*, the war served Borden as a sort of deus ex machina, providing an acceptable, even admirable, way out of a bad marriage.

Cather's lack of sensitivity to the death and destruction of combat reaches a truly arresting level by the end of *One of Ours*, which closes on a ludicrous apotheosis of the war. The novel goes so far as to affirm Claude's death in battle not as a necessary sacrifice to the cause but as a way for him to be spared the "desolating disappointment" that he would experience with a postwar return to normalcy and an inevitable loss of his "beautiful beliefs" in his own country and in France. Claude's mother "feels as if God had saved him from some horrible suffering, some horrible end" because the termination of the war lets loose a "flood of meanness and greed [that] had been held back just long enough for the boys to go over." The novel ends with a disturbing fantasy of a wave of veteran suicides motivated by feelings they share with Claude or his mother: "one by one the heroes of that war" cannot "bear" the fallen "world they have come back to . . . [and]

quietly die by their own hand" (205). Troubling here is Cather's obliviousness or indifference to actual reasons for World War I suicides, which occurred during the war and after—namely fear, physical damage, and psychological trauma.[55]

La Motte's book begins with one such attempted suicide; the first lines of the initial story, "Heroes," are: "When he could stand it no longer, he fired a revolver up through the roof of his mouth, but he made a mess of it. The ball tore out his left eye, and then lodged somewhere under his skull" (5). The story presents some horrifying and "disgusting" details about this uncooperative patient who perhaps still wants to finish himself off: "from his bleeding mouth he shot great clots of stagnant blood, caring not where they fell. One fell upon the immaculate white uniform of the *Directrice*, and stained her, from breast to shoes. . . . They told him it was *La Directrice*, and that he must be careful." But he "took aim afresh, and again covered her with his coward blood. Truly it was disgusting" (6).

La Motte's story eventually becomes an intense meditation on the insanity of war, as "the night nurse [she herself] was given to reflection" (8). The man is to be nursed back to health so he can be "court-martialed and shot" for attempting suicide. Nursing in this case "truly . . . seemed a dead-end occupation" (7). Also, La Motte realizes that while there is ostensibly a difference between the man wounded by attempted suicide and the other patients wounded by German artillery, the distinction is artificial because the others' supposed "ideals," which make them willing to serve, are "imposed" on them, by "a handful of men," "higher up." In reality, "they were all harnessed to a great car, a Juggernaut, ponderous and crushing, upon which was enthroned Mammon, or the Goddess of Liberty, or Reason, as you like" (9–10).

The story ends with a piece of information that literalizes La Motte's metaphor: she overhears one patient saying to another, "Dost thou know, *mon ami*, that when we captured that German battery a few days ago, we found the gunners chained to their guns?" (11). La Motte has forcefully proved her point, but the attempted suicide has dropped out of the story by the end. Focused on pressing the point of her "reflection," La Motte has used this man's story for her own purposes, and the reader never learns what happens to him. Does he die in the hospital? Is he nursed back to health and then executed? Is he somehow spared?

We know the answer to this question from the *directrice* herself. "Rosa," a chapter in Borden's *The Forbidden Zone*, picks up the story of the failed suicide. In it, Borden "plead[s] for the man's life" with a "General" who explains why he must be executed, "But, Madame, we have epidemics in the trenches. Panic seizes the men. They blow their brains out in a panic. Unless the penalty is what it is . . . the thing would spread. The same penalty applies to men who wound themselves. That's the favorite device of a coward. He puts the muzzle of his rifle on his foot and fires." But Borden argues with the General because she knows that the man in question "was not afraid of being killed, but of not being killed." She has heard him repeating the name "Rosa" in a "broken-hearted, high and hollow . . . child's voice." He "shot himself in despair because the Germans" had for too long failed to "shoot him; and a woman called Rosa let him down, or perhaps she died. Perhaps he simply wanted to go to her." The general brushes her off, but Borden takes what action she can to help this man who keeps ripping off his bandages and is clearly determined to end his own life. She tells a night nurse, "When Rosa [as she begins to call him, since he won't say his name] pulls off his bandage tonight, leave it off." Again this "night nurse" may well be La Motte, especially as Borden describes her as for "a minute hesitating," in response, for professional reasons: "She was highly trained. Her traditions, her professional conscience, the honour of her calling loomed for a moment before her, then her eyes lighted. 'All right,' she said."[56]

If the night nurse depicted in "Rosa" is indeed La Motte, then we have again their points of view on each other: La Motte's subtle but consistent derision of Borden and Borden's apprehension of La Motte as somewhat dehumanized by her professionalism. La Motte seems to be typically ironic regarding Borden here, and again about her awkward and unprofessional presence in the hospital. She notes Borden's "immaculate white uniform" and the hospital directive not to spit up blood on "*La Directrice*," contrasting the uniforms of real nurses, which, as opposed to those of playacting ones, do not remain immaculate. She calls the man's blood "coward blood" and implies it is the nature of his blood drenching Borden's uniform that makes it "truly disgusting"—but the reader understands that this is not La Motte's own perception of the man; rather, it belongs to the male "Medecin Major" or chief doctor, who finds the man's attempted suicide "incomprehensible," given how, "in these days, it was so easy to die with honour upon the battlefield" (6).

Meanwhile, Borden, in stark contrast to her description of the night nurse in "Moonlight," seems here to grant La Motte more humanity and compassion. We learn in Borden's story that, perhaps due in part to her own intervention, and the professional nurse's compliance—and the man later gives "a look of recognition . . . , perhaps even a faint look of gratitude"—the patient does manage to die in the hospital a few days later and does not have to get nursed back to health only to face a firing squad.[57]

It is clear that Borden does the man "justice," both in her actions and in her telling of his story, while La Motte's version of the man's tale seems more like fodder for the expert nurse's reflections on unprofessionalism and war propaganda.

La Motte and Cather not only shared a belief in egalitarian meritocracy. Their investment in their beliefs was so strong as to seem fanatical. Thus, at times and certainly when it came to the issue of meritocracy in particular, they also shared a tunnel vision that made them not only insensitive to others' concerns but seemingly out of touch with other basic human realities. Yet given the prewar exclusion of women from many jobs considered impossible or inappropriate for them—which the wartime emergency essentially disproved when they filled in for men called to military service—and given also the general, discriminatory, and unmerited dominance of men in the occupational fields they themselves belonged to and struggled to compete in, perhaps Cather's enthusiasm for wartime opportunities and La Motte's fixation on professionalism were not fanatical at all.

PART THREE

Combatant War Literature

My father . . . went into battle in August (Marbach sector) and saw the whole bloody show, including Meuse-Argonne and occupation of the Rhine. Marksman, three Bronze Stars . . . From a southern Mississippi hardscrabble farm. Amazing how that war transformed horizons.

—WILLIAM BRUMFIELD, *on Lewis Floyd Brumfield, who after the war earned a master's degree at the University of North Carolina and obtained a government job advising farmers*

CHAPTER SEVEN

A War Hero in an Antiwar Tale?

Thomas Boyd's *Through the Wheat*

Through the Wheat (1923) no longer gets its due. Most today see it as a simple and straightforward antiwar novel. Critics tend to ignore or underplay significant aspects of its content and radically reduce its complexity. In Steven Trout's excellent *On the Battlefield of Memory* (2010), he concludes that the novel is "among the bleakest of all American First World War narratives. . . . Boyd's novel tells a brutally simple and, one would think, relatively ambiguous story. . . . The only plot, per se, resides in [the protagonist] Hicks's harrowing descent, after one firefight too many, from gung-ho warrior to battle-fatigued zombie."[1] But Boyd's publisher, Charles Scribner's Sons, did not see the book that way, and neither did a host of reviewers. There was striking disagreement in the assessment of the book when it came out. Scribner's did not advertise Boyd's book as an antiwar novel. The jacket blurb, presumably written by editor Max Perkins, promised, "The author has not been content with the surface indications of war; he has plunged through the nightmare of fear, horror, and privation to bring up into the light the beaten gold of the spirit which has passed through the test by fire."[2] While one reviewer did describe Hicks's trajectory as "spiritual disintegration" and the *New York Times* review basically concurred, F. Scott Fitzgerald, who helped convince Scribner's to take on the book, wrote a review in which he claimed that the book "strikes one clear and unmistakable note of heroism, of tenuous and tough-minded exaltation, and with this note vibrating sharply in the reader's consciousness the book ends."[3] Edmund Wilson evidently perceived a double-sidedness to Boyd's novel. In one review, he remarked that the book's "tone," "if persisted in, should ultimately discourage humanity with war altogether."[4] In another, he wrote,

"This is probably the only account on record of what it meant to be a hero in the Marines."[5]

One reason the book's complexity has been reduced is that some contemporary reviews of the book are based on, and the ultimate verdict on the novel today is derived, to a significant degree, from its last sentence: "The soul of Hicks was numb" (266). As the 1923 *New York Times* review noted: "The effect of attack after attack, numberless tragedies day after day, unceasing danger, was to deaden [Hicks's] senses completely. His companions concluded, not without reason, that he was mad. He wandered about under fire with perfect composure—not because he was more brave than his fellows, but because he was psychologically dead."[6] In addition to Trout's characterization of Hicks having become a "battle-fatigued zombie," another present-day critic, Mark Whalan, refers to Hicks's "psychological and emotional numbness."[7]

"The soul of Hicks was numb" was not Boyd's original choice for the last sentence, or even his second choice. The original sentence was not only very different but apparently it mystified editor Max Perkins so much that he pressed Boyd to change it to something simpler and clearer. Whether one knows that the line was changed or not, too much significance has been put on it in characterizing the novel as a whole, especially since there are other sentences near the close of the book that beg for a more complex comprehension of its ending.

Another reason Boyd's novel has been oversimplified is that it is assumed to fit the supposedly typical "disillusionment narrative" of a naïve, enthusiastic recruit convinced of the wartime propaganda who has his illusions shattered as he experiences a disappointing realization about the real nature of modern war and the army. As Mark Whalan puts it, "The best known American writing about WWI was written by a new generation of male participant-writers, and generally represents the War as being responsible for soldierly disillusion and psychological trauma." He acknowledges both "ambulance drivers" and "combat veterans" together fashioning "a powerful myth of the War, asserting that American soldiers had entered the War idealistically and were buoyed by the immense propaganda circulated by the Committee on Public Information. Yet combat was shockingly brutal and callous, army life was characterized by institutional injustice and ineptitude, and the ideals of democracy and freedom that justified American participation were reduced to little more than an ironic joke."[8]

This received wisdom, which has stood for decades now, is, as I discussed at length in part I, simply wrong about the noncombatant writers who make up the Lost Generation. But even when it comes to the best known combat-soldier writing, it is only roughly applicable. In most cases it is woefully inadequate. Critics have tended to exclude Hervey Allen's memoir as not conforming to this disillusion "genre," but they have included *Through the Wheat*, Laurence Stallings's *Plumes*, and Victor Daly's *Not Only War* even though they present real challenges to such a description. William March's *Company K* is the purest example of this "disillusionment narrative" or most faithfully traces this "arc of disillusionment" that shows soldiers coming to the harsh realization of the horrible realities of war that fly in the face of the propaganda about it.[9] (But, as we explore in chapter ten, *Company K* omits central aspects of March's own experience, and he chooses this "myth of the War" for unexpected reasons.) Restoring of the historical context concerning the new army, however, allows us to perceive significant threads in texts that have been all but "invisible" to previous critics.

In a typical encapsulation of Boyd's novel, Whalan writes:

> *Through the Wheat* is a powerful recreation of the fog of war. Its protagonist, Private William Hicks, is a fine soldier hollowed into a sense of psychological and emotional numbness by a series of harrowing battles where he sees most of his comrades die. There is little overall narrative, just a rhythm of fear, respite, alternately anxious and listless waiting, and the hallucinatory intensity of combat. Near the end, Hicks advances alone under enemy fire and inspires his comrades to press the assault. Yet this supposed act of heroism is actually a symptom of acute combat fatigue. The novel closes with Hicks so disoriented and traumatized that he is unable to distinguish the living from the dead, or differentiate a pastoral landscape from the bloody aftermath of battle.[10]

This account is more or less right about one major thread of the novel, but it mostly misses another. It underplays how Hicks develops into "a fine soldier" and what this means for him, in terms of his sense of self and his sense of his officers, as well as his sometimes uncanny behavior in combat—which gives the novel a good deal of the "little overall narrative" that it has.

When the book came out, a deputy general of the Kentucky American Legion attacked it in a letter: "Perhaps I am not qualified to criticize literary work of any kind but in my honest and humble opinion this book is absolutely rotten. In the first place, it very emphatically states from cover to cover that the leadership entrusted to the American Army officers was a farce and the system of the United States Army was a joke."[11] There is also no question that *Through the Wheat* is highly critical of the American army and its officers, but the writer's condemnation of the book is, like the critic's, too sweeping. Boyd's work is more complicated. Certain officers and certain aspects of "the system" of the US Army are deeply affirmed in the novel.

The *New York Post Evening Post Literary Review* called *Through the Wheat* "the best war book since 'The Red Badge of Courage.' "[12] The two novels tell a similar story of their protagonists' transformations into effective soldiers. In each of them, a serious mistake on the part of the main character that could end in disaster instead leads to a fortuitous turn of events that launches his development. In Boyd's book, that turn of events is a sage intervention by a thoughtful veteran officer.

Despite the deputy general's impression, crucial to Hicks's story is a high-ranking officer he respects. Major Adams makes a momentous and wise decision regarding Hicks, a decision that changes the entire course of his service—and leads to his being a "fine soldier" when he might otherwise have ended up in the brig for life or even executed.

Hicks's position at the start of *Through the Wheat* resembles that of Andrews in John Dos Passos's *Three Soldiers* or Anthony in Fitzgerald's *The Beautiful and the Damned*. Hicks is stuck doing months of manual labor, growing "disconsolate" about it and highly critical of the army. (Boyd himself had a similar wartime experience.)[13] But there are from the beginning crucial differences between Boyd's text and those of his Lost Generation counterparts. The differences can be found in Hicks's particular criticisms of officers and complaints about his being used for manual labor.

> For nine interminable months William Hicks had been in France . . . , acting out the odious office of the military police, working as a stevedore beside evil-odored blacks, helping to build cantonments and reservoirs for new soldiers ever arriving from the United States.
>
> And he was supposed to be a soldier. He had enlisted with at least the tacit understanding that he was some day to fight. At the recruiting office in Cincinnati the bespangled sergeant had told him, "Join the marines and see some real action."
>
> But was this action? Was this war? Was this for what William Hicks had come to France? Well, he told himself, it was not. Soldiering with a shovel. A hell of a way to treat a white man. There were plenty of people to dig holes in the ground, but not many of them could qualify as sharpshooters. And Hicks swelled his chest a trifle, noticing the glint of the metal marksmanship badge on his tunic. (1–2)

As long as he is doing nothing but labor, Hicks feels that "life was worth very little," and that "existence" is "unbearable" (1, 2).

Hicks's anger over his misuse is immediately directed at the officers running things. The deeper problem for Hicks and his fellow soldiers, as they wait to get into the action, is not the drudgery and boredom, but, as one of them puts it, having "God-damned mail-order shavetails [newly trained, untested officers] tellin' me what to do and what not to do. That's what I hate" (41). In the narrator's more sophisticated rendition, "The grinning weakness which men called authority had followed [Hicks] since the day of his enlistment." Hicks might have no problem with authority—and not see it as weakness—if the leaders were really there to "further the accomplishment of a common motive," but in fact "most of the men . . . had enlisted or had been made officers and gentlemen . . . for the purpose of aiding their personal ambitions" (4–5).

Hicks and his fellow marines' disdain for most officers does not stop once they get into combat. They see their superiors as incompetent at modern warfare. At one point Hicks or a buddy comments that their lieutenant belongs at headquarters "with the rest of the dummies" (90). At another, his captain is described as a romantic Texan who would like to disregard what he had "learned [of] modern warfare from the books supplied by the nearest officers' training camp" because he "sentimentalized the attack": "How much finer it is, [Captain Powers] thought, to attack as General Sam Houston attacked; to march steadfastly upon the enemy and make them surrender at the point of a sword or bowie-knife. The only rift came in his realization that he had no sword, not even a bowie-knife" (110–11). During one firefight, Hicks hears an officer yell, "'Close in there, Hicks,' . . . and Hicks asked whether the men were not being killed swiftly enough without grouping them together more closely" (190).

The charge against officers in *Through the Wheat* is more serious than in *Three Soldiers* and *The Beautiful and Damned* (which concern characters in the Services of Supply or not serving overseas). Their stupidity and self-promotion is not merely demeaning and potentially psychologically abusive. It leads to avoidable failures to achieve combat objectives and unnecessary casualties.

Moreover, in its depiction of the dynamic between officers and men, Boyd's novel breaks ranks with Fitzgerald and Dos Passos even before it takes the reader onto the battlefield. Hicks and most of his fellows avoid Andrews's problem of "order shock" (and that of other characters in *Three Soldiers*) by talking back to their officers whenever possible. When they can get away with it, either because they are in the dark or on the move in groups, the marines are strikingly insubordinate to their leaders, calling a sergeant a "dirty German spy" (9); telling a lieutenant to "shut up" and asking him, "Where do you think you are at, anyway?" (45); and saying to a sergeant, "who the hell gave you permission to give us permission to talk?" (56).

This insubordination, as well as the criticism of officers' ignorance of modern combat tactics, stems from a crucial difference between Hicks and the noncombatant protagonists of Dos Passos and Fitzgerald, a difference that also makes Hicks's response to mundane work distinct from that of his noncombatant counterparts. The marines' refusal to accept subordination, their serious criticism of superiors, and their dissatisfaction with manual labor all come out of pride in their status—their having qualified to be marines—and their know-how. Hicks does not like "the hopelessness of routine [or] the bullying of petty officers" (224), which sounds like a complaint Andrews might make. But, unlike Andrews, he does not let the mundane labor or the constantly being ordered around break him down or tamper with his sense of worth.

Hicks has enlisted and has been accepted to be a combat soldier, or, more properly, a combatant.[14] Therefore, he is confident that he does not belong unloading ships or building cantonments. In distinction to Andrews's personal sense that he is cut out for something better than manual labor, Hicks's is an estimation that comes *from* the US military. To put it another way, like Andrews, Hicks has been assessed and assigned by the US military—in addition, his marksmanship has been evaluated and affirmed. But that assessment and measurement, which according to Dos Passos gives Andrews his "real" identity, his "real self," has deemed Hicks worthy of combat. (A similar distinction existed between Boyd and Dos Passos. A marine had "to pass a number of examinations before being formally inducted," a feat Boyd successfully accomplished, while Dos Passos was determined not fit for combat on account of his vision.[15])

Hicks's private rant about his being misused is racially motivated—"a hell of a way to treat a white man," he thinks.[16] But a sense of racial superiority is not the only basis on which he reassures himself. He can, thanks to the validation of the military, tell himself, "There were plenty of people to dig holes in the ground, but not many of them could qualify as sharpshooters." Hicks uses the word "people" here and not "black people": his "plenty of people" comprehends not only the "blacks" he complains to himself about working beside but lots of whites as well. There is an obvious sense of pride and distinction in his statement, "But was this [manual labor] action? Was this war? Was this for what William Hicks had come to France? Well, he told himself, it was not." Most men in the American Expeditionary Forces had in fact come to France to do labor service and so could not say this to themselves. Hicks has been designated for combat, and as a sharpshooter. On top of that, to be a marine was exceptional. Marines made up a very select group, just 54,690 out of the 4,412,533 men in the US armed forces.[17] It is not accidental or incidental that Boyd's book includes the subtitle "A Novel of the World War I *Marines*" (emphasis added). If we, as twenty-first-century readers, do not tend to notice the assertions of prideful distinction in military status, it is because we are thoroughly used to a world of meritocratic evaluation, selection, and assignment (and also used to a Marine Corps whose contemporary slogan is "The Few, the Proud . . ."). But meritocratic selection was not familiar in 1917.

Hicks's induction into the Marine Corps is only the first step in the story of his development into a fine soldier. Central to this narrative trajectory is his positive encounter with a seasoned officer who must make a decision about Hicks when he makes a blunder—and thus a positive encounter with "the system of the United States Army." As in Stephen Crane's Civil War tale *The Red Badge of Courage* (1895), a shameful, and punishable, action on the part of the main character is the ironic trigger for his development. But with Boyd's book, one might say, the deus ex machina of a "Red Badge of Courage" is replaced with an official vote of confidence.

Crane's Henry Fleming runs from the line in panic in his first moments in combat, and, later, trying to accost and halt a fellow Union soldier when the whole unit is in frantic retreat, he gets bloodied as the man angrily hits him with his rifle. When Fleming returns to his unit, he lies to his comrades, telling them that he received his head wound in battle. It is on account of being perceived as a brave soldier that Fleming then becomes one. So a fortuitous blunder away from the lines makes possible his real courage.

In *Through the Wheat*, Hicks falls asleep on guard duty and could face a court martial. Instead, Major Adams, a highly decorated veteran officer, with experience dating back to the war "in the Philippines," decides to "let [the matter] drop," after explaining to Hicks that the reason is because "some day you might make a good soldier" (26, 27–28). Hicks from then on purposely tries and eventually manages to fulfill his "prediction" (31). Hicks's arc of transformation is thus similar to Fleming's, but with an important difference: the perception that he is a "good soldier" is not a mistake based on a lie but rather the experienced, and essentially correct, judgment of a career officer.

In other words, Hicks is not saved and transformed by a lucky accident; he is recognized by a superior to have what it takes. Two things are important here: Adams is an excellent officer and manager of men who makes a sound personnel decision, and Hicks is again individually affirmed, this time by a man whom he and "half the battalion" "adored and held in awe" (26). Crane observes that a man becomes what he is seen to be by his peers, but he does so with cynical irony. Boyd makes a similar observation but without the cynicism, and it is not peers who pass this judgment but an "impersonal" "authority" (26). Sheer dumb luck and a fabrication saves Fleming and gives him a new identity he then embraces; the meritocratic "system of the United States Army" reaffirms an "impersonal" assessment of Hicks (previously made at marine induction and at training camp), into which he can grow. To stamp someone with an identity based on an evaluation is a powerful procedure of meritocracy. The effect is to instill (or undermine) confidence. Another effect, in the case of selection and validation, perhaps especially when either a second chance is granted, or no other institution has before provided such a chance, is to create a desire to reward the faith that has been placed in one.

It could be argued that Hicks *is* lucky that he is not judged here by an insecure, neophyte officer who might pass him on to a court-martial made up of a "group of morons sitting in solemn judgment [who] might decide to give him" life imprisonment or perhaps even worse: Major Adams says the court-martial "judges would have hung you as an example" (27–28). And given how many officers in *Through the Wheat* seem to be motivated by "personal ambitions" (5) or are incompetent—one "company commander" fires on his own men, having "forgotten" that "the raiding party was still out" (37)—Hicks does seem fortunate to come before Major Adams, whose "authority was as impersonal as the fourth dimension" (26).[18] Adams himself acknowledges the potential incompetence of army officers. When Hicks tries to blame his falling asleep on cold water in the shell hole where he was posted, Adams replies, "And you didn't think to bail it out? I knew that officers were so damned dumb that they needed dog-robbers [batmen or aides], but I didn't know that enlisted men were" (27).

But something other than luck is at issue here. Hicks's being assigned to the senior, veteran officer for judgment is the way things are *supposed* to work. Meritocracy is not infallible, as the presence of so many dubious officers demonstrates. It is simply an attempt at a rational approach to the evaluation and assignment of men. In calling for the army's meritocratic experiments, Secretary of War Newton D. Baker had expressed the desire to obtain "something more scientific than the haphazard choice of men, something more systematic than [arbitrary] preference or first impression."[19]

While all of the insubordination of Hicks and his fellows indicates a pride in their military status as marines, some of it implies a growing experience and knowledge of combat that some officers, especially newer ones, are lacking. The insubordination in combat sometimes goes beyond words, as the marines regularly disobey orders they consider stupid and pointlessly dangerous. When Hicks gets an order from the Texan Captain Powers, "in a Shakespearian voice . . . to return to his squad and lead them in a charge of the machine-gun nest," he responds, "Aye, aye, sir." But he thinks to himself, "Like hell we'll advance. . . . The poor fool." And after he gets back to his squad he suggests another tack (97). Likewise, when an officer yells, "Close in there, Hicks," Hicks simply fails to comply with this particular command while continuing to obey the general order to advance (190). These examples of a strict failure of military discipline are also cases of an alternative, failsafe command system kicking in and functioning—preventing men from being unnecessarily wasted in operations or procedures that are doomed to failure or senselessly risky. The alternative system that gets activated in *Through the Wheat* is arguably a meritocratic one, for Hicks knows that he better understands the combat situation than his officers in these instances.

His willingness to disobey a ridiculous command (when he can get away with it) partly issues from an expanding confidence that was initially stoked by the military's various recognitions of him—as a marine, as a sharpshooter, and as a potential "good soldier." And there is no question that Hicks evolves into a good soldier. He readily volunteers for dangerous assignments, and he accomplishes some notable acts of bravery. In one sequence, on a perilous water run he and another man have volunteered for, shells start bursting nearby as the German artillery hones in on them. Hicks's companion says he wants to "throw [his canteen] away and run." But Hicks talks him into persisting: "Yes. . . . And we die of thirst. Come on, it's not far now." The next shell "violently throw[s]" them, but they get up and keep going (120). In another sequence, Hicks and a second soldier carry three wounded men to safety one after another—from the front line to a "first-aid station"—under heavy shelling as well as a gas attack. Not only does Hicks risk being hit in the continuous bombing, but he gives his own gas mask to one of the wounded soldiers. When his "litter bearer" partner is killed by a "shell casing" that also leaves his gas mask "in shreds," Hicks "took up his night's vigil beside the wounded man," his coat wrapped around his head (since he has no mask) as "the bombardment continued most of the night." In the morning, Hicks's legs are burning "with an awful pain" caused by the gas, and he is unable get up. When he and his unconscious charge are finally found by a patrol, he tries to speak but passes out (156–60). That afternoon, he wakes up "in an evacuation hospital" (169). Boyd performed a similar "act of bravery" which garnered him a citation and a medal: he and fourteen other marines "in spite of the terrific machine gun and artillery fire, . . . volunteered and rescued wounded in the open, carrying them to places of safety at the risk of their own lives."[20]

No mention is made of Hicks being likewise decorated.[21] But his effectiveness as a soldier is also registered—and recognized by his peers and officers—in his longevity and almost continuous readiness for service. His short stint in a hospital after the gas attack is the first time Hicks is wounded seriously enough to be sidelined. After his return, the reader learns he is in fact one of only a "handful of the original members of the platoon" (219). Boyd was also in a unit that suffered a high rate of casualties. Casualties numbered 450 at an encounter with Germans near the village of Bourshes, but Boyd "was among the few not seriously injured." At the Battle of Soissons, the unit lost "50 percent in the first half hour," but Boyd again "was one of the few in his unit to escape injury."[22]

The upshot of Hicks's exceptional endurance is that he comes to have a special status in the company. The commanding officers now cut him extraordinary slack. Off the front one morning, "when the whistle was blown for drill, Hicks was still drunk from . . . the night before. But being one of the handful of original members of the platoon, little by way of reprimand was said" (218–19). In another instance, Hicks is stopped by a green lieutenant ("who had received at least ninety days' training") for being "out of uniform." The lieutenant is aghast at Hicks's answers to his interrogation and says, "Private, consider yourself under arrest." Hicks replies, "Aye, aye, sir," and starts "to walk away," essentially ignoring the junior officer. The latter threatens him further "with a charge of disobedience," but Hicks responds in the same way, ignoring him (203–5). There is no follow-up to this "arrest" or the threat of a further charge. Apparently, nothing comes of them; presumably, a senior officer who knows Hicks and his record, perhaps Major Adams again, lets this matter drop as well. But what is clear from this encounter is that Hicks is unconcerned about breaking nonessential rules when outside of battle, and the top officers extend him exceptional privileges as an unofficial reward for his continuous and excellent combat performance.

Hicks is not "out of uniform" due to neglect; rather, his tampering with his uniform is an attempt to individualize himself in much the same way that wearing medals might. According to one critic, William March's *Company K* and Joseph Heller's World War II satire *Catch-22* can both be seen as "testaments to the utter insignificance of individuality in a world of modern, mass-produced war," men's "names and their experiences totally absorbed into the dismal roll-call of sacrifices to a whole vast, impassive, war-breeding system."[23] Dos Passos seems to assert something similar about the army's reduction of a man to a name and number, whether he is a casualty or not. But Boyd's novel suggests something very different. The army *uniform* is of course a powerful symbol of this denial of individuality. Recall how, in highly significant acts of separation from the mass and of assertion of individuality, Andrews in *Three Soldiers* and Ernest Hemingway's Henry in *A Farewell to Arms* both discard their uniforms.

Hicks does not toss away his uniform, nor does he attempt to leave the army; rather, he modifies his dress in an act that he himself does not quite understand. "Hicks, having thrown away most of his equipment, had annexed . . . parts of uniforms of all descriptions. On his head was a bright red kepi which formerly belonged to a French Colonial. A pair of soft leather boots that reached above the calves of his legs had been salvaged from some officer's bedding roll. His blouse had been discarded and his shirt was unbuttoned at the throat. Hanging in cowboy fashion, a forty-five calibre Colt flapped against his right hip. From his left side was a Luger pistol that he had taken from a dead German officer." Why Hicks has done this he "did not know. He only knew that . . . he was highly pleased with the equipment he had substituted for" his army issue (203–4). Perhaps his bizarre outfit is an intuitive act of self-expression or instinctive way of cataloguing his encounters with various comrades and foes. Many soldiers collected war souvenirs.[24] Wearing them on one's person was less common, however.

A link also exists between Hicks's wearing of the French colonial's red kepi and his shifting view on race. After his racist complaint early in the story about being made to work next to "blacks," he gains a respect for black soldiers after watching and "marvell[ing]" at the bravery and toughness of black "Foreign Legion" soldiers with their "red, brimless, stovepipe hats." Uniquely among the troops he has encountered, they do not even "cry" out when shot (196–97).[25]

The "cowboy" imitation is a matter distinct from souvenir collecting and seems to indicate that Hicks is mythologizing himself. Maybe Hicks, who has not been officially decorated for his actions in battle, is providing his own improvised decorations. Regardless, his dressing himself in this way furthers the process of his distinguishing himself in the military and the war. There is no mutinous intent; he continues to participate fully in the actions of his unit and to take the usual precautions for the safety of his comrades and officers—even if he is putting himself at greater risk of a sniper's bullet by sporting the brightly colored cap. When the new lieutenant is "horror-stricken" that Hicks has failed to salute him, Hicks informs him, "You don't salute officers at the front, sir" (204)—because that would put officers in greater danger of being singled out by the enemy.

Though petty officers and even some of Hicks's comrades begin to question his fitness or sanity, the officers in charge continue to have faith in him. After he is "arrested" for being out of uniform and after he shows up drunk to roll call, "the platoon commander" assigns Hicks alone the crucial task of finding the French army so the Americans can work with them in concert on an assault. This affirmation clearly makes Hicks proud and feeds his confidence: "Importantly he adjusted the strap of his helmet. . . . To his leg he buckled his holster. . . . He liked the feel of the pistol against his thigh. It made him feel equal to any danger. He was a Buffalo Bill, a Kit Carson, a D'Artagnan" (238). He feels so sure of himself and so proud that he abandons the trench he is walking in. "Progress" there "was too dreary for his mood. He climbed out and commenced to stride along the open field, his chest inflated, his chin high." His sense of importance takes on grand, even absurd, proportions: "He thought of the men lying along the trench, huddled together . . . , and he felt motherly toward them. He thought of the Allied armies waiting for the war to be over, so that they might return to their homes and families, and he felt protective toward them. He thought of President Woodrow Wilson, bearing the burden of the saving of civilization on his thin, scholarly shoulders, and he felt paternal toward him. Hicks it was who had been ordered to find the French army" (238–39).

Near the end of the book, when Hicks has apparently begun to have trouble distinguishing the living from the dead and seems to be taking ridiculous risks with his own safety, one of his assistants warns the captain, "Sir, you hadn't better send Hicks out on that outpost. . . . Because sir, he's crazy." But the captain needs a leader of a "squad" who is also "an automatic rifleman," so he unceremoniously dismisses the assistant's warning: "Be off with you" (264).

Though it is easy to miss, as Hicks's progressively abnormal psychological state is a more striking development at this point in the novel, what the reader is witnessing here as well, in Hicks being allowed violations of discipline while still being chosen for important missions, is another example of meritocracy in action. And these developments are related. Whalan is right that as "Hicks advances alone under enemy fire and inspires his comrades to press the assault, . . . this supposed act of heroism is actually a symptom of acute combat fatigue."[26] Yet Hicks's perception, while obviously distorted, and his resulting behavior, while clearly reckless, do not mark a complete break with the way he has previously thought and acted; rather, there is continuity, with an extreme intensification. Hicks's confidence in his abilities as a soldier has been growing all along—partly because he has come through numerous bloody battles mostly unharmed but also because he has been again and again validated by the superiors he respects. That confidence has now reached unrealistic proportions. He is merely irritated by enemy machine-gun fire but no longer afraid of it. When it comes to the experience of the military's meritocracy, Hicks is a sort of polar opposite of Andrews and Anthony Patch, relentlessly demeaned by their superiors. Hicks has had so much reinforcement from above that it has contributed to his losing perspective.

This loss of perspective does not end horribly for Hicks, as the reader might expect. His perception is altered. In one combat scene, he sees "an enormous olive . . . supported by legs" and later "a combination of olive and turtle" (260) before he recognizes what is actually before him is a German soldier. And his sense of fear is at points overwhelmed by petty irritation: "Bullets spattered furiously all around. Hicks minded them less than the perspiration which ran down his face in little, itching rivulets" (261). Moreover, he takes seemingly unnecessary chances. At one point, his fellows, taking cover, "looked at him agape as he strode toward the enemy's line," exposing himself to possible sniper fire, to retrieve a "discarded rifle" he left there the day before (264–65). Nevertheless, he is neither killed nor wounded by the book's end, which finishes with the aftermath of a battle. Luck certainly plays a role, but something more is at issue here.

Even during his "enormous olive" hallucination, he knows all along that it is an adversary and a danger. Once he spots the "olive" hiding "behind a bush," he immediately becomes alert and focused—and stops playing in his head the word game he has invented to keep his mind occupied while lying flat and still to avoid the "hail of bullets" that confronts the platoon. He does not expose himself here, with peril imminent, but rather "crawl[s]," "bellied to the ground." When "a shell hole yawned in front of him," he takes advantage of it: "Like an alligator slipping into the water, his body slid down to the bottom." He then expertly sets up his automatic rifle for long-range accuracy: "He stuck the tripod in the bank a foot from the top of the hole." He fires twice, and the German is dead.

Likewise, his lack of what would seem to be a healthy fear does not prevent him from reacting appropriately in the heat of battle. Though the next German he spots is presumably contributing to the bullets spattering "furiously all around," the man does not inspire fear in Hicks but rather irritation. His reaction is to observe, "Wasn't that another atrocious-looking helmet behind the bush to the left?" But he promptly dispatches this other German with a "volley of shots" (260–62).

Boyd's portrait is of an uncannily effective soldier; Hicks's effectiveness clearly stems from experience in combat but also from his extraordinary coolness under fire. He may seem dangerously fearless and thus reckless, but in the middle of a firefight, his lack of fear seems to allow him an exceptional clarity that makes him a more formidable killer without putting him at greater risk. Fear can be dangerous as well as helpful in battle; it can lead to panic or distraction and thus mistakes. But at this point Hicks is simply immune to such errors. Boyd's comparison of Hicks in the shell hole and an alligator in water implies that he has become like that notoriously successful reptile predator—his self-protective stealth has become so second-nature that it is comparable to instinct operating in the natural environment for which the animal is evolutionarily suited.

Through the Wheat does record the physical carnage and psychological trauma of modern combat. But reducing the book to an antiwar "disillusionment narrative" does not square with what Boyd produced. His novel does not simply portray "combat [as] shockingly brutal and callous," nor does it simply depict "army life [as] characterized by institutional injustice and ineptitude." Both combat and the military are, in Boyd's work, double-sided. Yes, Hicks must routinely endure "the bullying of petty officers" (224) and the often dangerously incompetent instructions and actions of newer army officers. But the major ultimately in charge of the unit is a wise, experienced leader, who motivates Hicks to become a fine soldier. Likewise, combat is horrifying and heartless: indeed, Hicks loses his best friend, Pugh, late in the novel, which contributes to his psychological dissociation. But combat is also an intensely challenging proving ground, where Hicks excels, and thus gains confidence as well as the recognition of his peers and commanders.

As mentioned above, the reputation of the novel stems in large part from its concluding sentences: "No longer did anything matter, neither the bayonets, the bullets, the barbed wire, the dead, nor the living. The soul of Hicks was numb" (266). But the sentences that precede these two suggest the other side of Hicks's combat experience. The other men had watched him "agape as he strode toward the enemy's line." After he bravely and perhaps recklessly retrieves his rifle, "He turned and walked toward his platoon. . . . He raised his chin a little. The action seemed to draw his feet from the earth" (266). Hicks has previously raised his chin after he was appointed to an important task, and here again the gesture no doubt indicates pride. But what does the next line mean? Could it be suggesting that Hicks, swelling with pride, feels like he is walking on air? That seems hardly possible given the final line of the novel—"The soul of Hicks was numb." Was the author alluding to another meaning, a contemporary idiom now lost to us?

But actually, if Hicks is walking on air here—if he is psychologically above the surface of the earth and the fray—then the next line makes a kind of sense that the *New York Times* review and subsequent commentators have missed. "No longer did anything matter, neither the bayonets, the bullets, the barbed wire, the dead, nor the living" not because his senses are deadened but because he has momentarily transcended this world. Such a reading would square the ending with the novel's final battle sequence, in which his senses were transformed and heightened, hardly muted. In this regard, the claim by the *Times* reviewer that he "wandered about under fire" is simply inaccurate, a case of overlaying a reading of the ending "onto" the previous battle scenes. In the midst of the final firefight, Hicks's movements are incredibly controlled and adept.

In *War and Society*, sociologist Miguel Centeno records that "soldiers report that the end of a battle"—which this is for Hicks—"was one of the happiest moments of their lives," in part because of the "retrospective relief of survival."[27] As Winston Churchill famously wrote in an 1898 publication, "Nothing in life is so exhilarating as to be shot at without result."[28] Siegfried Sassoon's British narrator-protagonist, after a raid in which there were "two killed and ten wounded," in *Memoirs of an Infantry Officer* (1930), about World War I, "felt a wild exultation. Behind me were the horror and the darkness. . . . It was splendid to be alive."[29] Centeno elaborates: "The very intensity of combat, requiring extreme concentration and cooperation with a close group, also provides a rare form of joy. . . . The concept of happiness or contentment being found 'in the present' may find one its most extreme versions in battle, when warriors have no choice but to focus on the 'here and now' if they are to survive; what Robert Graves [author of the World War I memoir *Good-bye to All of That* (1929)] called 'life's discovered transitoriness.'"[30] However, the contradictory movement of Boyd's final sentence remains. The last line pops up like a roadblock, indicating either a dead end to this line of reasoning or a U-turn in the text.

Perhaps Boyd decided, when all was said and done, on another sharp turn here; the last paragraph is full of such zigzags. But as noted above, "The soul of Hicks was numb" was not in the original manuscript submitted for publication. It was added after editor Max Perkins, as Boyd's biographer, Brian Bruce, put it, pushed for a "more definitive" conclusion to a book whose last scene, he thought, "left the reader confused about the main character's . . . mental state."[31] The last scene, whether it ends with the original last line or the published one, is quite complex and difficult, and Perkins evidently wanted something simpler and easier to make out. He asked Boyd if he meant by the final paragraph that "Hicks had arrived as a soldier," but Boyd said that was not what he intended.[32] Nor was "The soul of Hicks was numb" even the second choice that Boyd came up with for the last line. The original last line was apparently, "Hicks was exalted: lost in the absolute." As a first alternative Boyd proposed, "Hicks was exalted: Gethsemanied," but Perkins rejected that as well.[33]

Gethsemane is the garden Christ and his disciples frequented and the location where he was betrayed by Judas. Boyd alludes to it earlier in the novel, when Hicks contemplates a hill that will be difficult to take: "There it rose—a Gethsemane—towering in the air, austere and forbidding" (235). Boyd is linking Hicks's experience to Christ's, including Christ's amazement and sorrow, as well as his coming betrayal by Peter as well as Judas, as he senses his death closing in.[34] But in both of the lines that did not make it into the final text, Boyd calls up a spiritual dimension to Hicks's "mental state." Whether his spiritual experience is associated with Christ or not, "Hicks was exalted." The word recalls Fitzgerald's statement that *Through the Wheat* "strikes one clear and unmistakable note of heroism, of tenuous and tough-minded exaltation, and with this note vibrating sharply in the reader's consciousness the book ends."[35] Fitzgerald could assert such a one-sided overall reading of the book that is diametrically opposed to the one-sided assessment critics today assert not simply because he had the original last sentence but because that sentence jibes with other scenes in the book and with other sentences in the final paragraph. (After all, other reviewers who never saw the original last line shared Fitzgerald's assessment, as did Scribner's.) The original and first-alternative last lines not only square with the previous few lines, which refer to Hicks's pride and his feeling that his feet have left the earth, but recast his indifference to everything earthly ("no longer did anything matter").

When Boyd wrote to Perkins suggesting the "Gethsemanied" line, he explained his intention for the ending: "Hicks is supposed to have reached the stage where nothing matters; where he'd risen above his surroundings."[36] Boyd was seeking a complex, even mystic, depiction of a soldier experiencing both the elation and loss or emptiness of spiritual transcendence or of "the absolute." This complexity or double-sidedness remains in the last paragraph, despite the last line having been simplified to "The soul of Hicks was numb."

Looking back on the long history of the reception of the Boyd's novel, it might be said that the book's overall meaning was reduced in complexity and bent toward an antiwar interpretation even before its publication. In essence, Perkins's editorial input on the last line unwittingly initiated a trend toward this oversimplification, which has carried the day in recent scholarship, despite great initial disagreement among reviewers about the book's valence.[37] The reality is that *Through the Wheat*, including its ending, has an irreducible complexity comparable to that of our greatest American war literature, from Crane's *The Red Badge of Courage* to Michael Herr's Vietnam War chronicle *Dispatches* (1977).

Boyd wanted to represent Hicks's physical suffering, shell shock, and horror over the deaths of his close friend and others, *as well as* his general effectiveness in combat, along with his pride in his performance and his recognition for it, including moments of "exaltation" at the front. That seems to be the reason why the last scene in particular confused Perkins (and his cousin, Richard Evarts, to whom he showed the book to make sure of his reading). But, though Boyd changed the last line, he resisted "any wholesale changes" to the ending because, as Bruce reasonably surmises, he "wanted to communicate the effect of modern warfare on the men who fought."[38] There seems to be little doubt that Boyd was aiming for a complex portrait of the effects of both modern combat and the modern military.

Hicks's experience, or his heterogeneous mix of experiences, reflects Boyd's. On the one hand, Boyd faced mental and physical suffering, as well as frustration with some of his officers. He was gassed on October 6, 1918, and treated in France for lung and throat problems due to phosgene gas and smoke inhalation. The injury was painful and temporarily debilitating—his war story, unlike Hicks's, ended in various army hospitals and an eventual return to guard duty with the army of occupation.[39] But he was aware that he was relatively lucky. When he was hospitalized, he wrote to his mother, "I have no cause to complain as it took me almost nine months to get [the injury] and besides it isn't very serious."[40] Meanwhile, "in common with many First World War Marines and doughboys, Boyd [like] his counterpart Hicks [was] contemptuous of most officers, who range[d] from pompous generals to inept 'ninety-day-wonder' lieutenants."[41] Boyd ended up being sent home in April 1919 in advance of his unit, for reasons that are not clear from his military record "but possibly," as Bruce puts it, "related to battle fatigue." Boyd complained of "nervousness" when examined by a physician at the end of May at the US Naval Hospital at Great Lakes, Illinois, and a couple of months later, after his discharge, a government doctor reported that he was suffering from "hysteria."[42]

On the other hand, there is Hicks's undeniable appreciation of aspects of the military and the war. This appreciation issues to some degree from Boyd's own relatively disadvantaged and fairly troubled upbringing. Though Hicks's background does not come into the story, the novel has a keen consciousness of status—as do Crane's and Herr's war books—and of the opportunities provided by the military's meritocracy to men of non-elite backgrounds. As Bruce observes: "Compared to Boyd, Fitzgerald and Hemingway had all the advantages. Both Hemingway and Fitzgerald were born into middle-class or upper-middle-class homes and had at least one devoted parent and the opportunity to receive a first-class education. Boyd grew up a virtual orphan without his father" (who died while his mother was pregnant) "and separated from his mother," who, after her husband's death was "destitute financially and emotionally" and in no condition to care for Thomas Boyd when he was born. When Thomas was a baby, his mother became a drug addict (because she was treated with morphine for severe headaches after an operation), and Thomas grew up in the homes of several different relatives, as his mother moved in and out of his life for the next fifteen years, part of the reason for his "sporadic education."[43]

Sociologist Centeno writes, "The temporary glory and importance given to actions [in war] may represent for many a rare moment of dignity and self-respect."[44] This phenomenon seems to apply both to Boyd and to his character Hicks. Boyd's letters to his mother during the war indicate his pride in being a marine. And, much like Hicks, Boyd disliked initially being put on work detail (unloading ships, constructing barracks, digging latrines, and serving on guard duty) and was gratified that he was destined for combat, writing to his mother about "having enlisted to fight and not do guard duty."[45] Moreover, he had an encounter with Major Adams, the real name of the officer who decided Boyd's fate after *he* broke the rules while on guard duty.[46] Boyd, who had achieved the rank of corporal and was soon to take his sergeants' exam, was "busted down" to private by Adams, but the major did not hand him over to a court-martial: because he "recognized Boyd's value as a soldier."[47] After this, Boyd "received straight '5s'—the highest possible markings—in his service-record book for military efficiency, obedience, and sobriety."[48] Boyd ended up seeing more combat than "the vast majority of American soldiers who served in France during the First World War."[49] He was promoted back to corporal in early 1919, and along with his citation from the US Second Division, he received the Croix de Guerre from the French Army.[50]

Boyd's highly autobiographical novel attempts to capture the heterogeneous and irreducibly complex experience of an American marine in World War I for the general reader. At the same time, it speaks directly to combatants like himself who were still suffering war's post-traumatic effects—physical wounds (Boyd's lungs were permanently damaged[51]), "nervousness" or "hysteria" or shell shock, and grief and sometimes guilt over buddies who died, but also loss of the emotional intensity, the intense camaraderie, the sense of the exceptional importance of one's employment, the extraordinary pride in one's military validation and status, and the uncanny spirituality of the battlefront.

Paul Edwards has written of two of the most famous British war memoirists, Siegfried Sassoon and Robert Graves, that they were "split." Sassoon's pseudonymous Sherston was eventually split between a desire to protest the war and a desire to excel at it; Graves "shows a contradictory desire to perform well in a publicly validated role and simultaneously debunk the project in which he has achieved excellence."[52] Several years before either of them published their war stories, Boyd—who in his shorter time of service saw as much action as either of them, though not in the trenches—did something similar in his. *Through the Wheat* is a story split between the horrifying and incredible human costs of war and the pride of being remarkably effective at it, split between a comic awareness of the blunders of most officers and a sincere awe of the few good ones. However, unlike Sassoon and Graves, who both came from privileged families and both got commissions on that basis, Boyd received, from the newly meritocratic US armed forces, a special sense of validation that he had not before experienced anywhere else, coming as he did from a deprived and troubled background. That sense of accomplishment or recognition seems to shine through in Hicks's intoxication at points with his prowess and with the trust placed in him. Such a thrill is especially compelling given that his story is from a private's point of view and not an officer's.

Through the Wheat is a classic American war novel that has not yet received its due. For some reason, it has almost always been assumed that it must be either a hero tale or an antiwar book when it is approximately both but perhaps finally neither. Maybe the assumption is based on a questionable sense that Boyd is not a sophisticated writer. In truth, the book is, on the whole, stylistically effective and successful—written in a spare prose and authentically representative of the language and slang of World War I marines. Fitzgerald thought so highly of it that, along with prevailing on Scribner's to publish it, he actually served as its editor. (Boyd accepted all of his edits, some significant, including the deletion of a discussion of Hicks's background.) As he praised it, "The whole book is written in the light of one sharp emotion and hence it is as a work of art rather than as a text book for patrioteer or pacifist that the book is arresting. . . . To my mind, this is not only the best combatant story of the great war, but also the best war book since 'The Red Badge of Courage.'" He later wrote to Boyd privately of *Though the Wheat* and his book of war short stories, *Points of Honor* (1925): "I think they are about my favorite modern books."[53]

CHAPTER EIGHT

The Intimate Seductions of Meritocracy

Laurence Stallings's *Plumes*

Plumes is about a man initially enthusiastic about participating in the war who ends up a badly wounded veteran with an amputated leg. It is beyond a doubt a story about becoming disillusioned with war. In fact, the main character Richard Plume's disillusionment is particularly striking and intense because he comes from a southern family with a long tradition of military service dating back to the Revolutionary War, and his loss of belief in the rightness and righteousness of serving one's country in the military alienates him from his family and his upbringing. Because of this alienation, he cannot return home after the war. Indeed, the book initially comes across as a simple, straightforward example of the "disillusionment narrative" that is supposed to characterize much of American writing about World War I. The protagonist's disillusionment seems to reveal the way in which World War I was fundamentally different from previous American wars, specifically in its dependence on an unprecedented level of government propaganda and in the unprecedented destruction of modern technological combat.

However, this simplified interpretation of the novel does not hold up. Richard's reasons for differing from his progenitors and souring on war are unclear. The fact is, many of Richard's ancestors were also badly wounded or maimed, and the book makes quite clear that modern weaponry has not made things worse in this regard. Moreover, Richard, an intellectually savvy college graduate, was not taken in by the nationalist propaganda. And so the reader is left wondering why Richard's reaction to being maimed in war is, after all, so different from that of his ancestors. If it is not due to the particular savagery of this first modern war, or to the empty political rhetoric that helped drive that war, then what is the reason?

It turns out that the key factor in Richard's different reaction is the military's unprecedented meritocracy, which has shaped not only his postwar reaction to his injury but in fact his original enthusiasm for the war. Because of the army's new organization—and despite his self-image—Richard cannot be like the ancestors he emulates. The new army has changed the whole experience of military service, and this transformation sets Richard apart from his forebears. Because a meritocratic system of power (with broad, or in this case, national reach) works on the intimate level of granting one a personal identity that is widely recognized, it has the power to change a man's relationship to himself, his peers, and his family. Whether one's initial branding is demeaning, as with Andrews in John Dos Passos's *Three Soldiers*, or flattering, as is the case with Richard, the system has fundamentally changed the source and nature of one's identity. Thus, it has the power to disrupt all previous sources of identity, including those of family, class, and ethnicity.

Laurence Stallings is supposed to be, according to Mark Whalan, one of the writers who "fashioned a powerful myth of the War, asserting that American soldiers had entered the War idealistically and were buoyed by the immense propaganda circulated by the Committee on Public Information."[1] Steven Trout essentially concurs:

> Stallings underscores the blindness inherent in Plume's gung-ho attitude toward war, a blindness shared by his ancestors. A genealogical history of the Plume family, presented near the beginning of the novel, reveals that its male members (war lovers one and all) all pay dearly for their martial enthusiasm. After plunging into war, few escape death or mutilation. And, economically, the family is worse off after each conflict. However, those Plumes who manage to return home from the battlefield, typically missing an arm or a leg, never talk of their physical suffering and financial sacrifice; instead, they dutifully take their place in commemorative rituals that stress the virtues of war for the next generation. Thus, Stallings makes it clear from the beginning that his protagonist is a dupe—in a line of dupes. However, after multiple operations on his leg, which leave him in constant pain, Plume resolves that he will defy family tradition and reject the role of the stoic war veteran. Thus, he refuses to return to Georgia, where a comfortable college appointment awaits him, and takes up residence in Washington, DC, where he flirts with political radicalism, seeking some way to protest against cultural forces that have led to his physical ruin.[2]

There are problems with these readings and with characterizing *Plumes* as a disillusionment narrative. To begin with, Richard Plume did not enter the war "idealistically" and thus he was no "dupe," in the sense of being naïve about the nationalist propaganda. But whether he was less of a dupe than his ancestors were is debatable. Arguably, he is more of a dupe because, even though he is uncomfortable with his motives for enlisting, he is nonetheless seduced by the army's unprecedented meritocracy as well as traditional promises of masculine glory. Second of all, critics have not asked why Richard "defies family tradition" after he is wounded. Given how similar to his ancestors he is supposed to be, and that so many of them came back from war wounded or maimed, it is worth wondering why Richard has a different response to his own injuries. The technological capacity of modern firepower to damage the human body does not seem to be what makes the difference. Stallings goes out of his way, in fact, to point out the "superstition among the ignorant that the World War was more cruel than any other." Noah Plume, who served in the Revolutionary War and suffered "a round blue hole in his groin, must there have experienced sensations and misgivings identical, in so far as physiology is concerned, with those of the German assault regiments at Verdun."[3] Nor are Richard's multiple surgeries, as Trout implies, what makes his experience, and thus his reaction, different from his ancestors. After the Revolutionary War, the same Noah Plume underwent "eighteen months of eighteenth-century surgery . . . where four strong men with straps and braces were the surgeon's most prized assistants" (13).

Richard is not as much like his ancestors as the book at certain points implies that he is. He begins to depart from their behavior long before he decides to reject their postwar role of the stoic war veteran or the "happy old cripple" (172). The reason he will not play this role has everything to do with why and how he got into the war in the first place. And his initial reasons and his enlistment were significantly different from those of his ancestors precisely because of the unprecedented mobilization and organization of the American army during World War I, which is to say, partly because of the propaganda about masculinity but mostly because of the new meritocracy. Given the unique mobilization, Richard has been encouraged and invited to have "personal" stakes in the war distinct from the communal stake of defeating the enemy and protecting the country—new chances for and experiences of social affirmation and promotion, which he is attracted by, though not entirely comfortable with, because his ancestors did not have these chances. But having such personal investments also means that he cannot accept his maiming as they accepted theirs—because his maiming has quashed this new social validation. With an army that now recognizes and validates abilities, disability comes to have a new meaning as well.

At points Richard seems to want to be, and the narration seems to want to present him as being, just like his ancestors. However, he cannot be just like them, given that the American army is no longer like the one they experienced. To begin with, the fact that Richard has gone to college, something he has in common with some of his Plume forefathers, means in this war that he will have special consideration to be an officer, something those college-educated forefathers did not experience. *Plumes* is cagey on the issue of Richard's difference from his military forebears, to the point of being entirely misleading at times. The novel is painstakingly set up and structured to make the reader think that, when it comes to war, Plume behaves just like his ancestors until after he is wounded. At the same time, there are clues and allusions that undermine this family likeness, revealing, on the sly as it were, that Richard behaves quite distinctly from the start. Thus, to understand *Plumes* it is necessary to understand not only how Richard's attitude to war differs from that of his progenitors but why the book obfuscates these differences.

Passages in the novel *provisionally* exemplify the standard disillusionment narrative. Richard feels at points that he "was seduced into [joining the army] by men like Taft who went about speaking for Wilson's participation in the war" (128). He talks of the "diet of shining swords that I was fed" as a child and youth (129). He speaks of his "[u]nquenchable anger at . . . the ignorance that victimized me" (171). When he is laid out on the battlefield wounded, the horrific truth about war comes to him, demolishing all the patriotic and sentimental lies that have been told. He is outraged at just how duped he has been.

> [T]his was no play-school. . . . This was It, and IT had got him. Who cared about Belgium and the Lusitania? Richard Plume, center of the universe, had life stolen from him. Stolen, by God, by those scoundrels who were not there upon the ground with him. The God-damned scoundrelly orators were not there—were not with him. They'd piece-meal stolen his life among them. The low, calculating scoundrels.
>
> Parades and parades and parades. Esme [his wife]. He had given her up and she had given him up [in his going to war], and back home thousand of loose-lipped seriously drooling sons-of-bitches were talking pompously of supreme sacrifices made pompously. What a fool to have given her up for them. . . . Oh, the millions of them back home who were not there on the

ground with eight or ten in their legs from a point-blank burst of a light Maxim.

. . . What price supreme sacrifice? (243–44)

But what makes *Plumes* a novel that both rewards reading and rewards analysis is that Stallings does not leave the matter there. Richard mitigates his claims of being victimized. His "unquenchable anger" is "unquenchable anger at myself and at the ignorance that victimized me" (171). When he mentions the childhood "diet of shining swords I was fed," he is actually comparing himself to the "German boy" who shot him and got shot in return, and who he imagines was "fed the same diet" but "earlier and in stronger quantities . . . from babyhood" (129). When he speaks of being "seduced," he admits that he is "no longer angry because I was seduced into it by men like Taft. . . . They were duped just as I was. I overestimated their intelligence. That poor old devil in the White House [Wilson] swallowed the same aphorisms fed me." Summing up his personal catastrophe, he concedes to his colleague Gary, "I'll admit that I fell under the freight train while attempting to steal a romantic ride" (128).

As at least one reviewer noticed at the time, the book has an "integrity that allowed Richard Plume, and Stallings as well, to understand his own culpability" in his tragic story. As Joseph Wood Krutch wrote in review for the *Nation* in 1924, already aware of the politicized "myth of the War" that has wrongfully been attributed in part to Stallings, "Surely this Richard, actually glad in the beginning to leave his instructorship and his wife to seek in France the romance of combat, is more typical of the soldier than the now more familiar figure of the completely unwilling victim of capitalist or political trickery."[4]

Whether Richard was "more typical of the soldier," he represents the willing victim of propagandistic "trickery." Because he is married, he is eligible for a draft deferment. Richard and his wife are both aware of this. Esme thinks, "If he fought a draft board he'd never get over it" (54), though he would not have had to fight very hard, given that she is pregnant with their child. But it is not the case that he is fully taken in by the propaganda. If he is susceptible to the propaganda about manhood—because it links up with his family's martial traditions—he is not a victim of the political propaganda, and, again, he does not enter the war "idealistically." He and Esme are both college educated. A graduate by the time he enters the army, he is working as a biology instructor and referred to as "Professor Richard Plume" (48, 54). Like Miranda and Adam in Katherine Anne Porter's "Pale Horse, Pale Rider," the couple are intellectually mature enough to be fully conscious of the propaganda campaign and its power and to be downright unconvinced about the political rationalizations for war.

The narrator of *Plumes* treats the wartime patriotism with irony. On the day Richard is leaving, he and Esme attend a ceremony at the college to honor him. When the dean makes a high-minded little speech that combines patriotic and Christian themes, "Esme, though she was very unhappy [about his going], smiled at this deification of Richard's impulsiveness" (53). The reader is also introduced to a townswoman named Mrs. Kershaw, a mouthpiece of the nationalist propaganda, who speaks with unwitting hyperbole of "one of those Belgian women . . . ravaged by every soldier in Germany," to which the narration wryly adds: "The ravages weighed heavy on Mrs. Kershaw's mind" (56). As Richard prepares to the board the train, he and Esme both think things they want "to shout" to the other but "they would not say." About his going to war, Richard thinks, "What an ass I'm making of myself!" And Esme wants to say to him, "You left me . . . at the end of six months of perfect happiness to rush off to shoot at people who never harmed us" (57). He later realizes that he knew "in the back of his mind" at that moment that he was "a fool" for going (244).

In his attraction to the romance of war, Richard is like the Plume men before him—but in going to France, he seeks something more than romance. And this other agenda sets him apart from his ancestors.

Richard shares what Steven Trout characterizes as the Plume family's "gung-ho attitude toward war." Trout notes that *Plumes* portrays "attraction to war—particularly as an expression of manhood—[as] . . . deeply rooted in the male American psyche."[5] The book starts with Richard's own description of his family's attitude to war. Chapter 4 begins much the same way, except it is the narrator who makes generalizations about the Plumes and war. In his enthusiasm for war and dedication to manhood, Richard is without question a "chip off the old hickory block," as his father says (26).[6] Yet there is a discrepancy between the Plume family's attitudes and Richard's actual experience.

"The Plumes seldom concerned themselves with military rank," yet Richard does concern himself with rank. "The Plumes themselves rarely reached the commissioned grades of national heroism" (51), but Richard reaches the commissioned grade of lieutenant. Richard contradicts the rules that are being asserted here, yet the narration hides or downplays his distinctness by implying that he achieves his rank by accident, without seeking it.

When the issue of a concern with military rank comes up, the narrator tells us that all we need to know about Richard's commissioned status is that it comes by the end of his service. Richard's case is thus comparable to one Civil War ancestor who does make captain as a result of his actions on the battlefield but "only two months before being" killed (51). The implication in this passage is that Richard, like his ancestors, does not care about attaining commissioned rank but gets it anyway: "Suffice to say that Richard reached this [rank] before he was discharged" (52).

But the odd tension in the text inheres in the fact that it does not truly "suffice to say" this. Earlier in the book, the narrator imparts that Richard was an officer before he hits the front and later suggests that he was an officer while still in the states. So it is not the case that Richard has merely attained that rank by the end of the war, by the time peace is negotiated "at Versailles," as the narrator misleadingly implies (52). Richard has definitely had that rank before seeing action, in the spring of 1918, as we learn in the first scene in the book: he "was the platoon's officer" as "his Sam Browne belt and Colt's 45" attest (4), and "the Sam Browne and Golden Bars of their vested rank" reinforce this point a couple of pages later (6). He may be an officer even before he leaves his hometown: as Richard says goodbye to his wife and boards the train that is presumably taking him to a training camp, other passengers see a "young officer off to war" (57).

Why this disparity in the text? Was Stallings himself a bit split or mixed up about how he wanted to present Richard Plume? The book is highly "autobiographical" and thus very personal.[7] Stallings grew up in Georgia, and two of his great uncles died in the Civil War. He attended Wake Forest College in North Carolina, the model for Woodland College, which Richard attends, where he likewise majored in classics and biology and met and eventually married the daughter of one of his professors.[8] In the war, Stallings was maimed in the same manner as Plume; he was likewise a commissioned officer before he finished his training stateside. In fact, Stallings clearly took the necessary bureaucratic steps to become an officer when the opportunity presented itself. According to his service record, he initially joined the Marine Corps Reserve as a private on May 29, 1917, and began active duty July 25. But he "was disenrolled on 9 October 1917, as a Private, to accept appointment as a Second Lieutenant in the regular Marine Corps," at which point he headed off to training camp at Parris Island, South Carolina.[9]

In sum, when it comes to the issue of rank or status, the narrator implies at one point that Richard is more like his ancestors than he actually is. But the reader discovers this discrepancy because the narrator is forthcoming about Richard's history at other points. What we get is the portrait of a character, and perhaps an author as well, who is not only concerned about rank but concerned with—or embarrassed about—being concerned about rank.

Something similar might be said about the concern with military decorations. When we learn that Richard was a second lieutenant by the time of Versailles, the narrator adds, modestly, "But it would be an imposition upon the reader to clutter this account further with martial trumpetings . . ." (52, suspension points in original). We thereby learn that there are other military achievements that might be "trumpeted" but that the narrator is going to hold them back, in keeping with the fact that "War to the Plumes" was only "a question of how did it start, when is it starting, where does one enlist" (51–52). (Stallings himself earned the Croix de Guerre and a Silver Star.)[10] Nevertheless, just a few pages later the narrator tells us about a medal Richard already has. When he is saying goodbye to his wife, he is wearing his "rifleman's medal. . . . A trinket he hoped some day to augment with other things equally valuable" (56, suspension points in original).

Why does Richard's attitude to war differ from that of his ancestors? And why does the narrative at times obscure the fact that he is different—and contradict itself when it comes to the issue of military status?

When the topic of the Plume lack of concern with military rank comes up, the narrator is not referring to the ranks that the Plumes have held but rather how they felt about their officers: "To be sure, they saluted their officers with reasonable alacrity, but never with a dog-like devotion" (51). The Plumes have not been officers because of their "social background." The very first sentence of the book tells us, "The Plumes have been in this country two hundred and fifty years, and not one of them was worth as much as $25,000" (3). In chapter 4, the connection between their modest economic standing and their noncommissioned status is made clear. In the Plumes' view, "an officer was a man who wished to carry to the field of combat some silly notion surviving from his social background" (51). But with World War I, that tradition of commissioned status in the US military being awarded on the basis of social standing has suddenly been broken. Richard is the first Plume to enter an American army that is partly meritocratic.

The military's partial meritocracy means that if Richard goes into the war a private, his superiors will not necessarily be men of a more exalted "social background" than himself; indeed, some might very well be socially inferior—and perhaps different ethnically as well. It also means that Richard, though he comes from a family of modest means—his parents "did not have a great store of money" (29)—is eligible to be a commissioned officer from the start. In fact, he has a better chance than most men of modest family backgrounds because of his education. Since his parents "set great store by books" (29) and his father is the head of a high school, he has gone to college. (College men had the privilege of taking a qualifying exam for officers' training school before entering the army.) In fact, there is another Plume family tradition—albeit not universal among his male ancestors—of going to Woodland College. There were "those Plumes too poor or too harum-scarum to attend it," but there also are some "who did attend" (34). So not only has the army changed in experimenting with meritocracy, but the army has changed the meaning of college in terms of opportunities for military rank.

Richard may be "a chip off the old . . . block," but he feels and behaves differently from his ancestors because the army he is joining is significantly different from the armies they joined. Having gone to college does not set Richard apart from his Plume forebears, but having gone to college in the World War I era does. Richard's father has read somewhere "that heredity was nine parts environment to one part grandfather" (26), and some version of that claim is surely operative here in Richard's deviation from his grandfather and other progenitors. If the US Army of World War I were like US armies of wars gone by, Richard would also behave like they did. But the social or institutional environment has radically changed. How can he not feel differently about commissioned rank when he is now especially qualified for it, and when his being merely a private will mean potentially having to "indulge" (51) officers who are socially inferior? He feels differently about military rank because rank implies something different now that it is awarded meritocratically. Therefore he acts differently by seeking a commission. His ancestors felt commissioned rank in past American armies was "silly" (51) because it was based on the dubious superiority of an accident of birth, but commissioned rank in a meritocracy is not "silly" by definition. The whole idea of meritocracy is that it substitutes for an arbitrary system one that is sensible, or to use President Woodrow Wilson's words, "practical" and "scientific."[11] "War to the Plumes was not a thing of personal attributes" (51), but it cannot help but be so for Richard because "personal attributes"—one's skills, capacities, physical fitness, intelligence—now matter to the army.

All the Plume men have rushed off to war. "'Not one of them,' said Richard, 'had anything worth going to war about'" (3). But Richard does. In a sense, the previous Plumes had something worth going to war about; it gave them a way to manifest and express their manhood. And Richard, too, is involved in a "romance of combat" that has everything to do with his southern family mythology and upbringing, which is committed to a martial definition of masculinity. But we understand what Richard means. Evidently, the Plumes have not gone to war to protect themselves, their families, or their property, and the same is true now of Richard; as Esme wants to tell him, you are "rush[ing] off to shoot at people who never harmed us." But war did not offer Richard's ancestors validation that translated into personal promotion. Now it does offer this to Richard. In addition, the public has, as a result of World War I propaganda, adopted his family's equation of military service and manliness. So Richard gets an official approval from the community luminaries—witness his sending-off ceremony at the college chapel, which he is "uncomfortable" with but nonetheless prepares for by excessively polishing his army boots (53–54).

His stake in the war goes beyond his ancestors'; he has a reason for going they never had. Another thing that Esme wants to "shout" at Richard but does not say is that he is leaving her and going to war to "get the glory" (57). Richard, unlike his forefathers, is involved in a romance of status or "glory" that comes from an awareness of the national propaganda about manhood and the realities of promotion in the wartime moment and the new army. This awareness makes him at once proud and uncomfortable.

Given the changes in the new army, Richard can hardly be expected to act the way his progenitors did. Yet no doubt that expectation remains because change in the army has happened so suddenly that Richard, the narrator, and maybe even the author have not quite processed its implications. *Plumes* contains unresolved and apparently unprocessed contradictions concerning Richard's attitude toward rank and military service. It is certainly possible that Stallings, at first enjoying significant military promotion and then suffering a traumatic wound that leaves him one of "the army of . . . [the] disabled" (169), just like Richard—and writing and publishing his book within half a dozen years of the beginning of that ongoing trauma—has not been able to thoroughly digest both what has happened to him and how it is that changes in the social environment of the military have made his experience so different from that of soldiers in previous American wars.

The book's contradictions about Richard's attitude to rank perhaps reflects Stallings's own conflicted feelings about the issue. But it certainly registers the narrator's difficulty or discomfort with Richard's distinct concern about rank, singular as it is for a Plume. Richard himself expresses discomfort with his decision to go to war, and this unease is yet something else that sets him apart from his forebears. The sense of being "ashamed . . . for going" (56) centers on his leaving Esme alone and pregnant, but Richard is not the first Plume to leave a wife and child; Noah Plume, who went to the Revolutionary War, left his wife home with "four" children (12). However, abandoning a wife with children or a child to come had a different valence when Noah Plume did it—merely out of patriotism, duty, or manhood—with nothing to gain in terms of advancement. Richard's situation is different because leaving for war offers him personal promotion. In other words, Richard's discomfort about his going to war may be focused on his betraying Esme and shirking his marital and fatherly duties, but the fact that it is shame he feels is made possible by his unique reasons for leaving. If he was not conflicted about his reasons, then he might feel bad about leaving, but he would not necessarily feel "ashamed" and "an ass" (56, 57) for doing so. If he were leaving purely out of a sense of manly duty to his nation, then both he and Esme would be bearing their separate burdens. But because that is not the case, Esme reasonably wants to say to him, "You get the glory. I bear the child" (57).

Though the novel is largely autobiographical, there is a significant discrepancy between the author's story and that of his character. When Stallings went off to war, he was not yet married (he got married upon his return, in 1919), and he and his future wife did not have a child until 1928.[12] Why might Stallings want to change *these* important details when there is so much correspondence between Richard's prewar and wartime history and his own? It seems that Stallings is looking for a way to treat—to both address and obscure—the "shameful" issue of Richard's concern with status.

On the one hand, Richard's being married with a pregnant wife draws our attention away from his motivations for going—which include his interest in military promotion and decoration—to the fact of his leaving her. His shame seems to stem from leaving, not from his reasons for leaving. On the other hand, giving Richard a pregnant wife, and thus eligibility for a draft deferment, makes his going much more clearly a result of his own desire and will. His personal reasons for going become more inescapable: they cannot be chalked up to compulsion or duty.

The painful issue of shame over status, which we saw with the Lost Generation writers in part I, recurs here, but with a difference. Richard is not, like William Faulkner's Cadet Lowe in *Soldiers' Pay* and F. Scott Fitzgerald's Anthony Patch in *The Beautiful and Damned*, embarrassed about failing to become an officer and a combatant; he is embarrassed about caring so much about succeeding. As a result of Richard's leaving Esme, she sees him as "such a child" (54). Cadet Lowe in Faulkner's novel and Nick in Ernest Hemingway's "A Very Short Story" each end up being seen by a woman as "a child" or "a boy" because of their relatively low military status. Here,

Richard ends up "a child" in Esme's eyes because of his concern with a military status he achieves. "A man" in Richard's position would presumably stay home and fulfill his duties as a husband and a father (as the draft regulations expressly allow), but Richard, still under the sway of a boyhood inculcation in battlefield fantasies, is all the more childish for caring about the "glory" that can begin stateside with an officer's uniform, "polish[ed]" boots, and a "rifleman's medal" (54, 56).

In "more exclusive wars" (54), like most of the ones his ancestors fought, Richard might be able to get a sense of "exclusivity" and martial recognition without going out of his way and thus without thinking about it. But the World War I draft has made this war inclusive, so, if Richard wants the special validation he feels he warrants, on account of his intelligence, education, "physique," and Plume-inherited "Nordic magnificence" (4, 6), he has to actively seek it out. Given the realities of this mobilization, there is something ignominious or even illicit for Richard in his relationship to war. The illicit quality comes out in his admitting that he "fell under the freight train while attempting to *steal* a romantic ride" (128, emphasis added).

The result of the discomfort with Richard's concern over status, expressed in different ways by the narrator, by Esme, and by Richard himself, is that it makes Stallings's book an odd disillusionment-with-war narrative comparable to those of the British memoirists Siegfried Sassoon and Robert Graves, but even more fractured than theirs. If Graves and Sassoon's alter-ego Sherston were split between a desire to show the evils, blunders, and horrors of war and yet to get recognition for participating in and excelling at it (see chapter seven), then Stallings's narrative is doubly split: first, between those conflicting desires in Richard and, second, between Richard's and the narrator's pride in Richard's military accomplishments and their shame about his concern with achieving them. In Sassoon's *Memoirs of an Infantry Officer*, Sherston eagerly attacks enemy trenches in part to gain a Military Cross, only to later throw the ribbon in the Mersey River in disgust as he contemplates making an official protest of the war.[13] Similarly, in *Plumes*, the narrator tells us Richard earned a "rifleman's medal" and hoped to earn others, and also indicates that Richard performed heroically on the battlefield. Then after the war, Richard teams up with a radical antiwar agitator who was in fact jailed during the conflict for his political work. But *Plumes* is further split in a way that Sassoon's novel is not. Stallings's narrator, as we have seen, both alludes to and withholds "further . . . martial trumpetings," and we never learn exactly how Richard acquitted himself that day on the battlefield when he was injured—though we find out enough to know that he definitely did some things worthy of "trumpeting." He shot the "German boy" who machine-gunned him (129), and we can deduce that he somehow captured the machine gun itself (he tells the men who evacuate him, "get belt from that light Maxim for souvenir"). Beyond that, things get hazy. Stallings uses, in advance of Faulkner, some unpunctuated streams and bursts of dialogue and consciousness: "tell your C.O. sixty in those woods in that clump sixty" (247). Presumably Richard repeats the word "sixty" because the men cannot believe he actually killed "sixty" of the enemy.

In real life, after Stallings had his kneecap blown off, he still managed to throw a grenade that "wiped out the entire [machine gun] nest. When he came to, he was in the hospital."[14] For "that wound" and "his courage during this incident," he "received the Croix de Guerre and the Silver Star."[15] The only hint that Richard likewise threw a grenade is his mostly cryptic comment to the stretcher bearers, possibly about the "souvenir" machine-gun belt they should retrieve, "don't mind shrapnel who minds shrapnel" (247). Graves and Sassoon give us clearly and in detail both sides of their split attitude to the war; Stallings is, meanwhile, so agonizingly conflicted that we can be sure of the splits but not all of the details—which makes sense given the severity of his and Richard's wounds and trauma.

The reason why Richard is the first Plume openly to turn against war, why his postwar reaction is so different from that of his forebears, is not simply the gravity of Richard's injury or his postwar physical trials. Why does Richard experience his physical ruin differently from, say, Noah Plume, who, because of his "mutilated feet," returned from the Revolutionary War to his wife and four children, "not as a provider, but as an eldest child able [only] to do small chores"? After all, in contrast to Richard, Noah was not ashamed of his mutilation. It is true Noah "had won a war" (12–13), but so has Richard. Why has Richard experienced "ruin" (112) or a "downfall" (261) when Noah did not?

To begin with, the victory in World War I begins to seem hollow soon after the war ends. Once the Versailles peace treaty turns out to be punitive, and then US participation in the League of Nations is defeated by the Senate, the American people know that the war has obviously not achieved the aims that Wilson and his government public relations agencies had promised. In addition, Richard finds himself in a nightmare postwar world. His treatment by the corrupt and mismanaged federal Veterans' Bureau is disgraceful; moreover, the financial benefits for wounded veterans are simply not sufficient. *Plumes* depicts not only permanent war wounds but also demobilization indignities that maimed soldiers experience as they plummet from heroes to disabled men, from soldiers selected for the American Expeditionary Forces to "the army of disgruntled disabled" (169). Complementing the physical suffering is the social demotion: "this awful descent in importance from soldier to ex-soldier these men had known in three years," their injuries compounding their depreciation, making them in "the social scheme . . . vagrants [who] had fallen so low" (290).

The unpopularity of the war soon after its end, along with the nation's failure to take care of its former soldiers, affect Richard's reception, as a wounded veteran, by the general public and government. But it does not change his reception at home, where he is to be embraced and treated as a hero. Richard's parents want to take care of him and his family "and wait upon them the remainder of [their] lives." Esme's parents want to do the same (80–81). So even this war's failures, geopolitically and in terms of veteran care, while definitely mattering, do not fully explain Richard's unique response: he refuses to return home to the college appointment that awaits him.

The book makes clear that Richard does not want to come back home and "drive everyone crazy" (170) with his "bitter" new "point of view about war" (80). But why he already has a bitterness none of his ancestors had, despite their wounds and suffering, is still unexplained. To be clear, his antiwar feelings and his decision not to return home come before he realizes that his government financial support is insufficient (164–69) and also before his disturbing encounters with the Veterans' Bureau (291–96). If we simply take it for granted that Richard has seen the light about war, while his ancestors remained duped, we let ourselves off easy. We are not analyzing fully; we are projecting a contemporary viewpoint while ignoring significant facts about the text and not taking into account meaningful contradictions within it.

After his visit to his Woodland home at Christmas, Richard imagines that the dean of the college and his parents have told him "something that came to this: 'We are all proud of you for making an ass of yourself' " (80). And thus, in addition to not wanting to hurt his "too kind" "folks" (80) with his antiwar sentiments, Richard has a second reason he does not want to return home: he believes that at home he would not only be admired but, as in American society at large, pitied—seen as a fool or "an ass."

Here he is wrong. The dean does not think he has made an ass of himself; this is what Richard hears because this is what he feels. The dean and Richard's family are sincerely proud of him, as he finally realizes much later in the story when he meets his cousin the congressman, Jabez: "Jabez Plume was like Zachary [Richard's father] and shared in his respect for Richard's scars. . . . It was genuine, awkward. Plume blood had been spilled on glory's altars. Jabez . . . was touched." "Why didn't this boy come to me?" he says to Richard's mother. "I would have done anything for him." And he is still ready to help Richard. "We are proud of the distinction he has lent us" (327).

Simply put, Richard, in distinction to his wounded forebears, feels like "an ass" because he has tried "to steal a romantic ride" while they "regarded [war] adverbially. It was a question of *how* did it start, *when* is it starting, *where* does one enlist" (51–52, emphasis added). Richard, the first to experience a meritocratic army, regarded war in terms of nouns or adjectives—"personal attributes"—he had no choice. Because Americans could not simply enlist for this war and be guaranteed participation in combat, Richard also had to ask, "What does one need to do to qualify for combat? Do I have those attributes?" And though he is not also obliged to care "what rank can someone like myself qualify for," the new organization of the army makes it is difficult not to.

Once one starts thinking about participation in war in terms of health, physical fitness, abilities, and so on, then war means something different from what it meant during previous conflicts. A combat wound can permanently deprive a soldier of the very attributes the military used to select him. It is no accident that the book begins with an emphasis on Richard's physical build—his "beautiful" "physique" is in evidence as he showers (4). Later, on the battlefield, we are given his exact height and weight details: he is "six feet one and weighing two hundred and seven pounds in . . . football condition" (243). Though the shower sequence is not literally a scene depicting army measurement of naked recruits, as we get in *Three Soldiers*, it is an echo of that procedure, especially because it is, singularly in the book, from the point of view of a higher-ranked officer, a captain, who observes Richard approvingly. Richard is what army photographs of such scenes of measurement sometimes referred to as a "prize specimen."[16] One of the effects of meritocratic evaluation, assessment, and assignment is that one cannot help identifying oneself in terms of the traits with which one has been associated. This is true even if those traits and that assessment are complimentary. Richard, like Dos Passos's Andrews, has been branded by the military. The fact that his branding is positive does not simply mean that he has been affirmed and selected; it also means that the basis of his own identity has changed, and that new identity is vulnerable to damage. When Richard is physically wounded, his identity is thus injured as well. In a system of power in which one can be a wartime winner before hitting the front—by being selected for combat or officers training—one can also be a loser after the war is over. In a system of power that identifies ability, one can also be, or become, identified as disabled. That is why Richard is the first Plume who can feel resentment as well as misery.

The Plume ancestors could not lose their self-respect once they enlisted in the war; whatever happened to them—including death and mutilation—they had fulfilled their masculine duty. They were no less masculine or dutiful for having been maimed—in fact, their scars proved their service (and some of them "romance[d] about [their] wounds" [80]). They did not expect, and usually did not get, promotion or validation from the army; thus they did not lose that status and affirmation when the war was over; they simply expected respect from their families and to be taken care of by them when they returned home. They could be miserable because of their pain and physical limitations, but they did not have resentment over being manipulated and stripped of a personal sense of value (307).

But in the new army, and in a society that is mobilized to support the draft and the war, men selected for combat service will experience, after the armistice, a "descent in importance from soldier to ex-soldier," which is "awful" if one is maimed but hard enough if one is simply demobilized and returned to a society no longer concerned with the war. Even if one is not mangled under the wheels of the glamorous military "freight train," to use Richard's metaphor, one is tossed off the train at war's end. If you have the right qualifications, the military meritocracy validates you and makes you feel special, and then, with your discharge, leaves you high and dry.[17] Richard's ancestors may have been duped by an ideology that linked masculinity and martial participation, but Richard is duped by a military meritocracy in which men are flattered for their useful abilities but expendable when they are no longer of use.

Like the antiwar Jewish activist Meyer, whom Richard teams up with after the war and whose forebears have been "rubbed raw" by being racially stigmatized (307), Richard now experiences stigmatization. In a world where one is identified for one's abilities and disabilities, Richard is right that only an "ass" would risk himself physically. Richard cannot believe that his folks back home see things differently because his way of viewing himself and others has been profoundly inculcated by his experience of being assessed and classified by the army. But his folks have not been subjected to these meritocratic procedures of power; thus, they are not influenced or "poisoned" by them.

Given his terrible injury, Richard wants his experience to mean something. And it does—even though it may not be in the way he intends. Part of Richard's not wanting to go home was to make sure that his son did not grow up to "repeat [my] experience" (163), but he gives up on this aim at the end, telling Esme he cannot prevail over the cultural forces that glorify war, and adding, "I'll go home with you any time you say" (347). "I'm through," Richard says, admitting a sense of defeat in regard to his son (though it still remains to be seen whether he has failed, as the book ends with Richard's friend Gary educating young Dickie as to the awful truth of war).

But Richard's experience has still been redemptive. He himself has changed for the better. Early in the book, he is very self-centered, an aspect of his personality that presumably played a role in his seduction by the propaganda (about service) and military meritocracy and that his army selection and promotion also augmented. The prime example of his self-occupation comes when he leaves pregnant Esme in the lurch, seeking instead his own "romantic ride." At the moment he is injured, the narration's insistent repetition of his considering himself the "center" of things has the effect of critical irony: "Richard Plume had led Crocker [a soldier under his command] to his death. Crocker would die. But the center of the universe . . . . [suspension points in original] Ah! That wasn't Crocker. Richard Plume, center of everything, and nothing else mattered, was bleeding to death and the cold . . . would finish . . . off . . . the center of all living things" (243). By the end of the book, Richard has become socially conscious and active in helping other social unfortunates, something he admits to Meyer he never would have done "if I were . . . sound physically" (307). It is also hard to imagine him teaming up in activism with a "wiry little wild Jew" (274) before he was maimed.

Richard also grows less prejudiced. The book is structured to make us see this clearly: in the first scene, Richard picks a fight with a black Senegalese soldier and addresses him with a racial slur: "You Sambo." The narrator makes clear that Richard's feeling of racial superiority—his sense of "Nordic magnificence"—is tied up with his affirmation by the military, his "vested rank" (5–6). After the war, and late in the book, when he reinjures his leg and is facing amputation in Walter Reed Hospital, his bunkmate is an African American officer named Jackson. The army might have been segregated, but the army hospital is not.

Richard's response to Jackson, while still not entirely devoid of southern prejudices, is a major transformation from his intoxication with his superiority at the start. Lieutenant Jackson, like Richard, went from "college into war"—and commissioned rank. Jackson's sharing Richard's rank seems to matter in the amendment of Richard's racial attitudes. If the army meritocracy has confused and even crippled Richard's sense of himself, it has also perhaps helped alter his view of black men. In any case, Richard offers Jackson his hand, as they lie in adjacent beds, and he twice worries about seeming "condescending" to Jackson. For his childhood inculcation in prejudice, Richard "inwardly cursed hundreds of Plumes." And "he resolved furiously to submit his post-war Liberalism to the acid test with Jackson in the coming months" (253). Though Richard cannot extirpate his prejudice about the mixing of the races, "his respect for Jackson" stops him from arguing with his friend Gary about it. In the end, "Richard was sure that he himself was without prejudice the day that Jackson was discharged" (266). He has passed the test.

Richard is ready to return home at the end of the book, not merely out of defeat, not simply because he has given up on trying to keep his boy, Dickie, from making his mistake. He is also making this decision for redemptive reasons. He is doing something significant for Esme, giving her something she wants and needs, and it involves a sacrifice on his part because, whenever the issue of war comes up, it will be difficult for Richard, as he will not be able to express his true feelings in all their intensity. But this decision is also possible because Richard has come to understand that his family is not infected by the "meritocratic" mind-set that would see him as "fallen so low." They will not be seeing him in comparison to the prize physical specimen he was when he went off to war—and finding him wanting. And even if he never understands exactly why, he has also realized that his attitude about the war, what he calls near the end of the book his pursuit of "cheap glory," did not make him a chip off the old Plume block but rather put him in common company with a "million" men who behaved as he did (275, 274).

CHAPTER NINE

Not Only What You Would Expect

The Inside Story in Victor Daly's *Not Only War*

VICTOR DALY'S *Not Only War: A Story of Two Great Conflicts* (1932), the only novel of the war by an African American veteran, much like Thomas Boyd's *Through the Wheat* and Laurence Stallings's *Plumes*, has been underestimated by critics. It is generally treated as one of a number of African American texts that respond to the war or depict black soldiers, but all of the others, including short stories, are written by noncombatants or nonparticipants. Daly's is the only such work written by a black veteran. *Not Only War* is rarely accorded the special or sustained separate treatment it deserves. As a result, Daly's novel has never been recognized for what it is.

The critical tendency in regard to *Not Only War*, established in a contemporary omnibus review by Alain Locke, has been to suggest that his short book is complex but then, without bringing out its full complexity, to see it as flawed or lacking. Locke described the book as a "complicated novelette of the World War [that] . . . fails to move with the conviction necessary to good fiction"—unlike another 1932 novel he reviewed along with Daly's that he found a "quite moving story."[1] It is unclear exactly what Locke had in mind "by the *conviction* necessary to good fiction," but Daly keeps us distanced at certain key points from the main characters, who are, in addition, underdeveloped. Moreover, there is one specific piece of information he withholds—he tells us that the black protagonist soldier Montgomery (nicknamed Montie) Jason is court-martialed and stripped of his rank after a white officer named Bob Casper discovers him fraternizing with a French woman, but he does not tell us what Montie was charged with.

David Davis, the editor to whom we are indebted for a new (2010) edition of the novel finds Locke's criticism "both unwarranted and curious," asserting that the book "explores the social construction of the color line, its obvious sexual connotations, and its less obvious international contradictions as powerfully and with as much conviction as any novel." But then he himself also suggests that "the book does have some melodramatic aspects," for example the ending "seems overly sentimental."[2] Montie meets a wounded Bob Casper on the battlefield and decides, despite his natural resentment of Bob, to try to save him, risking his own life. Bob thanks him and seems to repent of his racism—"war isn't the only hell I've been through lately," he says to Montie—and they die "with their arms about each other" (69–70).

In *The Great War and the Culture of the New Negro* (2008), Mark Whalan has presented the most specific and complex version of this mixed assessment. He shows that this sentimental scenario—of the wounded white soldier who repents on the battlefield of his racism to a black soldier who has come to his aid and whom he has sometimes personally wronged—is common to several African American stories of the war. He goes on to suggest that there was historical validity to the idea that "no-man's-land," the area between the trenches, was a race-less space where equality could be realized and humanity could be achieved.[3] As Whalan puts it, building on the work of British military historian Joanna Bourke, "the terrain's very deathliness configures it as an egalitarian space; the differences in how individuals are embodied in representation according to race become unsustainable in an environment that is so hostile to the integrity to the body." He also quotes historian Stephen Kern, who writes of no-man's-land, "class, rank, and nation were leveled; World War I assaulted far more of the hierarchical structure of privilege than its participants had ever expected."[4]

A groundbreaking US army panel famously recommended the abolishment of segregation in the military just after World War II partly because they came to the similar conclusion, based on military experiences in that war, that combat is the great equalizer. The members of the Gillem Board, in their report, "Utilization of Negro Manpower in the Postwar Army Policy" (1946), claimed that in situations of combat, where white soldiers faced mortal danger, they had no objections to being aided by African American replacement troops.[5]

Thus, Whalan illuminates a historical reality that suggests these charged scenes between black and white soldiers were not entirely wishful. But he also admits that such climactic, battlefield-conversion scenes, Daly's included, "which imagine . . . that racial injustice can be swept away by the shared experience of crisis and mutual danger" are still "highly formulaic" and were "regularly lampooned by a later generation of writers."[6]

Though Daly's story seems to fit the mold Whalan describes, it actually does not. That it resembles in its ending other African American stories may be due to Daly's wanting to "correct" them. He alone among these writers knew what really happened on and off the battlefields of France when white and black troops encountered each other. (He also knew how and why such encounters happened.) In any case, these stories were partially right—perhaps they were based on real tales of the front that circulated in the black community and immediately got mythified—and Daly's was bound to intersect with them, while radically extending them.

Daly's book seems contrived and sentimental to twenty-first-century readers for two reasons. First, we do not know the specifics of how black soldiers interacted with white soldiers, as well as French women, in France in World War I. Second, critics have misread Bob Casper's last words to Montie—by looking at them out of the context of the complex story Daly tells about these characters' relationship, or in the context of the endings of these other World War I tales. Thus we have seen those words as an apology and evidence of a conversion, when Bob is actually saying something different and much more startling. Daly's ending is not largely sentimental or contrived but rather is profoundly based in fact and reflects a very specific reality, not known except by insiders, about the racial politics in France—a reality that these other stories Whalan groups together do not address.

Something analogous can be said about those things that are arguably "unmoving" about Daly's novel, as well as about those things that are missing. Once we consider that this book may have been meant principally for an insider audience, the book's "unmoving" quality and its omissions appear as purposeful authorial decisions or strategies.

Before we get to the insider story of what happened in France, we need to situate Daly's novel in the broader and much more widely known history of domestic race relations in America before, during, and just after World War I. When the United States joined the war, many African Americans hoped that "if we roll up our sleeves and plunge into this thing, that the Government will reward the race for its loyalty" (12), as Montie puts it. He in fact is echoing the controversial position that W. E. B. Du Bois famously took in "Close Ranks," an essay published in the *Crisis* in July 1918. "Let us, while this war lasts, forget our special grievances and close our ranks shoulder to shoulder with our own white fellow citizens and the allied nations that are fighting for democracy," Du Bois wrote. "We make no ordinary sacrifice, but we make it gladly and willingly with our eyes lifted to the hills."[7]

This was indeed "no ordinary sacrifice," and other African American leaders pilloried Du Bois for his "apparent conciliation" and even treachery in this editorial, given that the army was considering him for a captaincy in the Military Intelligence Branch.[8] Black leaders involved in fighting for equality before the war, including the board of directors of the NAACP, which had been founded in 1909, were deeply split on this issue of "closing ranks" and more generally on how to take advantage of the "unique opportunity" World War I presented to the black community. The United States had declared it was fighting the war "for Democracy," yet it was obviously not, in the eyes of African Americans, practicing democracy at home.[9] In an editorial addressed to President Woodrow Wilson, A. Philip Randolph, and Chandler Owen, the two most vocal opponents of Du Bois's position, wrote: "Lynching, Jim Crow, segregation, discrimination in the armed forces and out, disfranchisement of millions of black souls in the South—all these things make your cry of making the world safe for democracy a sham, a mockery, a rape on decency and a travesty on common justice."[10] In Daly's novel, Montie's friend Roscoe articulates the point of view of black Americans who did not trust the US government to reward them for "closing ranks" but rather believed the nation's white leadership would be happy to use them for its own ends and then drop them: "what have we got to do with this war, anyhow? It's a white man's war. He started it. Let him finish it. There's nothing in it for us" (12).

Roscoe turns out to be right, historically speaking. African Americans served in the war, but the US government did not reward the black community. Black veterans returned home to find intensified and more violent racism. As historian Chad L. Williams writes, "The war inflated the hopes of African Americans that a new era of democratic opportunity lay on the horizon. Instead, these hopes were met by a wave of racial violence unmatched since the end of the Civil War. . . . An estimated twenty-five race riots, large and small, erupted throughout the nation. . . . James Weldon Johnson . . . label[ed] the bloody demobilization months of 1919 'The Red Summer.' "[11] Montie realizes Roscoe is right while still in France, after his unjust court-martial for being "friendly with white girls": "his mind traveled to the war itself, to the destruction, and suffering, and death . . . to the hundreds of . . . black boys who were rotting up there. For what good purpose, he asked himself. Came in answer all the high-sounding phrases that lull men's reason to sleep, and allow them to be led off like sheep to the slaughter—to make the world safe for democracy—war to end war—self determination for oppressed people. But they didn't mean black people. Oh no, black people don't count. . . . Maybe Roscoe . . . was right after all. It was a white man's war" (60–61).

Daly's book has been seen as exemplifying works that make "a case for African American citizenship through military service."[12] And in his journalistic agitation for civil rights after the war, Daly certainly made this case. But perhaps he wrote the novel for other reasons. In his review of Daly's book, Locke also "marvelled that with all the fiction of the war, the paradoxical story of the American Negro fighting a spiritual battle within a physical battle has just now been attempted," fourteen years after the war's end.[13] Part of the reason such a story took so long to come out is that Daly was the only black veteran to write a novel of World War I, and only black veterans knew this "paradoxical" insider story. But Daly's wait of a dozen years to write and publish *Not Only War* suggests, too, that with the novel he was not getting out an important and timely message for which he found other venues or media. David Davis asserts that "the book was intended specifically for an African American audience."[14] But is it possible that Daly wrote the book mainly and even more specifically for other African American *veterans*?

Daly's novel was "Dedicated to the Army of the Disillusioned," and though much of the black community was disillusioned by the ungenerous and brutal postwar reality that it confronted, perhaps the book was literally meant for those African American soldiers who had, like him, served in France. Daly's work may be like Ernest Hemingway's *The Sun Also Rises* and *A Farewell to Arms* and F. Scott Fitzgerald's *The Great Gatsby*, intentionally distancing us from certain characters and refusing to provide certain seemingly relevant pieces of information because it is intended for a specific group of readers who, the author knows, will have special relationships to those characters and who can fill in the blanks from their own experience. Maybe Daly's "failure" to present believable or fully developed characters is a purposeful tactic meant to make possible an insider reader's special experience of the book: the black veteran reader can project himself onto Montie Jason and imagine Bob Casper as specific white officers he encountered.

Unlike his character Montie Jason, Daly was from the North, attended integrated public schools in New York City, and went to Cornell University. He was according to Davis, from "the northern black bourgeoisie," or the "talented tenth," as Du Bois called "this group of educated and advantaged people."[15] He was also one of the very select group of black commissioned officers trained at Fort Des Moines, the African American officers training camp that Montie applies to but is rejected from. Montie is unusual for being a college student, but his southern background and noncommissioned rank were much more representative of the black combat veteran experience than Daly's.

In fact, Montie's college-student status is something Daly seems to need so he can bring seamlessly into the story this token, segregated officers training camp, whose existence issued out of a controversial compromise between some African American leaders and the US government, which Du Bois also supported and many black commentators likewise denounced, since it involved accepting segregation.[16] More generally, Montie's college qualification and the Des Moines camp demonstrate the limited meritocratic opportunities for African Americans in the US army, despite its obvious and at times brutal discrimination. Montie's story involves encountering *both* the army's rabid racial discrimination as well as the restricted meritocratic opportunities it extended to black men, which makes his military experience not merely dreadful but schizophrenic.

Locke also faults Daly's novel for lacking "a poetic style."[17] But, again, the novel's fairly simple and straightforward diction—as well as its short length—might be devices to make the book accessible to as many black veterans as possible, many of whom had a minimal education. In an interview Daly gave years after the book's publication, he went out of his way to state, "My writing was not influenced by any Black authors." He said he had heard of Locke and James Weldon Johnson but had not read them in his last year at "an all white high school." He added that he went on to meet them both, but he made no comment about how he regarded them. With his own fiction, including *Not Only War*, he was up to something different from what other "Black authors" or writers associated with the Harlem Renaissance were doing.[18]

Daly would also have known that combat-veteran readers had particular vulnerabilities, and perhaps he was being sensitive to his primary audience. What Locke does not consider when he notes that *Not Only War* "fails to move" general readers is that its "unmoving" quality may not be a failure but instead a strategy on Daly's part not to move insider readers too much—causing them post-traumatic distress.

Like Hemingway's *A Farewell to Arms* or *The Sun Also Rises*, *Not Only War* has both a public and a private face. It tells a private story that is fully appreciated only by a particular audience. Hemingway is satisfying noncombatant readers embarrassed by their wartime experience who are looking to be validated and to have their demons exorcised rather than revisited—and he respects their needs for both privacy and affirmation (see chapter four). (As we saw in chapter two, John Dos Passos does not protect his noncombatant veteran readers of *Three Soldiers* in this way; he rehearses his and their anguish in excruciating psychological detail and, perhaps for this reason, puts a virtual coded warning at the beginning of his book.) Daly might well be, like Hemingway, respecting the privacy and sensitivity of a traumatized audience—not divulging the details and the extent of black veterans' suffering and trying to give them relief or catharsis, not further pain—in keeping the story from being too psychologically revealing or too "moving."

Daly refers to this pain in a short foreword to the book: he addresses not the "physical" hell of war, "branded . . . for all time" by William Tecumseh Sherman, but "another gaping, abysmal Hell": "a purgatory for the mind, for the spirit, for the soul of men" (3). The foreword's reference to the suffering depicted in the book may be intended, much like Dos Passos's epigraph, to let a specific traumatized potential reader know what he will be getting into in reading *Not Only War*. As with Dos Passos's untranslated epigraph, Daly's foreword seems to be both an invitation and a caution.[19] But perhaps Daly, in contrast to Dos Passos, is wording the book's second short message (the first, again, is that the book is "dedicated" to black veterans) in what is a carefully abstract and largely metaphorical manner, as a way of indicating that the suffering addressed will be handled sensitively by the author.

In addition, and unlike Hemingway, who was writing about something potentially traumatizing but not taboo, Daly had a story to convey about sexually crossing "the color line" that was, regardless of whether he wrote it with a particular traumatized audience in mind, simply too controversial to be explicitly or fully told in a public forum in 1930s America. He and his black veteran comrades had witnessed or undergone experiences of sexual "miscegenation"—as it was called by white Americans—that was specific to France, and a world away from what sexually crossing the color line entailed in the United States, and especially the South. Almost everything about this highly charged experience was different in France: A white woman could be frank and open about her willing role or involvement in a relationship with a black man. A white man would be shocked at this different reality and frustrated by his relatively limited power to punish the black participant (lynching an American soldier was not an option in France). A black participant would experience the complex effect of all of these differences. Therefore, Daly told this taboo story implicitly and, as it were, secretly. As a result, it is easy for a contemporary reader to miss a good deal of it. But because crossing the color line was central to the black soldier's experience in France, this implicit story would hardly have been lost on an African American veteran audience.

The foreword's allusion to the book's apparent subject—this other hell—is literal as opposed to metaphorical in one regard. It distinguishes the two ways one can enter into it: "actually born [into it] or unconsciously sucked" (3). Is Daly referring to the two different types of black soldiers who experienced the racist American army in France, namely those from the South and those from the North? Langston Hughes coined the phrase "Jim Crow shock," to describe the American Expeditionary Forces (AEF) experience of black soldiers who were not from the South.[20] This group would include Daly, who "had never been to the South when he wrote the book."[21] But given that both of the main characters are from the South—one black and one white—this foreword would thus be pointing to an experience (of being "unconsciously sucked" into this other "Hell") that properly belongs to no one in the book. It is possible that the foreword is not about the content of the book so much as it is about its intended readers. However, would Daly really want to say that northern black men did not know the hell of racial degradation before being "unconsciously sucked" into it by the experience of the army?

It seems more probable that, with this second means of entering into this other hell, Daly is describing not the black soldiers' experience in France but the white ones'. It can hardly be an accident that white soldier Bob Casper's last words in the book's last scene are, "war isn't the only hell I've been through lately" (69), practically quoting from the foreword. What Daly seems to be telling his black veteran readers before the story starts is that he is going to help them understand part of their experience in France, including the abuse they were subjected to there by the army, partly by shedding light on what the white soldiers went through.

Although Whalan's revelation of the special, colorblind quality of no-man's-land challenges a *strictly* sentimental understanding of the final scene of *Not Only War*, other problems of melodrama or believability remain.[22] The very fact that our black protagonist soldier encounters his white soldier nemesis wounded in no-man's-land seems, to a twenty-first-century reader, melodramatic or contrived. It seems simply too neat to be realistic, given that there has previously been an ugly conflict between these characters.

Recall that Casper is the man responsible for having Montie Jason court-martialed and deprived of his noncommissioned rank after he discovers that Jason is having a relationship with a white French woman. Yet Daly also does not reveal the charges on which Montie is court-martialed.[23] This omission adds to the book's sketchiness and seems to diminish the realism of the story, as this sort of lack of detail has the effect of reducing its verisimilitude. Montie had been ordered to billet at the white woman's house by his commanding officer—all the more reason why the grounds of the court-martial should be made clear. Given his southern racist background, Bob may not like Montie fraternizing with a white woman, but he presumably would have had to find some violation to charge him with.

A general reader, then or now, feels frustration at these omissions and contrivances. But what if we knew, as Daly's fellow black veteran readers would have, that "Daly based the last battle on his experiences with the [African American] 367th [Regiment] attempting to rescue two white units, one American and one French, whose attack had failed"—and that, specifically "for this action," all the troops in Daly's regiment were awarded the Croix de Guerre by the French?[24] The information changes our sense of the ending because now we know that this scene is not, at least in its broad outline, contrived but rather refers to a well-known actual event in which black troops went out to rescue white soldiers. Admittedly, it does not clear up the "contrived" quality of the ending completely; there is still the over-neatness of Montie encountering a white officer who has verbally abused him and had him officially punished for sexually crossing the color line.

But what if we knew, in addition, that predating this rescue mission, there was incredible, ongoing racial tension between white officers and African American troops within Daly's own Ninety-Second Division, and that this tension in fact centered on the issue of sex between black soldiers and French women? As Chad L. Williams writes in *Torchbearers of Democracy*, "Having survived the racial nightmare of the Ninety-second Division, Daly was more than familiar with the army's unjust treatment of black officers as well as white officers' paranoid obsession with restricting access to French women."[25] We know generally that "the protection of white womanhood, central to white male southern identity, traveled across the Atlantic and, with it, fears of black male sexuality as a threat to the stability of the domestic color line." But if we want to understand how a black veteran reader would have experienced Daly's book, and in particular the ending, we need to be more familiar with the specific racist tension that existed in the Ninety-Second Division—and understand that the rescue mission Daly obliquely represents inevitably took place in that environment. According to Williams,

> After an alleged wave of rapes and attempted rapes committed by black soldiers enflamed the sensitivities of American army officials, the Ninety-

> second Division came under obsessive scrutiny. The division, with its contingent of black officers and rigorously trained fighting men, became a potent symbol of black manhood and, as such, was cast as threat to white womanhood. The burden of proof consistently rested on the Ninety-second Division to provide evidence exonerating black soldiers . . . , even in situations where a white soldier had been identified by the victim. Within the gossip circles of the AEF's white officers, the Ninety-second became derisively labeled "the rapist division."[26]

American military officials released to French officers of the Ninety-Third Division an infamous memo entitled "On the Subject of Black American Troops," essentially informing them of Jim Crow and asking them to enforce it and to restrict fraternization with African Americans.[27] In the same vein, the commander of the Ninety-Second "produced an explicitly restrictive memo directed at his own men." Citing "the increasing frequency of the crime of rape, or attempted rape," by black soldiers, he implicitly accused black officers of failing to control their men and charged "white officers to take action": "*All* are expected to pull together to prevent the presence of colored troops being a menace to women." The commander, Maj. Gen. Charles Ballou, threatened that if the "rape" problem was not seriously addressed, Gen. John J. Pershing, commander of the AEF, would "send the 92d Division back to the United States, or break it up into labor battalions, as unfit to bear arms in France."[28] (Ballou had previously served as the commander of Fort Des Moines, where Daly himself was trained and commissioned; as commander, he had at times been beloved by his black trainees.[29]) He presented the warning and the charge to white officers to police their black charges as being "in the broader interest of the colored race."[30] Later, General Ervin, who succeeded Ballou in command of the Ninety-Second, issued "Order No. 40—a proclamation that Negroes should not speak with or to French women. Carrying out this order the Military Police overseas undertook to arrest Negroes found talking to French women."[31]

Historical facts corroborate the details of the novel's final scene. In the real mission for which Daly's regiment received the Croix de Guerre, African American soldiers, who had been harassed, abused, and threatened by white officers for their supposed sexual transgressions, ended up attempting to rescue wounded white American troops, a mission in which black soldiers died. In other words, the only poetic license that Daly *may* have taken with the setup of this final scene was to have his two *representative* characters of different races meet up, but that is just the sort of "heightening" or "compression" of a real situation that realistic literature engages in all the time. (For example, the three soldiers in Dos Passos's novel run into each other by chance at just about every stage in the course of his novel, more than randomness would seem to allow.)

And what of Daly's omission of the charge Montie faces at his court martial? Daly and his black comrades in the Ninety-Second knew that they could be arrested and court-martialed merely for talking to a French woman. Black veteran readers would have recognized the novel's action as reflecting a reality with which they were all too familiar.

The actual events to which Daly's book alludes were ugly and traumatic: the racist accusations and abuse by white officers certainly, but even the ultimate outcome of the heroic mission. As historian Adam P. Wilson comments, while the French awarded the black troops with distinguished medals, "the Americans rewarded them with a return to discrimination."[32] In the years following the war, Daly and many other African Americans who saw combat were traumatized veterans who had suffered not only from shell shock but also from "Jim Crow shock." Taking these psychological realities into account, it becomes more understandable why Daly waited more than a decade to write this novel. It was perhaps simply too painful early on, before a significant number of years had elapsed. The fact that the book is as schematic as it is has perhaps a similar explanation.

But even with all this insider knowledge, does the final scene still not seem sentimental, melodramatic, or wishful? Yes, the historical facts make realistic Montie's decision—which seems initially angelic—to put aside his "furious" feelings and risk his life to save the man who "had taken shelter behind his official rank to insult him . . . [and] had preferred charges against him, that had caused him to be court-martialed and reduced to the ranks" (68). But, arguably, Bob's reaction—even though he is sure to lose his leg and might lose his life, and despite the fact that Montie, in attempting to rescue him, takes a "risk [that Bob himself says] is too great"—still seems too good to be true. He says to Montie, "God, but you're a prince, . . . war isn't the only hell that I've been through lately" (69).

Bob's last words are taken to mean, as Adam P. Wilson puts it, that Bob has, even before this moment of sacrifice on Montie's part, experienced something on the order of a "desire but inability to abolish the racial hatred within himself."[33] Examples from other stories point us toward this interpretation. To return to Mark Whalan and his cataloging of climactic repentance scenes between African American and white soldiers in World War I:

> No-man's-land becomes a space of moral revelation, a transformative environment that, as Eric Leed has proposed, shares many similarities with

> those spaces used in various rites of passage, rites that often result in a "change of character." . . . All the writers see no-man's-land as a highly charged moral space; [Florence] Bentley [in "Two Americans" (1921)], [Jessie] Faucet [in *There Is Confusion* (1924)], and Daly, describe it has a "hellish" place of punishment and retribution, yet one where past sins are confessed and repented. . . . [A]ll of the white soldiers . . . have been guilty of harsh discrimination against African Americans, and all repent of this behavior. As [the white] murderer [of the black man's brother back in Georgia] in "Two Americans," says, "I'm thinkin' if those folks back home could see this Hell that hate has made over here—maybe they would get a light on some things."

Whalan finds such scenes, not only in Bentley's story and Faucet's novel, but also in African American writer Seamon Cotter Jr.'s "On the Fields of France" (1920), white writer Hendrik van Loon's "The Way of War" (1924), and white filmmaker D. W. Griffith's movie *The Greatest Things in Life* (1918).[34]

Is not Daly's sequence, like those in these other texts, a "highly formulaic" one "which imagines that racial injustice can be swept away by the shared experience of crisis and mutual danger"?[35] No wonder Wilson and other commentators conclude that Daly's ending is "hopeful . . . , suggesting the possibility of racial harmony."[36] It is, strictly speaking, possible that Bob is lying or exaggerating, caught up in the emotion of the moment. But, again, given that Daly puts in Bob's mouth (with the words "war isn't the only hell . . .") a version of the last line of the foreword, "Not only War is Hell," which itself echoes the novel's title, it seems hardly possible that these last words of the antagonist are not to be taken with the utmost seriousness.

The problem with our accepting Bob Casper's moral transformation is not that Bob thanks Montie for helping him or calls him "a prince"; whether he in addition thinks that Montie is a fool, he cannot help but feel the black man's nobility in this intense and life-threatening moment. The problem is not even that, in this heightened moment, he might fleetingly question his racism entirely and put some of his prejudices aside if he lived—probably holding on to others. It seems believable that injured white soldiers would "lose some of their prejudices in the extreme conditions of the battlefield, especially when faced with the selfless heroism of black soldiers," as Whalan puts it at one point.[37] The Gillem Board, which recommended abolishing segregation in the armed forces after World War II, discovered precisely this. The problem is that Bob seemingly claims that he has been through hell "lately" as a result of an inner conflict over his own racism, after his discovery of Montie with the French woman and before this present scene.

This apparent claim seems unbelievable, and thus Daly's ending is wishful or sentimental—unless Wilson and other commentators are not reading Bob's words in the right way. Maybe the "hell" Bob has been through has not been about wrestling with his racist beliefs.

But how could that possibly be? Are we supposed to imagine that Daly relies on a climactic but typical no-man's-land scene involving soldiers of the different races yet produces a fundamentally different result? There is good evidence to think so. To begin with, the timing or arc of Bob's transformation differs from the other stories Whalan cites, in which a moral conversion occurs entirely in the "charged moral space" of no-man's-land. Again, Bob has been going through "hell . . . lately." Moreover, on the battlefield, even though he is badly wounded and likely not to make it out, he never actually confesses past sins and never repents of them or even apologizes to Montie.

Also relevant is Daly's perspective as the scene's author. Some of the tales Whalan discusses appeared before Daly's book in *The Crisis*, a journal to which Daly himself contributed stories.[38] His 1950s claim that his "writing was not influenced by any Black authors" may be essentially true, but it is hard to imagine that he was unaware of those stories.

Remember that Daly, among all the artists that Whalan cites, is the only black veteran. In fact, Davis states that "very few, if any, black writers other than Victor Daly had actual experience in combat."[39] It is true that numerous African American veterans appeared in published works in the 1920s, but James Weldon Johnson nonetheless claimed in 1930 that "the Negro novel of the World War is still unwritten."[40] Davis explains that "no novel had yet featured a black soldier in active duty as a primary character. To that point, black soldiers had been depicted more as symbols than as characters. *Not Only War* is the African American novel of World War I."[41] The advertisement in *The Crisis* for *Not Only War* read "At Last! The Negro Novel of the World War."[42] Maybe this was not hype. Daly underwent and thus knew things about the black veteran experience that these other writers who depicted black veteran characters did not.

In a book that is regularly elliptical and only becomes comprehensible when we reestablish the specific historical context of the African American experience in France during World War I, which Daly alludes to but mostly withholds, perhaps because he is counting on his reader to know it, Bob's words—whose meaning seems obvious to us, as modern-day readers interpreting them either in Whalan's literary context or in a broader historical but less relevant context of American race relations over the last hundred years—may not mean what we think they mean. This is especially true with events and words in the novel that deal with the sexual crossing of the color line in France. That material, as Daly well knew, was largely taboo and could not be explicitly aired in a published work. We need to re-situate Bob's last words in their particular World War I context—including the limitations Daly faced regarding what could be written on this taboo subject. In perceiving that Bob's words have a self-evident meaning, we have in fact lifted them out of both that context and the text.

Whalan characterizes the climactic, battlefield-conversion scenes, while "formulaic" and "regularly lampooned by a later generation of writers," as deserving of further consideration because of "the way [they] defamiliarize American racial politics goes further than a liberal and patriotic faith in the supreme bond of a shared nationalism."[43] In particular, citing Richard Dyer, Whalan observes that the wounding of "the white male body, deeply threatening to the white imagination at the time, is indulged in by all of the authors of these narratives, and in nearly every work, this horror is exacerbated by the white soldier's helplessness in the hands of a black soldier." And citing British military historian Joanna Bourke, he adds that "for many men the experience of being wounded or maimed in conflict involved a dramatic loss of agency and physical ability that they understood in terms of becoming infantilized, feminized, or losing sexual potency." He continues: "The sudden removal from the privileged position in a whole series of dichotomies—adult/child, man/woman, sexual/non-sexual being—was configured in the *Crisis*, *Not Only War*, and *There Is Confusion* primarily in racial terms, as black soldiers took control of the lives of their incapacitated and passive white comrades."[44] In Daly's case, the "sudden removal from the privileged position" has already started for Daly's white soldier before he is wounded on the battlefield.

Bob's crisis of demotion, or his "hell," begins when he discovers Montie in a relationship with the French woman Blanche Aubertin. Bob is not lying when he says has been through hell lately, but he is not referring to a crisis of conscience either. He is referring to the fact that from that moment at Blanche's house, his status, and the white supremacist world he has counted on, has largely collapsed.

Chad Williams notes that, in its witch hunt for black-soldier rapists, the army leadership was having a hysterical reaction to the "potent symbol of black manhood" that the Ninety-Second Division represented, given "white male southern . . . fears of black male sexuality as a threat to the . . . color line."[45] Daly's novel echoes this theory and takes it even further by showing that this hysteria was exacerbated by the shock of finding themselves in a sexual competition with black soldiers for cultured and desirable white women, a competition they were losing.

That Daly's book has not regularly been seen this way is a salute to his presentation of this story entirely by showing rather than telling, with no authorial commentary—a procedure Hemingway or Stephen Crane would have approved of. Nevertheless, the sexual crossing of the color line and the sexual competition between Bob and Montie are absolutely central to Daly's novel—and, again, none of its significance would have been lost on a black veteran. This theme begins just half a dozen pages into novel, with Bob's meeting a "colored girl" (10) named Miriam, with whom he will become involved, and who just happens to be the first "girl in [Montie's] life . . . who made any difference" (22).

Bob's first meeting with Miriam is made possible by extraordinary wartime conditions, in that Bob would not usually, as he puts it to himself, "ride down to the Junction beside two niggers!" Though he finds Miriam "damned good looking" and wants to ride with her, in peacetime he would be constrained because "what would folks think" (10). But Bob needs to catch a ride because he is late for a train that will take him to meet a captain who will "fix it" so he can get into officers "Training Camp." The "competition would be keen" to get "appointed" to the camp, and, despite his privileged social status, Bob understands he is not guaranteed a place (9). But he also knows that he has a connection because of his exalted family, and, if he misses his train, "it may cost me my commission." Bob finally takes the ride because he figures that he can rationalize the generally unacceptable fraternization with black women on the basis of "an emergency of war." "Hell, during war-times folks do all sorts of things" (10–11).

But if the unusual wartime conditions make possible Bob's initial ride with Miriam, his sexual conquest of her—and his essentially winning out in the competition with Montie for her—is due to the status quo in the Jim Crow South. Miriam recognizes that "Southern white men . . . could only seek friendship with comely colored girls for one purpose—a social equality that existed after dark." However, Bob has the power to get her something she wants, as she is a teacher "restricted," because of her partial college education, to working for low pay in the "county schools of the south," and he is the "son of the Chairman of the School Board." If Miriam is unable to get a teaching job, she will be stuck doing "domestic service" for whites. (If Miriam's family had been better off financially, she could have finished college in the North and gotten a teaching job up there.) Though at first she imagines, naïvely it seems, that she can get Bob to help her without sleeping with him (25–27), they soon end up sexually involved.

The competition between Bob and Montie is obvious—though both are initially in the dark about the other, and Montie never learns about Miriam's involvement with Bob, though Montie's friend Roscoe does. Daly also makes it plain that Bob's dalliance with Miriam prevents her from developing a relationship with Montie, which seemed at the start of the book a sure thing. Because Miriam is busy with Bob, Montie literally cannot get a single date with her. "I've been here [to the place she's staying] five nights straight without getting any glimpse of you," Montie tells her. He asks her to give him one evening before he himself has to go off to camp—hopefully, the one officers training camp for black recruits at "Ft. Des Moines, Iowa." But she will not break her previous "engagement" with Bob, and Montie leaves, angry, aware that she is "dated up for to-night" (31–32). The next thing Montie hears about Miriam is that she has left town suddenly (38). He can only "conclude . . . bitterly that she had quit him cold" (39). Daly makes it abundantly clear that in the competition for Miriam, Bob's power as a high-status white man trumps anything Montie can mean to her—though she genuinely likes Montie, and he is offering her a serious relationship.

In this first round in the competition the book sets up between Bob and Montie, Bob wins at every turn. Bob receives his commission and gets Miriam just as he wants her, as "a helluva good buddy" (18). Meanwhile, Montie finds that "his name was not included in the quota that went from his state to the Officers Training Camp at Ft. Des Moines" (39), and he loses the opportunity to pursue a promising relationship with the only woman he has ever really cared about. If the competition for admission to training camp among white men is "keen," among African Americans, who have a single such camp and only one graduating class (1,200 candidates are admitted and 639 will succeed), it is stupendous. The first half of the book, which takes place in the United States, makes clear that the wartime "emergency" has hardly challenged "the supremacy of the white race" or Bob's belief in it (8). In particular, it has not threatened Bob's supremacy over Montie when it comes to access to military positions and black women.

But the sexual competition between Bob and Montie has a second round in France, which comes out quite differently, much to Bob's surprise and dismay. Something commentators have generally ignored is that Bob does not simply happen on Montie "socializing with white women" (59) and become "furious" merely over that. He has gone to Blanche Aubertin's house out of his own sexual interest in her. Bob has heard from a fellow officer that she is "the prettiest mamaselle in this town." He also learns that she is "the village high brow" and lives in a "big house" (56). "There was an air of refinement and culture about the place. Its location beyond the town smacked of aloofness. The high garden wall that enclosed it, clothed it with exclusiveness," Daly tells the reader. "One could see that they weren't ordinary peasants" (50). The reader has also learned that Blanche's father is off serving "in Paris with the Intelligence Service" (54). Perhaps critics have missed Bob's interest in Blanche because he was initially taking his fellow officer Warner to see her. But when the man passes out from drink, Bob decides to make his own approach to Blanche, planning to ask her to go on "a drive": "Here's where I put a fast one over on Warner. . . . What a lark!" he thinks (57–58).

Things begin to turn sour for Bob when Blanche informs him that Warner "insulted me . . . a few days ago. Now you want to insult me in my own home." Then, before he can apologize to her and explain, Montie appears, due to Blanche's raised voice. It is in this context—of seeking a sexual "lark" with the prettiest French woman in town, who is also rich, educated, and desired by his fellow white officers—that Bob gleans that Montie is already involved with her. Bob's subsequent reaction may be hysterical and racist, but he is not imagining things. Daly has let his reader know, with a light touch, that Montie and Blanche have slept together. He obliquely alludes to the fact in the line that follows on an evening of fairly intimate discussion between them and ends chapter 12: "Sergeant Jason did not report for duty quite so early the next morning" (55).

The situation becomes even more humiliating for Bob when, due first to being in Blanche's presence and second to Montie's being there in the house on the authority of his "Company Commander," Montie answers Bob's hostile questions in a "cool manner," then with "asperity," and finally talks back to him with barely suppressed rage, "I see . . . , you carry your dirty southern prejudice with you everywhere you go" (58–59).

Bob insults Montie, calling him a "nigger" (59), and he threatens to have him reduced to ranks. He has the last word between them. And he retains the power to court-martial Montie. But his victory is, significantly, limited. To begin with, as Davis crucially points out, Bob's ability to take vengeance on Montie is restricted from the extremes it would take at home—both men know that in the South Montie would be lynched.[46] However, the undermining of Bob's usual southern prerogatives as a white man go much further.

While Bob can still officially strike back at Montie, in this confrontation, which takes place entirely with Blanche there, Bob's humiliation is deepened and his ultimate defeat is effected, in terms of his competition with Montie over her, when she tells him unmistakably "to leave my house" (58–59). To say the least, this is not how things would play out with a rich, educated white woman in the South discovered with a black man she is clearly involved with. In this situation, the high-class white woman—shockingly for the white man—prefers the African American man, and rejects the white man, shames him, and sends him away. Bob does not even have the power to immediately remove Montie from Blanche's home. And while Bob gets the last word in the argument, the sequence does not end there, or on a high note for Bob. Daly adds to the end of the chapter a single, understated line that conveys the extent of the psychological impact this event has had on Bob: "Miriam's weekly letter to Bob went unanswered that night" (59).

Miriam had been the prize Bob had won in a competition with Montie that Bob was cognizant of. Bob knows who Montie is, evidently because Miriam has told him. Probably because Miriam has asked Bob to do so—out of guilt over her treatment of Montie—Bob has pushed for Montie's promotion, and now Bob says, "I had those chevrons put on your sleeve" (59). But at this point, after the confrontation with Montie in France, Bob can only feel—due to his own warped racism—that Miriam is not much of a prize compared to the high-class, white Blanche (whose whiteness Daly hammers home by giving her a name that in French means "white"). He can only feel that Montie has beaten him out for the real prize. It is no wonder that he does not write Miriam that night: she has been devalued for him, now that he cannot help but compare her to Blanche.

Bob's previously absolute confidence in his own superiority has, as a result of the sequence at Blanche's house, been badly damaged. That assault on Bob's ego may well tarnish his sense of his conquest of Miriam. Bob can hardly avoid realizing, after he experiences Blanche's preferring a black man to him, that he won the competition for Miriam on the basis of his powerful social connections, through his father, not on the grounds of some innate attractiveness and superiority based on his whiteness. Bob's own racial scale of values has exploded in his face, disfiguring him in his own eyes, which is why, in the foreword, Daly refers to Bob's way of entering the mental or spiritual hell of racism as being "unconsciously sucked" into it (as opposed to "born" into it). Bob did not realize that his own white supremacist beliefs could make him vulnerable to a sudden vertiginous loss of self-confidence. All he had to do was encounter an educated white woman outside of American culture.

The racial reversal, in which the hierarchy is turned on its head, goes even further. Bob's painful experience, in which his own racism is turned back on him, is intensified by the fact that Blanche judges him—and indeed stereotypes him—in part on the basis of his skin color and the social position that comes with it. The "terrible mistake" that Bob feels has "been made" (58) by Blanche about his intentions with her is, in fact, based on a prejudice that Blanche has developed about white officers, which Bob essentially confirms:

there has been no mistake from her point of view. Her experience with the American army in France has, before Bob shows up, taught her two things about white men that she is displeased with: First, "all the [American] officers were white men" because they have evidently, and arbitrarily and unjustly, in her eyes, excluded black men. Second, these white officers, again acting out of an arrogant but apparently undeserved sense of their own superiority, do not treat French women with respect but rather see them as available for casual sex. Bob's friend Charlie Warner has insulted her on the street, by stopping her, asking her name and her place of residence, and also condescendingly calling her "keed" (kid). The first fact makes her "frown" and the second makes her "indignant" (54). When Bob uses Charlie's name as a calling card with Blanche and offers to take her out, he not only associates himself with the man who has insulted her, he insults her again, in her own house, by assuming it is acceptable to come, as a perfect stranger, with no proper introduction to the house of a well-bred or "nice" French woman and ask her out on a date—seeming to treat her, and perhaps indeed treating her, much as a Frenchman would treat a "common" working-class or peasant woman. With his southern white arrogance, intensified by his status as an officer in a country he is defending, Bob does not think to consider that he is operating in a foreign culture, with its own upper-class mores and sensibilities.

Bob is, in fact, not exactly the same as Warner; as soon as he grasps that Blanche was insulted by his friend, he wants to issue "an apology" (58). And this is precisely the point—that Bob *is* different, but it makes no difference in Blanche's eyes. Whatever Bob's intentions were, he has been sullied in Blanche's mind by his status as a white officer and his association with the rude one that she has encountered. She judges Bob on the basis of the stereotype she has of white American officers—notwithstanding that he never shows her anything that would dissuade her from the first impression he gives her by "mistake." Just after he thinks of apologizing, Montie shows up, and then he behaves in a bullying, arrogant, and uncouth fashion that only confirms her impression.

Daly's depiction of white American officers' casual and forward treatment of French women is, by all accounts, based in reality: it jibes with portrayals by contemporary white authors, including soldier-writers, as well as those of historians. Dos Passos and Willa Cather depict soldiers who discuss the looseness of French women generally and look for or find opportunities for casual sex with them. Laurence Stallings and Maxwell Anderson's fantastically successful play *What Price Glory?* is to a large degree a "comedy" centered on two profane-talking American officers involved with the same French woman, Charmaine, the daughter of the local tavern owner in the town where they are stationed. When the old Frenchman they call "Cognac Pete" comes to demand from one of them both marriage for his daughter and money, he says: "the Americans arrive. They are big and strong, and they always demand [or take] what they want. They are not accustomed to our mores or practices, but—for God sake!—why do they choose the one flower of my life [his daughter], when they can find [sex] anywhere with the prostitutes who want them."[47] As historian Joshua S. Goldstein flatly puts it in his *War and Gender* (2001), "Doughboys behaved badly towards French women."[48]

Daly's depiction of the reversal here that shocks and debilitates Bob—that many French women came to prefer black soldiers to white ones—is also factually based. Williams documents that French townspeople, most of whom were women (the men were "dead, maimed or at the front"), were generally apprehensive at first about black American soldiers, based on French prejudices about black French-colonial Africans as well as white American racist propaganda. However, "after interacting with African American soldiers, many French civilians began to discard these racial stereotypes." As one black soldier wrote, "the people found us different and learned to love us."[49]

Daly seems to concisely represent this process. When Montie first shows up at the Aubertins' house, Blanche's grandmother greets him, and she is initially scandalized by his asking for a room to sleep in. "'Non, non, officier,' cried the old woman, making ready to close the door." She has been told that only white officers will be billeted in her house, and she describes Montie to Blanche, who is inside the home, as "'Un noir,' . . . then by way of further explanation, she added, 'un Americain.' Montie smiled to himself . . . , 'A nigger first—an American afterwards.'" But almost immediately, the old woman's attitude changes; when she realizes that he speaks some French, she "showed unusual surprise—and interest" (50–51). In addition, Montie does not behave in a pushy or arrogant way, but, aware of the awkwardness of the situation that the French women have been put in (given that they were misled that only commissioned officers would be billeted with them), he acts "very hesitantly" and with extreme politeness (50).

"[T]he generally fond view the French had of African American soldiers did not come from a natural proclivity toward racial equality on their part," writes Chad Williams. Rather, "One [of] the most significant factors in shaping how the French interacted with and viewed African Americans was their contentious relationship with white American soldiers. White soldiers . . . held French civilians in low regard. They accused

French merchants of intentionally inflating prices and, even more unsettling, refusing to conform to American racial customs. The behavior of some white Americans reflected their national and racial arrogance, causing many French merchants and hostesses to prefer the *soldats noirs*."[50] Black officer Lester Granger remembered, "The French liked the Negro officers better than they did white American officers, because . . . we were 'plus gentil.' The average white American in France in that day—so far as I could see—was the advance cartoon of the bumptious American overseas today [in 1940]. Almost none knew any French. A number of us did know quite a bit. Almost none was interested in the culture, in the history, in the monuments of France. They herded around in public places and made remarks and made passes." A black officer named Charles Houston concurred: "The general contrast between our attitude and the typical attitude of the white officers was so great that the townspeople took our side and after we had been in the district a month all the lies the white officers tried to spread about us fell on deaf ears." Still another black soldier, Walker Jordan, enjoyed seeing a French storekeeper turn away white soldiers, telling them, "Allez! Allez! Le blanc soldat no bon—ugh! [Go! Go! The white soldier no good—ugh!]"[51] Lieutenant Osceola McKaine wrote of his—and Daly's—367th regiment, "The Buffaloes [the nickname of that regiment] have been tres polit and have made friends."[52] In Daly's novel, black veterans would have recognized Blanche's very different reactions, to Montie on the one hand and Bob and his white friend Warner on the other, as typical.

Montie's and Blanche's becoming sexually involved was also reflective of the black veteran experience. As Williams reports, "In a . . . 1918 letter to his church in Chicago, 370th Infantry chaplain William Bradden wrote that some of the regiment's men had 'fell willing victims to cupid and married even though they knew more about the French language than I do about an Aeroplane.' In his reply to the United States Military Institute survey question, 'was there much consorting with local women,' a black veteran of the 317th Ammunition train [of Daly's Ninety-Second Division] responded: 'Yes a plenty.' "[53] Daly himself wrote in the black journal *The Messenger*, "over one thousand Negro stevedores intermarried with white French girls."[54] While this number is almost certainly wildly inaccurate when it comes to literal marriages, Daly was probably using "intermarried with" as a euphemism for had intimate relationships with. This is also how Williams, one of the leading experts on the African American soldier experience in World War I France, interprets Daly's comment. Statistics are not available, but in regard to sexual relationships, Daly's number is plausible.[55] Second Lt. James B. Morris summed up the situation succinctly when he wrote in his memoirs, "It seemed ironic that white women whom we would be lynched for looking at back home were throwing themselves at us over here."[56] While we are familiar with the phenomenon of black artists, and specifically musicians and writers, expatriating to France after the World Wars to escape American racism, the number of black soldiers who expatriated to France after World War I was actually quite small. Though of "important symbolic value," "their presence most likely numbered less than two dozen," according to Williams.[57] Meanwhile, we are less familiar with the phenomenon of interracial relationships during the war.[58]

Not Only War depicts—cryptically, to be sure, for the general reader but quite obviously for a black veteran—how the racial politics in France cut both ways. Sometimes the white soldiers and officers ended up psychologically bloodied as well. Montie, especially on the day of the court-martial instigated by Bob, experiences in France the "Hell on Earth" that was racism and concludes, "Prejudice was here to stay" (62). But Bob, too, as Daly enigmatically indicates in the final scene, has, as a consequence of their meeting at Blanche's house, "been through" his own "hell." In addition, Daly explores in these reversals in France the way the black veteran experience is not only hell—not only Jim Crow degradation and abuse.

While no-man's-land might have been the only zone where race was erased, there was another domain in France where the "playing field" of the racial power-game was largely leveled: in American soldiers' relationships with the French citizens. Historians Williams and Jennifer Keene both cite a story related by Charles Houston, a black officer, that resembles some of the "crossing-the-color-line" action of Daly's novel.

> Two French 'sporting girls' had spurned their white American officer companion for a black officer who drew their interest by his ability to speak French. The white captains, incensed, confronted the uppity black lieutenant. Houston and another officer happened to be passing by and observed the argument. Seemingly out of nowhere, two trucks "loaded with white enlisted men," led by one of the aggrieved white officers, arrived on the scene with orders to lynch the African American officers. It was around 10:30 or 11:00 at night, in a deserted plaza save for the presence of four black officers and a mob of white soldiers, and southern-style racial justice had again reared its ugly head on French soil.[59]

Houston continues: "The officer who led the mob began to yelp about 'niggers' forgetting themselves just because they had a uniform on, and it was time to put 'a few in their places,' otherwise the United States would not be a safe place to live after they get back. The enlisted men were milling around us. None offered us any violence, possibly because it is a most serious offense in the Army for an enlisted man to strike an officer, and these men were not sure they could get away with it." Keene adds, "Houston and his comrades took advantage of their hesitation to argue that as officers" they would not, as Houston put it, have "anything to do with enlisted men, but that there were four white officers and four of us, and they could either fight it out one by one or all together so long as it was an officers' fight."[60] "The exchange grew more heated with the whites claiming they would not lower themselves by fighting 'niggers' and the blacks countering that the white officers were cowards. A white captain from the military police finally arrived to lecture the officers 'on disgracing the uniform in a public brawl and order us back to our hotels,' Houston recalled."[61]

Keene concludes: "It is hard to imagine a group of aroused working-class whites hesitating to attack middle-class black professional men because they feared serious repercussions from the civilian criminal justice system. Civilian lynch mobs during the war killed 36 and 60 African Americans in 1917 and 1918, respectively, including several black soldiers home on leave. Only one charge of an intra-military lynching, however, ever surfaced. . . . [T]he record of one known intra-military lynching as compared to 96 civilian mob killings suggests that the military was a safer place than civilian society to challenge the racial status quo."[62]

The American military brass could instruct the French to avoid fraternization with black soldiers; it could order black soldiers themselves to cease such fraternization; it could order white officers to police such fraternization; it could punish black soldiers with court-martial for fraternizing with white women; it could threaten to cashier or send home entire divisions if the fraternization did not cease. But, as Houston's story, and many other such firsthand accounts demonstrate, the military was not willing to allow—and did not permit—white soldiers and officers to use violence against black men in uniform, for they had the status of members of the US Army. Meanwhile, much of the French citizenry, which, again, was mostly female, did not care to be told by the American military authorities how to behave in their own country (perhaps especially toward soldiers that were, as they saw it, fighting and dying for France). Thus, fraternization did not stop. As Williams puts it, "Black soldiers, consciously defying their superiors, found interracial democracy, so to speak, in the company of French women."[63]

Houston's true story and Daly's novel both indicate that World War I France was for black soldiers—despite the intense and often hysterical racism of the white military brass, officers at the front, and noncommissioned soldiers—not solely a place of abuse and indignity. Daly's book suggests, and recent military historians such as Keene, Williams, and Wilson have shown, that it is not quite right to say, as the 1974 study *The Unknown Soldiers: Black American Troops in World War I* did, that the war meant nothing but more of the same in terms of the "humiliation and degradation of black Americans."[64] France was also a space of limited black empowerment.

It is no coincidence that some historians date the Harlem Renaissance from February 17, 1919, the day that returning black soldiers of the 369th Infantry Regiment, called the Harlem Hellfighters—marched up Fifth Avenue in New York City to Harlem, where they received a hero's welcome from an "interracial" crowd of "black and white New Yorkers."[65] Nor is it a coincidence that Daly himself, after the war, "devoted his life to securing civil rights for African Americans." As Davis puts it, "the book itself marks the struggle for civil rights before the movement."[66]

But the tendency among historians and literary critics has been to see the postwar civil rights agitation as a reaction to the experience of racism in the American army, a construction of events that misses something important. Keene suggests that African American political agitation began with soldiers' actions while in the army. She explains how things are generally viewed:

> In 1919, W. E. B. Du Bois penned an editorial for *The Crisis* entitled "Returning Soldiers" in which he urged black veterans of the First World War to make their dismal encounters with unrelenting racism in the wartime army count by taking up the cause of civil rights. . . . Nearly every discussion of black soldiers' experiences uses Du Bois's exhortation to explain the mood of this disillusioned generation of black veterans who injected a more insistent and militant tone into the postwar civil rights movement. This widely accepted narrative connects the individual wartime suffering of soldiers in a racist American army to veterans' postwar collective political activism.

Keene goes on to offer a more complex narrative: "Rather than waiting until they left the army to begin their fight for civil rights, many of the 380,000 African American soldiers who served during the First World War engaged in that struggle from the moment they put on the uniform. Black soldiers staged work slowdowns, ignored orders restricting their contact with French civilians, challenged white authority openly, wrote individual letters of protest, and signed petitions in collective efforts to better their conditions within the military."[67]

Keene's correction of the timeline for the intensification of civil rights agitation is not just a matter of getting the dating right. Part of the reason for this wartime outpouring of black resistance and protest was that, as Keene also shows, "black soldiers faced fewer risks than black civilians who violated the racial status quo."[68] Beyond enjoying certain basic rights as soldiers that African American civilians in the South did not have, some black soldiers also experienced other positive wartime opportunities provided by an undeniably racist army. That some black soldiers were trained in arms and put into combat, that some were made officers, that some were given the chance, whether they were combat soldiers or not, to visit a foreign country and people that did not have a history of slavery and Jim Crow meant that many African American soldiers had a mixed wartime experience that was not merely dismal and humiliating but also empowering and confidence building. Their horribly demeaning army treatment *provoked* many to become politically active, during the war or after, but the rights and opportunities that their limited meritocratic and mostly discriminatory participation in the army nonetheless provided also gave many a pride, status, and awareness that at the same time *inspired* a more militant and insistent civil rights agitation.

Daly had before the war experienced little in the way of the hardships of discrimination, "with the exception of his limited career opportunities," as editor Davis remarks.[69] And, as Williams concludes, his "racial and political consciousness [was] significantly hardened" by the experience of the army's racial discrimination in France. Yet Daly's World War I experience was also affirming in some ways. In addition to the African American reception by the French, which he witnessed and wrote about in the novel, he was, as mentioned, one of the few to be selected for officers training camp, the most significant meritocratic opportunity the army offered to black men. He was also in the successful half of the training class that graduated from the program. He even seemed to have had an unusually encouraging experience of "interracial solidarity" at training camp. Davis reports that Daly "wrote exuberant letters back to his [college] fraternity brothers from camp telling them, for example, that 'the spirit that exists between white & black troops is A#1, they mingle freely and exchange mutual help to an almost amazing degree.'"[70] Meanwhile, Daly's plans for political activism probably began during the war, in the company of other black officers. Williams suggests that Daly "more than likely took part or was at least privy to the secret meetings held by Osceola McKaine and other fellow officers of his regiment," members of the Ninety-Second Division who started in France the League for Democracy—"officers . . . (all colored) . . . interested in the formation of a secret organization or society among all colored troops in the A.E.F. whose object is the promotion of social equality between colored and white after demobilization," as an alarmed US Military Intelligence Division report put it.[71]

Southern politicians' alarm at African American participation in the army, limited and discriminatory though that participation was, may have been virulently racist but it was by no means delusional: these white supremacist officials understood that putting African Americans in uniform, arming them, making even a limited number of them officers, and introducing them to a people who did not share America's particular race prejudice would be a threat to the Jim Crow status quo. It is also no coincidence that the African American regiment that marched up Fifth Avenue on February 17, 1919, was one that saw combat, fought with the French, was under French command, and included more than 100 men who won French or American medals, including the first two Croix de Guerre medals awarded to US soldiers.[72] As Arthur George Gaston, a member of the 317th Ammunition Train of Daly's Ninety-Second Division, recalled, the French accepted "Negro soldiers as equals of any other soldiers and of themselves." He found France "different for a Negro," where he "could be accepted as an equal, as a friend." The result was that "I could feel it surge in me . . . this new sense of confidence, of being equal."[73]

Critics have assumed that Daly's decision to end the book with his two characters dead with "their arms about each other" (70) is a straightforward one: that he simply wanted to leave the reader with a "hopeful" final image, "suggesting the possibility of racial harmony."[74] The fact that Montie is "perfectly safe" (68) before he decides to try to save Bob's life emphasizes the African American sacrifice that was made in the war cause. Although the ending delivers those messages, it is also more complex.

First of all, if Montie and Bob have reconciled, it is not only because Montie risks his life to save Bob's but because Bob has, due to the social conditions in France, been on the receiving end of his own vicious racism. They now have shared the experience of hell that Daly mentions in the foreword and Bob refers to in the last scene. It is hardly to be overlooked that it is the white character who is given, at the end of the book, the climactic line, "war isn't the only hell that I've been through lately." Montie apparently understands what Bob means: "'Don't worry about that now. Here we go,' said Montie, cheerfully" in response (69). Maybe that "cheerfully" is not only a way of spurring a wounded Bob on but also represents Montie's inevitable satisfaction upon discovering that Bob, too, has suffered from the racism he abused Montie with. Montie may be "a prince" (69), but he is also only human.

Second, perhaps Daly wants to end Montie's story not only by underlining the black soldiers' bravery, nobility, and sacrifice but by leaving us with a scene of African American agency and empowerment. Montie's wartime journey has reflected the strange mix of meritocratic and social opportunity, on the one hand, and abusive discrimination, on the other, that black soldiers experienced in France. He wants to be a commissioned officer, and though the "camp examination" shows that he is "physically fit," he is also considered "awfully young" (36), so he is rejected, which was almost inevitable given the limited number of candidate spots open to black men. He does not want to end up in a "labor battalion" but rather as a soldier with a chance to "work my way up through the ranks and get a commission, after all" (39). By enlisting, he partially succeeds in this quest. He gets promoted to corporal and then sergeant partly because Bob puts in a good word for him—"he's pretty well educated. I think he'd make a darn good non-com" (41)—but also partly because he is an able soldier whom his lieutenant works closely with. (He never makes commissioned officer though this was possible, and nearly 600 more African Americans got a commission beyond those of the Des Moines segregated officers training camp, making the total of such black officers in the US army during World War I around 1,200.)[75] He wants to get out of the South and eventually overseas, and he does get "a trip to New York" (39) and makes it to Europe. In France, he experiences an equality with a French woman that many African American soldiers referred to in their letters and memoirs. When Bob verbally assaults him, he confidently stands up for himself, and he gets to see Blanche stand up for him as well, telling Bob to get out of her house. He is also unceremoniously court-martialed on Bob's authority.

By ending with this last scene on the battlefield, we are left with Bob psychologically and physically diminished and Montie in a position of superiority on both of these levels. He makes the choice whether to help Bob or consign him to certain death; he has the physical power to help him, and he gets the psychological validation of learning that Bob has been mentally brutalized by his own racist beliefs.

Montie's story might have gone on. Montie says to himself after his court-martial that "Prejudice was here to stay," and he has certainly learned—as his friend Roscoe warned him from the start—that black service in the war was not going to wipe out discrimination. But what that would mean for many black veterans was that the fight against prejudice—the other "Great Conflict" Daly refers to in his subtitle—which predated the war and intensified during it, would go on afterward, with redoubled effort and boldness on their part.

Daly could have incorporated some of his postwar experience into Montie's story. Daly himself was decorated for his participation in his regiment's rescue mission of white French and American troops. He survived the war and returned home to the United States where his experience of and battle against discrimination continued. He wrote articles in 1919 and 1920 educating "American citizens about African Americans' role in the conflict" and calling attention to housing discrimination against black New Yorkers.[76] In 1921 he won a discrimination suit against a restaurant in New York City that "had refused him, his wife, and his mother-in-law service." In 1934, a couple of years after he published *Not Only War*, "he joined the US Department of Labor, where he worked to integrate retail stores and transportation systems."[77] He would be employed there for the next thirty years.

Daly's decision to end Montie's journey with death on a French battlefield was neither idealistic nor fatalistic. He surely wanted to honor those black veterans who made the ultimate sacrifice, some of whom had died trying to save white troops. But he also wanted to end on a moment and in a place where blacks and whites were more nearly equal and both vulnerable—not simply in the hell of combat but also in that other social hell into which Montie was born in the segregated South and into which Bob got unconsciously sucked outside of the United States in a foreign country that neither knew nor respected Jim Crow.

CHAPTER TEN

Too Glorifying to Tell

The Unspeakable in William March's *Company K* and Hervey Allen's *Toward the Flame*

William March's *Company K* (1933) and Hervey Allen's *Toward the Flame: A Memoir of World War I* (1926) seem completely different sorts of books. *Company K* is a novel with 113 chapters, each narrated by a different soldier, covering all phases and aspects of the American soldiers' experience from training camp to transport ship to combat to postwar life. *Toward the Flame* is a continuous "personal narrative" of one soldier recounting a single "drive from the Marne to the Vesle during the fateful months of July and August, 1918."[1] But the two books have a striking commonality in that they are both strangely silent on the issues and experiences of personal and social promotion, affirmation, and opportunity in the new army. This silence is odd since the authors both experienced such validation, and for both of them it is hard to believe that military validation was not meaningful. March came from a poor family, and his service with the Marines opened doors for him after the war that fairly quickly led to his becoming a successful and wealthy man. Allen had matriculated at, but failed to graduate from, the Naval Academy. His stint in World War I was actually a return to the US army: he had previously served in the 1916 skirmish with Mexico.[2] In unraveling the riddle of these books' shared silence, it turns out to be revealing to look at them together.

Both books also share extremely unusual narrative tactics. Again, March's book has over one hundred separate narrators; Allen's abruptly ends midscene in the midst of a perilous battle sequence—the reader can infer that something terrible has happened but does not know exactly what. Are these two shared aspects—one concerning excluded content, the other concerning highly distinctive stylistic devices—somehow related?

As we saw in part I, the male Lost Generation or noncombatant writers (with the exception of E. E. Cummings) were tortured by having essentially been denied, or demoted from, the social privilege that they had always previously enjoyed on the basis of their familial, ethnic, and economic backgrounds. John Dos Passos, Ernest Hemingway, F. Scott Fitzgerald, and William Faulkner wrote fairly straightforwardly in their early works about these embarrassing or emasculating experiences. In their later works they continued to address them, albeit in cryptic or oblique ways, attempting to come to terms with them by transposing them.

The combatant writers, of various social backgrounds, had different responses to their meritocratic validations and thus showed their protagonists experiencing these successes very differently. Thomas Boyd, who had a disadvantaged upbringing, has his protagonist, Hicks, thrilled at times by the recognition of his abilities. Laurence Stallings, who grew up middle class, had a main character, Plume, from a similar social background, and a narrator who both seem confused by or uncomfortable with the achievement of rank and medals. Victor Daly's Montie is willing to join a racist military in the hopes of the black community being rewarded with equality. He is glad to be personally promoted, but his friend Roscoe sees the army as fundamentally exploitative of black people. Roscoe seems also to register his distrust of the meritocratic tokenism that can seduce Montie into fighting a "white man's war" by jokingly calling Montie "Major-general."[3] And Roscoe's wariness is validated when Montie is unjustly court-martialed and demoted out of racist prejudice. All these authors address issues of meritocracy, even if, in *Plumes*, the text is itself contradictory on the subject.

March and Allen go out of their way to avoid these issues entirely, though both authors were promoted and decorated. March ended up a sergeant and Allen a first lieutenant, and both received the Croix de Guerre. March got major US Army citations as well, including the Distinguished Service Cross (second only to the Congressional Medal of Honor).

Perhaps Allen, used to social affirmation and meritocratic recognition within his upper-middle-class milieu, was not impressed by his officer rank and decoration and thus kept silent on the subject of military status. He went to an "exclusive boys' prep school" then attended college at the University of Pittsburgh, and his postwar success, which was eventually tremendous, was not dependent on his connection to the military. But his background also indicates that he cared about the military from his youth. He attended the Naval Academy at Annapolis, though he did not finish there because of a stomach problem three years into his studies that caused him to fall below the required weight. By the time the United States entered World War I, he had served in a National Guard unit in the border war with Mexico and participated in the war "preparedness" movement as a college student. (While at university, "during a demonstration of campus pacifists, he [even] commandeered a cannon and fired it to express his disgust.")[4]

As for March, his father was a "timber cruiser" in Florida, and his parents "were, from all accounts, poor and had to struggle to raise their large family" of eleven children, two of whom died in infancy. March, born in 1893, "obtained very little consistent education, and then mainly in small backwoods schools" in sawmill towns.[5] He left home at 16 and never finished high school. He put himself through two years of college but could not afford to finish. His army experience involved not only a striking affirmation for a young man from an impoverished background; it led to important postwar opportunities that dramatically changed his socioeconomic status.[6]

In a preface to the 1934 edition of *Toward the Flame*, Allen revealed that he purposefully attempted to be unconcerned with issues of pride and status when writing his memoir. He explained there that he had "tried, insofar as anyone can, to eliminate the big 'I' of little ego and to substitute for it only the first person singular of the fellow who happened, under certain circumstances, to be around" (xxii). Perhaps we can see a similarity here to *Plumes*: Richard Plume, who, like Allen, is an officer, is clearly uncomfortable with his concern about rank and medals. But Stallings nevertheless addresses rank and medals, and thus we are able to get a sense of the source of Richard's discomfort: he is the first Plume to experience a meritocratic army, and that change in military organization makes it impossible for him to behave like the forefathers he emulates. Meanwhile, Allen never fully discloses why he decided to exclude "the big 'I' of little ego." Perhaps in that slightly mocking descriptor we can read a discomfort with "ego" that is similar to Richard's, but, nonetheless, and in distinction to the case in *Plumes*, we do not get hints as to the origin of that unease.[7]

Allen asserts that his aim in writing the book was to give a "*cross section of the citizens in arms*." He did not want to relate a "personal adventure," but instead to objectively report events experienced by "one of many of the National Guard units of the American army," from an impersonal point of view (xxii, emphasis in original).

But strange aspects of Allen's text indicate that something more is at issue here. Allen gives the impression that he would have been more comfortable excluding himself entirely from the book, if that were somehow possible in a memoir. A weirdly apologetic, tautological line in the original

1926 preface reads, "As a personal narrative told in the first person it is only natural that I appear in it myself" (xx). The author's excuse for appearing in his own "personal narrative" makes the reader aware that something *unnatural* might be at work.

Moreover, Allen's dedication to limiting his personal involvement in his own narrative goes beyond eliminating his ego, or else his definition of ego is quite broad—whichever is the case, this makes his book very different from Stallings's. It is also makes it, in one particular way, downright bizarre for readers. Allen's story ends midscene, with the narrator and his men under attack at a village called Fismette, one of them crying "Oh! God!" (277). In the original edition, which literally ends with the sentence "*Here ends this narrative*," the reader would have to infer or even guess that Allen stopped here because at this juncture he got wounded. The only explanation in the original preface is that the story is "broken off when the film burned out" (xx).

In the 1934 preface of a reissued edition, whose "personal narrative" still ended midscene, Allen offered up that he followed the rule "When the fighting ends the story stops" in delimiting his narrative, which led to its radically abrupt ending. Thus in stark contrast to *Plumes*, Allen, as he also explained in 1934, "did not inflict upon my readers certain personal sufferings and physical indignities that followed." Allen in fact held back in 1926 *all* of the "sufferings and . . . indignities that followed," not just "certain" ones; in addition, the reader of the original publication never even finds out how he was wounded or how he got out alive—though one might imagine that his wounding and escape form part of "the story . . . [of] the night attack on the village of Fismette," with which he claims to have "ended the story." How he got out, in particular, is all the more mysterious because, as the reader of the 1926 edition understood, "most of the defenders of that place had ceased to exist." Allen's reason for excluding these events was, as he explained in 1934, "I felt that [what followed after the narrative cuts off was] important to me alone" (xxii–xxiii).

Many readers of Allen's 1926 book did not see it that way, after having spent more than two hundred pages in the company of the author. As he admits in the 1934 preface, he had in the eight-year interval received "many letters and innumerable questions as to what *did* happen to me" (emphasis in original). His reply is brief and elliptical:

> in the early morning hours after the attack, and in the company of one sergeant, I managed to return to headquarters where I was promptly tagged by our regimental surgeon and sent to a base hospital.

> To him, and to that surgeon, whoever he was, who in a certain field hospital saved my eyes from the effect of mustard gas and tended other injuries, I should like at this time to express what the word "gratitude" only too coldly conveys. But that is another story. (xxiii)

Readers of either the 1926 or 1934 edition could not help but be struck by Allen's abrupt ending and his discomfort including anything that smacked remotely of ego or pride, including basic self-concern. But neither preface explains Allen's *personal* motivations behind these choices, especially as his assumption that the story of his wounding was "important to me alone" proved to be so mistaken.

William March does not draw attention to the personal exclusions he has made. There is no preface that explains why he has produced a novel with 113 separate narrators. But clearly his overall storytelling strategy is striking. Faulkner is famous for his multiple narrators, but when it comes to sheer numbers, March considerably outdoes the more renowned modernist-experimentalist author. And while critics have paid attention to March's obvious intention to give every member of a fictional army company a voice, and thus to attempt to achieve a certain objectivity, or an appearance of objectivity, they have not paid attention to the exclusions of his own personal story that the book entails. March inserts bits and pieces of his own experience into the book by attributing them to some of his 113 fictional soldiers. His biographer, Roy S. Simmonds, identifies the most salient of these cases. But what Simmonds does not do (and again no critic has done) is to identify or examine those aspects of March's own remarkable story that he leaves out entirely. Exploring these aspects seems all the more called for because, in talking to people about some of those experiences, March manifested curious behavior—and had seemingly conflicted attitudes. This curious behavior is something Simmonds does report.

March criticized Erich Maria Remarque's *All Quiet on the Western Front* (1929), at the time seemingly "the war book to end all war books"—as Simmonds calls it—as not entirely successful because "the German author had confined himself mainly to the experiences of one man, the book's first person narrator, and had thus presented a far too one-sided, ostensibly autobiographical picture."[8] The converse criticism might be leveled at March, namely that he excluded major aspects of his own experience and oddly presented a picture that was also one-sided in part because it was not autobiographical enough. Simmonds explains that "March's concept had been to write a book in which the background of the war, so vividly described in the narratives of previous writers, could be simply taken for granted, thus allowing him to concentrate almost exclusively on the *reactions* of men to war."[9] But it is precisely a whole side of March's reactions that are not in *Company K*.

One thing March leaves out of the novel is his own misrepresentation of his war wounds. Just after he returned home, in 1919, he told several people, including his boss, Harry Hardy Smith, that he "had only six months to live because of the wounds he had received." March's sister Marie and a friend and business associate named McRae both asserted that March "had a silver plate inserted in his skull as a result of the wounds he received at Belleau Wood, but there is no evidence that this was so." And "as late as 1937 . . . , March was still maintaining that at the time of his discharge he was 'in pretty bad physical shape' due to the effect of gas," though "his marine records show that when he was demobilized his physical condition was rated excellent." As Simmonds sums up, "In later life, [March] admitted that the wounds he received at Belleau Wood had been superficial and did not amount to much. He was, also . . . wounded during the fighting at Blanc Mont, as his citations record, but . . . he was not hospitalized afterward. It is reasonable to assume that these wounds he received were even more superficial than those he had received in the earlier engagement."[10]

Another thing March does not include in *Company K* is his reaction to his medals, promotions up from the ranks, and strong service record. March had a phenomenally successful war service as a marine: he was promoted to corporal and sergeant, had an exemplary record, and was among the most highly decorated American soldiers in World War I. In addition to the Croix de Guerre, he was recognized with a particular pair of medals from the American army "that to anyone with a knowledge of the military services, is literally mind-defying."[11] How March felt about these recognitions, some received while in France, some after he returned to the states, is entirely absent from *Company K*.

When the issue of his medals, promotions, and record came up among friends and family, he again led people astray. Simmonds relates that he "wished to give the impression" that he did not care about these things, especially the citations. His sister and McRae believed that March was nominated for the Congressional Medal of Honor; "according to McRae, March . . . was . . . so disinterested that he refused to fill out the necessary papers for it, throwing them instead into the wastepaper basket."[12]

But Simmonds questions these reports, as well as March's real feelings about his achievements, as "official records do not show that March was ever recommended for this particular award. He was, however, awarded the Navy Cross on November 11, 1920, the second anniversary of the armistice.

He certainly did not reject" this honor.[13] Regarding March's supposed indifference to his army recognitions: "The evidence all points the other way, for he invariably mentioned his military honors in the routine biographies he supplied on request to editors. He liked to stress that although he did not consider himself a soldier, he had risen to the rank of sergeant in the marines and that, on discharge, he had been given an exemplary character marking of three fives, explaining, again with obvious pride, that this was something very rarely awarded." When March traveled to London in the mid-1930s, he took his medals with him. As his biographer reasonably observes, "Surely a man who is indifferent to his medals does not take them with him on journeys all over the world."[14]

March's biographer implies that his feigned disinterest in his military achievements was tied to "survivor's guilt": "There is little doubt that March, like many of his returning veterans, felt an inescapable sense of guilt at having survived the war, when so many of his comrades had been killed or horribly and incurably wounded."[15] He also asserts, "There is no doubt that for March the gradual composition of *Company K* was in some part an exercise in self-therapy."[16] It is not much of a leap to see March's omissions from his novel of his own feelings about his combat achievements and military validation as stemming from the same source of survivor guilt.[17]

Hervey Allen's biographer Stuart E. Knee likewise suggests that Allen suffered from survivor guilt—specifically a "guilt over" what happened at Fismettes, the setting of the last scene of his memoir. This was a town that a US major general, R. L. Bullard, felt could not be taken or held given the layout and the men at his disposal, but his decision was overruled by a French commander, and the results were catastrophic for Allen's company.[18] Allen may not have known about Bullard's position at the time he drafted the book in 1918 and 1919, though he probably was aware of it by the time the book was published seven years later; in any case, he only included it in the reissued 1934 edition. When Allen realized there were only four of the men in his cadre left alive and "he saw it was hopeless"—they were blocked from Fismettes by the German force, and there was no chance of helping to defend the town—he "and three others made for the river." As Knee puts it, "His decision to cross and not to die in defense of Fismettes was one which triggered a veritable light show of nightmares for months to come. He blamed himself for deserting those [in other groups] who were left, but this was not the case." Allen's intention in heading back to the town of Fismes across the river was to inform his superiors of the disastrous situation so the greatly outnumbered American troops left in Fismettes could be reinforced and rescued. He feared "that anyone short of an officer would not be taken seriously at Headquarters, so . . . felt compelled to swim. . . . 'How we got back . . . I don't know, but we did. . . . Terribly unstrung,' gassed, and with a right knee struck by shell fragments, he made his report [to Headquarters] and was admitted to Field Hospital 109. Ironically, it was all for nought. 'The Colonel got a relief started right away,' but the initial Fismettes troops were wiped out."[19]

Allen's biographer, like March's, does not speculate about how the author's survivor guilt might have affected the shape of his book—only that his writing was part of the process of healing his "shellshock" and "expiat[ing] some residual guilt over Fismettes." Knee has documented that while Allen healed for more than a month in the hospital from battle wounds, "he was tortured by night with the hallucination that people were whispering about him. Truthfully, having seen so many die, he was, for a time, ashamed to have survived at all"; he later confessed that he had "contemplated suicide."[20] It is easy to see a connection between survivor guilt and Allen's refusal—or inability—in *Toward the Flame* to include a scene depicting his literal *survival* of the disastrous battle at Fismette, where most of the members of his unit died. In fact, as Allen puts it in the 1934 preface, "I *can* now, after sixteen years" (xxiii, emphasis added), thereby implying that previously he simply could not do it.

But the term "survivor guilt" is perhaps misleadingly narrow about the guilt that shaped the exclusions or omissions March and Allen made from their books. The narrowness of the term makes it "difficult" for March's biographer "to appreciate exactly what March's reasons were for wishing to install in people's minds the fiction of his precarious physical condition" when, after returning home, he told friends and family he was near death.[21] Apparently, March was not just guilty about having survived but of having come through the war relatively intact while he not only saw "so many of his comrades" killed but so many "horribly and incurably wounded." March's "fiction of his precarious physical condition" was, one imagines, generally not a plea for pity or concern but rather an attempt to deny a reality about his relative good health that also made him feel guilty. March may also have suffered from a related guilt of having done so well in the war and having been so thoroughly recognized when so many of his comrades had their lives destroyed or ended by it—thus his pose of indifference to his medals and honors. These related syndromes might, for the sake of clarity, be called "promotion guilt" and "abledness guilt."[22]

Allen seems to have suffered from similar guilt complexes. One way to identify the material that Allen considers a matter of "ego" and has thus suppressed from the 1926 text is to examine what he added to the 1934 version. His other substantive change was to include an addenda that follows the narrative proper. What the addenda makes clear, through military letters by Maj. Gen. Bullard and comments by the American Commander-in-Chief Gen. John J. Pershing, is that the attempt to hold Fismette was a terrible French command blunder (278–82).

It is reasonable to speculate that Allen limits himself from expressing in the 1926 text any judgment or disapproval of his superiors' strategic and tactical decisions—unless they are blatantly wrongheaded. Indeed, the sort of criticism of officers that crops up often in Boyd's *Through the Wheat* is almost entirely absent from Allen's memoir. There are only a couple of instances of it, and perhaps not accidentally, one of them is the occasion for perhaps the wittiest passage in the whole book, a stylistic flourish generally lacking from his prose: Allen says about a tactical discussion among his superiors that he overhears, "here was a quarrel about how to fight somebody else conducted in solecisms in which the premises of all parties to the controversy were entirely wrong. It was almost legally magnificent. It was more than that—it was military. I lit a cigarette" (149–50). Perhaps Allen's style revs up at this moment because of the tension involved for him in allowing himself this bit of "egocentric" judgment.

Allen rarely allows himself to express his pride in being an officer, performing his duties under difficult conditions, or being in the know (when most men are in the dark). When such instances do arise, they are undercut or dimmed by being framed as complaints. So we learn about Allen's sole responsibility at one point for the men in his unit in the form of a gripe about being "left . . . the only officer with the company. . . . Living as close to [the troops] as I had to do in the woods, the men nearly nagged me to death. Robin Hood must have had his nerves shattered by forest intimacies" (29). Again, Allen employs a literary adornment as a way to defuse the anxiety this small assertion of ego perhaps incites. And when we find out that Allen is considered a good officer it comes not only by way of a dissatisfaction, but a dissatisfaction that, importantly, he shares with other officers. There was "a general growl at the policy of getting rid of certain officers, not personally on the right side of the powers, by sending them home to train troops instead of sending *us*, 'the hard workers'" (88–89).

One of the rare—if not indeed unique—mentions of his "pride" is mitigated by his citing chemical "gas" in the same breath: "I swallowed a whole mouthful of gas and pride to think that Glen and I were probably the only two lieutenants in the whole division who really knew the exact location and status of things at the time" (72). The way Allen remembers this emotion is telling of his survivor guilt: a memory of feeling pride sparks a self-punishing recollection of ingesting poison. As with the previous example, Allen's inclusion of another officer in the anecdote mitigates the self-assertion.

Allen is able "to a remarkable degree . . . [to] succeed . . . in achieving his objective" of keeping his "ego" out of the story, according to Steven Trout.[23] But he succeeds because this objective is not simply an intellectual decision but a psychological imperative. If Allen crosses the line into what feels like too much self-promotion or even self-concern, he triggers his guilt. Whether "the medicine [of writing] worked" to alleviate his being "troubled at night by memories of the war" (xxiv) or (as his biographer asserts) "to expiate some residual guilt over Fismettes,"[24] it was indeed because Allen was able to "rid himself of his subjective war by trying to make it objective in writing" (xxiv).

No doubt remembering or reminding himself of all the strain and suffering he himself went through helped reduce his guilt over Fismettes, as did his recording and essentially memorializing the pain, maiming, and death that his compatriots experienced. Allen's text focuses on the psychological and physical ordeals associated with the harrowing conditions of modern combat: the exhaustion; the terror ("I was so frightened myself I could scarcely get the men together" [46]); the gruesome humor (for example on encountering a "headless man" [52]); "the longings for persons one loves . . . so physical and acute that it makes a man ill" (64); the "nerve strain" brought on "by being shelled more or less for a month or so" (91); "the feeling of utter yearning and despair, the fear of the last indignities ahead, and the knowledge that the war might go on for years and years, [which] brought mental and physical paralysis to the individual" (63).

Allen began his self-treatment with the "medicine" of writing in a "hospital in France" as he healed from his Fismettes injuries, at which point he completed "about half" of the memoir (xx). Next, he did something else that also helped alleviate his guilt: he asked to rejoin his unit, then in the Argonne, though he "was debilitated both mentally and physically." So a month and a half after the final events recorded in his memoir, he was back at the front line, and, soon enough, he was "wounded in action again." This time, he was "cited for bravery and given the Croix de Guerre, but a couple of weeks later, he was back at the front line yet again, "having 'cracked up,' been gassed, [and] limping slightly but perceptibly from his Fismettes wound."[25]

It might have seemed that Allen had done plenty to purge himself of his remorse over Fismettes by this point, but after his return home in 1919 he was still haunted "by memories of the war and often unable to sleep" (xxiv).

It was then that he wrote "the other half" of the book.[26] "The medicine worked," according to Allen, or, perhaps more accurately, it did some work of healing him psychologically. By 1933, when he wrote the preface for the 1934 reissue of the book, he was able to briefly discuss in print his survival at Fismettes. By 1940, he could refer to his decision to return to his outfit in the Argonne, after being seriously wounded at Fismettes, as motivated by "[w]hat I now regard as a silly sense of duty."[27] And so his guilt was, finally, one imagines, expiated.

William March's guilt, though it might have dissipated over time, apparently haunted him his entire life. When he first returned home after the war, he had "recurring nightmares, waking in the night with a 'screaming need' and taking a drink from the bottle of whiskey he always kept by his bedside."[28] His suffering came to center on one particular incident from his wartime experience, one he represented in *Company K*. As Simmonds puts it,

> Although in later years March was generally noncommittal concerning his exploits in battle, one story crops up several times in the reminiscences of friends and acquaintances, a story which he clearly felt impelled to tell over and over again, almost as a form of expiation. The peripheral details may vary . . . , but the central traumatic incident is horrifyingly constant. . . . [T]he crux of the story is that William came face to face with a young German soldier—a desperate boy with blond hair and blue eyes. William instinctively lunged at the German with his bayonet. The boy stumbled and the bayonet pierced his throat, killing him instantly, his eyes wide open and staring into William's face. The young German's death was to haunt William all his living days, even intruding into his dreams. Although he attempted to lay the ghost, as it were, in the Private Manuel Burt section of *Company K*, he evidently did not succeed and there is evidence that even up to a few years before his death he was still struggling to rid himself of the insistent, terrible memory of the boy's face and staring eyes. It is certainly not without significance that at various stages of his life March experienced hysterical conditions related to both his throat and eyes.
>
> These psychosomatic symptoms . . . , when they manifested themselves in the throat condition, were serious enough to warrant sustained psychoanalytic treatment [in the mid-1930s].[29]

In short, neither the writing of *Company K*—which his biographer called "a form of therapy" and a way of "exorcising his own private demons"[30]—nor psychiatric therapy nor the passage of time fully worked to heal March.

As I have suggested, March suffered, immediately after the war, from abledness guilt and promotion guilt, along with the survivor guilt his biographer identifies. But both of these related types of guilt no doubt were made even more intense by the fact that his sterling war record and his lies about his poor health (perhaps meant to ease his abledness guilt) were instrumental to his success after the war. On account of his war record, the army provided him with a chance to study journalism at the university in Toulouse for a few months.[31] One imagines that this opportunity was meaningful to March, who had not been able to afford to finish college.[32] In addition, that service record, along with the fabrication that he had only six months to live, helped him land the job in a shipping company, launching his successful and prosperous career.[33] Again, this is particularly significant for a man who grew up in poverty.

Soon after returning from the war, in 1919, March left Tuscaloosa, Alabama (where his family now lived), and managed to get a modest job as a private secretary to a Mobile lawyer named Smith. "March volunteered information about his war exploits, showing Smith his medals and citations. Smith was apparently left with the impression that March had only six months to live because of the wounds he had received. It is not clear how this misunderstanding—if it was a misunderstanding—on Smith's part arose, but it was soon to have fortunate and far-reaching consequences for March." Smith had business dealings with John B. Waterman, who was in the process of founding the Waterman Steamship Corporation—and who happened to be a war veteran himself. "Smith suggested that Waterman might like to give his young employee . . . a job, and Waterman agreed, more out of a sense of pity for the returned veteran than anything else. Smith had apparently passed on to Waterman his understanding that March was doomed to an early grave, and Waterman, remembering his own involvement in the Spanish-American War, was sympathetic to the idea of employing wounded veterans." March would eventually rise to the rank of vice president of the Waterman company, and his Waterman stock holdings were finally worth $3 million.[34] Already by the mid-1920s—several years before he published any of the material that would eventually constitute *Company K* and evidently before he even began writing it—the company was growing and expanding, and March was being promoted. He was made manager of the "traffic department" in 1924, and in 1926 he was given the responsibility to open up a "branch office in Memphis." In 1928, when he began writing stories, he was given the same task in New York City.[35]

There is a strange irony in March's postwar success. Perhaps he lied to Smith about his health with the intention of seeking career help, but it is possible that such lies about his physical condition had already become habitual and reflexive, as a way to lessen his guilt.[36] In either case, if the lie about his ruined health had originated as a means to ease one aspect of his survivor guilt (that of coming through the war relatively healthy and certainly "abled"), the irony is that, in leading to greater success, this lie actually served to intensify another aspect of that survivor guilt (namely his guilt over the postwar promotion and success that the war helped bring him).

Hervey Allen also enjoyed dramatic career success, but it did not intensify his survivor guilt. Presumably, Allen's success was not guilt inducing, in contrast to March's, because Allen succeeded on the basis of his later writing, and his war service had essentially nothing to do with making him a wealthy man and a household name. In 1933, he published *Anthony Adverse*, a 1,224-page historical novel set in the Napoleonic era, which sold a million copies by 1935 and 2 million by 1947.[37] It was made into a successful Hollywood movie in 1936. The reissue of *Toward the Flame* in 1934, Steven Trout surmises, "probably had as much to do with Allen's sudden name recognition and marketability as it did with the respectable following that the original edition . . . had inspired among World War I veterans."[38]

Allen's dissipating guilt regarding the war would not have been reactivated or intensified by his success. March, by contrast, owed the break that set him up in his career to his war service. And March's economically disadvantaged childhood made his adult success all the more dramatic, and that much more dependent on his war and army experience. His life and fortunes changed fundamentally with the war, mostly because the meritocratic opportunities and affirmations he experienced with the military opened doors for him.

March's promotion guilt militated against including in *Company K* any of the positive reactions he had to being promoted and decorated by the military and any of the positive effects the war had on his life. There is a character in the novel who earns a combination of medals quite similar to that of March. Yet this character's experience of heroism in combat and recognition—so meaningful to March and so important to his postwar success—is presented in a negative light.

Private Dresser's incredibly distinguished set of medals—the French Croix de Guerre, the Distinguished Service Cross, the Medal Militaire, and the Medal of Honor—is similar to March's (honored with the Croix de Guerre, the Distinguished Service Cross, and the Navy Cross for Valor). In Dresser's chapter, we learn about the brave actions he performed to earn these decorations, but we never find out how he feels about receiving them. We only learn that in his life after the war they do not mean much. Dresser returns to his lowly "old job" in his hometown hardware store and "has been there ever since"; moreover, the people he encounters back home simply find it hard to believe that the mere clerk in front of them is the same man who won these commendations on the battlefield. "In my home town people point me out to strangers and say, 'You'd never believe that fellow had a hat full of medals, would you?' And the strangers always say no, they never would."[39] If anything, these medals become for Dresser a source of pain, an uncomfortable reminder of the status crash he experienced after the war. Though he risked his life to do heroic things in the war, and was once highly validated and respected for having done so, he has been repaid by becoming a mild curiosity for the townsfolk.

There is no character in *Company K* who is also highly decorated in a similar manner and who is proud of his medals, or ambivalent about them given a sense of survivor or promotion guilt. Also, no character attends a European university as an army reward for his military service. And no one's war record happily helps him get launched in a promising career.

In one chapter of *Company K*, a former soldier parlays a serious war wound—the loss of his foot—into success, specifically a successful bid for a seat in Congress. But this potentially uplifting story is a cynical and depressing one. This character, Lieutenant Fairbrother, happens to be a warmongering opportunist who runs his campaigns on fear (255–56). There is also a respectable veteran in the novel who moves to Birmingham, Alabama, after the war, invests in a successful business, and has "enough money laid by in safe bonds to keep us comfortably for the rest of our lives." But his tragedy is that he was once a promising pianist who lost most of his left hand in the war (230–31).

In a similar vein, March's dramatic stories of fortunate and unlikely survival are told against the backdrop of the deaths and wounding of numerous others. There are two characters in the book who are referred to as having "lucky" escapes (111, 156), but in both cases the incidents involve, and emphasize, many casualties. Private John McGill's chapter begins, "I went out on raiding parties time after time where every man except myself was killed or wounded." It ends, "Before going over the top many of them would put their hands on my forehead, hoping thereby to become lucky themselves, but whatever the power that protected me, it never worked for anyone else" (110–11). In another chapter, Private Samuel Quillin survives a bomb blast that kills everyone else and leaves him without "a scratch": the story ends with the doctor telling him, "Twenty-six men were taken out of that dugout, and you're the only one that came out alive" (155–56).

In short, bits and pieces of March's experience are represented in *Company K*, but if those experiences were not actually traumatizing or dreadful, March transforms them so that they become so. In this sense, the modus operandi of March's novel is a sort of opposite of the procedure Hemingway employed. In his own life, Hemingway embellished his war record and the story of his wounding to make himself look better (see chapter four). March, meanwhile, downplayed his war record and lied about his wounds to make himself look less fortunate. Hemingway, out of embarrassment over his noncombatant position and service, created narrators who were war heroes (most obviously with *A Farewell to Arms*). March, out of guilt over his coming through the war physically intact, over his decorated success as a combatant, and over his postwar success helped along by his war service, created characters whose medals seem meaningless after the war or whose postwar success was either ugly and sinister or undermined by drastic war wounds.

Company K can accurately be described as an example of the disillusionment narrative; it is, in my estimation, the only major American World War I work that fits that bill. Through its 113 narrators, it takes the reader from the innocent idealism of the men on their way by boat to France—believing they are "saving civilization and dedicating [their] lives to [their] country" (22)—through their experiences of the horrors of combat, the stupidities of junior officers that pointlessly cost lives, and the war crime of a senior officer who orders the shooting of German prisoners, and ultimately to their jaded and ironic consciousness about the corrupt and degrading American endeavor that they were duped into joining, and that they have paid for with physical maiming and disabilities, mental trauma, and death. Even in death, they cannot escape being used, no longer as cannon fodder but as propaganda fodder. One of March's characters throws away his dog tags specifically to avoid having his name used to feed the myths of patriotic war, yet he becomes hallowed as the "Unknown Soldier" buried in Arlington Cemetery (178–82). Try though they might, after the armistice, to break "the chain" (182) and turn their horrible experience into a lesson that might "enlighten" people about "the senseless horror of war"—one former private creates the "Society for the Prevention of War"—their efforts will ironically contribute to the next generation's embrace of it: "[S]ome one began organizing a company of National Guard in our town about that time and my disciples, anxious to protect their country from the horrors I had described, deserted my society and joined in a body" (228–22). The future clearly belongs to that opportunistic veteran officer who presciently sees another war on the horizon but hysterically imagines enemies of America everywhere. He warns of the rising "militarism" in Italy and the threats posed by Japan and Germany, but also by England and France, and advocates US military preparedness. He is the lieutenant who uses his maiming in the war to get elected and reelected to the House of Representatives (255–56).

But this disillusionment trajectory does not correspond to March's own experience. Rather, this bleak disillusionment "myth,"[40] which March perhaps helped create and certainly participated in, served his needs, and in particular his psychological need to exclude from the novel most of the fortunate aspects of his army and war experience—or to transform them into something dismal.

March's novel is not only shaped by the exclusions and transformations of his own experience. It is also focused, as a result of the author's own trauma, in a manner that is not commonly recognized. The central event in March's novel is the shooting, in cold blood, of a group of German prisoners by the members of Company K. No other important American World War I book has such a center. But the valence of this scene is generally not fully or accurately understood.

Philip Biedler writes a fairly representative take on the novel in his introduction to the 1989 reissue of the book: "As with Hemingway, mixed with the violence and brutalization, there is some talk of loss of illusion, of betrayal through patriotic lies. Yet in March, more than in any of his contemporaries, this too is ultimately subsumed into a depth of horror that goes far beyond any Lost Generation conceit. . . . [I]n narrative after narrative, there is mainly just one fundamental fact of modern warfare: the fact of violent, ugly, obscene death" (xiv–xv). This may be roughly true. And it may also be the case that "throughout *Company K*, the narratives of individual soldiers become a litany of callousness, brutality, and degradation. This is most clearly reflected in a single incident lodged both literally and figuratively at the center of the book, something that might be thought of as the novel's primal scene: the execution of twenty-two German prisoners" (xvii–xviii). But Biedler's description does not fully explain why March chose to place this incident at the center of his book.

In the first chapter of *Company K*, Private Joseph Delaney, apparently the author (or editor) of the book about his "own company," and his wife discuss including in this book "the part about shooting prisoners." His wife thinks it should be taken out "because it is cruel and unjust to shoot defenseless men in cold blood," and "it isn't typical." "It may have been done a few times. I'm not denying that, but . . . [i]t couldn't have happened often." Delaney does not challenge her assertion but simply asks, "Would . . . an air raid be better?" He implies that "killing harmless people [you] are not even fighting" by aerial bombing is just as cruel. "Would [an air raid] be more typical?" "Yes," replies his wife, "That happened many times, I understand" (14–15).

It can be deduced from their discussion that shooting prisoners is distinctive on two counts. It is atypical, and it is "unjust." It does not make sense that March was interested in foregrounding an event *because* it was atypical; as Delaney says, he wants the book "to be a record of every company in every army" (13)—in other words, representing what is completely typical. (Simmonds demonstrates that March had a similar aim.) So if March was going to include something he—or at least his fictional book editor or author—considered atypical, he must have had a strong reason. Was March interested in highlighting the unjust acts committed by the American army?

Previous to the publication of *Company K*, March published, in 1931 in the journal *Forum*, a collection of sketches called "Nine Prisoners" that, as his biographer explains, "was eventually to form the central incident of the book: the arbitrary shooting of a group of unarmed German prisoners by the marines and the emotional effect on the men who carried out their captain's orders." And "it created an immediate furor among many of the magazine's readers." The response was mixed, but "many . . . letters abused [March], for example, for 'having murdered the good name and good sense of millions of American soldiers.'"[41]

One letter bothered March enough for him to respond in print; "for the first and last time, he felt it necessary to defend and justify his work in public." Here was an opportunity for March to give details of an actual shooting of German prisoners by American soldiers—if he had actual facts and he aimed indeed to call attention to "unjust" acts committed by the American Expeditionary Forces—and giving such evidence would presumably be the strongest defense of his publication imaginable. But March did not choose to do so. "My story . . . is, so far as I am aware, strictly fiction," he wrote. He went on to say that "there is . . . nothing in the story to indicate that its characters are drawn from the Marines or the American Army at all." It seems that March's aim was not to expose an unjust action by the Americans but instead, as he put it, "to make the men and their reactions universal in their implications, beyond military boundary lines."[42]

One can perhaps understand why March, after this experience with "Nine Prisoners," would include an initial chapter in *Company K* attempting to explain his intentions for the book. On the very first page of the novel, he nearly reiterates his explanation for his 1931 story: "This book started out to be a record of my own company, but . . . I want it to be a record of every company in every army" (13). Despite this disclaimer, many readers of *Company K* were scandalized by the episode of the shooting of German prisoners by American troops. This time around, the publisher of the book "asked March if he could quote chapter and verse in relation to an actual incident where such a thing did happen." Here was another opportunity for March to expose an unjust action by the American army, if that was indeed his intention, but, again, he did not. "March refused to be drawn [in]. . . . March felt it was better that there be no attempt by him or his publishers to prove or justify any material in the book, as this might involve living persons and be more than a little embarrassing, in more ways than one, to all concerned."[43]

Simmonds implies that March did in fact know of an actual event in which German prisoners were shot by American soldiers—despite March's claim that "Nine Prisoners" was "strictly fiction." (Military historian Jennifer Keene is "fairly certain" that such incidents did occur though she has not come across an official army record substantiating a shooting of prisoners; what she has come across are "anecdotal reports by American soldiers themselves.")[44] One thing is for certain: if March knew of such a real, unjust event, he was not interested in exposing it. And given the incendiary nature of representing such an episode—of which March was completely aware after his experience with the 1931 story—it is hard to believe that he thought the modest and subtle disclaimer in his first chapter would prevent a storm of indignation about *Company K*, especially as the conversation that follows it between Delaney and his wife, also in the first chapter, could be seen to imply rather that such events did take place, and that March was well aware that the scene would again be controversial.

So why then was March set on including such an episode when the pursuit of "justice" or "exposing injustice" was clearly not his aim? Maybe he wanted the controversy—to help sell books. But if that was his purpose, why bother with the caveat or disclaimer in the first chapter? The episode must have been psychologically important to March, so important that he was not willing to part with it, even though he knew it would cause him some trouble.

In his 1931 letter in response to the angry reader March wrote that he "hoped to make the men and their reactions universal in their implications." He was interested in men's "reactions" to the shooting of prisoners that are "universal": the most common reaction of the characters in the book who participate is guilt. This is the reaction of Private Richard Mundy, who afterward "fell to the ground and pressed [his] face into the fallen leaves," repeating, "I'll never hurt anything again as long as I live" (137). Private William Nugent, after the war, kills policemen—the way he sees it, "the cop of my outfit made us" shoot prisoners—he does not deny committing murder when he is caught, and he waits impassively to get the death penalty (210, 209). After the war, Private Everett Qualls blames the misfortunes he experiences on his being "guilty" for shooting prisoners. When his baby dies, he again thinks of his participation in the execution, takes out his "service revolver," and fires the gun into his mouth (221–23).

Company K is, arguably, centered on guilt, and guilt also shapes its exclusions and transpositions. The central episode generates intense guilt in the participants, two of whom cannot rest until they have sealed their own deaths. The longest episode of the novel by far—nine pages—is Private Manuel Burt's chapter, in which March gives a version of his own suffering over his bayoneting of the young German. The short chapter that follows Burt's, by Private Colin Urquhart, strikingly and starkly asserts, "All I know, surely, is that there should be a law, in the name of humanity, making mandatory the execution of every soldier who served on the front and managed to escape death there" (254). This bald and radical statement—obviously expressing self-hatred and coming directly after Burt's chapter, as a sort of conclusion or moral to his story—seems also to issue out of March's guilt.

March's biographer Simmonds observes that "a large proportion of his work can perhaps be said to be *emotionally* autobiographical, rather than *factually* autobiographical." And his ultimate assessment of the *emotional* content of March's novel is in pretty close agreement with mine. "The principal theme of *Company K* demonstrates how the collective madness of war . . . reacts upon the individual soldier, driving him into insanity or an unbearable sense of guilt."[45] But where we differ is in the understanding of the source of March's guilt: Simmonds thinks that the "psychic scars . . . [of] World War I were, to a large degree, exorcised through the process of writing *Company K*" and that "his war experiences no longer posed an overriding problem" by the mid-1930s, when he went into psychoanalysis in London—though he admits March could never shake the image of the face of the German he bayonetted. "By then," Simmonds speculates, March was dealing with "the emotionally crippling nature of his childhood, stemming possibly from his relationship to his father, together with the conscious and unconscious conflict arising from the duality of his nature, manifesting itself in the two personalities of . . . the business tycoon and . . . the author."[46] In implying that March was uncomfortable with his business tycoon status, and that he was also somehow suffering over his childhood, Simmonds approaches the real issue behind the author's ongoing guilt.

A significant part of the unending wellspring of March's suffering, resulting in his obsession with the German boy he killed and his psychosomatic symptoms, came from the guilt he experienced as a result not only of his survival in relatively good physical condition but of his success in the war and after. His ongoing guilt was a result in particular of the lucrative opportunities the war opened up for him, while for so many others that he had encountered it had been the end, or left them so physically or mentally shattered that it may as well have been.

The letter that got under March's skin, that he felt compelled to reply to in 1931, was not the one that accused him of "having murdered the good name and good sense of millions of American soldiers." It was one that asserted that March was "one of these peace-at-any-price people, who, having either never been a soldier at all or having been stationed at some camp during the war, believes himself an expert on the horrors of fighting. . . . That such a person should be accepted as a qualified observer of war is ridiculous."[47]

March wrote a long letter in response, of which his disclaimer about the American execution of German prisoners was only the beginning. He went on to set the record straight about his having been in the war:

> I resent bitterly any inference that because I have written such a story I lack either patriotism or physical courage. To those who do imply such things, let me say that I enlisted, voluntarily, when war was declared, that I participated in all action that my regiment saw; that I was discharged honorably with the highest possible rating for a Marine—a perfect 5, given, I understand, rarely. I was awarded for personal bravery under fire every decoration except the Congressional Medal of Honor, and as a result of wounds I received in action, I shall never be entirely well again so long as I live. I dislike mentioning these things: I do it now merely to defend myself.[48]

The contents of this public letter cannot simply be taken at face value. But it is important to note that in order to "defend" himself, March admits to the medals he at other times acted as if he did not care about, is honest about *not* having been awarded the Congressional Medal of Honor, and evinces a pride in his awards and especially his perfect rating as a marine. He also identifies strongly with his service in war. And he admits that he does not like mentioning "these things." This last statement seems to be an honest one insofar as it jibes with his general tendency to downplay his medals and service. And it presumably relates to his survival-related guilt—or more specifically, a kind of promotion guilt that was in some ways new with this war and US mobilization and was thus, perhaps, an especially American phenomenon: what we might call "merit guilt."

Perhaps March is also compulsively telling his habitual lie—again out of survival-related guilt—about having come out of the war permanently damaged. But the vagueness of his comment about his well-being might indicate that he, in his mind, is honestly referring to the fact that, because of *psychological* "wounds . . . received in action," he will never "be entirely well again" mentally.

What March says next, if it is not a lie made in defending himself, is surprising given that he will, a couple of years later, publish what many critics consider the most antiwar American novel to come out of World War I. "My present attitude toward war is this. If there were a war impending, my conscience and my special knowledge would impel me to do what I could to prevent it. Failing that, I would make the best of a bad situation and reenlist immediately in any combat unit which would accept in its ranks a battered, half-blind old hulk."[49] I do not think that March is lying here. The fact that he says he would first try to prevent another war, given his "conscience" and "special knowledge," is obviously sincere. His assertion that he would, if necessary, join in another war at this point may or may not be true, but it suggests that what is driving March, in his personal suffering and in *Company K*, is not an antiwar agenda so much as a sense of "conscience"—or of guilt. In order to assuage his guilt, Hervey Allen returned to his unit after his serious wounding at Fismettes. March seems to indicate here his readiness, or at least his fantasy, to do something similar.

But what is also very striking for us, after the whole journey of this examination of the major American writers of World War I, is that what sticks in March's throat enough for him to respond in print—when some of the other letters he ignores are equally or even more accusatory—is the accusation that he was "never . . . a soldier" or was only "stationed at some camp during the war." March's sense of self, his identity, or his ego (to use Allen's term) is deeply tied to his having served as a combatant. The assertion that he was a noncombatant is a falsehood he simply cannot brook. He must set the record straight in public.

The final paragraph of March's letter underlines this fundamental distinction between those who have served at the front and those who have not. He writes, "from the tone of those [letters] that have been addressed to me personally, I have learned one thing: it is futile and it is hopeless for any man who actually served on the line to attempt to make well-meaning, romantic folk share his knowledge: there is, simply, no common denominator."[50] Steven Trout takes it for granted that "the respectable following that the original edition" of Allen's *Toward the Flame* "inspired [was] among World War I veterans." March's letter does not indicate that he is writing only for veteran combatants, but they are certainly his principal audience. American writing about World War I did not invent the category of literature meant primarily for an insider readership. But it involved this phenomenon on a mass scale, first, because of the unprecedented, traumatic experiences that the World War I mobilization and combat entailed and, second, because of the sheer number of men that mobilization involved and who thus needed to come to terms with the events that befell them, either as combatants or noncombatants. These two different forms and experiences of participation in war were often not only quite distinct to begin with, but their difference was made astronomically greater by its being highly fetishized in the popular imagination.

In *Memoirs of an Infantry Officer*, British World War I veteran Siegfried Sassoon is quite honest about his feelings of gratification upon receiving the Military Cross, or M.C., a decoration he hoped to earn: "Books about war psychology ought to contain a chapter on 'medal-reflexes' and 'decoration-complexes.' Much might be written . . . about medals and their stimulating effect on those who really risked their lives for them." He also admits that "[t]his gratifying little event"—that of learning that his "M.C. had come through"—"increased my blindness to the blood-stained future."[51]

Later in the conflict, Sassoon decided, while still in the army, to make an official protest of the war. Given the dire consequences that awaited a soldier for such an action—a court-martial and then prison—he was ready to "martyr" himself. Though he truly had come to think the war was being prolonged for corrupt reasons, it is hard to imagine that his plan of "forcing them to make a martyr of me" did not also involve some emotional compulsion—some guilt.[52] (Only the intervention of his friend and fellow officer Robert Graves, called David Cromlech in the memoir, convinced Sassoon to give up his plan of going to prison and instead to accept a medical leave for shell shock. Graves tells him, perhaps lying to him, that the army would not court-martial him and "won't make a martyr out of you" but rather would treat him as "insane."[53])

During his moment of protest, his Military Cross was on his mind, and in a gesture he considered "[w]eighted with significance," he threw his M.C. ribbon "into the mouth of Mersey" river. But instead of sinking, it "floated away," and he immediately thought of the awards he had won in fox-hunting competitions: "One of my point-to-point cups would have served my purpose more satisfyingly, and they'd meant much the same to me as my Military Cross."[54] The two sorts of prizes made him *feel* a similar gratification. His eagerness to perform well in trench raids and gain a Military Cross was similar to his ambition to win riding cups, which "six years before . . . had seemed a significant way of demonstrating my equality with contemporaries"—by whom he meant men of the same class as himself. (The British military system made meritocratic distinctions within existing social class divisions; commissioned officer positions were almost entirely restricted to men of the upper classes.) "And now I wanted to make the World War serve a similar purpose, for if only I could get a Military Cross I should feel comparatively safe and confident."[55]

The gratification of military affirmation involved not only an "increased . . . blindness to the blood-stained future" at the time but also, later, when the dust settled, a guilt about the blood-stained past, at least in men who were sensitive. March was undoubtedly a sensitive man. The intense gratification that he must have felt over his military achievements and recognition—stronger than Sassoon's one might imagine, given that Sassoon came from a privileged background and got his officership on that basis before he set foot in France, while March had an underprivileged upbringing and earned his promotions through his performance at the front—came back to haunt him in the form of merit guilt or "medal complexes." The "Dangling Man" in Saul Bellow's World War II–era novel of that name (1944) is appalled by the very idea of "climbing on the backs of the dead."[56] Meritocracy will not always provoke such repulsion or guilt, but it is likely to do so when an army fighting a war is meritocratic—and some men are dying while others are winning promotions and recognition.

Conclusion
War *and* Meritocracy Literature

THE RELATIVELY RECENT RECOVERY of the history of the US Army during World War I means that all of the literature of the conflict appears in a dramatically new light, including the texts written by some of America's most celebrated writers. Classifying works as pro- or antiwar, as has been the tendency, is too blunt a procedure. It has missed the fundamental and crucial distinction between the male noncombatant and combatant experiences.[1] This is not to say simply that combatants experienced the war more intensely—though this distinction definitely applies in the cases of F. Scott Fitzgerald and William Faulkner, who never made it to Europe, and arguably in those of ambulance drivers John Dos Passos and E. E. Cummings as well. Ernest Hemingway, however, was badly wounded as a noncombatant. Rather, the distinction between combatant and noncombatant matters because, socially speaking, combat roles were validated and noncombat positions were not. American recruits, most of whom got nowhere near the front, experienced distinct kinds of disillusionment depending on their wartime experience. Moreover, there is a basic distinction between antiwar sentiments and anti-military ones, which have all been classed together as protests of war. Noncombatants tended to be disillusioned about the army or the society that failed to validate them; since their service in the war was affirmed in many ways, white combatants did not tend to experience this form of disillusionment—though, given the official discrimination of the army, black ones did. To put this more strongly, we have thought of American World War I combat veterans as alienated from society, but, by and large, the intense veteran alienation generated by World War I belonged to noncombatant veterans, who felt alienated not only from society at large that failed to recognize their service but from the army they had served, which treated noncombatants as relatively unimportant. That alienation was also felt by African American veterans, combatants and noncombatants alike.

Likewise, when it comes to women writers, categorizing works as pro- or antiwar is too sweeping and not very revealing. Women were not subject to military rejection or selection and assignment, as men were. But the war nonetheless created both opportunities for women and expectations for their participation. Women worked as nurses and drove ambulances in the war zone; they also took over home front jobs vacated by men, sometimes performing tasks that had previously been considered either inappropriate or impossible for women. This extraordinary moment of opportunity for women, along with the meritocratic opportunity created in the army, was not lost on women writers used to second-class citizenship in the form of occupational exclusion or discrimination, especially those, such as Willa Cather, who could sympathize with men from the working classes who also suffered from limited socioeconomic opportunity. At the same time, women were pressured to support the war in various ways, and young women in particular found themselves drawn into the war hysteria concerning masculinity.

Willa Cather's Pulitzer Prize–winning *One of Ours* is deliriously pro-war, but not out of patriotism. Thus, it is very different from most such writing: the novel is unsparingly critical of pre- and postwar American culture, society, and business, which Cather sees as suffocating, non-egalitarian, and corrupt. Her book is pro-war for the same reason it is pro-military. In direct opposition to works by the privileged male Lost Generation writers, her novel is explicitly enthusiastic about the unusual social opportunities the war and the American army created for working-class men, as well as for women. Cather calls the war "a miracle so wide in its amplitude that . . . the roughnecks and the low-brows were caught up in it. Yes, it was the rough-necks' . . . golden chance."[2] Ellen La Motte's nursing memoir *The Backlash of War* was obviously antiwar. It was banned in England, France, and the United States. But Cather and La Motte, who could not have been farther apart on their views of war, actually had much in common when it came to the issue of meritocracy. The female protagonist in Porter's high-modernist "Pale Horse, Pale Rider" consciously detests the wartime propaganda with which she is bombarded and the wartime jingoism that demands unthinking pro-war sentiment (and so shares with Cather's narrator a distaste for American business and industry). Yet her seemingly straightforward antiwar attitude is complicated by her unconscious embrace of one portion of the propaganda instrumental to the mobilization of men for service: that concerning the masculine desirability of men in uniform and the suspicion of those out of it.

Thomas Boyd's *Through the Wheat*, Laurence Stallings's *Plumes*, Hervey Allen's *Toward the Flame*, Victor Daly's *Not Only War*, and William March's *Company K* all depict the horrors of combat and its physical and psychological devastations. These works, written by combat soldiers of different class and racial backgrounds, in obvious ways resemble European literature of the conflict more than those by the Lost Generation authors do. But it has to be added that most of these works do not fit the supposedly standard antiwar disillusionment story of an idealistic recruit under the sway of the wartime propaganda who enters the service and comes to a disappointing and disturbing awakening about the true nature of modern war and the army. This literature, too, is inflected and complicated by the unique American experience of a partly meritocratic and partly racist military, which makes it different from European World War I literature. Only *Company K* fundamentally fulfills the disillusionment story schema—and, as we saw in chapter ten, there are psychological compulsions that drove March to suppress other aspects of his experience that did not fit this formula. In some of these works, the mixed experience of that peculiar army helped shape the perception of combat itself: combat, though horrifying, could provide opportunities to prove oneself worthy of promotion, increased responsibility, and decoration—as is the case in the books by Boyd, Stallings, and Daly. It could also provide an escape or antidote to certain intolerable aspects of army life, such as the vicious racism in *Not Only War* and "the bullying of petty officers" in *Through the Wheat*.[3]

"Steven Trout suggests that [World War I] became America's forgotten war partly because none of the . . . multiple and conflicting accounts"—some patriotic and hopeful, some haunted and disillusioned—"ever became enshrined as the singular national memory," writes critic Mark Whalan.[4] But perhaps another reason for the "forgotten-war" status is that the army history was quickly forgotten. The army did not advertise its sometimes controversial meritocratic programs. Also, most noncombatant participants felt cheated or mistreated by the army and were thus ashamed to talk about their experience. The Lost Generation writers who did refer to it in fiction often did so in an indirect or even coded way. Meanwhile, those whom the army selected for combat went through other primary traumas, which either overshadowed the experiences of military affirmation and promotion or caused combatant writers also to be, like the Lost Generation authors, reluctant to speak about these things, though out of guilt and not shame.

But the thread of the army's meritocracy, and its effects, runs through combatant writing nevertheless. These military practices and their consequences are central to understanding the motivations and challenges of the protagonists of *Through the Wheat*, *Plumes*, *Toward the Flame*, and *Not Only War*, and they are relevant in coming to grips with the focus and exclusions of *Company K*. Stallings's *Plumes* has a disillusionment trajectory that is not the "standard" one precisely because the main character's story is profoundly shaped by the new army's practices. Boyd's *Through the Wheat*, in an even greater departure from the supposedly standard narrative, presents an arresting mix of contradictory trajectories: of both traumatization and success as a soldier. Even Daly's *Not Only War*, though dedicated to the "Army of the Disillusioned" and chronicling the American Expeditionary Force's intense racial persecution of African American doughboys, tells an inside story also involving a different side to the black experience in France. March, in *Company K*, and Allen, in *Toward the Flame*, both attempt, due to the psychological trauma of war-related guilt, to completely avoid representing their own affirmations and promotions in the war.

Though these books tend to focus on the brutality of the modern battlefield and the reality of shell shock and other forms of what we today call post–traumatic stress disorder, they are also, like the Lost Generation novels, concerned with status, though the status issues are not about being undervalued by the army in the context of a new and short-lived meritocracy. In the works by combatant authors, one finds sometimes an exploration of "demobilization injuries" that follow the loss of wartime status as well as the declining popularity of the war. One also discovers a focus not on "mobilization wounds" due to meritocratic rejection but on "mobilization boons," "mobilization confusions," and "mobilization guilt"—along with survivor guilt—due to meritocratic selection or affirmation or postwar opportunities opened up by combat service and validation. These works represent crises experienced by men chosen to be combat soldiers or officers who faced status crashes after the armistice when they returned home to uncelebrated jobs, or who felt guilt about their promotions during the war or after, given the casualties among their compatriots.

Postwar social demotion was especially intense for soldiers or officers who were maimed, such as the author Laurence Stallings and his character Richard Plume, but it was also operative for working-class or poor men for whom the war had meant extraordinary opportunity and affirmation, such as some of the characters in *Company K*.[5] Meanwhile, wartime social promotion could be especially marked for men from nonelite or even disadvantaged backgrounds who were decorated for extraordinary battlefield performance. Jay Gatsby is the famous literary example of such a man, born to a poor, ethnic American farming family, but authors Victor Daly, William March, and Thomas Boyd experienced this, too. Daly's novel presents a special case, in which the black soldier protagonist experiences, during the war, meritocratic selection, frontline promotion, and unprecedented social opportunities for equality in France, as well as racist abuse, exclusion, and demotion.

Almost all of the accomplished American war literature of this era might share the title Daly gave to what turned out to be the only World War I novel written by a black veteran, *Not Only War*. And in all of this literature, the experiences of status change are mixed and complex. Even in Daly's novel, though a reader might well expect nothing but degradation for the African American soldier protagonist, given the army's notorious policies and practices of racial discrimination, that turns out not to be the case. When read with insider knowledge of its particular historical context, Daly's story of black war service and sexually crossing the color line in France is quite different from other African American World War I tales, and something much more shocking than literary critics have taken it to be. The lasting American literature of World War I, indeed, might be more precisely categorized as "war and meritocracy literature," as it represents the first large-scale American encounter not only with the shock of modern war but with the shock of meritocracy.

NOTES

Introduction: The Shock of War and Meritocracy

1. Frederick R. Karl, introduction to William Faulkner, *Soldiers' Pay* (New York: Liveright, 1997), viii.

2. Michael Reynolds, *The Young Hemingway* (Oxford: Blackwell, 1986), 18–20. In regard to Hemingway's doctoring of his uniform, Steven Trout explains, "Hemingway removed the Red Cross insignia from his Milan-tailored tunic before being photographed in 1918." Trout, pers. comm., March 24, 2017. See also Steven Florczyk, *Hemingway, the Red Cross, and the Great War* (Kent, OH: Kent State UP, 2014).

3. Reynolds, *The Young Hemingway*, 23, 22.

4. Carlos Baker, *Ernest Hemingway: A Life Story* (New York: Scribner, 1969), 36.

5. Frederick R. Karl, *William Faulkner: American Writer: A Biography* (New York: Weidenfeld & Nicolson, 1989), 110.

6. Biographer Kenneth S. Lynn suggests this about Hemingway in his *Hemingway* (New York: Simon & Schuster, 1987), 73.

7. Baker, *Ernest Hemingway*, 44.

8. David M. Kennedy, *Over Here: The First World War and American Society* (New York: Oxford UP, 1980), 149.

9. Jennifer Keene, *Doughboys, the Great War, and the Remaking of America* (Baltimore: Johns Hopkins UP, 2000), 2.

10. Selective Service Act of 1917, Sec. 3, www.legisworks.org/congress/65/publaw-12.pdf, accessed July 12, 2017.

11. Keene, *Doughboys*, 2.

12. Along with the draft, "the military's new emphasis on the 'management of men' was similar in many ways to trends of the corporate scientific managers who attempted to control the growing labor force" and shared this Progressive Era ethos. Nancy Gentile Ford, *Americans All!: Foreign-Born Soldiers in World War I* (College Station: Texas A&M UP, 2001), 4. Though the most renowned Progressives initially presented a unified front in opposition to American involvement in the war, many ultimately broke ranks and, whether out of pragmatism or idealism, came to identify with Wilson's approach. Kennedy, *Over Here*, 33–35.

13. Howard Zinn, *A People's History of the United States* (New York: Harper Perennial Modern Classics, 2005), 364.

14. "At the beginning of the war, the regular army contained roughly 127,588 officers and men. Approximately 80,446 National Guard officers and men were in federal service along the Mexican border, with an equal number serving in the states. The army anticipated filling the divisions reserved for National Guard and regular army troops with volunteers in the summer of 1917, but the expected numbers failed to materialize. Army officials soon realized that they would have to use draftees to bring these volunteer-oriented divisions up to combat strength and also funnel conscripts into the national army units reserved exclusively for draftees." Jennifer Keene, pers. comm., November 2, 2016.

15. Kennedy, *Over Here*, 147.

16. Ibid., 148.

17. Ibid., 148–49.

18. Nancy Gentile Ford, *The Great War and America: Civil-Military Relations during World War I* (Westport, CT: Praeger Security International, 2008), 37.

19. A War Department General Order decreed the use of the cards for soldiers and required in addition that every soldier be interviewed. General Order No. 46, US Army *Personnel Manual* (November 1, 1918), chapter V, 1; Records of the Committee on Classification of Personnel (407.5.2) (hereafter CCP) in the Records of the Adjutant General's Office (Record Group 407), National Archives, College Park, MD.

20. In April 1918, the federalized National Guard units were officially absorbed into the national army, or new army. While soldiers may have still identified with their guard units, they were henceforth technically in the regular army. Though Wilson had run on a platform of keeping the United States out of the war, World War I had made the federal government aware that America was in no position to fight a war, whether the country entered the conflict or not, and this reality was now perceived of as a dangerous vulnerability. Keene, pers. comm., November 2, 2016. See also Russell F. Weigley, *History of the United States Army* (New York: Macmillan, 1967), 345–48. The chairman of the House Military Affairs Committee, James Hay, came up with the plan, ratified by the House and incorporated into the 1916 National Defense Act, that provided for a "National Guard under increased federal supervision" and, specifically, "the federal government . . . curb[ing] political patronage in the Guard by reserving the right to qualify state officers for equivalent federal commissions." Weigley, *History of the United States Army*, 348, 345.

21. *The Personnel System of the U.S. Army* (Washington, DC, 1919), 1:178, 47, CCP. W. Johnston, adjutant general, endorsed Walter Dill Scott's "more careful and scientific system" of selecting and classifying men. Letter of July 11, 1917, quoted in ibid., 47.

22. Lt. Col. W. V. Bingham, "Army Personnel Work: With Some Implications for Education and Industry," 3, CCP; "Committee on Psychology" (report, dated 1918), 8, Medicine and Related Sciences Division of the National Research Council, National Archives, College Park, MD. See also Raymond E. Fancher,

The Intelligence Men: Makers of the IQ Controversy (New York: Norton, 1985), 119; *Personnel Manual*, chapter V, 4.

23. Director Walter Dill Scott to the Secretary of War, "A Plan for the Proposed CCP," August 4, 1917, CCP; Daniel J. Kevles, "Testing the Army's Intelligence: Psychologists in World War I," *Journal of American History* 55 (1968): 579.

24. Robert M. Thorndike and David F. Lohman, *A Century of Ability Testing* (Chicago: Riverside, 1990), 46.

25. Memorandum for the Chief of Staff, 31 July 1917, quoted in Jennifer Keene, "Raising the American Expeditionary Forces: Early Decision Making in 1917" (unpublished ms), 15.

26. Jeremy A. Crang, *The British Army and the People's War, 1939–1945* (Manchester: Manchester UP, 2000), 9–10.

27. Keene, "Raising the American Expeditionary Forces," 14–16, 13; Kennedy, *Over Here*, 159–60. The military would officially be desegregated by President Harry S Truman in 1948, and in practice it ended segregation by the middle of the Korean War. Neil A. Wynn, *The Afro-American and the Second World War* (London: Paul Elek, 1976), 126. This no doubt likewise helped pave the way for desegregation outside the military in the 1954 US Supreme Court decision of *Brown v. Board of Education.*

28. See Ford, *Americans All*, 14, 112–36, and Richard Slotkin, *Lost Battalions: The Great War and the Crisis of American Nationality* (New York: Henry Holt, 2005), 7, 93, 110. The phrase "100 percent Americanism," newly fashioned in the era, is quoted in Kennedy, *Over Here*, 67.

29. Ford, *Americans All*, 74–75, 73.

30. Ibid., 3.

31. Ibid., 74–75, 73.

32. Fitzgerald, *The Great Gatsby* (New York: Scribner, 1992). Subsequent page references in text. See chapter one for a discussion of the pertinent information in *A Farewell to Arms.*

33. Fitzgerald's novel is unique among Lost Generation fiction: in it, a noncombatant veteran author has a protagonist who is given a great boost by the meritocracy. Fitzgerald's silence on the mechanism of Gatsby's army selection and promotion to lieutenant and then captain in the training camps is only the beginning of the oddity of the reading experience created by the combination of noncombatant author and war-hero protagonist. See chapters one and four.

34. Hemingway "said he had not taken the Stein epigraph seriously. He had meant to contrast her splendid bombast against the simple statement of Ecclesiastes." Michael S. Reynolds, "False Dawn: *The Sun Also Rises* Manuscript," ed. Harold Bloom, *Modern Critical Interpretations: Ernest Hemingway's* The Sun Also Rises (New York: Chelsea House, 1987), 120.

35. Ezra Pound, "Hugh Selwyn Mauberley [part I]," www.poetryfoundation.org/poems/44915/hugh-selwyn-mauberley-part-i, accessed July 15, 2017.

36. Kennedy makes the same observation in *Over Here*, 151.

37. Ralph D. Casey, *What Is Propaganda?* (1944), quoted in Adam Poltrack, "A Bill of Goods: How Advertisers Sold the Great War and Created the Lost Generation" (MA thesis, City University of New York, May 2016), 7.

38. Poltrack, "Bill of Goods," 10; StephenVaughn, *Holding Fast the Inner Lines: Democracy, Nationalism, and the Committee on Public Information* (Chapel Hill: U of North Carolina P, 1980), 30; Jia-Rui Cook, "The Posters That Sold World War I to the American Public," *Smithsonian Magazine*, July 28, 2014, www.smithsonianmag.com/history/posters-sold-world-war-i-american-public-180952179/#40JjyjSVbGm8twTp.99, accessed January 4, 2017.

39. Relying on an advertising division led by "five prominent figures in the trade," Creel's committee placed copy in $1.5 million worth of donated ad space; it also sponsored 75,000 speakers to give approximately 750,000 pro-war speeches around the country. Creel quoted in Poltrack, "Bill of Goods," 22; Stephen R. Fox, *The Mirror Makers: A History of American Advertising and Its Creators* (New York: Morrow, 1984), 75.

40. Poltrack, "Bill of Goods," 7; Cook, "Posters That Sold World War I"; Mordecai Lee, *Government Public Relations: A Reader* (Boca Raton, FL: CRC, 2008), 79.

41. Poltrack, "Bill of Goods," 21; Mark Tungate, *Adland: A Global History of Advertising* (London: Kogan Page, 2007), 19.

42. Kennedy, *Over Here*, 162.

43. See T. J. Jackson Lears, *No Place of Grace: Antimodernism and the Transformation of American Culture, 1880–1920* (New York: Pantheon, 1981), xiii–xviii; John Higham, "The Re-orientation of American Culture in the 1890s," in *The Origins of Modern Consciousness*, ed. John Weiss (Detroit: Wayne State UP, 1965), 27, 35, 40, 46; Ann Douglas, *The Feminization of American Culture* (New York: Farrar, Straus and Giroux, 1977), 327; Keith Gandal, *The Virtues of the Vicious: Jacob Riis, Stephen Crane, and the Spectacle of the Slum* (New York: Oxford UP 1997), 10–12.

44. Kennedy, *Over Here*, 151, 163–66.

45. Ibid., 149.

46. Jennifer Keene, "Hemingway: A Typical Doughboy," in *War+Ink: New Perspectives on Ernest Hemingway's Early Life and Writing*, ed. Steve Paul, Gail Sinclair, and Steven Trout (Kent, OH: Kent State UP), 54–55. Enlistment was no longer possible in infantry, artillery, or engineering units, but, for example, doctors or railroad men, whom the army needed and for whom the army was essentially in competition with the civilian sector, were still welcome to enlist. Keene, pers. comm., November 2, 2016.

47. Keene, "Hemingway: A Typical Doughboy," 54.

48. Ibid., 54–55.

49. Arthur Hoyle, "Henry Miller's Women, Part Two: Orgasm," *Huffington Post*, June 24, 2014, www.huffingtonpost.com/arthur-hoyle/henry-millers-women-part-_b_5523954.html, accessed October 27, 2016. According to some com-

mentators, including Hoyle, the author of this article, Miller was a "pacifist." But pacifists do not tend to look for exemptions from military service by working for the War Department.

50. Karl, *William Faulkner*, 111.

51. Kennedy, *Over Here*, 166.

52. Virginia Spencer Carr, *Dos Passos: A Life* (Garden City, NY: Doubleday, 1984), 149, 156.

53. Christopher Sawyer-Laucanno, *E. E. Cummings: A Biography* (London: Methuen, 2006), 141.

54. Arthur Mizener, *The Far Side of Paradise: A Biography of F. Scott Fitzgerald* (Boston: Houghton Mifflin, 1951), 71; Matthew J. Bruccoli, *Some Sort of Epic Grandeur: The Life of F. Scott Fitzgerald* (New York: Harcourt Brace Jovanovich, 1981), 86, 94.

55. Perhaps the most famous such text is Sandra M. Gilbert, "Soldier's Heart: Literary Men, Literary Women, and the Great War," in "Women and Violence," special issue, *Signs: Journal of Women in Culture and Society*, 8.3 (Spring 1983): 422–50.

56. Keene, "Hemingway: A Typical Doughboy," 58; Harold Wool, *The Military Specialist: Skilled Manpower for the Armed Forces* (Baltimore: Johns Hopkins UP, 1968), 17.

57. Keene, *Doughboys*, 51.

58. Keene, "Hemingway: A Typical Doughboy," 58; Wool, *Military Specialist*, 17. This percentage breakdown applies to the army, but the number of Marines, in general designated for combat, was so small a percentage of the AEF—just over 1 percent—that their inclusion does not change the ratio.

59. Keene, *Doughboys*, 55.

60. Ibid.

61. Keene, "Hemingway: A Typical Doughboy," 58–59.

62. Richard S. Faulkner, *Pershing's Crusaders: The American Soldier in World War I* (Lawrence: UP of Kansas, 2017), 350. The song, created by members of the SOS, went

> Mother, Take Down Your Service Flag, You're Son's in the SOS.
> He's S.O.L., but what the hell,
> He never suffered less.
> He may be thin, but that's from gin,
> Or else I missed my guess.
> Mother, Take Down Your Service Flag, You're Son's in the SOS.

63. Keene, *Doughboys*, 55.

64. CTCA pamphlet quoted in Nancy K. Bristow, *Making Men Moral: Social Engineering during the Great War* (New York: New York UP, 1996), 113–14.

65. As opposed to prostitutes, who also swarmed the camps and presented a similar kind of problem for moral and health reformers. Mary E. Odem, *Delinquent*

Daughters: Protecting Adolescent Female Sexuality in the United States, 1885–1920 (Chapel Hill: U of North Carolina P, 1995), 122; Bristow, *Making Men Moral*, 126.

66. Bristow, *Making Men Moral*, 117. For another CTCA report, see Odem, *Delinquent Daughters*, 122.

67. Odem, *Delinquent Daughters*, 122.

68. Reform and psychological studies quoted in Ellen K. Rothman, *Hands and Heart: A History of Courtship in America* (Cambridge, MA: Harvard UP, 1987), 243.

69. Faulkner, *Soldiers' Pay*, 158–59.

70. E. Deantonio, M.D. to G. B. Perkins, Capt., 10565-501G/24, Military Intelligence Division of the War Department General Staff, National Archives.

71. Lloyd Brown, NPR interview, 2009. "I was looking for the ladies," Brown reiterated in another interview. "National Museum of Marine Corps Dedication; World War I Veteran Reflects on Service," Nov. 10, 2006, www.cnn.com/TRANSCRIPTS/0611/10/cnr.05.html, accessed July 14, 2016.

72. Quoted in Kendall Taylor, *Sometimes Madness Is Wisdom: Zelda and F. Scott Fitzgerald* (London: Robson Books, 2002), 2.

73. Bristow, *Making Men Moral*, 114–15.

74. Ibid., 127, 129–30. Because of the national emergency of the war and the need for healthy troops, the Commission on Training Camp Activities was given unprecedented powers to crack down on sexual vice. Ibid., 135–36. Under the Selective Service Act and what was called the American Plan, "the military could arrest any woman within five miles of a military cantonment." And under "the new health laws, when women were arrested, their civil rights were suspended." Ruth Rosen, *The Lost Sisterhood: Prostitution in America, 1900–1918* (Baltimore: Johns Hopkins UP, 1982), 35. Detained women were to be subjected, involuntarily, to a medical exam. The Department of Justice gave the CTCA this power, under the doctrine of the police power of the state and "the constitutional right of the community" with regard to "infections and communicable diseases." Allan M. Brandt, *No Magic Bullet: A Social History of Venereal Disease in the United States Since 1880* (New York: Oxford UP, 1985), 85. "If found infected, a woman could be sentenced to a hospital or a 'farm colony' until cured." Rosen, *Lost Sisterhood*, 35.

75. Bristow, *Making Men Moral*, 117.

76. Mizener, *Far Side of Paradise*, 75.

77. John Whiteclay Chambers, ed., *The Oxford Companion to American Military History* (New York: Oxford UP, 1999), 752. To be quite specific about these numbers, this includes the army, of 3,893,340 men and the Marines of 54,690. Another 462,000 were in the navy, bringing the armed forces total to around 4.4 million, but the combatant and noncombatant numbers here do not include sailors. The navy often did dangerous "convoy" or "mine" work, accompanying US transport ships across the Atlantic, starting in the summer of 1917, and

laying a "mine barrage" in 1918 at the neck of North Sea to prevent neutral nations from trading with Germany. Keene, pers. comm., November 2, 2016. The figures come from the provost marshal's report, made after the war. *Second Report of the Provost Marshal General to the Secretary of War on the Operations of the Selective Service System to December 20, 1918* (Washington, DC: GPO, 1919), 227.

78. Nancy Ford, pers. comm., October 15, 2016.

79. Stephen Jay Gould, *The Mismeasure of Man* (New York: Norton, 1981), 195.

80. Keene uses the phrase in regard to Hemingway in "Hemingway: A Typical Doughboy."

81. Quoted in ibid., 62.

82. Faulkner, *Pershing's Crusaders*, 356.

83. Trout, pers. comm., March 24, 2017; Richard Rubin, *The Last of the Doughboys: The Forgotten Generation and Their Forgotten War* (New York: Houghton Mifflin, 2013).

84. Steven Trout, pers. comm., October 20, 2016.

85. Jennifer Keene, pers. comm., October 19, 2016.

86. Trout, pers. comm., October 20, 2016.

87. Keene, pers. comm., October 19, 2016.

88. Dan Carlin, "Hardcore History 55—Blueprint for Armageddon VI" (podcast, May 5, 2015), episode 4, www.dancarlin.com/product/hardcore-history-55-blueprint-for-armageddon-vi/, accessed August 17, 2016. For the sake of clarity, it should be pointed out that "the term 'shell shock' accumulated meaning during the First World War, initially signifying the effects of 'concussive power' on the nervous system, but ultimately coming to be associated with any form of mental illness tied to combat experience." Trout, pers. comm., March 24, 2017.

89. Roy S. Simmonds, *The Two Worlds of William March* (Tuscaloosa: U of Alabama P, 1984), 71.

90. Stuart E. Knee, *Hervey Allen 1889–1949: A Literary Historian in America* (Lewiston, NY: Edwin Mellen, 1988), 45.

91. Hervey Allen, "Preface to This Edition," in *Toward the Flame: A Memoir of World War I* (Lincoln: U of Nebraska P, 2003), xxiv.

92. Knee, *Hervey Allen*, 45.

93. Brian Bruce, *Thomas Boyd: Lost Author of the "Lost Generation"* (Akron: U of Akron P, 2006), 22.

94. See Knee, *Hervey Allen*, 47.

95. Adam P. Wilson, *African American Army Officers of World War I: A Vanguard of Equality in War and Beyond* (Jefferson, NC: McFarland, 2015), 141.

96. Philip D. Beidler, introduction to William March, *Company K* (Tuscaloosa: U of Alabama P, 1989), x. March received "the French Croix de Guerre and *both* the Distinguished Service Cross and the Navy Cross for Valor." This feat is confirmed in Simmonds, *Two Worlds of William March*, 17.

97. Quoted in Margaret R. Higgonet, introduction to *Nurses at the Front: Writing the Wounds of the Great War* (Boston: Northeastern UP, 2001), xxx. The first quote comes from Goldman; the next three are from Gilbert, Goldman, and Marcus.

98. Pearl James extends this sort of consideration to Fitzgerald's veteran narrator Nick Caraway in *The Great Gatsby* (even though, again, Fitzgerald did not himself experience combat) in *The New Death: American Modernism and World War I* (Charlottesville: UP of Virginia, 2013), chapter 2.

99. David Davis, the editor of the recent reissue of *Not Only War*, cannot be sure, but he never came across any information that Daly was wounded. Pers. comm., October 21, 2016.

100. Robert Graves, *Good-Bye to All That* (Providence: Bergen, 1995), 297, 291.

101. Bruce, *Thomas Boyd*, 46; Phyllis C. Robinson, *Willa: The Life of Willa Cather* (New York: Doubleday, 1983), 228.

102. Maxwell Anderson and Laurence Stallings's play *What Price Glory?* (1924) was a smash hit on Broadway, with its run of 435 performances. Based on the length of the run and the size of the theater, somewhere in the neighborhood of 300,000 people probably saw it. John Wilkins, Bay Area Theater Director, pers. comm., August 16, 2016. King Vidor's war movie *The Big Parade* (1925), adapted from literary works by Stallings, recorded a profit of $3.5 million and was probably the second most successful film of the silent era. (The most successful was 1915's *The Birth of a Nation.*) It would turn out to be MGM's largest grossing movie until *Gone with the Wind* in 1939. The film "was so successful that it ran on Broadway for two years; made Vidor famous as a director; won stardom for its lead, John Gilbert; and helped establish Metro-Goldwyn-Mayer financially." Joel W. Finler, *The Hollywood Story* (London: Wallflower Press, 2003), 24, 152; Melvyn Stokes, *D. W. Griffith's* The Birth of a Nation (Oxford: Oxford University Press, 2007), 3; Joan T. Brittain, *Laurence Stallings* (Boston: Twayne, 1975), 23. And the 1930 American movie adaptation of *All Quiet on the Western Front* won both Outstanding Production (now called Best Picture) and Best Director. The Official Academy Awards Database, http://awardsdatabase.oscars.org/search/results, accessed December 11, 2017.

103. Bruce, *Thomas Boyd*, 46. Dos Passos quickly became "as famous as Wrigley's," and seven months after publication he got a royalty check for $8,000 on a book that sold for two dollars. Carr, *Dos Passos*, 185, 190 (quote is from Jack Lawson). For the original book price, see www.abebooks.com/Three-Soldiers-Dos-Passos-John-George/126261274/bd, accessed August 17, 2016.

104. The publisher was Knopf. Robinson, *Willa*, 228, 230.

105. Bruce, *Thomas Boyd*, 56–57, 45–46. By 1924, the book was in its seventh printing.

106. George Garrett, introduction to Laurence Stallings, *Plumes* (Columbia: U of South Carolina P, 2006), xv–xvi.

107. Lynn, *Hemingway*, 360, 365.

108. Allen, "Preface to This Edition," xxi.

109. Simmonds, *Two Worlds of William March*, 73.

110. Bruce, *Thomas Boyd*, 46.

111. As well as the public tastes of the theater- and film-going public.

112. But as a result of this criterion, the poets T. S. Eliot and Ezra Pound, though they attempted to join the war effort and, like a number of the Lost Generation prose writers, experienced meritocratic rejection, are not included. Harry Crosby presents a similar case; he was a Lost Generation poet who served as an ambulance driver and saw intense combat action. And the poet Alan Seeger, who joined the French Foreign Legion and died at the Battle of the Somme, is not included, not only because he only published poetry but also because he was killed before the United States entered the war.

113. For example, in his review of my *The Gun and the Pen* in the *Journal of Military History*, military historian Peter S. Kindsvatter cites these three authors as belonging, after Hemingway, Fitzgerald, and Faulkner, to the next "tier of post–World War I authors." *Journal of Military History* 73.3 (July 2009): 979–81.

114. In his classic text, *World War I and the American Novel* (Baltimore: Johns Hopkins UP, 1967), Stanley Cooperman features, along with all of the soldier-writers I have chosen to focus on here with the exception of Daly, who is not addressed, Theodore Fredenburgh (*Soldiers March!*, 1930), James Stevens (*Mattock*, 1927), and Elliot Paul (*Impromptu*, 1923). These novels fit the other criteria I am using here; they take up issues of meritocracy as well as combat. For example, in *Soldiers March!*, the main character, Eddie Zorn, enters the army with the intention to "work his way up," much like the character Dan Fuselli in Dos Passos's *Three Soldiers*. He realizes that "The fellows that make the grade have got to be as hard as the conditions they live under. . . . Old rules don't work." Quoted in Cooperman, *World War I*, 137, 139. I have not included these three novels, or the novels of other soldier-writers, not because they are irrelevant or would not reward analysis but simply because I am limited in space and can only adequately address a limited number of authors and texts—and these authors' novels do not fit the criterion that their books have recently been reissued.

115. Edith Wharton's *A Son at the Front* (1923) does not fit this criterion, as her book is about a "son" in the French army, not the American one.

Part One: War Literature by Noncombatant Males

Epigraph: Frank Friedel, "Supplying the Troops: The Services of Supply," in *Over There: The American Experience in World War I* (Short Hills, NJ: Burford, 2003), available at www.worldwar1.com/dbc/freidel.htm, accessed August 11, 2016.

Chapter One: Noncombatant Mobilization Wounds

1. F. Scott Fitzgerald, *The Great Gatsby* (New York: Scribner, 1992), 137, 138. Subsequent references in text.

2. Gay Wilentz, "(Re)Teaching Hemingway: Anti-Semitism as a Thematic Device in *The Sun Also Rises*," *College English* 52.2 (February 1990), sees a typical Anglo-American prejudice with Hemingway: "Hemingway's treatment of Robert Cohn" as issuing from his feeling "threatened by the hordes of immigrants entering his country through Ellis Island" (191). Walter Benn Michaels, *Our America: Nativism, Modernism, and Pluralism* (Durham, NC: Duke UP, 1995), also interprets the author's prejudice as typical of the nativism of the era, but with much more specificity about that nativism and its relation to modernism. Carlyle Van Thompson, *The Tragic Black Buck: Racial Masquerading in the American Literary Imagination* (New York: Peter Lang, 2004), sees Gatsby as African American.

3. For a poster with the phrase "Big Game," see Nancy K. Bristow, *Making Men Moral: Social Engineering during the Great War* (New York: New York UP, 1996), illustration following 112. The "Big Show" appears in David M. Kennedy, *Over Here: The First World War and American Society* (New York: Oxford UP, 1980, 210, 223. Fitzgerald's phrase comes from "I Didn't Get Over" (1936), quoted in Arthur Mizener, *The Far Side of Paradise: A Biography of F. Scott Fitzgerald* (Boston: Houghton Mifflin, 1951), 68. Hemingway referred to the war as a great show. Carlos Baker, *Ernest Hemingway: A Life Story* (New York: Scribner, 1969), 36.

4. Quoted in Miguel A. Centeno and Elaine Enriquez, *War and Society* (Cambridge, UK: Polity, 2016), 48.

5. See Matthew Frye Jacboson, *Whiteness of a Different Color: European Immigrants and the Alchemy of Race* (Cambridge, MA: Harvard UP, 1998), and Karen Brodkin, *How Jews Became White Folks and What That Says about Race in America* (New Brunswick, NJ: Rutgers UP, 1998). Jacobson observes that the Holocaust was a turning point in regard to the American conception of Jews—and in regard to the rise of the conception of "ethnicity" (187–88).

6. The history of blacks in World War I has been known since the publication of Arthur E. Barbeau and Florette Henri, *The Unknown Soldiers: Black American Troops in World War I* (Philadelphia: Temple UP, 1974). This history about ethnic Americans has much more recently been recovered in Nancy Gentile Ford, *Americans All!: Foreign-Born Soldiers in World War I* (College Station: Texas A&M UP, 2001); Richard Slotkin, *Lost Battalions: The Great War and the Crisis of American Nationality* (New York: Henry Holt, 2005); and my own *The Gun and the Pen: Hemingway, Fitzgerald, Faulkner, and the Fiction of Mobilization* (New York: Oxford UP, 2008).

7. F. Scott Fitzgerald, *The Beautiful and Damned* (New York: Signet, 2007), 249–50. Subsequent references in text.

8. Bristow, *Making Men Moral*, 127, 129–30.

9. "The term *charity girls* originally referred to young women, generally of the working class, who used sexual relations as barter in the heterosocial world of commercial amusements in the late nineteenth century." Bristow, *Making Men Moral*, 117.

10. "The aviation service attracted [Fitzgerald] as the romantic equivalent of the Civil War cavalry." Matthew J. Bruccoli, *Some Sort of Epic Grandeur: The Life of F. Scott Fitzgerald* (New York: Harcourt Brace Jovanovich, 1981), 74. Hemingway said he wanted to "get into aviation when I am 19 and get a commission." Quoted in Peter Griffin, *Along with Youth: Hemingway, the Early Years* (New York: Oxford UP, 1985), 51. Faulkner "sought a commission in the air corps." Frederick R. Karl, *William Faulkner: American Writer: A Biography* (New York: Weidenfeld & Nicolson, 1989), 110.

11. Mizener, *The Far Side of Paradise*, 71.

12. "Fitzgerald also fell off his horse at a parade and was ordered to take riding lessons." Bruccoli, *Epic Grandeur*, 86, 94.

13. The story was called "The Offshore Pirate." Quoted in ibid., 93.

14. Ernest Hemingway, *The Sun Also Rises* (New York: Scribner, 1986), 31. Subsequent references in text.

15. Michael Reynolds, *The Young Hemingway* (Oxford: Blackwell, 1986), 18–19.

16. Masculine icon Theodore Roosevelt helped to establish this attitude. He had criticized Red Cross ambulance work for able-bodied men of draft age, and Hemingway was old enough to be drafted in September 1918, when the minimum draft age was lowered to 18: "Let . . . a man of fighting age . . . do his utmost to get into the fighting line—Red Cross work, Y.M.C.A. work, driving ambulances, and the like, excellent though it all is, should be left to men not of military age or unfit for military service, and to women." Reynolds, *The Young Hemingway*, 23. Given such a prevailing attitude, "it is little wonder that Hemingway, along with other Red Cross men, began to invent a different war life for himself," as Hemingway biographer Michael Reynolds puts it (ibid.).

17. Michael S. Reynolds, "False Dawn: *The Sun Also Rises* Manuscript," ed. Harold Bloom, *Modern Critical Interpretations: Ernest Hemingway's* The Sun Also Rises (New York: Chelsea House, 1987), 121, 120.

18. Hemingway's comparably straightforward "A Very Short Story," published a year before the densely symbolic novel, is informative here: a nurse dates an injured American soldier but then rejects him for a high-ranking Italian officer of an elite combat squad; she also demeans their relationship as "only a boy and girl affair." Ernest Hemingway, "A Very Short Story," in *In Our Time* (New York: Macmillan, 1986), 66. See chapters two and four for further discussion of this text.

19. Ernest Hemingway, *A Farewell to Arms* (London: Granada, 1980), 88–92. Subsequent references in text.

20. Rod Andrew Jr., "Soldiers, Christians, Patriots: The Lost Cause and Southern Military Schools, 1865–1915," *Journal of Southern History* 64.4 (1998): 680, 679.

21. Elizabeth Sudduth of the rare books division at the University of South Carolina, which houses the Fitzgerald papers, checked the fact that Fitzgerald never made captain with Fitzgerald experts Judy Baughman and Matthew Bruccoli. Pers. comm., May 25, 2007. In later years, Fitzgerald fantasized in his private "ledger" about being a hero in battle—and being a captain. Bruccoli, *Some Sort of Epic Grandeur*, 93.

22. Ford, *Americans All*, 80, 82.

23. Ibid., 3.

24. William Faulkner, *The Sound and the Fury* (New York: Vintage, 1956), 243. Subsequent references in text.

25. E. R. Johnstone to R. Bayard Cutting, letter titled "The Training School at Vineland New Jersey," 1918, p. 1, Committee on Provision for the Feeble-Minded, National Archives, College Park, MD, refers to identifying the "feeble-minded."

26. Ford, *Americans All*, 67–87; "Extract From Military Intelligence Bulletin No. 17," Part A, 1–2, 10565-414/1, Military Intelligence Division of the War Department General Staff, National Archives.

27. "Rating Sheet for Selecting Captains," "Form No. 1051" (1917–18), 1–2, and "Officers' Training Camps, 1917, Individual Rating Sheet for Selecting Candidates In Each Training Unit," Committee on Classification of Personnel in the Army in the Adjutant General's Office, National Archives. On the tests, see letter from E. I. Du Pont De Nemours and Company, Military Sales Department, February 23, 1918, in Medicine and Related Sciences Division of the National Research Council, Committee on Psychology, National Archives.

28. Kennedy, *Over Here*, 188.

29. Again, the military extended equal opportunity to immigrant and ethnic Americans (about a third of the draft) because they determined they could not afford the "luxury" of ethnic prejudice on top of the racial discrimination that the government imposed on the army (blacks accounted for nearly 15 percent of draftees) and still win the war.

30. Stephen Jay Gould, *The Mismeasure of Man* (New York: Norton, 1981), 218–21.

31. Kennedy, *Over Here*, 188. In fact, northern schools were so much better that northern black men outscored southern whites on the tests. These results had no practical application during the war, however, because of the military discrimination against African Americans. Alan M. Osur, *Blacks in the Army Air Forces during World War II: The Problem of Race Relations* (Honolulu: UP of the Pacific, 2005).

32. Rabbi Lee J. Levinger, *A Jewish Chaplain in France* (New York: Macmillan, 1921), 121, 123.

33. William Faulkner, *Soldiers' Pay* (New York: Liveright, 1997), 42.

34. James G. Watson, "Faulkner and the Theater of War," in *Faulkner and War: Faulkner and Yoknapatawpha, 2001*, ed. Noel Polk and Ann J. Abadie (Jackson: U of Mississippi P, 2004), argues that Ames is "drawn from . . . the experience of soldiers of the Great War . . . who inspired the young Faulkner's envy and despair in 1918. . . . Looking back from the moment of composition in 1928–1929 to the fictional moment of 1910, Faulkner borrowed from and, where necessary to the fiction, recast his intense experience at Yale [on his way to Canada] and in the R.A.F. when the Great War had been a constant point of reference and gauge of his morale" (30).

Chapter Two: The Horrors of War Mobilization

1. John Dos Passos, *Three Soldiers* (Mineola, NY: Dover, 2004). Subsequent references in text.

2. Stanley Cooperman uses the phrase "World War I novel of protest" in *World War I and the American Novel* (Baltimore: Johns Hopkins UP, 1967), 85.

3. When World War I veteran Lloyd Brown was asked why he was not homesick as a 16 year old in the service, he answered, "Well, I had a lot of my shipmates, and going to different countries, and going ashore, and going to dances and meet some young ladies and so forth in different countries, and learn *how to speak French* and so forth" (emphasis added). "Interview with Lloyd Brown," June 28, 2005, Veterans History Project, http://memory.loc.gov/diglib/vhp/story/loc.natlib.afc2001001.31443/transcript?ID=sr0001, accessed July 14, 2016. Victor Daly includes a scene in which enlisted men rely on their noncommissioned officer "to do the talkin' for us" when it comes to arranging being billeted in a French home. Daly, *Not Only War: A Story of Two Great Conflicts* (Charlottesville: UP of Virginia , 2010), 49–50.

4. He continues: "I hear your M.P.'s are very strict. You must be able to toss the word the minute you see a skirt, and make your date before the guard gets onto you." Willa Cather, *One of Ours* (n.p.: Seven Treasures, 2009), 130. And despite the concerted attempt of the US army to enforce chastity for members of the AEF (it was against orders to engage in sex, and they were barred from brothels), about 70 percent of American soldiers who went to Europe had sex there. Allan M. Brandt, *No Magic Bullet: A Social History of Venereal Disease in the United States Since 1880* (New York: Oxford UP, 1985), 114.

5. My translation.

6. Cooperman, *World War I and the American Novel*, 84–86, quote on 85.

7. Historian Jennifer Keene concurs with this assessment. Pers. comm., October 19, 2016.

8. William Faulkner, *Soldiers' Pay* (New York: Liveright, 1997), 3. Subsequent references in text.

9. Frederick R. Karl, *William Faulkner: American Writer: A Biography* (New York: Weidenfeld & Nicolson, 1989), 115–16.

10. As mentioned in chapter one, next time we encounter the epithet "slobbering and moaning" in the Faulkner oeuvre it will belong to Benjy in *The Sound and the Fury*, who is obviously like Mahon in certain ways but also shares Lowe's emotional excesses, as well as his remaining a "child" into adulthood.

11. I am indebted to Steven Trout for pointing out to me that "Lowe is not the only noncombatant humiliated in Faulkner's fiction. In *Flags in the Dust* (originally published as *Sartoris* [1929]), a Marine veteran taunts Horace Benbow, a detested 'Y-man' (i.e., noncombatant YMCA worker), as he returns from Europe to his hometown in Mississippi." Pers. comm., March 24, 2017.

12. Ernest Hemingway, "A Very Short Story," in *In Our Time* (New York: Macmillan, 1986). Subsequent references in text. *In Our Time* is actually Hemingway's second published book, following *in our time* (1924); this slim volume included vignettes that reappear in *In Our Time* but not the short stories.

13. It should perhaps more accurately be called a "Sincerely, Jane Letter," as Luz remains in the war zone, doing war work, and Nick has returned home to the States.

14. Kenneth S. Lynn, *Hemingway* (New York: Simon & Schuster, 1987), 88.

15. Ibid., 88, 95.

16. Tim Auld, "Ernest Hemingway and the 'Dear John' Letter from His First World War Love," *Telegraph*, June 14, 2014, www.telegraph.co.uk/history/world-war-one/10561536/Ernest-Hemingway-and-the-Dear-John-letter-from-his-First-World-War-love.html, accessed July 5, 2017.

17. Lynn, *Hemingway*, 98.

18. This takes on additional meaning as we explore Hemingway's other tales of a wounded soldier and his nurse in chapter four.

19. F. Scott Fitzgerald, *The Beautiful and Damned* (New York: Signet, 2007), 250–51. Subsequent references in text.

20. Matthew J. Bruccoli, *Some Sort of Epic Grandeur: The Life of F. Scott Fitzgerald* (New York: Harcourt Brace Jovanovich, 1981), 93.

21. Dos Passos was born Jack Madison; his mother was not married to his biological father, John R. Dos Passos Sr. See Carr, *Dos Passos*, 14.

22. While serving as an ambulance driver, Dos Passos got into some trouble with the Red Cross authorities for pacifist sentiments expressed in letters he wrote. He was recommended for a discharge by a Red Cross major. Another trouble he faced was a failure to show up to the draft board when he was called just after his departure for Europe to be in the ambulance corps. He wanted simply to stay in Europe to continue to participate in some way in the war, and he tried various avenues, but they did not work out; his extremely poor eyesight got in the way with the American Field Service. In the end, despite attempted interventions by powerful allies, he was ordered to report to the draft board back in the United States. He managed, with the help of an influential connection named James Brown Scott, a major in the Judge Advocate General's Department, to get

his delinquency charge with the draft board dropped. Eager to get back to the war and afraid "that it might end before he could back," he was apologetic with the draft board chairman and won over the medical examiner. Virginia Spencer Carr, *Dos Passos: A Life* (Garden City, NY: Doubleday, 1984), 146–53.

23. Ibid., 153.

24. Quoted in ibid., 156.

25. Ibid., 160.

26. Ibid., 164.

27. Ibid., chapters 1–11.

28. Jennifer Keene, pers. comm., May 11, 2017.

29. H. L. Mencken, "Portrait of an American Citizen," *Smart Set* 69 (October 1922): 140–42.

30. Review of *Hickoxy's Army, Being a Short History of Headquarters Company, 306th Field Artillery, 77th Division, A.E.F.*, *Quarterly Journal of the New York State Historical Association* 2.4 (October 1921): 270–71.

31. Steven Trout, *On the Battlefield of Memory: The First World War and American Remembrance, 1919–1941* (Tuscaloosa: U of Alabama P, 2010), 3.

32. Carr, *Dos Passos*, 186–87.

33. Ibid., 186.

34. Ibid., 164.

35. "Some recent work on shell shock has pointed out the high numbers of noncombatants who suffered from it, concluding that shell shock is as much about fear as it is about exposure to shells." Keene, pers. comm. May 11, 2017. Hervey Allen makes a similar point about "gas shock" in *Towards the Flame*, namely that men could develop "gas shock" simply from constant false alarms about gas. But whether shell shock is the result of actually being shelled or of possibly being shelled, the point here is that uncontrollable fear is the psychological issue for the sufferer.

36. Jennifer Keene, pers. comm., November 2, 2016.

37. There are plenty of such examples of the arbitrariness of the army's meritocracy, but one other example comes from John Lewis Barkley's World War I memoir *Scarlet Fields* (Lawrence: UP of Kansas, 2012). "Barkley was barred initially from service as an infantryman, despite his extraordinary skills as a marksman, because of his stuttering." Trout, pers. comm., March 24, 2017.

38. Carr, *Dos Passos*, 164.

39. Ibid.

Chapter Three: Saved by French Arrest and Imprisonment

1. Christopher Sawyer-Laucanno, *E. E. Cummings: A Biography* (London: Methuen, 2006), 104.

2. Or an autobiography or memoir by his own account. Ibid., 205. Cummings himself wrote that "the appeal of the book is largely documentary." Ibid., 202.

3. E. E. Cummings, *The Enormous Room* (New York: Modern Library, 1934), 313. Subsequent references in text.

4. Sawyer-Laucanno, *E. E. Cummings*, 104.

5. The scene in the jail cell opens a chapter called "En Route." The narrator is en route to a destination prison he has not yet reached (23).

6. Sawyer-Laucanno, *E. E. Cummings*, 120. "Camp du Triage" is glossed as "concentration camp" in the introduction to *The Enormous Room* (iii).

7. When Cummings the writer is later, after he is drafted, subjected to the American army and its evaluative procedures, he is validated rather than rejected. This army experience of Cummings the writer, though it is beyond the scope of *The Enormous Room*, occurs before the book is published. See below.

8. As Karsten Piep, *Embattled Home Fronts: Domestic Politics and the American Novel* (Amsterdam: Rodopi, 2009), asserts about Hemingway's Frederic Henry, Dos Passos's Andrews, and Cummings in *The Enormous Room* (10–12).

9. Sawyer-Laucanno, *E. E. Cummings*, 120–21.

10. Again, Cummings does go into the US Army later in the war but chose not to depict that experience in *The Enormous Room*. See below.

11. A variation on this derogatory witticism appears in Faulkner's *The Sound and the Fury*, in Quentin's section: "Land of the kike home of the wop." William Faulkner, *The Sound and the Fury* (New York: Vintage, 1956), 155.

12. Sawyer-Laucanno, *E. E. Cummings*, 141.

13. Ibid., 141–42.

14. Cummings quoted in ibid., 142.

15. Ibid., 140–41.

16. Ibid., 141.

17. Cummings letter, quoted in ibid., 143.

18. Ibid., 142.

19. Poem quoted in ibid., 143–44.

Chapter Four: Hemingway's Thrice-Told Tale

1. For a wonderful recent example, see Pearl James, *The New Death: American Modernism and World War I* (Charlottesville: UP of Virginia, 2013), chapter 3.

2. Ernest Hemingway, *A Farewell to Arms* (London: Granada, 1980), 232. Subsequent references in text.

3. Jennifer Keene, "Hemingway: A Typical Doughboy," in *War+Ink: New Perspectives on Ernest Hemingway's Early Life and Writing*, ed. Steve Paul, Gail Sinclair, and Steven Trout (Kent, OH: Kent State UP, 2014), gives me credit for proposing this reconnection: "Gandal's work, however, proposes a way to reconnect the Lost Generation writers to their fellow veterans" (61). My take on Hemingway, Fitzgerald, and Faulkner, essentially summarized in chapter one above, was first published in *The Gun and the Pen: Hemingway, Fitzgerald, Faulkner and the Fiction of Mobilization* (New York: Oxford UP, 2008).

4. Keene, "Hemingway: A Typical Doughboy," 61–62.

5. William Faulkner, *Soldiers' Pay* (New York: Liveright, 1997), 48.

6. Keene, "Hemingway: A Typical Doughboy," 62.

7. F. Scott Fitzgerald, *The Great Gatsby* (New York: Scribner, 1992), 158.

8. Ernest Hemingway, *The Sun Also Rises* (New York: Scribner, 1986), 101. Subsequent references in text.

9. John Dos Passos, *Three Soldiers* (Mineola, NY: Dover, 2004), 11, 10. Subsequent references in text.

10. There are other 1920s noncombatant texts, which I do not have the space to address here. Another example is James Stevens's novel *Mattock* (1927), a comic and bitter book all about the noncombatant experience and its frustrations.

11. John Dos Passos, *1919*, in *U.S.A.* (New York: Library of America, 1996), 663. Subsequent references in text.

12. Perhaps more accurately, Dick is simply the denizen of an upper-crust milieu, and certainly the super-rich could actually have had the kind of experience in the World War I army that Dick does—though of course Dos Passos did not come from such a milieu, and even Cummings, the most elite member of the Lost Generation, did not have a family with this kind of pull. (Either way, the book is arguably incoherent here, as Dick's brother is not privy to such privilege on his own, without Dick's help.)

13. Michael Reynolds, *The Young Hemingway* (Oxford: Blackwell, 1986), 21–22.

14. In his 1927 short story "In Another Country," in *The Complete Short Stories of Ernest Hemingway* (New York: Scribner, 1998), the American narrator muses: "I had been wounded, it was true; but we all knew that being wounded, after all, was really an accident" (208).

15. Kenneth S. Lynn, *Hemingway* (New York: Simon & Schuster, 1987), 85.

16. Reynolds, *The Young Hemingway*, 21.

17. Lynn, *Hemingway*, 98.

18. Just this sort of noncombatant resentment for a pilot is represented in the famous post–World War II movie *The Best Years of Our Lives* (1946). The pilot character is played by Dana Andrews.

19. Michael S. Reynolds, "False Dawn: *The Sun Also Rises* Manuscript," ed. Harold Bloom, *Modern Critical Interpretations: Ernest Hemingway's* The Sun Also Rises (New York: Chelsea House, 1987), 120. See also Reynolds, *Hemingway: The Paris Years* (Cambridge, MA: Basil Blackwell, 1989), 295.

20. Reynolds, *Hemingway: The Paris Years*, 340; Reynolds, "False Dawn," 120.

21. Jack M. Bickham, *Writing Novels That Sell.* (New York: Simon & Schuster, 1989), 61.

22. Hemingway's anti-Semitism has been much discussed. On Hemingway's problems with ethnic Americans, see Gandal, *The Gun and the Pen*, chapter 4.

23. We learn that Cohn is 34 years old (9), was "married five years," and then spent "three years" in Europe (4–5). If the action of the book is set in the present (the book is published in 1926), this would mean that Cohn was 25 in 1917,

definitely of draft age. It also means that he got married in 1918—perhaps with express purpose of avoiding service. The significance of this information about Cohn's age and domestic circumstances are the sort of thing so easily lost to view over time, but it would hardly have been lost on a World War I veteran in the 1920s. Just imagine how conscious a Vietnam-era reader, especially a veteran reader, would have been about a similar character's age and circumstances that explain his lack of service.

24. Reynolds, *The Young Hemingway*, 21–22.

25. Keene, "Hemingway: A Typical Doughboy," 60.

26. Reynolds, *The Young Hemingway*, 21.

27. Ellen Andrew Knodt, "Suddenly and Unreasonably: Shooting the Sergeant in *A Farewell to Arms*," in *Hemingway's Italy: New Perspectives*, ed. Rena Sanderson (Baton Rouge: Louisiana State UP, 2006), argues that Henry has a sort of hysterical fit during this episode, and his unloading an entire clip at the fleeing sergeants indicates intense emotion rather than a stoic attitude. That is plausible, and his failure to have any emotional reaction later may be due to his immediately repressing the event. But my point here is not about what Henry is actually feeling but how he appears to a "casual" reader (and not a professional literary critic).

28. See Gandal, *The Gun and the Pen*, 47–48.

Part Two: War Literature by Female Participants and Nonparticipants

Epigraph: Alice Paul was an activist who historians believe secretly cut a deal with President Woodrow Wilson to end her wartime prison hunger strike in exchange for his support for the constitutional amendment granting women's suffrage. *The Great War*, PBS documentary, aired April 10–12, 2017; Christopher Capozzola, *Uncle Sam Wants You: World War I and the Making of the Modern American Citizen* (New York: Oxford UP, 2010), 114.

Chapter Five: The Mobilization of Young Women

1. After encountering various female characters, written by Lost-Generation male writers who pretty obviously suffered from masculinity issues as a result of their noncombatant status (again, Hemingway and Faulkner lied about their service, and Fitzgerald "regret[ted]" in the 1920s "not getting overseas during the war"), it is refreshing and revealing to get a female author's portrait of a young woman experiencing the wartime moment. It is also illuminating to have the tables turned and to meet noncombatants depicted by a woman writer, and seen through the eyes of a young woman who is dating a soldier and officer. In this regard, it is particularly revealing to see how that young woman character understands the noncombatant's resentful attitude toward her—because it sheds light on the portraits of women we get in Lost Generation male literature.

2. Porter quoted in a 1956 *Denver Post* interview, in Joan Givner, *Katherine Anne Porter: A Life* (New York: Simon & Schuster, 1982), 128.

3. Katherine Anne Porter, *Pale Horse, Pale Rider: Three Short Novels* (New York: Harcourt, Brace, 1967), 147. Subsequent references in text.

4. Porter's depiction of the environment of the super-patriotic home front, and Miranda's silent capitulation to its expectations, is realistic, according to historical accounts. Christopher Capozzola uses the term "coercive voluntarism" in *Uncle Sam Wants You: World War I and the Making of the Modern American Citizen* (New York: Oxford UP, 2010), chapter 3: "The Obligation to Volunteer: Women and Coercive Voluntarism." See also *The Great War*, PBS documentary, aired April 10–12, 2017.

5. Porter's insight here sheds light on the reason that noncombatant male Lost Generation authors often gave their female characters a malevolent aspect. Hemingway's Luz and Brett, Faulkner's Margaret Powers and Caddy Compson, and Fitzgerald's Gloria and Daisy are all involved with soldiers; they all have male multiple suitors; most of them have extramarital affairs; some of them treat men cavalierly, and Brett in particular, it is revealed at the bullfights, has a taste for blood.

6. It may be that Miranda's sense of Chuck has perhaps been unfairly tarnished by her knowledge of such men.

7. According to Jennifer Keene, pers. comm., February 27, 2017, women did not hand out white feathers in the United States, as English women did.

8. Following Judith Butler's notion of performing gender. Butler, "Subversive Bodily Acts," in *The Cultural Studies Reader*, 3rd ed., ed. Simon During (New York: Routledge, 2007), 371–82.

9. F. Scott Fitzgerald, *The Beautiful and Damned* (New York: Signet, 2007), 286–87. See chapter two above for a more thorough description of this scene.

10. See, for example, the confrontation with the "Y.M.C.A. man" over his charging soldiers for hot chocolate in Thomas Boyd, *Through the Wheat: A Novel of the World War I Marines* (Lincoln: U of Nebraska P, 2000), 43.

11. Steven Trout, pers. comm., March 24, 2017. Richard S. Faulkner, *Pershing's Crusaders: The American Soldier in World War I* (Lawrence: UP of Kansas, 2017), writes, "Few engineers experienced . . . [frontline combat danger and] excitement. Both division engineers and pioneer infantry regiments spent their time in the vital mission of repairing and maintaining the vital routes to the front" (510).

12. Faulkner, *Pershing's Crusaders*, 350.

13. Virginia Spencer Carr, *Dos Passos: A Life* (Garden City, NY: Doubleday, 1984), 156.

14. President Woodrow Wilson said, "The federal government has pledged its word that as far as care and vigilance can accomplish the result, the men committed to its charge will be returned to the homes and communities that so generously gave them with no scars except those won in honorable conflict." Allan M. Brandt, *No Magic Bullet: A Social History of Venereal Disease in the United States Since 1880* (New York: Oxford UP, 1985), 101, 96.

15. Givner, *Katherine Anne Porter*, 128.

16. Ibid., 127.

17. Ibid., 129.

18. Porter in a 1969 interview, quoted in ibid., 128.

Chapter Six: "A Miracle So Wide"

1. Willa Cather, *One of Ours* (n.p.: Seven Treasures, 2009), 95. Subsequent references in text.

2. Ernest Hemingway, *Torrents of Spring* (New York: Scribner's, 1930), 89, quoted in David M. Kennedy, *Over Here: The First World War and American Society* (New York: Oxford UP, 1980), 219. In a letter to Edmund Wilson, he wrote, "Wasn't that last scene in the lines wonderful? Do you know where it came from? The battle scene in *Birth of a Nation.* I identified episode after episode, Catherized. Poor woman, she had to get her war experience somewhere." From Hemingway, *Selected Letters, 1917–1961*, ed. Carlos Baker (New York: Scribner's, 1981), 105, quoted in Steven Trout, "Antithetical Icons? Willa Cather, Ernest Hemingway, and the First World War," *Cather Studies* 7 (2007), http://cather.unl.edu/cs007_trout.html, accessed September 16, 2016.

3. Quoted in Phyllis C. Robinson, *Willa: The Life of Willa Cather* (New York: Doubleday, 1983), 228–29.

4. "Sergeant, Elizabeth Shepley, 1881–1965," Social Networks and Archival Context, http://socialarchive.iath.virginia.edu/ark:/99166/w6rf68d3, accessed October 8, 2016.

5. Robinson, *Willa*, 223.

6. Ibid., 231–32.

7. Margaret R. Higgonet, introduction, *Nurses at the Front: Writing the Wounds of the Great War* (Boston: Northeastern UP, 2001), xiv.

8. Ibid., ix, xxxvi–xxxviin21.

9. Stein quoted in ibid., xi.

10. Ibid., xiii, ix.

11. Christine E. Hallett, *Nurse Writers of the Great War* (Manchester: Manchester UP, 2016), 84.

12. Gertrude Stein, *The Autobiography of Alice B. Toklas* (1933), chapter 6, http://gutenberg.net.au/ebooks06/0608711.txt, accessed October 20, 2016.

13. Higgonet, introduction, xiv.

14. Ellen La Motte, "An American Nurse in Paris," *Survey*, July 10, 1915, 335.

15. Ellen La Motte, *Backwash of War*, reprinted in Higgonet, *Nurses at the Front*, 59. Subsequent references in text.

16. Higgonet, introduction, xviii.

17. Ellen La Motte, *The Backwash of War* (1916), 172, www.gutenberg.org/files/26884/26884-h/26884-h.htm, accessed July 19, 2017. Borden has her own version of this story, called "Enfant de Malheur," in her book on World War I

nursing. In it, Borden is interested in the spiritual redemption of this man, who is a former criminal. La Motte would no doubt have found such an aim inappropriate to the institution. Higgonet observes that La Motte finds Borden at times "concerned with emotional rather than physical care" (introduction, xvii).

18. Hallett, *Nurse Writers of the Great War*, 78.

19. Steven Trout, *Memorial Fictions: Willa Cather and the First World War* (Lincoln: U Nebraska P, 2002), claims she did a decent job.

20. She also heard about the war from "Western boys" whose war injuries were being treated in "Polyclinic Hospital in New York" in the winter of 1918, returning "soldiers who came to call on her" at her home, and newspaper stories and memoirs by and about soldiers. Robinson, *Willa*, 221–23.

21. Robinson, *Willa*, 66, 76–77.

22. Higgonet, introduction, ix, xiv.

23. Ellen La Motte, *The Backwash of War*, new ed. (New York: G. P. Putnam's Sons, 1934), v–vii.

24. Higgonet, introduction, xxv–xxvi.

25. "Thanks to the persistence of the pioneer female administrators of hospital-based nursing schools in applying Nightingale's model, the standards of classroom and on-the-job training had risen sharply in the 1880s and 1890s, and along with them the expectation of decorous and professional conduct." Shawna M. Quinn, *Agnes Warner and the Nursing Sisters of the Great War* (Fredericton, NB: Goose Lane, 2010), 15–16.

26. La Motte, "An American Nurse in Paris," 334, 335.

27. Ibid, 335.

28. Ibid.

29. Ibid., 336.

30. Hazel Hutchison, *The War That Used Up Words: American Writers and the First World War* (New Haven: Yale UP, 2015), 142.

31. Hallett, *Nurse Writers of the Great War*, 84–85.

32. Robert S. Nelson, "The Art Collecting of Emily Crane Chadbourne and the Absence of Byzantine Art in Chicago," in *To Inspire and Instruct: A History of Medieval Art in Midwestern Museums*, ed. Christina Nielsen (Newcastle: Cambridge Scholars Publishing, 2008), 146, www.academia.edu/3625724/The_Art_Collection_of_Emily_Crane_Chadbourne_and_the_Absence_of_Byzantine_Art_in_Chicago, accessed October 20, 2016.

33. Hallett, *Nurse Writers of the Great War*, 84–85.

34. Quoted in ibid., 84.

35. Higgonet, introduction, xxxvi–xxxviin21.

36. La Motte, *Backwash of War*, 202–4.

37. Higgonet, introduction, xxxvi–xxxviin21.

38. Nelson, "Art Collecting of Emily Crane Chadbourne," 145.

39. Ibid., 144.

40. A 1919 letter she wrote to her cousin expressed her feelings: "I shall never forget that it is owing to you entirely that I was able to give up my work in Baltimore and to have the leisure to undertake the work that I had always wanted to do, that is, write. Without your help all these years that would have been impossible. I should have just had to go on doing work which finally grew to be dull and mechanical, and could never have afforded to live while I tried to make myself known as a writer. I wonder if you can ever know how grateful I am for that, dear Alfred. I have said so, at times, but I don't believe I can ever make you know what it really means" (ibid., 226n71).

41. Stein, *Autobiography of Alice B. Toklas,* chapter 6.

42. Ibid.

43. Higgonet, introduction, xi.

44. Stein, *Autobiography of Alice B. Toklas,* chapter 4.

45. Ibid.

46. "La Motte's public health role was also characterized by an awareness of the potential of women professionals in a heavily male-dominated field." Hutchison, *War That Used Up Words*, 143.

47. Higgonet, introduction, xiii.

48. Carlos Baker, *Ernest Hemingway: A Life Story* (New York: Scribner, 1969), 44.

49. Jack Kerouac, *Vanity of Duluoz: An Adventurous Education* (New York: Penguin, 1994), 148.

50. Higgonet suggests this is probable (introduction, xvii).

51. Mary Borden, *The Forbidden Zone*, in Higgonet, *Nurses at the Front*, 94–95.

52. Higgonet, introduction, xvi.

53. Hallett, *Nurse Writers of the Great War*, 78–79.

54. La Motte, *The Backwash of War* (1916).

55. "There were suicides during and after WWI—most connected with 'Shell Shock.' " Nancy Ford, pers. comm., January 8, 2015. See also Annessa Stagner, "Healing the Soldier, Restoring the Nation," *Journal of Contemporary History* 49.2 (April 2014): 255–74. Steven Trout points out that "Cather obliquely refers to Charles Whittlesey of the Lost Battalion in this section . . . [and] attributing his death to some sort of postwar disillusionment with America is especially absurd. Whittlesey likely committed suicide because he could no longer endure his sense of guilt over losing so many men in a pointless action deemed 'heroic' by the US Army." Trout, pers. comm., March 24, 2017. Cather evinces more of the same insensitivity to the psychological costs of war in portraying her one character who obviously suffers from shell shock—the amnesiac "Lost American"—as having been made happier by his condition. Cather, *One of Ours*, 150–51.

56. Borden, *Forbidden Zone*, 125–27.

57. Ibid., 127.

Part Three: Combatant War Literature

Epigraph: William Brumfield, pers. comm., February 16 and 21, 2017.

Chapter Seven: A War Hero in an Antiwar Tale?

1. Steven Trout, *On the Battlefield of Memory: The First World War and American Remembrance, 1919–1941* (Tuscaloosa: U of Alabama P, 2010), 7.

2. Quoted in ibid., 8.

3. Ibid., 7–8; *New York Times* review, quoted on back cover of Thomas Boyd, *Through the Wheat: A Novel of the World War I Marines* (Lincoln: U of Nebraska P, 2000).

4. Quoted in Trout, *On the Battlefield of Memory*, 8.

5. Edwin Howard Simmons, introduction to Boyd, *Through the Wheat*, v. Subsequent citations to the novel in text.

6. *New York Times* review, in Boyd, *Through the Wheat*.

7. Mark Whalan, "Literature (USA)," in *1914–1918-Online: International Encyclopedia of the First World War*, ed. Ute Daniel, Peter Gatrell, Oliver Janz, Heather Jones, Jennifer Keene, Alan Kramer, and Bill Nasson, http://dx.doi.org/10.15463/ie1418.10349, accessed September 2, 2016.

8. Ibid.

9. Ibid.

10. Ibid.

11. Brent G. Nunnaly, quoted in Brian Bruce, *Thomas Boyd: Lost Author of the "Lost Generation"* (Akron: U of Akron P, 2006), 56.

12. Quoted in ibid., 55.

13. Ibid., 12.

14. Technically, a Marine is not a combat *soldier*, which designates a man in the *army*, but I am referring to the role of the Marine as a combatant.

15. Bruce, *Thomas Boyd*, 11.

16. Hicks's comment suggests "another implication for writers feeling disillusioned by being assigned noncombatant work. These assignments are challenging their racial identities as 'white,' not just their class or ethnic identities. . . . Their sense of 'white privilege' [is] attacked. . . . Hicks escapes that fate, but doesn't that leave the other, less-meritorious feeling also 'less white'?" Jennifer Keene, pers. comm., May 11, 2017. Indeed, such a feeling was possible even in losing out in a competition with certain ethnic Americans, since, for example, in this period, Jewish and Italian Americans were not considered white (along with Arab and Chinese Americans). See Matthew Frye Jacboson, *Whiteness of a Different Color: European Immigrants and the Alchemy of Race* (Cambridge, MA: Harvard UP, 1998), and Karen Brodkin, *How Jews Became White Folks and What that Says about Race in America* (New Brunswick, NJ: Rutgers UP, 1998).

17. Jennifer Keene, *Doughboys, the Great War, and the Remaking of America* (Baltimore: Johns Hopkins UP, 2000), 215n2.

18. In Boyd's short story "A Little Gall," in *Points of Honor* (1925), an enlisted man gets five years in Leavenworth for merely drunkenly talking back to an officer.

19. Newton D. Baker, quoted in Nancy Gentile Ford, *The Great War and America: Civil-Military Relations during World War I* (Westport, CT: Praeger Security International, 2008), 37.

20. Bruce, *Thomas Boyd*, 19; Citation in the 2d Division General Order #53 on 12 September 1918 for an action on 19 July, quoted in Simmons, introduction, xi.

21. This may be because Boyd's awards came later, after the fact, and the narrative of *Through the Wheat*, which closely mirrors Boyd's real war experience, and ends just after a battle scene, is strictly chronological.

22. Bruce, *Thomas Boyd*, 17–18.

23. Philip D. Biedler, introduction to William March, *Company K* (Tuscaloosa: U of Alabama P, 1989), xxi.

24. Jennifer Keene, "Hemingway: A Typical Doughboy," in *War+Ink: New Perspectives on Ernest Hemingway's Early Life and Writing*, ed. Steve Paul, Gail Sinclair, and Steven Trout (Kent, OH: Kent State UP), 54.

25. Of course, this may be simply a matter of exchanging a couple of denigrating stereotypes of black men as more animal or savage ("they are made for hard labor"; "they smell bad") for an ennobling one ("they don't feel pain").

26. Whalan, "Literature (USA)."

27. Miguel A. Centeno and Elaine Enriquez, *War and Society* (Cambridge, UK: Polity, 2016), 46.

28. Winston S. Churchill, *The Story of the Malakand Field Force* (1898; reprint, London: Kessinger, 2004), 107, quoted in http://desertonfire.blogspot.com/2009/07/source-of-famous-churchill-quote.html, accessed September 2, 2016.

29. Siegfried Sassoon, *Memoirs of an Infantry Officer* (London: Faber & Faber, 1930), 39.

30. Centeno and Enriquez, *War and Society*, 46.

31. Bruce, *Thomas Boyd*, 52–53.

32. The Perkins quote is from a March 5, 1923, letter; Boyd's response came in a March 7 letter. Brian Bruce, pers. comm., August 11, 2016.

33. Bruce, *Thomas Boyd*, 53. Bruce has not seen a copy of the original manuscript and does not know if one exists. In the biography, he does not venture to guess what the last line originally was. He is now—after he and I discussed it via email and phone—basing his presumption about what the original last line was on the correspondence between Perkins and Boyd. What he knows for certain, from the letters, are the texts of these two alternative last lines and that Boyd suggested the "Gethsemanied" line in a letter dated March 7, 1923, then on March 12, suggested changing the "lost in the absolute" line to the "numb" line, which appears in the published version. Bruce, pers. comm., August 11, 2016. I agree with his conclusion. And one further piece of evidence that points to "Hicks was exalted: lost in the absolute" as the original last line in the manuscript sub-

mitted to Scribner's—and that makes it fairly certain that "Hicks was exalted" was in any case part of the original last line—is Fitzgerald's review, quoted above and below, which speaks of the book's "exaltation, and with this note vibrating sharply in the reader's consciousness the book ends." Quoted in Trout, *On the Battlefield of Memory*, 8.

34. The Gospel of Mark (14:32–33) has "amazed" as well as "heavy" and "sorrowful." The Gospel of Matthew (26:37–38) has only "heavy" and "sorrowful."

35. Quoted in Trout, *On the Battlefield of Memory*, 7–8.

36. Boyd's March 7, 1923, letter continues: "That is all there is to the ending. I don't see what I can do with it. It's a delicate point, and if I tried to make it more obvious, I might bungle." Bruce, pers. comm., August 11, 2016.

37. Trout, *On the Battlefield of Memory*, 7.

38. Bruce, *Thomas Boyd*, 52–53.

39. Ibid., 21.

40. Ibid., 22.

41. Simmons, introduction, ix.

42. Bruce, *Thomas Boyd*, 21, 23–24.

43. Ibid., xiii, 4–5. Simmons, introduction, claims that Boyd "was well schooled" (v), but Bruce's details indicate otherwise.

44. Centeno and Enriquez, *War and Society*, 46.

45. Bruce, *Thomas Boyd*, 11–13.

46. According to Bruce, *Thomas Boyd*, he fell asleep on duty (13), but Simmons, introduction, relates the infraction as sitting down and taking off his rifle belt (viii).

47. Bruce, *Thomas Boyd*, 11–13.

48. Simmons, introduction, viii.

49. Bruce, *Thomas Boyd*, 22.

50. Ibid., 19–20; Simmons, introduction, xii.

51. Bruce, *Thomas Boyd*, 27.

52. Paul Edwards, "British War Memoirs," in *Cambridge Companion to the Literature of the First World War*, ed. Vincent Sherry (Cambridge: Cambridge UP, 2005), 24–25, 28.

53. Bruce, *Thomas Boyd*, 48–52, 55, 79.

Chapter Eight: The Intimate Seductions of Meritocracy

1. Mark Whalan, "Literature (USA)," in *1914–1918-Online: International Encyclopedia of the First World War*, ed. Ute Daniel, Peter Gatrell, Oliver Janz, Heather Jones, Jennifer Keene, Alan Kramer, and Bill Nasson, http://dx.doi.org/10.15463/ie1418.10349, accessed September 2, 2016.

2. Steven Trout, *On the Battlefield of Memory: The First World War and American Remembrance, 1919–1941* (Tuscaloosa: U of Alabama P, 2010), 135.

3. Laurence Stalling, *Plumes* (Columbia: U of South Carolina P, 2006), 11. Subsequent references in text.

4. Quoted in George Garrett, introduction to Stalling, *Plumes*, xvi.

5. Trout, *Battlefield of Memory*, 135.

6. "Old Hickory" was Richard's grandfather, named after "General Jackson" (13–14).

7. Joan T. Brittain, *Laurence Stallings* (Boston: Twayne, 1975), calls it "an autobiographical novel" (30).

8. Ibid., 18, 17, 19–20, 30.

9. Ibid., 20. Brittain attained Stallings's service record from the Department of the Navy (ibid., 105n8).

10. Ibid., 21.

11. David M. Kennedy, *Over Here: The First World War and American Society* (New York: Oxford UP, 1980), 149.

12. Brittain, *Laurence Stallings*, 15, 23.

13. Paul Edwards, "British War Memoirs," in *Cambridge Companion to the Literature of the First World War*, ed. Vincent Sherry (Cambridge: Cambridge UP, 2005), 25.

14. Roland Neel, Stallings's friend, quoted in Brittain, *Laurence Stallings*, 20.

15. Ibid., 21; Steven Trout, afterword to Stallings, *Plumes*, 349.

16. "Taking the Measurements of a Prize Specimen" was the title of one photograph. US Military Records, World War I, photography section, 165-WW-479, National Archives.

17. There was monetary compensation after World War I for veterans and a special pension for wounded veterans, but the US government and the military eventually came to recognize that there was a fundamental problem with only this form of support after demobilization. Near the end of World War II, Congress passed the GI Bill in part to solve the problem; money for college specifically meant money that would translate into social promotion.

Chapter Nine: Not Only What You Would Expect

1. Alain Locke, *The Critical Temper of Alain Locke: A Selection of His Essays on Art and Culture*, ed. Jeffrey C. Stewart, Critical Studies on Black Life and Culture 8, ed. Henry-Louis Gates (New York: Garland, 1983), 212.

2. David Davis, introduction to Victor Daly, *Not Only War* (Charlottesville: U of Virginia P, 2010), viii, xix. Subsequent references to the novel in text.

3. Ibid., xix. Mark Whalan, *The Great War and the Culture of the New Negro* (Gainesville: UP of Florida, 2008), 69–81.

4. Whalan, *Great War*, 74.

5. The Gillem Board's "Utilization of Negro Manpower in the Postwar Army Policy" (1946) made the connection between interracial troop behavior in combat and ending segregation. Bernard Nalty, *Strength for the Fight: A History of Black Americans in the Military* (New York: Free Press, 1986), chapters 11, 13.

6. Whalan, *Great War*, 73.

7. Du Bois quoted in Chad L. Williams, *Torchbearers of Democracy: African American Soldiers in the World War I Era* (Chapel Hill: U North Carolina P, 2010), 75.

8. Williams, *Torchbearers of Democracy*, 75. As historian Adam P. Wilson, puts it: "The institution of Jim Crow had effectively replaced the institution of slavery as a means of suppressing blacks, entrenching itself securely in the core culture of white America and in the mindset of the nation. . . . Jim Crow and segregation denied African Americans the equality and freedoms they envisioned occurring from slavery's end and hoped governmental Reconstruction would ensure. Black Americans continued to face discriminatory treatment. Additionally, inadequate support from government leaders and American society discouraged their attempts to gain equal education, health care, housing, and voting rights." Adam P. Wilson, *African American Army Officers of World War I: A Vanguard of Equality in War and Beyond* (Jefferson, NC: McFarland, 2015), 6.

9. Ibid., 6–7. See also Williams, *Torchbearers of Democracy*, 75–76.

10. Wilson, *African American Army Officers*, 39.

11. Williams, *Torchbearers of Democracy*, 224–225.

12. Davis, introduction, vii–viii.

13. Locke, *Critical Temper of Alain Locke*, 212.

14. Davis, introduction, viii.

15. Ibid., ix.

16. Wilson, *African American Army Officers*, 39–44.

17. Locke, *Critical Temper of Alain Locke*, 212.

18. "An Interview with Victor Daly," in Daly, *Not Only War*, 97. Daly goes on to name two black authors he was not influenced by, one being Alain Locke.

19. And maybe especially as he reminds his prospective reader that one can be "unconsciously sucked" into this "abysmal Hell," but this is not the primary meaning of that phrase in the foreword, as I discuss below.

20. Kimberley L. Phillips, *War! What Is It Good For? Black Freedom Struggles and the U.S. Military* (Chapel Hill: U of North Carolina P, 2012), 76.

21. Davis, introduction, xii.

22. Whalan is also challenging the characterization of the final scenes in other African American World War I tales—as strictly sentimental. But these other tales remain largely sentimental while Daly's does not.

23. Davis, introduction, xviii.

24. Wilson, *African American Army Officers*, 141.

25. Williams, *Torchbearers of Democracy*, 335.

26. Ibid., 167.

27. Ibid., 160.

28. Williams, *Torchbearers of Democracy*, 167–68.

29. Wilson, *African American Army Officers*, chapter 3.

30. Williams, *Torchbearers of Democracy*, 168.

31. Emmet J. Scott, *Scott's Official History of the American Negro in the World War* (1919; reprint, New York: Arno Press and the New York Times, 1969), 442.

32. Wilson, *African American Army Officers,* 141.

33. Ibid.

34. Whalan, *Great War*, 72–73.

35. Ibid., 73.

36. Wilson, *African American Army Officers,* 141.

37. Whalan, *Great War*, 72.

38. Davis, introduction, xi.

39. Ibid., xxviii.

40. Ibid., xxix.

41. Ibid., xxix.

42. "Interview with Victor Daly," 95.

43. Whalan, *Great War*, 73.

44. Ibid., 73–74.

45. Williams, *Torchbearers of Democracy*, 167.

46. Davis, introduction, xviii.

47. Maxwell Anderson and Laurence Stallings, *What Price Glory?* in *Three American Plays* (New York: Harcourt, Brace, 1926), 33, my translation. The soldier who is translating for the captain translates the first part as "the soldiers take what they want." Steven Trout, pers. comm., March 24, 2017, observes that in the 1925 film *The Big Parade*, based on Stallings's writing, "American soldiers (all of them white) paw at French women, including the heroine Melisande, who nearly has to fight off a band of sex-starved Doughboys. The film's realistic depiction of AEF members engaged in the predatory pursuit of 'casual sex' sits uneasily next to its central love story."

48. Joshua S. Goldstein, *War and Gender: How Gender Shapes the War System and Vice Versa* (Cambridge: Cambridge UP, 2001), chapter 2, www.warandgender.com/wgwomwwi.htm, accessed September 7, 2016.

49. Williams, *Torchbearers of Democracy*, 162–63. This phenomenon was also attested to by two of the female African American welfare workers in France who worked with the AEF (of which there were only a few): "The relationship between the colored soldiers, the colored welfare workers, and the French people was most cordial and friendly and grew in sympathy and understanding, as their association brought about a closer acquaintance." Addie W. Hunton and Kathryn M. Johnson, *Two Colored Women with the American Expeditionary Forces* (Brooklyn: Brooklyn Eagle Press, 1920), 182, https://archive.org/details/twocoloredwomenwoohuntiala, accessed July 25, 2017. They also attested to the smear campaign carried out against black soldiers by white troops. (183–84.)

50. Ibid., 163–64.

51. Ibid., 164.

52. Ibid., 166.

53. Ibid., 169.

54. Quoted in Davis, introduction, xviii.

55. Chad Williams, pers. comm., October 25, 2016.

56. Wilson, *African American Army Officers*, 92.

57. Williams, *Torchbearers of Democracy*, 267.

58. At the time, "the existence of these interracial romances was well-known, and further ammunition to the postwar southern insistence that black soldiers needed to be put back in their place in 1919—violently if necessary." Jennifer Keene, pers. comm., May 11, 2017. What makes Daly's story taboo is not the interracial relationship per se between a black American and a white French woman, but that a rich, educated white woman prefers a black soldier to a white officer, which causes the white officer psychological shock.

59. Williams, *Torchbearers of Democracy*, 170.

60. Jennifer Keene, "Protest and Disability: A New Look at African American Soldiers during the First World War," in *Warfare and Belligerence: Perspectives in First World War Studies*, ed. Pierre Purseigle (Leiden: Brill, 2005), 219–20; Williams, *Torchbearers of Democracy*, 170.

61. Keene, "Protest and Disability," 220.

62. Ibid. Keene acknowledges that a black soldier claimed there was one other case of an intra-military lynching, but a postwar congressional investigative body, along with the NAACP apparently, doubted the claim.

63. Williams, *Torchbearers of Democracy*, 170.

64. Arthur E. Barbeau and Florette Henri, *The Unknown Soldiers: Black American Troops in World War I* (Philadelphia: Temple UP, 1974), 20.

65. Williams, *Torchbearers of Democracy*, 215–19, quote at 217.

66. Davis, introduction, x–xi.

67. Keene, "Protest and Disability," 215, 217.

68. Ibid., 219.

69. Davis, introduction, ix–x.

70. Ibid., x.

71. Williams, *Torchbearers of Democracy*, 281, 272.

72. *New York Times*, October 1919, www.oldmagazinearticles.com/WW1_Black_veterans-pdf, page 2, accessed August 26, 2016; "369th Infantry Regiment: 'Harlem Hellfighters,'" www.blackpast.org/aah/369th-infantry-regiment-harlem-hellfighters, accessed August 28, 2016.

73. Williams, *Torchbearers of Democracy*, 166.

74. Wilson, *African American Army Officers*, 141.

75. Keene, "Protest and Disability," 218.

76. Wilson, *African American Army Officers*, 137, 138.

77. Davis, introduction, xi.

Chapter Ten: Too Glorifying to Tell

1. Hervey Allen, *Toward the Flame: A Memoir of World War I* (Lincoln: U of Nebraska P, 2003), xx, xix. Subsequent references in text.

2. In this first stint of service with the Pennsylvania National Guard, he did not see combat and did little more than camp out at the Texas-Mexico border. Steven Trout, pers. comm., March 24, 2017.

3. Victor Daly, *Not Only War* (Charlottesville: UP of Virginia, 2010), 12, 35, 38.

4. Stuart E. Knee, *Hervey Allen, 1889–1949: A Literary Historian in America* (Lewiston, NY: Edwin Mellen, 1988), 1–41, esp. 14–15, 17, 28–29, quote at 17.

5. According to Dr. Edward Glover, an "eminent psychoanalyst" with whom March underwent analysis in London in the mid-1930s, March struggled all his life to come to terms with a "very difficult" childhood. Part of the difficulty sprang from the fact that March, a sensitive and perceptive child, could not have "failed to note the comparison between the mode of life to which he was shackled in sawmill towns and the more genteel existence enjoyed by his cousins in Mobile." Roy S. Simmonds, *The Two Worlds of William March* (Tuscaloosa: U of Alabama P, 1984), 2–4, Glover quoted at 4.

6. Ibid., 2–4, 9–11.

7. Allen, like Stallings, was from a middle-class family; like Stallings and Plume, he was a college graduate and a lieutenant in the army; unlike them, Allen attended the Naval Academy and served in the border "war" with Mexico, in 1916, during which time he was promoted from private to corporal to second lieutenant. When he rejoined the army in 1917, he entered as a second lieutenant and was in France promoted to first lieutenant. Knee, *Hervey Allen*, 1–41.

8. Simmonds, *Two Worlds of William March*, 62.

9. Ibid.

10. Ibid., 24–25, 27.

11. Philip D. Beidler, introduction to William March, *Company K* (Tuscaloosa: U of Alabama P, 1989), writes that March received "the French Croix de Guerre and *both* the Distinguished Service Cross and the Navy Cross for Valor" (x). This feat is confirmed in Simmonds, *The Two Worlds of William March*, 17.

12. Simmonds, *Two Worlds of William March*, 25.

13. Ibid.

14. Ibid., 25–26.

15. Ibid., 26.

16. Ibid., 71.

17. Survivor guilt was first prominently discussed in the 1960s in relationship to Holocaust survivors. In terms of combat survivors and World War I studies, Alexander Watson and Patrick Porter, "Bereaved and Aggrieved: Combat Motivation and the Ideology of Sacrifice in the First World War," *Historical Research* 83.219 (2010): 146–64, argue that survivor guilt was a motivating factor in combat, as well as in postwar writing. "Sacrificial ideology not only helped soldiers (and their families) to cope with the grief of bereavement but also channelled po-

tentially damaging 'survivor guilt' emotions into increased support for the war and determination to endure. The feeling that one 'owe[d] a debt . . . to the dead' appears to have been widespread among combatants; post-war memoirs, for example, often begin with dedications explaining that the work was undertaken out of some sense of duty to the fallen. While in peacetime, this perceived obligation was concentrated on perpetuating the memory of lost comrades, during the fighting itself, it usually focused on ensuring that their sacrifices were vindicated. Many soldiers thus adopted what modern psychologists might recognize as a 'survivor mission,' comprising a renewed commitment to victory, as the only way to ensure that comrades' losses would be rendered worthwhile and honoured" (161).

18. Allen, "Addenda," in *Toward the Flame*, 278–79.

19. Knee, *Hervey Allen*, 44–45.

20. Ibid., 45, 46.

21. Simmonds, *Two Worlds of William March*, 24–25, 27.

22. This awkward term is meant to signify a guilt over coming out of the war "abled" or not "disabled," as so many soldiers were seriously wounded or maimed.

23. Steven Trout, introduction to Allen, *Toward the Flame*, viii.

24. Knee, *Hervey Allen*, 46–47.

25. Ibid., 47.

26. Ibid.

27. Ibid.

28. Simmonds, *Two Worlds of William March*, 27.

29. Ibid., 23.

30. Ibid., 31.

31. Gatsby in *The Great Gatsby* and Andrews in *Three Soldiers* both take advantage of the opportunity to study at European universities.

32. At 16, March left home in Florida and moved to Mobile, Alabama, where he found a job in a law firm. With the money he saved, he went to Valparaiso University in Indiana, known then as the "poor man's Harvard," because he could be accepted without a high school diploma. After he earned that qualification at Valparaiso in a year, he was able, just after turning 21, to enter the law school at the University of Alabama in Tuscaloosa. But his education only lasted one more year because he ran out of money. At this point, he moved to New York and found another law firm job. He was living there, when, on Registration Day, June 5, 1917, he, along with nearly 10 million other American men, registered for service; he enlisted in the Marine Corps the following month and passed the physical. Simmonds, *Two Worlds of William March*, 9–11.

33. Ibid., 19, 27.

34. Ibid., 27–29.

35. Ibid., 29, 31.

36. March "told many people when he first returned from France that he had been advised he did not have long to live." Ibid., 23.

37. Knee, *Hervey Allen*, 253, 255–56.

38. Trout, introduction, xiv.

39. William March, *Company K* (Tuscaloosa: U of Alabama P, 1989), 225. Subsequent references in text.

40. Mark Whalan, "Literature (USA)," in *1914–1918-Online: International Encyclopedia of the First World War*, ed. Ute Daniel, Peter Gatrell, Oliver Janz, Heather Jones, Jennifer Keene, Alan Kramer, and Bill Nasson, http://dx.doi.org/10.15463/ie1418.10349, accessed September 2, 2016.

41. Simmonds, *Two Worlds of William March*, 53.

42. Ibid., 53–54.

43. Ibid., 74.

44. Jennifer Keene, pers. comm., October 19, 2016.

45. Simmonds, *Two Worlds of William March*, 322, 320.

46. Ibid., 316, 317.

47. Simmonds, *Two Worlds of William March*, 53–54.

48. Ibid.

49. Ibid.

50. Ibid.

51. Siegfried Sassoon, *Memoirs of an Infantry Officer* (London: Faber & Faber, 1930), 72, 71.

52. Ibid., 330.

53. Ibid., 330–31.

54. Ibid., 326.

55. Ibid., 24.

56. Quoted in Stanley Cooperman, *World War I and the American Novel* (Baltimore: Johns Hopkins UP, 1967), 138.

Conclusion: War and *Meritocracy Literature*

1. One reason critics have not perceived this distinction is that they have not known about the history of the unprecedented mobilization history of World War I. Other reasons have to do with trends in literary criticism. With poststructuralism, author biography went out of style in literary criticism and came to be seen as largely irrelevant to it (theorized, following Michel Foucault, as "the death of the author"). Since then, there has been a misguided inattention to what critics now call the "subject position" of the author beyond his or her gender, race, and sexuality (and sometimes class, though often the author's class is also ignored). Gender, race, and sexuality have the status in literary studies as the favored or important biographical differences that matter—in essence, critics now pay a limited and selective attention to author biography. It is always (and quite reasonably) essential to know, for example, whether a female character has been written by a woman as opposed to a man, or whether a black character has been written by an African American or a white person. Yet it is acceptable not to know whether a soldier character has been written by a combat soldier or a non-

combatant. (Granted this distinction may not always be crucial, but, for the reasons I have discussed, it was for Americans with World War I. Only the historical context can tell us what "subject positions" matter.)

The tendency of inattention to this last distinction, or indifference to the idea that a combat soldier might have something special and noteworthy to say about war or the combat experience, different from that of a noncombatant participant or even a nonparticipant, reaches its apotheosis in John T. Matthews's truly excellent and at times brilliant chapter "American Writing of the Great War," in *The Cambridge Companion to the Literature of the First World War* (Cambridge: Cambridge UP, 2005), which addresses no writing by American combat soldiers at all. Boyd, Stallings, Allen, March, and Daly are not mentioned, nor is there any acknowledgment that the piece lacks such writing. The distinction between noncombatant and combatant author just does not matter here. The point is that it simply has not been considered important in the field of literary studies.

The failure to make this distinction can result in misleading conclusions about American literature of World War I. Karsten H. Piep's at times fascinating and provocative *Embattled Home Fronts: Domestic Politics and the American Novel* (Amsterdam: Rodopi, 2009), for example, asserts, referring to Dos Passos, Hemingway, and Cummings, that for the World War I "generation of adventurous doughboys the 'great show' proves to be one protracted letdown" (111). But of these three, only Dos Passos was a doughboy who went to Europe as part of the army, and none of them were combatants. Similarly, the book asserts that "American soldier-poets, unlike numerous of their European counterparts, have rarely produced sheer combat novels or *Frontromane*"—"at the heart of these and similar American war novels by combatants . . . lies not the front experience as such, but the retreat from war" (28)—citing by name only Cummings's *Enormous Room* and Hemingway's *A Farewell to Arms*. But these two Lost Generation authors, both noncombatants, were not counterparts of European combatant writers, and the claim is simply inaccurate when it comes to American war novels by combatants.

2. Willa Cather, *One of Ours* (n.p.: Seven Treasures, 2009), 140.

3. Thomas Boyd, *Through the Wheat: A Novel of the World War I Marines* (Lincoln: U of Nebraska P, 2000), 224.

4. Mark Whalan, "Literature (USA)," in *1914–1918-Online: International Encyclopedia of the First World War*, ed. Ute Daniel, Peter Gatrell, Oliver Janz, Heather Jones, Jennifer Keene, Alan Kramer, and Bill Nasson, http://dx.doi.org/10.15463/ie1418.10349, accessed September 2, 2016.

5. Gatsby initially experiences this sort of demotion: just after the war, Wolfsheim finds the decorated army major in "the gutter." F. Scott Fitzgerald, *The Great Gatsby* (New York: Scribner, 1992), 179.

INDEX

1919 (Dos Passos), 23, 30, 81, 83–86

African American soldiers: combat and, 8, 25, 42, 173–77, 182–84, 196–99; draft and, 5, 8, 12, 15; empowerment of, 195–96, 198; French treatment of, 182, 192–93; "humiliation and degradation" of, 194–95; meritocracy and, 25, 37, 112, 119, 177, 196, 198; military discrimination against, 2, 7–9, 25, 196–97; military honors, 182–84; noncombatants and, 37, 42, 111–12, 172; in *Not Only War,* 179–82, 184–85, 197–98, 188–93, 226–27; officer positions, 25; in *Plumes,* 172–74; racism and, 76, 91, 140, 145, 170–71, 175–79, 183, 193–94, 201, 223; segregation and, 25, 37, 42, 112; sexuality and, 180–82, 185–89; veterans' experiences, 175–78, 184, 195–99; white officers and, 8, 37, 181; Wilson administration and, 7–8, 175. *See also* race; segregation

Allen, Hervey: critical reaction to works, 137; ego, 208–9, 220; on "gas shock," 243n35; limiting of personal involvement in narrative, 202–4; literary success, 27; Lost Generation literature and, 2, 28; on meritocracy in the military, 201–2; military service, 13, 200, 258n7; Naval Academy, 200; post-traumatic stress/combat injuries, 24–26, 209–10, 225–26; survivor guilt, 206–7, 212. See also *Toward the Flame*

All Quiet on the Western Front (Remarque), 204, 236n102

American Expeditionary Forces (AEF), 14, 21, 47, 59, 110, 179, 181, 233n58, 241n4, 256n47, 256n49. *See also* combatants; noncombatants

American Field Service, 242n22

American Legion, 22, 137

Anderson, Maxwell, 190

Anglo-Americans: *The Beautiful and the Damned* and, 52, 57; ethnic/racial bias, 36–37, 40, 42–43, 82, 238n2; femininity and, 120; *The Great Gatsby* and, 35, 41–42, 89, 91–92; Lost Generation's perspective and, 3, 10, 30; masculinity and, 30, 38; noncombatants, 89; *The Sun Also Rises* and, 36, 40–41, 82

anti-Semitism, 3, 8, 36, 40, 43, 92, 245n22. *See also* Jewish Americans

The Autobiography of Alice B Toklas (Stein), 116–17, 125

aviators, 38, 56, 88, 91, 120

AWOL soldiers, 54–55, 57–59, 65–66

The Backwash of War (La Motte), 30, 116–18, 121, 124, 126. *See also* La Motte

Baker, Newton D., 5–6, 142

Ballou, Charles, 181

The Beautiful and the Damned (Fitzgerald): Anglo-Americans and, 52, 57; Cummings and, 69–70; ethnic Americans and, 37; *The Great Gatsby* and, 91; humiliation in, 81, 87–88; hysteria in, 109; military rank and, 52; noncombatants and, 44, 81–82; officers and, 37–38, 52–53, 61, 88; post-traumatic stress and, 61; as psychological horror, 48; shame over status in, 164; *The Sun Also Rises* and, 92; *Through the Wheat* and, 138–39

Bellow, Saul, 222
Biedler, Philip, 215
bilingualism, 8, 40, 42
biographies/biographical writing: Allen, 24, 209; *The Autobiography of Alice B Toklas*, 116–17, 125; Boyd, 149, 152, 252n33; Cather, 115, 119; Cummings, 69, 76–77, 243n2; Dos Passos, 65–66, 83, 112; Faulkner, 13; Fitzgerald, 18; Hemingway, 22, 51, 83, 86, 88–89, 93, 239n16; March, 24, 204–7, 210–11, 216, 218; Porter, 23, 113; post-traumatic stress and, 25; Stallings, 160, 164, 254n7; "subject position" and, 260n1
black soldiers. *See* African American soldiers
Bonus March, 27
Bookman (magazine), 115
Borden, Mary, 25, 116–18, 124, 126, 128–32, 248n17
Boyd, Thomas, 30, 172; class and, 201; as combatant, 25; critical reception of work, 135, 137, 261n1; criticism of officers in work of, 208; Dos Passos and, 140; historical importance of works, 28; on horrors of combat, 225–26; "A Little Gall," 252n18; Lost Generation literature and, 2, 21, 28; on Marine Corps, 140–41; meritocracy and, 225–27; military honors, 25, 252n21; military service, 1–2, 25; post-traumatic stress/combat injuries, 25, 225; publication of *Through the Wheat*, 27, 135–36, 149–51, 252n33; upbringing, 151–52, 201; veterans as audience of, 47. See also *Through the Wheat*
Bradden, William, 192
Brandt, Allan, 112
Brown, John, 66
Brown, Lloyd, 17, 241n3
Brown v. Board of Education, 231n27
Bruce, Brian, 149, 151, 252n33, 253n46
Bullard, R. L., 206, 208
bureaucracy, 55, 65–66, 160
Butler, Judith, 247n8
Camp Devens, 76
Camp Gordon Plan, 8. *See also* ethnic Americans
Camp Leavenworth, 38
Camp Sheridan, 18, 38, 42
Camp Taylor, 18, 38, 41–42
Canada, 1, 5, 38, 49, 58, 62, 241n34
Casey, Ralph D., 11
Catch-22 (Heller), 144
Cather, Willa: biographical writing, 115, 119; commercial success of work, 27, 115; criticism, 114; French and, 47; gender and, 114; intended audience, 115; La Motte and, 118, 123, 128–32; Lost Generation literature and, 2, 29–30; meritocracy and, 118–21, 128–32; women and, 190, 224. *See also* meritocracy; *One of Ours*
censorship, 47, 117, 121
Centeno, Miguel, 149, 152
Ceremony (Silko), 99
charity girls, 16–18, 38, 49, 108, 239n9. *See also* sex
Christy Girls, 11. *See also* propaganda
Churchill, Winston, 149
Civil War (US), 4–6, 10–12, 14, 141, 160, 175
class: in Dos Passos's works, 53–54, 58–59, 62–64, 85; draft and, 11–12; in Fitzgerald's works, 35, 42–43, 52, 55–58, 91–92; in Hemingway's works, 51; masculinity and, 14–16, 38, 57–58; meritocracy and, 2, 6–10, 37–38, 56, 62–63, 99, 151–52, 155, 167, 173, 201, 222, 226–27, 261n5; noncombatants and, 10, 29; race and, 112–13, 188–90, 194; sexual revolution and, 17–19; wartime changes to social standing and, 7, 38, 56, 99, 151–52, 167, 226–27, 261n5; women and, 10, 16–18, 91–92, 108, 188–89. *See also* meritocracy
"Close Ranks" (Du Bois), 174
combatants: African American soldiers, 8, 25, 42, 173–77, 182–84, 196–99; in Allen's works, 209–10; in Cather's works, 118–19, 128–30; Cummings and, 76–77; decorations/medals awarded to, 25, 95; designation as,

13–15, 19, 47, 84, 141; in Dos Passos's works, 58–59, 67; *The Great Gatsby* and, 38, 41; in Hemingway's works, 79–80, 86, 89, 93–99; intelligence testing and, 42–43; in March's works, 206–7, 212, 214, 220–21; masculinity and, 2, 10–11, 14–17, 40; meritocracy and, 18–19, 154–71, 201, 206–9, 225–27; in *Not Only War,* 172–99; in "Pale Horse, Pale Rider," 103, 106–7, 110–12; patriotic war accounts and, 20; percentage of troops designated as, 19; in *Plumes,* 154–71; post-traumatic stress and, 25–26, 58; postwar compensation, 22; postwar literature and, 2–3, 10, 13, 23–31, 48, 80–86, 200–1, 223; social impact of status, 14–15, 48; in *Through the Wheat,* 135–53; veterans of combat, 41–42, 79–80; view of noncombatants, 15, 86, 106–7; women and, 17–19, 103. *See also* masculinity; noncombatants; *Through the Wheat;* wounds
combat injuries. *See* wounds
commissioned vs. noncommissioned officers. *See* officers
Commission on Training Camp Activities (CTCA), 16, 18, 234n74. *See also* training camps
Committee on Classification of Personnel, 6–7. *See also* meritocracy
Committee on Public Information, 11, 136, 155. *See also* propaganda
Company K (March): commercial success of, 27; as "disillusionment narrative," 137, 214, 225–26; guilt and, 218, 220; individuality and, 144; intended audience for, 47; meritocracy and, 212–13; military medals and, 205–6; narrators, 31, 200; "Nine Prisoners" and, 216–17; therapeutic nature of writing, 24, 31, 206, 210–11, 214, 217–18; trauma and, 214–15; war wounds in, 205. *See also* March
Congressional Medal of Honor, 201, 205, 219.
Cooperman, Stanley, 47, 237n114, 241n2
corruption in the military, 63, 166, 221
Cotter, Seamon, Jr., 183
Crane, Stephen, 37, 141–42, 151
Creel, George, 11, 232n39
The Crisis (magazine), 174, 184
Croix de Guerre, 25, 128, 152, 161, 166, 180–81, 197, 201, 205, 209, 212
Crowder, Enoch H., 13
cultural bias, 26, 42
Cummings, E. E.: antiwar view, 70–71; assignment to combat duty, 14, 76–77; difference from other Lost Generation writers, 30, 69–71, 76–77, 201; Dos Passos and, 70, 73–76; draft and, 76; happy tone of war writing, 69–71; identity and, 74–75; incarceration by French, 70–72, 75–76; La Motte and, 122; Lost Generation literature and, 28, 30; narrative voice in *The Enormous Room,* 71–75; "new dignity," 70, 73–74; as noncombatant, 2, 69–77, 223; privileged background, 2, 75–76; training camps and, 76–77; use of French in works, 47. See also *The Enormous Room*

Daly, Victor, 172–99; as combatant, 25–26; disillusionment and, 137; family background, 176–77; Lost Generation literature and, 2, 28–29, 31, 225–27; trauma and, 225–26. *See also* African American soldiers; *Not Only War;* race
Davis, David, 172, 174, 184, 188, 195–96
deferment, 12–13, 69, 92, 108, 158, 164. *See also* draft
"Diary of a Dud" (Maxwell), 80
disability, 44, 157, 163, 167, 169, 214
discipline, military, 24, 139–40, 143, 146; noncombatants and, 47–48, 55, 58–62, 64, 70–73
"disillusionment narrative," 136–37, 148, 155–57, 165, 214–15
Dispatches (Herr), 151
dissociation, 26, 35, 148
Distinguished Service Cross, 7, 201, 212, 235n96, 258n11
Division of Pictorial Publicity, 11. *See also* propaganda

Dodge, Raymond, 7
Dos Passos, John: biographical writing, 65–66; class and, 53–54, 58–59, 62–64, 85; commercial success of, 20, 27; Cummings and, 70, 73–76; draft and, 14, 53; ethnic Americans and, 54, 74, 85, 155; identity and, 63–64, 66, 73–74; Lost Generation literature and, 2, 28; meritocracy and, 61–64, 66–67; noncombatants and, 14, 19, 22–23, 47–48, 58–61, 84–85; training camps and, 53, 112; use of French language in works, 46–48; veterans and, 46–48, 59, 67; women and, 54–56, 64, 85. See also *1919; One Man's Initiation; Three Soldiers*
doughboys, 19, 21, 59, 80, 111, 151, 191, 226, 256n47, 261n1. *See also* combatants; noncombatants
draft: African American soldiers and, 5, 8, 12, 15; Civil War draft riots, 10; class and, 11–12; Cummings and, 69, 76, 244n7; deferments, 12–13, 108, 158, 164–65; Dos Passos and, 14, 53, 85, 242n22; ethnic Americans and, 240n29; Faulkner and, 1, 14; Fitzgerald and, 38; impact on army mobilization, 3–5, 229n12; masculinity and, 12; National Guard and, 230n14; noncombatants, 14, 19; propaganda and, 2, 9–12, 106, 108, 239n16; social impact of, 10–11; Woodrow Wilson and, 3–6, 10–12. *See also* class; Selective Service Act
Du Bois, W. E. B., 174–77, 195
Dyer, Richard, 185

Edwards, Paul, 153
Eliot, T. S., 46, 237n112
The Enormous Room (Cummings), 30, 47, 69–76. *See also* Cummings
ethnic Americans: Anglo-Americans bias, 36–37, 40, 42–43, 82, 238n2; *The Beautiful and the Damned* and, 37; bilingualism and, 8, 40, 42; in Cummings's works, 76; in Dos Passos's works, 54, 74, 85, 155; ethnic-specific companies, 8; *A Farewell to Arms* and, 40; *The Great Gatsby* and, 9, 18, 30, 35, 42, 89, 91, 226; in Hemingway's works, 41, 92, 245n22; identification of ethnic groups, 9–10; identity and, 155, 251n16; Lost Generation writers and, 37–38, 43–44, 201; military's equal treatment of ethnic groups, 2, 6–8, 37, 40–44, 155, 240n29; noncombatants and, 82; in Stallings's works, 161; women and, 38. *See also* anti-Semitism; German Americans; immigrants; Italian Americans; Jewish Americans

A Farewell to Arms (Hemingway): *The Beautiful and the Damned* and, 87–88, 91; commercial success of, 27; criticism, 86–87, 93–94; emasculation of characters in, 88–92; Hemingway's lie about combat service and, 1; individuality and, 145; intended audience for, 79–80, 95–97; Lost Generation literature and, 9, 79–81; love story in, 86–88; meritocracy and, 42; military awards in, 40, 96; noncombatants and, 20–23, 30, 42, 80–99, 214; *Not Only War* and, 176–77; significance of novel's ending, 78–79; view of military, 54. *See also* Hemingway
Faucet, Jessie, 183
Faulkner, Richard S., 15
Faulkner, William: intended audience, 80–81; lies about war record, 1–2, 39; masculinity and, 20, 23, 48–52, 93, 107, 111, 201; meritocracy and, 35–39, 55, 62, 164; noncombatants and, 1–2, 13–15, 19–20, 30, 44, 62, 68–69, 93, 223; sexual revolution and, 17; use of multiple narrators, 204. See also *Soldiers' Pay; The Sound and the Fury*
Fitzgerald, F. Scott: biographical writing, 18; class in works of, 35, 42–43, 52, 55–58, 91–92; Jewish Americans in works of, 44, 90–91; masculinity and, 88–89; noncombatants and, 88–89; officer rank and, 14, 38, 41; sexuality and, 52–53, 87; training camps and,

38–39, 41–42, 44, 52, 81–82, 87, 231n33; women in works of, 41–44. See also *The Beautiful and the Damned; The Great Gatsby*
Fitzgerald, Zelda, 18, 42
Flagg, James Montgomery, 11
Forbidden Zone (Borden), 126, 128, 130
Fort Des Moines "Colored Officers' Training Camp," 176–77, 181, 187
Foucault, Michel, 63, 72, 260n1
Fredenburgh, Theodore, 237n114
freedom, 66, 136, 255n8
French treatment of Americans: African American soldiers and, 182, 192–93; Cummings and, 70–72, 75–76

gender: American society and, 7, 29; discrimination and, 29, 63; gender bias, 26; masculinity and, 10, 12; mobilization of army and, 10, 103, 109; reversal of roles, 12, 16, 19, 114. *See also* masculinity; sex; women
German Americans, 35, 41, 59, 82. *See also* ethnic Americans
GI Bill, 7, 254n17
Gibson Girl, 11. *See also* propaganda
Gilbert, John, 236n102
Gilbert, Sandra, 26
Gillem Board, 173, 183, 254n5
Glover, Edward, 258n5
Goldman, Dorothy, 26
Goldstein, Joshua S., 191
Good-bye to All of That (Graves), 26, 149
Gould, Stephen J., 43
Granger, Lester, 192
Graves, Robert, 26, 149, 153, 165–66, 221
The Greatest Things in Life (film), 183
The Great Gatsby (Fitzgerald): Anglo-Americans and, 35, 41–42, 89, 91–92; *The Beautiful and the Damned* and, 91; class and, 35, 42–43; Daly and, 176; emasculation in, 90–91; ethnic Americans and, 9, 18, 30, 35, 42–44, 82, 89, 91–92, 226; noncombatants and, 23, 30, 36, 89; officer rank in, 9, 35, 42–43, 48, 89–90, 231n33; postwar social demotion and, 226, 261n5; race and, 238n2; *The Sun Also Rises* and, 88–89, 92. *See also* Fitzgerald, F. Scott
The Great War and the Culture of the New Negro (Whalan), 173
Griffith, D. W., 183

Harbord, James G., 33
Harlem Renaissance, 177, 195
Hay, James, 230n20
Heller, Joseph, 144
Hemingway, Ernest: Jewish Americans in works of, 36, 39–40, 82, 91–92; masculinity and, 86, 88, 90–92; noncombatants and, 36, 37–38, 44–45, 50–52, 79–99, 177–78, 214; race in works of, 91–92; sexuality in works of, 44–45, 50–51; training camps and, 40–41, 83; veterans and, 79–80, 83–84, 92; women and, 36, 38–41, 84; wounds and, 1, 20–23, 30, 39–40, 50–51, 83, 86, 92–98, 214, 223. See also *A Farewell to Arms; In Our Time;* masculinity; *The Sun Also Rises*
Herr, Michael, 151
Higgonet, Margaret, 116–17, 122, 124, 249n17
Houston, Charles, 192–94
Howard, Sidney, 115
Hughes, Langston, 179
"Hugh Selwyn Mauberley" (Pound), 9
Hutchison, Hazel, 123
Hut Service, 110
hysteria: propaganda and, 40, 103; sexual revolution, 16–17; war hysteria, 13, 105, 224. *See also* post-traumatic stress

identity: in Boyd's works, 142; Cummings and, 73–76; in Dos Passos's works, 63–64, 66, 73–74, 140, 155, 168; freedom from the system, 66; in March's works, 220; meritocracy and, 61–64, 66, 155, 168; military and, 7, 10, 66, 73–74; race and, 180, 251n16. *See also* individuality; meritocracy
immigrants, 6, 8–9, 37, 42–44, 120, 238n2. *See also* ethnic Americans

imprisonment: Cummings and, 69–77, 122; in Dos Passos's works, 53–55, 67, 112; March and, 214–21; in *Through the Wheat,* 142
individuality, 71–72, 74, 76–77, 144–45. *See also* identity
influenza, 57, 103, 105, 112–13
injuries. *See* post-traumatic stress; wounds
In Our Time (Hemingway), 20, 50, 242n12
intelligence tests, 6, 14, 42–43, 64, 127
Italian Americans, 40, 57, 96, 251n61. *See also* ethnic Americans

James, Pearl, 236n98
Jewish Americans: Anglo-Americans and, 82; in Cummings's works, 76; in Fitzgerald's works, 44, 90–91; in Hemingway's works, 36, 39–40, 82, 91–92; Holocaust and, 238n5; Jewish officers, 43; military's treatment of, 37, 43–44; in *Plumes,* 169–70; racial identity and, 251n16. *See also* anti-Semitism; ethnic Americans
Jim Crow, 175, 179, 181–82, 186, 193, 196–97, 199, 255n8. *See also* African American soldiers; race
Johnson, James Weldon, 175, 177, 184
Jordan, Walker, 192

Kafka, Franz, 65
Karl, Frederick R., 13
Keene, Jennifer, 15, 22, 80, 193–96, 217
Kennedy, David, 80
Kerouac, Jack, 127
Knee, Stuart E., 206–7
Krutch, Joseph Wood, 158

La Motte, Ellen: on "adventures," 117–18; Cather and, 118, 123, 128–32; criticism, 116–17; decision to leave war zone, 123–26; frontline experiences, 2, 26, 116–17; Lost Generation literature and, 2, 29–30; meritocracy and, 118, 121–22, 127–28, 132, 224; mobilization and, 121–23; publication of works, 121–22; Stein on, 116–18, 125–28. See also *The Backwash of War*
"The Last of the Belles" (Fitzgerald), 18
Last of the Doughboys (Rubin), 21
League of Nations, 166
Locke, Alain, 172, 176–77
Lost Generation authors: Cummings's unique place among, 69, 76, 245n12; humiliation and, 94; masculinity and, 10, 14–15, 55, 103, 164–65, 246n1; meritocracy and, 2, 37, 164, 231n33, 237n112; noncombatants and, 2–3, 10, 13–14, 20–23–27, 29, 48–52, 55, 136–37, 201, 231n33, 247n5, 261n1; origin of term, 9; postwar literature, 2–3, 9–10, 19–24, 28–30, 36, 80–82; trauma in writing of, 48–51; veterans and, 80; women and, 246n1. *See also individual authors*
lynching, 175, 178, 188, 193–94, 257n62. *See also* African American soldiers; race

March, William: combatants and, 2, 21; commercial success of, 27; disillusionment narrative and, 137; intended audience, 47; meritocracy and, 25; post-traumatic stress, 24–26; use of multiple narrators, 31. See also *Company K*
Marcus, Jane, 26
Marine Corps, 136, 138–44, 151–53, 160, 200, 205–6, 216, 219, 233n58, 242n11, 251n14, 259n32; ethnicity/race and, 25, 43; masculinity 11; meritocracy and, 14; *See also* combatants
masculinity: Anglo-Americans and, 30, 38; class and, 14–16, 38, 57–58; combatants and, 2, 10–11, 14–17, 40; combat injuries and, 23, 156; draft and, 12; emasculation, 36–37, 39–40, 48–52, 69, 88–89, 201; Fitzgerald and, 88–89; gender and, 10, 12; Hemingway and, 39–41, 86, 88, 90–92; Lost Generation literature and, 10, 14–15, 55, 103, 164–65, 246n1; meritocracy and, 19, 37–38; military service and, 12–14, 36–38, 58, 96, 105–9, 163, 169; noncombatants and,

14–19, 48–52, 110–11, 246n1; officers and, 16–19; propaganda and, 2, 10–11, 30; self-reliance and, 12; sexuality and, 38, 40–41, 64, 106–7, 185; Theodore Roosevelt and, 239n16; training camps and, 14–15; uniforms and, 109, 224; women and, 38–41, 48, 64, 103–4, 120, 159, 224. *See also* combatants; meritocracy; noncombatants; sex
Maxwell, Paul, 80–81
McKaine, Osceola, 192, 196
medical units: Cummings and, 30, 69–76, 122; Dos Passos and, 14, 47, 53–54, 84; Hemingway and, 1, 22, 38–40, 86, 93–96; La Motte and, 116, 122; meritocracy and, 223–24. *See also* noncombatants; Norton-Harjes Ambulance Corps; Red Cross
Memoirs of an Infantry Officer (Sassoon), 79, 141, 165, 221
Mencken, H. L., 58–59
meritocracy: ability and, 6–7, 62, 66, 77, 122, 127–28, 157, 168–69, 185; African American soldiers and, 25, 37, 112, 119, 177, 196, 198; Allen and, 201–2; British system of, 222; Cather and, 118–21, 128–32; class and, 2, 6–10, 37–38, 62–63, 155, 173, 201, 222; combatants and, 18–19, 154–71, 201, 206–9, 225–27; Cummings and, 71; Dos Passos and, 61–64, 66–67; in *A Farewell to Arms,* 42; federalization of National Guard, 6, 230n20; identity and, 61–64, 66, 155; intelligence testing and, 42–43, 71, 77; La Motte and, 118, 121–22, 127–28, 132; Lost Generation authors and, 2, 55, 164, 225–27, 231n33, 237n112; masculinity and, 19, 37–38; "meritocracy wound," 127; mobilization of army and, 2–3, 5–10; National Defense Act and, 6; noncombatants and, 37–38, 61–64, 223–25; officer selection and, 2, 7, 18–19, 42, 62, 141–42; *Plumes* and, 154–71; race and, 25, 112, 177, 196–98; sexual revolution and, 18; talents and, 5–7, 62–63, 120, 176; *Three Soldiers* and, 54–65, 77, 237n114; *Through the Wheat* and, 142–43, 146–47; women and, 18–19, 29, 119, 224. *See also* masculinity; officers; physical evaluations, military
military (US). *See* American Expeditionary Forces; combatants; draft; Marine Corps; meritocracy; noncombatants; officers; veterans
military awards/medals: African American soldiers and, 25, 182, 197; awarded by foreign governments, 128, 161, 182, 197, 201, 205, 212; Congressional Medal of Honor, 201; Distinguished Service Medal, 7, 201; in *A Farewell to Arms,* 40, 96; March and, 205–6, 211–14, 219; "medal complexes," 221–22; noncombatants and, 95; posthumous, 124; "rifleman's medal," 161, 165; Stallings and, 161; in *Through the Wheat,* 144. *See also* Congressional Medal of Honor; Croix de Guerre
military intelligence, 6, 175, 188, 197
Miller, Henry, 13
The Mismeasure of Man (Gould), 43
Mizener, Arthur, 18
mobilization of army. *See* draft
"mobilization wounds," 23, 45, 92, 99, 127, 226. *See also* wounds
Morris, James B., 192
My Antonia (Cather), 114–15, 120–21

NAACP, 175, 257n62. *See also* African American soldiers
Nation (magazine), 158
National Archives, 9
National Defense Act of 1916, 6
National Guard, 5–6, 13, 202, 214, 230n14, 230n20, 258n2
nationalism, 106, 154, 156, 159, 185
nativism, 37, 92, 238n2
Navy Cross, 205, 212, 235n96, 258n11
Ninety-Second Division, 180–82, 185, 192, 196–97
no-man's land, 110, 173, 179, 182–84, 193

noncombatants: African Americans and, 37, 42, 111–12, 172; alienation and, 22, 36–37, 75, 154, 223–24; Anglo-Americans, 89, 92; as audience for postwar literature, 26–27, 67–68, 177–78, 220–21; *The Beautiful and the Damned* and, 44, 52–53, 61, 81–82; civilian contractors, 11, 15; class and, 10, 29; Cummings and, 2, 69–77, 223; designation as, 13–14; disappointment and, 36–38; dissociation and, 35–36; Dos Passos and, 14, 19, 22–23, 47–48, 58–61, 84–85; draft and, 14, 19; emasculation and, 36–37, 39–40, 48–52, 69, 88–89, 201; ethnic Americans and, 40–44, 82; failure to distinguish between their experience and combatants', 2–3, 22, 260–61n1; in *A Farewell to Arms,* 20–23, 30, 42, 80–99, 214; Fitzgerald and, 36–41, 88–89; gender and, 103, 106–7; *The Great Gatsby* and, 23, 30, 35–36, 40–41, 89; Hemingway and, 36, 37–38, 44–45, 50–52, 79–99, 177–78, 214; Lost Generation literature and, 2–3, 10, 13–14, 20–27, 29, 48–52, 55, 136–37, 201, 231n33, 247n5, 261n1; March and, 220; masculinity and, 14–19, 48–52, 110–11, 246n1; mental/physical suffering and, 48–68; meritocracy and, 37–38, 61–64, 223, 225; military awards and, 95; officers and, 94, 96–98, 106–7; "Pale Horse, Pale Rider" and, 103; Porter and, 23, 106–13; post-traumatic stress and, 23–25; segregation and 37, 42, 112; in *Soldiers' Pay,* 44, 49–50; in *The Sound and the Fury,* 41–42; status and, 38–44; training camps and, 19, 22; veterans and, 20–22, 35–36, 47, 80, 83; women and, 18–19, 23, 39, 47–56, 84, 103–10; wounds and, 23–26, 92. *See also* American Expeditionary Forces; combatants; masculinity; medical units; Red Cross; survivor guilt

Norton-Harjes Ambulance Corps, 54, 70–71, 84

Not Only War: A Story of Two Great Conflicts (Daly): African American soldiers and, 179–82, 184–85, 197–98, 188–93, 226–27; criticism, 172–73, 177; final scene, 179–84; historical context of, 173, 175, 181–85; idea of hell, 178–79; intended audience, 177–78; present-day audience and, 174; race and, 173–79, 184, 187, 197; sex and, 178–81, 184–92, 227; training camps and, 176–77, 186–87, 196, 198. *See also* African American soldiers; Daly; race

officers: in *1919,* 84; African American soldiers and, 5–8, 37, 176–77, 180–82, 186–98; appointment of, 7; in *The Beautiful and the Damned,* 37–38, 52–53, 61, 88; commissioned vs. noncommissioned, 8–9, 16, 19, 25, 35, 37, 43, 55, 62, 76, 159–62, 170, 176–77, 179, 181, 191, 194, 198, 222; in *Company K,* 214; Cummings as, 76–77; elitism and, 5–7, 12; in *A Farewell to Arms,* 40, 42, 88; Fitzgerald as, 14, 38, 41; in *The Great Gatsby,* 9, 35, 42; in *In Our Time,* 50; Jewish Americans and, 43; in Lost Generation literature, 9–10, 25, 37–44, 55, 225–26; masculinity and, 16–19; in *Memoirs of an Infantry Officer,* 79, 165, 221–22; meritocracy and, 2, 7, 18–19, 62; noncombatants and, 94, 96–98, 106–7; in *Not Only War,* 172; in *Plumes,* 157, 160–62, 164–65, 170; race and, 8, 37, 181; Services of Supply and, 33, 84; in *Soldier's Pay,* 49; in *The Sun Also Rises,* 88; in *Three Soldiers,* 55, 57, 59–61, 77, 168; in *Through the Wheat,* 137–53; in *Toward the Flame,* 201–2, 207–9; in "A Very Short Story," 44, 87. *See also* meritocracy

One Man's Initiation (Dos Passos), 53–54

One of Ours (Cather), 27, 30, 47, 114–15, 118–21, 123, 129, 224, 241n4. *See also* Cather

Over Here (Kennedy), 80

Owen, Chandler, 175

pacifism, 69–70, 77, 153, 202, 233n49, 242n22
"Pale Horse, Pale Rider" (Porter), 23, 30, 103, 111, 158, 224. *See also* Porter, Katherine Anne
Paul, Alice, 101, 246
Perkins, Max, 27, 135–36, 149–51
Pershing, John J., 181, 208
personal narratives, 200, 203
physical evaluations, military, 1, 13–14, 38, 61–64, 73, 76–77, 107, 140, 162, 168, 185, 198
Piep, Karsten, 244n8, 261n1
Plumes (Stallings): combatants and, 201–3; commercial success of, 27; criticism, 172; as "disillusionment narrative," 137, 154–57, 225–26; meritocracy and, 31, 156, 161–71, 202–3; romance of war and 156–159. *See also* Stallings
Points of Honor (Boyd), 153
Porter, Katherine Anne: Lost Generation literature and, 2, 29–30; masculinity and, 103–6; mobilization and, 107–10; noncombatants and, 23, 106–13; propaganda and, 106, 111–12, 158–59, 224. *See also* "Pale Horse, Pale Rider"
Porter, Patrick, 258n17
postmodernism, 63, 66
poststructuralism, 63–64, 66, 260n1
post-traumatic stress, 25, 31, 60–61, 67, 99, 152, 177, 226. *See also* suicide; survivor guilt; wounds
postwar life, veterans and, 17, 25, 129, 155–56, 166, 176, 199, 226
Pound, Ezra, 9–10, 237n112
poverty, 2, 8–9, 12, 18, 41, 54, 82, 89, 200, 202, 211, 226. *See also* class; meritocracy
Preparedness Movement, 6, 202, 215
prison. *See* imprisonment
privilege. *See* class; meritocracy
propaganda: "disillusionment narratives" and, 136–37; hysteria and, 40, 103; Lost Generation literature and, 112, 117, 121, 132, 214, 224–25; masculinity and, 2–3, 10–15, 30, 104; noncombatants and, 22; *Plumes* and, 154–59, 163, 170; sexuality and, 106, 112
prostitution, 16, 18, 38, 191, 233n65, 234n74. *See also* charity girls
Pynchon, Thomas, 63

race: Anglo-Americans and, 36–37, 40, 42–43, 82, 238n2; class and, 112–13, 188–90, 194; in Cummings's works, 76; in Hemingway's works, 91–92; identity and, 180, 251n16; institutionalized racism, 7–8; intelligence tests and, 42; meritocracy and, 25, 112, 177, 196, 198; no-man's land and, 110, 173, 179, 182–84, 193; in *Not Only War,* 173–79, 184, 187, 197; in *Plumes,* 170–171; postwar literature and, 36–38; race riots, 180; sex and, 31, 38, 178, 180–81, 184–88, 192, 227, 260n1; in *Three Soldiers,* 82, 85; in *Through the Wheat,* 142, 145; veterans and, 174–75; wounds and, 173, 179, 181, 184–85, 197. *See also* African American soldiers; Jim Crow; lynching; segregation
Randolph, A. Philip, 175
rank: *See* meritocracy; officers
rape, 175, 181
The Red Badge of Courage (Crane), 138, 141, 151, 153
Red Cross, 1–2, 38–39, 84, 108, 120, 123, 229n2, 239n16, 242n22. *See also* noncombatants
Remarque, Erich Maria, 204
Revolutionary War, 154, 156, 164, 166
Reynolds, Michael, 88, 93, 239n16
Roosevelt, Theodore, 5, 12, 239n16
Rubin, Richard, 21

Sassoon, Siegfried, 79, 149, 153, 165–66, 221–22
Scott, James Brown, 242n22
segregation: desegregation of military, 231n27; Gillem Board and, 173, 183, 254n5; institutionalization of, 7–9, 37; military hospitals and, 170; noncombatants and 37, 42, 112; officer training and, 25, 177, 198; opposition to, 173, 175. *See also* African American soldiers; Jim Crow; race

Selective Service Act, 3–4, 13, 234n74. *See also* draft
sentimentalism, 59, 99, 117, 128, 139, 157, 173–74, 179, 182, 255n22
Services of Supply (SOS), 14, 21–22, 33, 47, 53, 84–85, 139. *See also* noncombatants
sex: African American soldiers and, 180–82, 185–89; Anglo women and, 38, 91; charity girls, 16–19, 38, 49, 108, 239n9; class and, 17–19; in Fitzgerald's works, 52–53, 87; French women and, 190–91; in Hemingway's works, 44–45, 50–51; homosexuality, 91, 126; masculinity and, 38, 40–41, 106–7, 185; military regulations against, 58, 234n74, 241n4; in Porter's works, 105–6, 108; promiscuity, 38, 41; race and, 31, 38, 178, 180–81, 184–88, 192, 227, 260n1; recruitment propaganda and, 11, 106; sporting girls, 193; WWI sexual revolution, 16–18. *See also* gender; prostitution; women
shell shock. *See* post-traumatic stress
Sherston, George. *See* Sassoon
Silko, Leslie Marmon, 99
Simmonds, Roy S., 204–5, 210, 216–18
slackers, 12–13, 104
Smith, Harry Hardy, 205
social status. *See* class; meritocracy
soldiers. *See* African American soldiers; combatants; noncombatants
Soldiers' Pay (Faulkner), 17, 23, 35, 44, 49–50, 80, 92, 107, 164
The Sound and the Fury (Faulkner), 23, 28, 30, 36, 41, 44
Spanish-American War, 5, 211
Spears, Edward Louis, 129
sports, 43
Stallings, Laurence: background, 201; commercial success of, 27; criticism, 28–29, 172; "disillusionment narratives" and, 225–26; meritocracy and, 25, 31, 202; noncombatants and, 2; post-traumatic stress and, 225–26; wounds and, 166. See also *Plumes*
Stein, Gertrude, 9, 116–18, 122, 124–27, 231n34
Stevens, James, 237n114, 245n10
subject position, 260n1
suicide, veterans and, 24, 129–31, 207, 250n55. *See also* post-traumatic stress; veterans
The Sun Also Rises (Hemingway): commercial success of, 20, 27; ethnic Americans and, 36, 40–41, 82; lies about author's combat status in, 1, 22–23, 86, 93; Lost Generation literature and, 23, 28, 30; love story in, 86–88; masculinity and, 39–41; noncombatants and, 22–23, 80, 88, 92–93; *Not Only War* and, 176–77; origination of term "Lost Generation," 9; wounds and, 30, 39, 45. *See also* Hemingway; noncombatants
survivor guilt, 206–7, 209–10; "abledness" guilt, 207, 211; promotion guilt, 207, 211–13, 219

Three Soldiers (Dos Passos): commercial success of, 20, 27; criticism, 58–59; Cummings and, 69–70; desertion in, 60–61; Dos Passos's biography and, 65–66; humiliation in, 77, 81, 168; identity in, 63–65, 145, 155; intended audience for, 46–48, 67, 83, 178; Lost Generation literature and, 22–23; meritocracy and, 54–65, 77, 237n114; race and, 82, 85; *Through the Wheat* and, 138–39; trauma in, 60–67; use of French in, 46–47; view of military in, 53–60; women in, 52. *See also* Dos Passos
Through the Wheat (Boyd): *The Beautiful and the Damned* and, 138–39; critical view of, 135–37, 150–52; final lines of, 136, 148–50; insubordination in, 139–43; luck in, 141–42; meritocracy and, 142–43, 146–47; officers in, 137–53; psychological state of protagonist, 146–48; publication of, 27, 135–36, 149–51, 252n33; race and, 142, 145; reception of, 136–37, 150–51; training camp in, 142; uniform as symbol of individuality in, 144–46; Woodrow Wilson and, 146; wounds and, 143–44, 147. *See also* Boyd

Torchbearers of Democracy (Williams), 180, 255n8, 256n49
Toward the Flame (Allen), 24, 27, 31, 200–2, 207, 212, 220, 225–26. *See also* Allen
training camps: African American soldiers and, 176; in *Company K*, 200; in Dos Passos's works, 53, 112; in Fitzgerald's works, 38–39, 41–42, 44, 52, 81–82, 87, 231n33; in Hemingway's works, 40–41, 83; influenza outbreaks in, 112–13; masculinity and, 14–15; noncombatants and, 19, 22; in *Not Only War*, 176–77, 186–87, 196, 198; sex and, 16, 38, 233n65, 234n74; in *Through the Wheat*, 142. *See also* charity girls; Commission on Training Camp Activities
transport ships, 200, 234n77
Treaty of Versailles, 26, 166
Trout, Steven, 59, 110, 135–36, 155–56, 159, 209, 212, 220, 225, 229n2, 232n46, 242n11, 250n55
Truman, Harry S., 231n27

uniforms: allure of, 16–17, 105–6; individuality and, 144–46; masculinity and, 109, 224; slackers and, 12–13, 108; tampering with, 1, 144, 229n2; veterans and, 1. *See also* combatants; officers
US Army. *See* American Expeditionary Forces; combatants; draft; noncombatants; veterans

van Loon, Hendrik, 183
venereal disease, 18, 44, 58, 78, 112–13, 234n74, 241n4. *See also* sex
"A Very Short Story" (Hemingway), 20, 23, 30, 44–45, 50, 86–87, 92, 96, 99, 164, 239n18
veterans: African American soldiers, 172, 175–80, 182, 184, 186, 192–93, 195, 198–99, 224, 227; alienation of, 223–24; Allen and, 212; American Legion organization, 22; as audience for postwar literature, 10, 20, 23–24, 27, 82–84, 246n23; back pay/compensation, 27, 254n17; Boyd and, 136, 138; combatants, 23–24, 26–28; Dos Passos and, 46–48, 59, 67; Hemingway and, 79–80, 83–84, 92; injuries, 23–24, 166; language in postwar writing targeted to, 3, 10, 41, 49, 65–66, 79, 82–83, 166, 193, 201; lies about being veterans, 1; March and, 206, 211–14, 220; memories of WWI, 17, 21, 241n3; noncombatants, 20–22, 35–36, 80, 83, 92, 96, 126; suicide and, 24, 129–31, 207, 250n55; term "Lost Generation" and, 9; Veterans' Bureau, 99, 166–67
Vietnam War, 85, 151, 246n23
volunteering for military service, 5, 12, 14, 53–54, 73, 86, 122–23, 143–44, 230n14

War and Gender (Goldstein), 191
The Waste Land (Eliot), 46
Waterman, John B., 211
Whalan, Mark, 136–37, 146, 155, 173–74, 179, 182–85, 225
What Price Glory? (Stallings and Anderson), 190
Whittlesey, Charles, 250n55
Williams, Chad L., 175, 180, 185, 191–96
Wilson, Adam P., 182–84, 195, 255n8
Wilson, Edmund, 87, 115, 135, 248n2
Wilson, Woodrow: African American soldiers and, 7–8, 175; army mobilization, 36, 230n20; Cummings and, 75; Du Bois and, 175; military drafts and, 3–6, 10–12; Paul and, 246; *Plumes* and, 157–58, 162, 166; propaganda and, 11–12; *Three Soldiers* and, 85; *Through the Wheat* and, 146; veterans and, 247n14
women: Anglo women, 10, 38, 91; class and, 10, 16–18, 54, 91–92, 108, 188–89; contemporary feminist criticism of female war writers, 25–26; discrimination and, 29; in Dos Passos's works, 54–56, 64, 85; ethnic Americans and, 38; in Fitzgerald's works, 41–44; French women, 46–47, 180–81, 190–91; in Hemingway's

women (*continued*)
works, 38–41, 84; imprisonment, 112; Lost Generation literature and, 2, 10, 25–26, 29–30, 55, 114–32; masculinity and, 38–41, 48, 64, 103–4, 120, 224, 159; in medical field, 2, 126; meritocracy and, 18–19, 29, 119–20, 224; mobilization and, 103–12, 132; noncombatants and, 18–19, 23, 39, 47–56, 84, 103–10; in *Plumes,* 159; postwar writing, 2–3, 25, 29, 114, 118–19, 224; race and, 174, 180–81, 185–87, 190–91; representation in the works of male writers, 26–28, 48, 54–55, 84–85; sexuality during the war and, 16–19, 48, 106–7, 190–94; societal expectations of, 120–24; suffrage and, 101; in *The Sun Also Rises,* 36, 39–40; training camps and, 16–19; viewed as "blood thirsty," 104, 107–8; war work, 29, 116–32, 224. See also *The Backwash of War*; Cather; charity girls; gender; La Motte; *One of Ours;* "Pale Horse, Pale Rider"; Porter, Katherine Anne; prostitution
World War II, 7, 99, 128, 144, 173, 183, 222, 254n17
wounds: Allen and, 207, 209–10; in *The Backwash of War,* 116–18; "demobilization wounds," 99; Hemingway and, 1, 20, 22–23, 30, 39–40, 50–51, 83, 86, 92–96, 98, 214, 223; lying about, 1, 86, 141; March and, 205–7, 211, 213–14, 219–20; masculinity and, 23, 156; medical treatment of, 116–18, 122–23; "meritocracy wound," 127; noncombatants and, 23, 26, 92; in "Pale Horse, Pale Rider," 104, 106, 112; phallic/genital, 44–45, 89–90; in *Plumes,* 154, 156–57, 163, 166–69; race and, 173, 179, 181, 184–85, 197; in *The Red Badge of Courage,* 141; self-inflicted, 130–31; in *Through the Wheat,* 143–44, 147; in *Toward the Flame,* 203–4; Veterans' Bureau and, 166–67. *See also* survivor guilt; "mobilization wounds"; post-traumatic stress

xenophobia, 8, 42, 44

YMCA workers, 110, 242n11. *See also* noncombatants